DATE DUE

MAR 2 0 1997	
MAR 2 4 1998	
DEC 1 8 1998 SEP 1 8 2001	
NOV 0 7 2002 MAY 1 3 2003	

GAYLORD   PRINTED IN U.S.A.

AFRICANS
IN THE
AMERICAS

AFRICANS IN THE AMERICAS

A History of the Black Diaspora

Michael L. Conniff
AUBURN UNIVERSITY

Thomas J. Davis
UNIVERSITY AT BUFFALO

CONTRIBUTING AUTHORS:
Patrick Carroll ▪ David Eltis ▪ Patience Essah ▪
Alfred Frederick ▪ Dale Graden ▪ Linda Heywood
▪ Richard Lobban ▪ Colin Palmer ▪ Joseph Reidy ▪
John Thorton ▪ Ronald Walters ▪
Ashton Welch ▪ Winthrop Wright

ST. MARTIN'S PRESS   NEW YORK

Editor: Louise H. Waller
Managing editor: Patricia Mansfield-Phelan
Project editor: Alda Trabucchi
Production supervisor: Alan Fischer
Art director: Sheree Goodman
Text and cover design: Kenny Beck
Map art: Maryland Cartographics
Photo research: Elnora Bode
Cover art:
  Title: *La charmeuse*
  Artist: Aziz Diagne
  Medium: Reverse painting on glass (reproduction of an original
  thiessoise reverse painting on glass)
  Size: Original work 24" × 36"

Library of Congress Catalog Card Number: 92-62717

8 7 6 5 4
f e d c b

For information, write:
St. Martin's Press, Inc.
175 Fifth Avenue
New York, NY 10010

ISBN: 0-312-04254-X (paperback)
     0-312-10275-5 (cloth)

PREFACE

Africans in the Americas offers a comparative and comprehensive survey of the African diaspora in the Americas. It seeks to convey to the college student and the informed general reader the intellectual challenge and excitement of the recent research that has greatly sharpened our understanding of the myriad ways that the African-American experience has shaped today's world.

The book portrays the elements of a common legacy, emphasizing shared and similar experiences among persons of African descent in the Americas. It paints an extensive mural of African American peoples from their origins in Africa through their dispersion in the diaspora down to contemporary times. It does not suggest a singular experience, as if African Americans lived the same life in all places and at all times. The false notion of a monolithic experience represents yet another effort to rob African Americans of their individuality and personality.

The book affirms Africa's vital, enduring contribution to the Americas and to the global community. An African-inspired ethos infused the Americas, and continues to fill the continents from north to south and at all points in between. It pulsates in the Mardi Gras and daily pace of Brazil's Rio de Janeiro and Louisiana's New Orleans. Its rhythms mark the tempo in Colombia's Cartagena and in Michigan's Detroit. It throbs in Mexico's Veracruz and in Panama's Colón. No Caribbean island lacks its beat. Region may strongly vary the mix, but no doubt exists about the universal source—Africans in the Americas.

These chapters also address the growing interest in global history and multicultural approaches in classrooms, which require a text with wide coverage, portraying Africans and their diaspora in the Americas as integral parts of world history. It also responds to specialists in African American Studies who have stressed the need to expand students' horizons to include Africa and Latin America in a full and coherent discussion of the African diaspora in the Americas.

Many persons contributed to the creation of this book, for it has been a collaborative project in the fullest sense of the phrase. The scholars who provided text, ideas, and illustrations work at the advancing edges of their fields. We take great pleasure in recognizing their outstanding contributions: Their writings form the core of this book.

Richard Lobban surveyed African history to 1500, emphasizing elements that later became important in the black diaspora.

John Thornton examined early relations between Africa and Europe and the initial experiences of Africans in the Americas.

Colin Palmer explored Africans' central roles in settling the Caribbean islands and establishing their preeminence in tropical exports.

Patrick Carroll synthesized his deep understanding of African life in the Spanish American mainland colonies prior to independence.

David Eltis analyzed the ending of the trans-Atlantic slave trade.

Ashton Welch tackled the difficult story of emancipation in the United States, while Dale Graden did the same for Brazil.

Linda Heywood and Joseph Reidy treated African Americans' postemancipation experiences as workers and entrepreneurs.

Ronald Walters, Karin Stanford, and Daryl Harris summarized the political and civil rights initiatives of American blacks.

Winthrop Wright delineated race relations in modern Latin America.

Alfred Frederick limned the continuing ties that bind Africa and the Americas.

Patience Essah depicted the lives and activities of women in the African diaspora, which were integrated into various chapters.

Bonham Richardson kindly supplied the story of King Ja Ja that opens Chapter 15.

We also express our appreciation for the critiques and suggestions of the following reviewers: Lillian Ashcraft-Eason, Bowling Green State University; L. G. Moses, Northern Arizona University; Hillard Pouncy, Swarthmore College; Patricia W. Romero, Towson State University; Stuart B. Schwartz, University of Minnesota; Quintard Taylor, California Polytechnic State University; Cortez Williams, University of New Mexico; and Julie Winch, University of Massachusetts—Boston.

We thank Don Reisman and Louise Waller at St. Martin's Press for their guidance and support, which brought this book into being. We thank also St. Martin's associate editor Frances C. Jones, editorial assistant Gabriela Jasin, copyeditors Susan Rothstein and Betty Pesagno, and photograph researcher Elnora Bode. In addition, Jennifer Pennington kindly helped with clerical and bibliographical matters, while Ethan Grant researched illustrations and performed last-minute editorial tasks. Special thanks go to Janet Frederick and Brenda M. Brock for their sustaining encouragement.

◆ NOTE ON BIBLIOGRAPHIC ESSAY

The annotated bibliographic essay that follows the Glossary offers sources available in English for additional explorations. The list is highly selective and for the most part features recent publications. Little attempt has been made to include the vast periodical literature available, documentary collections, unpublished theses, the rich non-English language sources, or time-honored studies in the field (unless they are mentioned in the text).

◆ NOTES ON TERMINOLOGY

To provide some uniformity of language, the text follows certain conventions worth noting here to avoid confusion.

African American as a noun refers to all persons of African descent anywhere in the Americas. It is used as synonymous with *black* and *Negro*. As an adjective, it similarly refers to artifacts or elements of the common experience and heritage of Africans in the Americas.

Hyphenated constructions using the prefix *Afro* refer to people or elements specific to place, as in *Afro-Brazilian, Afro-Cuban,* and *Afro-Caribbean. Afro-American* refers to African Americans within the United States or its colonial predecessors. To avoid confusion, the adjective "U.S." identifies the separate nation and "American" the broader Americas.

A *creole* may be any non-Indian person born in the Americas or a person of mixed descent, particularly one of mixed African and European descent. A creole whose parents are African and European is a *mulatto;* and, more broadly, any person of African and European racial descent may be referred to as a mulatto. Creole may also designate an element or culture created in the Americas or a mixture of elements or cultures in the Americas. It conveys the sense of "multicultural."

Many other frequently used terms appear in the glossary.

CONTENTS

xi

PART I

Africa, Europe, and the Americas

S ince the dawn of human life, Africa's peoples have spread outward via the land bridge connection with Asia, while others have flowed back into Africa. Over the centuries reciprocal migrations, cultural and technological exchanges, trades of plants and animals, and commerce followed a northeast-southwest axis. Much later, in the Middle Ages, growth in ocean travel fully connected Africa with the Far East and the European peninsula. Thus, well-worn exchange and migration routes within Africa were complemented by expanding overseas associations.

Land forms and geography affected relations between Africans and peoples of other continents. The entire continent tilted toward the northwest, with its lowest edge jutting into the equatorial Atlantic. Despite some breathtaking volcanoes and high plateaus, most of its surface was made up of rolling plains. Africa's soils were for the most part only mildly fertile and subject to leaching and erosion, as are most tropical soils. The benign climate offered constantly warm temperatures. Africa lacked regular invasions of cold air, however, so that rainfall could only be generated by tropical and monsoon weather, which were seasonal and erratic. Given sharp fluctuations in rainfall, Africans were forced to live near the major river systems that drained the continent—the Nile, Zambezi, Limpopo, Orange, Congo, and Niger—and to those that flowed into lakes.

Africans learned to become resourceful in dealing with the peculiar features of their land. For example, they practiced swidden, or slash-and-burn agriculture, along the rain-forested west coast and in the great Congo

Basin. They grazed cattle and other livestock in the sweeping savannas that covered a third of the continent. In arid upland plains, they cultivated irrigated fields and fished along lakeshores and meandering rivers. Where game was abundant, they hunted. They even adapted to the Sahara and Kalahari deserts, living in oases and importing necessary supplies. The leading threat to survival in Africa, drought, caused many Africans to migrate periodically to unaffected lands. The one natural enemy they did not have to contend with was harsh weather, because three-quarters of the continent lay in the tropics.

Africa's geographical and climatic conditions posed formidable obstacles to outside penetration; as a result, the interior of the continent remained a mystery to the rest of the world until the nineteenth century. Only hardened professionals ventured to cross the vast Sahara Desert that stretched clear across its northern bulge. In addition, all of Africa's major rivers contained rapids or falls within a thousand kilometers of their mouths, impeding inland navigation. Forbidding uplands cut by the Rift Valley lay along the east coast, while deserts and dense rain forests obstructed entry on most of the west coast. Finally, as if these obstacles were not sufficiently daunting, malaria, sleeping sickness, and yellow fever in central Africa further discouraged foreigners from traveling inland. At the same time, these physical impediments reduced other people's knowledge about Africans and their societies. (See Map I-1.)

The Europeans' conquest and occupation of the American continents in the sixteenth century abruptly added a western vector to Africa's overseas linkages. With wrenching suddenness, ships arrived along the Guinea coast and purchased slaves for the settlements in the New World. What began as a trickle became a torrent, and within a century the slave trade carried some eight thousand persons a year across the Atlantic. The African-American diaspora had begun.

In some ways Africa's history up to that point in time predisposed its leaders to participate in the slave trade, necessarily influencing the Africans' experiences in the Americas. First, the Africans themselves made widespread use of slaves in household, agricultural, and military settings, thereby making it easier to export people considered redundant in their societies. Africa's major empires and states organized and sanctioned the trade as a way both to manage and control population and to provide tax revenues. Second, the trade to Arabian and Asian markets established in earlier periods provided ready supply lines for the new Atlantic demand, and since slaves in Africa enjoyed many rights and protections, it was easier to justify and expand their enslavement. Finally, the relatively high level of material development in Africa—in the fields of metallurgy, animal husbandry, agriculture, mining, and construction—made these people especially valuable as workers in the Americas.

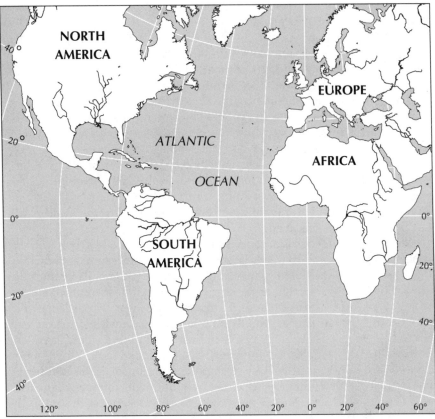

Map I–1   Africa, Europe, and the Americas

African slaves owed their condition to their birth, indebtedness, capture in war, or personal misfortune, and for their part traders dealt in slaves for profit. Therefore, this was simply an old system revitalized to supply new markets in the Americas. No one, however, foresaw the changed conditions and destructive forces the slaves would encounter in their new environment.

Many of the Europeans who traveled to Africa were drawn by curiosity and the lure of the exotic. Most wished to exchange some goods for money or commodities that could be resold at home for a profit; these included both slaves and a wide array of products. Others had more general political aims, hoping to push back Islamic advances and to win allies for their European states. Still other Europeans had religious motives, aspiring to convert Africans to their Christian faiths. These goals were not necessarily exploitative and were portrayed as being in the best mutual interests of Africans and Europeans.

The Europeans gradually associated the exploitation of slaves with African phenotypes, especially dark skin. Thus began the racist treatment of Africans and their descendants, a situation that continues to this day in the Americas. Some historians trace African enslavement in the Americas to economic factors, maintaining that the rise of a capitalist mode of production in the Americas created overwhelming demands for an exploitable labor force. In this view, racism was secondary, being an ideology invented to justify the enslavement of African peoples. But whatever the exact sources of racism, Africans lost their liberty, were perceived as subject people, and suffered dismal treatment following that perception. Therefore, whether these effects were a function of cultural chauvinism, capitalist imperatives, virulent racism, or a combination of all three could hardly have consoled the enslaved.

The slave trade created commercial and political links between Europeans and Africans that lasted into the nineteenth century. Generally, these were relationships of parity and occasional rivalry. To be sure, the Europeans, with their ships, firearms, and expanded commercial networks, were a powerful element; European capitalism, in particular, was an important organizing and motivating force. Nevertheless, African leaders were neither passive nor reactive in their dealings with Europeans and pursued their own goals, among which profits ranked high. When opportunities arose, they used military strength as rapaciously as the Europeans. For several centuries the peoples of the two continents interacted as equals and even as partners. Sadly, they cooperated most in the diaspora, the massive export of slaves to the Americas.

The first Africans who arrived in the Americas came soon after Columbus's first voyage, traveling as sailors, soldiers, and workers. They helped to conquer the Amerindian states and to reduce the natives to submission. They were soon joined by increasing numbers of slaves from Africa whose roles would be to do manual labor and to supervise native workers. Finally, the Europeans created the chattel slave, a person regarded as property whose entire existence was devoted to carrying out the orders of the master. The vast majority of Africans imported to the Americas came as chattel to labor on the plantations, farms, ranches, and other businesses of European and Euro-American owners.

Since most Africans in the New World did not have the protections that slavery afforded them at home, their existence in the Americas proved far harsher. The deeds of sale signed on African shores did not shield them in the Americas. Under these conditions, they had to adjust to the Euro-American societies founded by their masters, which at first meant recreating as much of Africa as they could for purposes of solace and survival. Later, it meant selectively adopting European culture, technology, aesthetics, and organizational principles. In the end, a creative recombination of diverse elements—African, Amerindian, and European—produced a new and unique African American civilization.

Part I begins with a survey from the dawn of human existence until the end of the fifteenth century, concentrating on the great kingdoms of the Nile Valley and the savannas and portraying developments by Africans themselves and those achieved in collaboration with others. The section goes on to trace the emerging relationships between Africa and Europe in the fifteenth and sixteenth centuries, based on exploration, trade, warfare, and religious conversion. Finally, Part I examines the Africans' early experiences in the Americas, mostly—but not exclusively—as slaves in economic enterprises.

Chapter 1
AFRICA TO 1500

50,000	*Homo sapiens* established in parts of Africa.
4000	Barley and wheat cultivated in the Nile Valley.
3100	Pharaohs unify Egypt.
2250–1575	Kerma rules in ancient Nubia (upper Nile).
1570–1090	Egypt's New Kingdom dynasty colonizes Nubia.
950	Kush state arises in Nubia.
814	Phoenicians establish capital at Carthage, Tunisia.
760–656	Nubia (Kushites) rules during Egypt's Twenty-fifth Dynasty.
500	Iron production reaches West Africa from the upper Nile Valley.
332	Greeks conquer Egypt.
30	Romans conquer Egypt.
B.C./A.D.	
300	Most Egyptians converted to Christianity.
640	Islam enters Egypt.
711	Moors from North Africa establish civilization in Spain.
1076	Almoravids conquer Ghana.
1235	Empire of Mali established.
1415	Portuguese conquer Ceuta in North Africa.

| 1468 | Songhai captures Timbuktu, the capital of Mali. |
| 1482 | Portuguese build Fort Almina (Ghana) to buy slaves and gold. |

Human beings trace their common ancestors to Africa some two to three million years ago—to the best of our current knowledge, to *Homo africanus* (also known as *Australopithecus*). These erect-statured, toolmaking hominids lived in the savanna grasslands of South and East Africa, and their social organization was based on their ability to discover, gather, and consume a diversity of foods from the environment. Hunting larger animals in particular required effective coordination. Communication and technology, though simple at first, allowed for some accumulation of knowledge and a rudimentary mastery over nature.

Perhaps two hundred thousand years ago, the more complicated forms of Stone Age hominids such as *Homo erectus* evolved from these societies. Then, with the retreat of European glaciers about fifty thousand years ago, new lands were opened for human habitation, and *Homo sapiens neandertalensis* spread farther into Asia and Europe. The several forms of humanity at the time were essentially indistinguishable: They all used heavy axes and other tools of stone, bone, wood, and horn, and they lived exclusively by hunting and gathering. The modern continents of North and South America were still unsettled by human beings.

About ten to fifteen thousand years ago, peoples of the Old Stone Age gave way to the more sophisticated *Homo sapiens sapiens* of the Mesolithic Age. These people still lived by hunting and gathering, but they had now discovered fire and used hunting nets, harpoons, jewelry, pottery, and woven cloth. Their cultures became more complex as well, as they developed separate folklore and oral traditions, animistic religions, marriage, and social differentiation. Gradually, some ancient societies became seasonally sedentary, with improved techniques for hunting animals in the savannas and near rivers. They also became more successful at gathering wild seeds and grains.

During the Neolithic Age the "Stillbay" and "Capsian" types of people, known for their finely chipped stone flake tools, evolved in parts of Africa. They appear to be the ancestors of today's Khoisan or Click-speaking peoples, as well as the San in the Kalahari Desert and the Pygmies in the Zairean rain forests. These groups were egalitarian and followed animistic or polytheistic religions.

Olduvai Gorge, East Africa, where archaeologists discovered evidence of early human ancestors during the 1950s. Anthro-Photo File.

◆ ANCIENT EGYPT

About six thousand years ago the Neolithic "food-producing revolution" occurred in northeast Africa. Plant cultivation and cattle herding probably first began in Turkey and Mesopotamia and quickly spread to the Nile Valley. In this era, wheat and barley were imported, and sheep, goats, and pigs were bred with local species. These innovations probably advanced up the Nile Valley and across the Sahara. As seen in the rock paintings found in the central Sahara dating to about 3000–5000 B.C., the hunters of the region were beginning to herd cattle and goats. In the following centuries farming and herding spread across the Sahara (which was not completely arid at the time).

Meanwhile, the peoples of the upper Nile developed agriculture based on the cultivation of millet and sorghum and the domestication of goats. Later, perhaps as early as four thousand years ago, camels and horses arrived from Asia, allowing migrations toward the west and south, across the savanna grasslands and the Sahel. Then sometime around 1000 B.C. a great migration began from a location in the northcentral African rain forests southward almost to the southern tip of the continent. These people, ancestors of today's Bantu speakers, also spread the use of other crops such as bananas, sugarcane, and yams (originally from Southeast Asia). Iron technology in Africa probably emerged earliest in the Nile Valley some twenty-five hundred years ago. Within several centuries smelting spread into the Lakes Region of East Africa, the savanna of West Africa, and on to southern Africa.

As African societies evolved, some peoples, living in comparative harmony with their resources and population size, continued to hunt, herd, and farm in small groups. Other societies evolved into states, kingdoms, and major empires.

Egypt was without question the first great civilization in Africa. Surrounded by hostile desert, Egypt arose as a populous settlement as a "gift of the Nile River," which flooded surrounding plains and thus supported game and wild plants. Straddling the strategic land crossroads between Africa, Asia, and Europe, Egypt also became a point for interchange between the Mediterranean and Red seas and the Persian Gulf. Many developments affecting the rest of Africa took place in or near the Nile Valley, such as the cultivation of plants and the development of metal smelting. Thus, Egypt's major role in forming early African civilizations has been well established.

In modern times, scholars often underestimated the contributions of ancient Egypt to European civilization. More than two millenia ago, when the Ptolemaic Greeks came to rule Egypt, they extensively adopted and interpreted Egyptian spiritual, material, political, aesthetic, and intellectual systems. Although later Greek authorities freely acknowledged their cultural debt to Egypt, during the nineteenth century many European writers, limited by their ethnocentrism and racism, decided that black Africa could have had nothing to do with Europe's rise to greatness. Some treated Egypt as Middle Eastern and divorced it from the rest of Africa, whereas others went further, asserting the preeminence of northern Aryan sources of Greek civilization to the virtual exclusion of Semitic, African, and Egyptian influences.

Beginning in ancient times, Egypt was a genuine crossroads of peoples and cultures, and its peoples were multiethnic and multiracial, as depicted in dynastic drawings of their rulers. They came from as far away as Asia Minor and Nubia, in the upper Nile Valley. As a prosperous, advanced society with an enviable commercial and strategic location, Egypt attracted many conquerors who would come with their soldiers and elites, enrich themselves, and carry off booty and advanced technology. In the past three millennia, for example, Egypt has been ruled by the Kushites, Libyans, Assyrians, Persians, Greeks, Romans, Christians, Arabs, Turks,

French, and English. As a prime cradle of human development, in some sense Egypt indeed belongs to all peoples.

In addition to their cultural debt to Middle Eastern civilizations, the Egyptians also borrowed from other African societies. For example, the Nubians may have developed the political institution of kingship that produced the pharaohs. They also contributed great varieties of animals and goods that made up a material stock for Egyptian civilization: cattle, sheep, goats, geese, and camels, as well as hides, ivory, leopard and snake skins, ostrich feathers and eggs, spices, wood, mats and rugs, rope, cloth, pottery, incense, minerals, and gold. Other regions of Africa sent soldiers, sailors, slaves, merchants, kings, and princes to Egypt. Basic theological ideas, such as divine rule, may have originated south of Egypt. So, too, aspects of Afro-Asiatic language and systems of matrilineal kinship were used throughout North Africa during early historic times.

As Egypt took, so also it gave. As a major center of power in the Middle East, Egypt deeply influenced the great religions that arose in this region: Judaism, Christianity, and Islam. Detailed studies reveal vast borrowings and connections among these great religions. Mohammed, for example, drew on the teachings of the early prophets in the Bible in composing the Koran. The prophet Moses was likely serving Pharaoh Ramses II when political instability compelled him and his followers to retreat into the Sinai wilderness. Because of Jewish subordination to Egypt, both the Torah and the Bible make frequent negative references to the Land of the Pharaohs.

◆ ANCIENT NUBIA AND KUSH

Nubia and its various subcultures also served as a channel of transmission for both African and Eurasian civilizations. Actually a string of settlements in the Nile Valley between Aswan and northern Sudan, Nubia experienced many of the same sweeping demographic, cultural, and economic changes as did Egypt to the north. Early Nubian societies supported themselves by agriculture, fishing, and hunting, and all of them had some social differentiation and developed religion. A major advantage they enjoyed was their access to grazing lands in the upper Nile Valley, where they developed an extensive cattle industry. Some four thousand years ago an independent Nubian state emerged at Kerma, which served as its capital for over five hundred years. (See Map 1–1.)

At the height of its development, Kerma had a sharply stratified society and complex division of labor. The Kerma kings had substantial wealth and power, as shown by their retinues of servants and huge burial mounds. They developed handsome red pottery, bronze statuary, and massive brick architecture. Archaeologists speculate that Kerma may have operated a profitable slave trade that supplied servants and soldiers to Egypt and beyond.

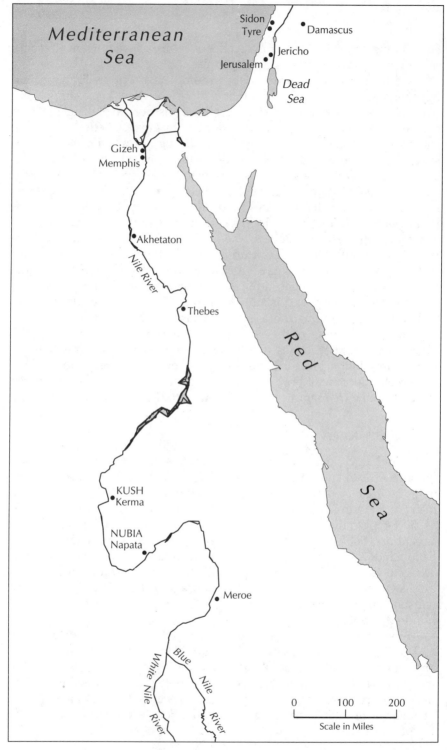

Map 1–1 Nubia and Kush, Showing Kerma, Thebes, and Meroe

Some three thousand years ago, the Egyptian pharaohs annexed Nubia, which they governed through appointed viceroys. They periodically stripped the valley of livestock, gold, and slaves, giving rise to rebellions and the eventual independence of the region. This new Nubian state was known as Kush, and it moved its capital to Karnak, in southern Egypt. Kush prospered from herding and advanced irrigated agriculture, which paid for large armies and supported an efficient state. Eventually, about twenty-five hundred years ago, Kush took over the entire Nile Valley, including the weakened Egypt. By then Nubia had suffered frequent attacks from Libya and Assyria and had to maintain standing armies to defend itself. It was during one such attack that the Nubians were introduced to the camel, which would revolutionize transportation in the continent. The Kushite leaders and their Phoenician and Jewish allies fought to defend their Mediterranean states.

◆ PHOENICIAN EXPLORATIONS

In the ninth century B.C., the Phoenicians, peoples who came from ancient Lebanon, began a campaign of expansion around the eastern Mediterranean, which culminated in the founding of their great city of Carthage in modern-day Tunisia. Carthage became the center of a vast trade network that penetrated the Sahara and linked many Atlantic ports via ship. Rather than defend their routes alone, however, the Phoenicians struck deals with other states for trade and protection. Phoenician exports of cedar to ancient Egypt date back five thousand years.

Phoenician (or Punic) captains, navigating by the North Star, ventured further than any earlier Mediterranean sailors and became the unchallenged masters of the seas. The unique circular design of Carthage harbor could accommodate 220 seagoing ships at once. Many of these ships were three times the size of those used by Columbus two thousand years later. Under state commission, Phoenician masters sailed beyond the Straits of Gibraltar to Brittany and perhaps to the Azores and England. Another brave expedition appears to have reached modern-day West Africa. Herodotus claimed that they were the first to circumnavigate the continent of Africa in a three-year voyage, an extraordinary feat for the era.

The Carthaginians also organized overland trade that brought ivory, gold, slaves, animal skins, spices, gums, and other products across the Sahara. Often these valuable items were traded only for salt, which was lacking in Central Africa and highly valued for its taste and preservative qualities. Over many millennia, this unbalanced exchange may have contributed to the unequal levels of living between North and sub-Saharan Africa.

At the height of Phoenician development, the contemporary Olmec civilization arose across the Atlantic, on a plain occupied by modern

Veracruz in Mexico. Archaeologists are uncertain about the origins of this culture, but according to one account, Olmec ancestors arrived by ship from far to the east, allowing for a possible contact with Carthage. Several facts lend credence to this hypothesis: Olmec phenotypes and art were different from those of the later Mayan people, and Olmec sculptured heads, with their broad noses, full lips, and tightly curled hair, are remarkably African-looking. They also used helmets similar to those worn by Kushite soldiers. Did the great land power of the period, Kush, allied with the world's great sea power, Phoenicia, conduct vast naval explorations some twenty-six hundred years ago? Future studies might resolve this question.

In the centuries following these possible Kushite-Phoenician ventures, rival powers invaded and managed to wrest control of the lower Nile from the Kushites, breaking their contact with the Mediterranean. Even so, the Kushites continued to develop their advanced culture by adding their own features to borrowed Egyptian hieroglyphics, religion, and architectural style. They even created their own unique alphabetic written language, complete with vowels and separated words, unlike Egyptian hieroglyphics.

Seeking greater security from invasions from the north, the Kushite rulers relinquished their claim on Egypt and withdrew up the river to Merowe, their second capital. Their alphabetic writing expanded, and it has become known as the mostly untranslated Meroitic cursive. They built many new pyramids in the Sudan, which were smaller but more numerous than those of Egypt. Through their exports of cattle, elephants, and other livestock to the Greeks and Romans, Kush prospered and expanded iron production. Sometime around 350 B.C., however, Kush was invaded by the Axumites, a people from Ethiopia, and its remarkable civilization ended.

◆ CLASSICAL TIMES: GREEKS AND
   ROMANS IN AFRICA

The Greeks, whose rise to prominence owed so much to Egypt, invaded North Africa in about 332 B.C., taking control from its Persian rulers. The conqueror Alexander founded and built a great classical city which he named after himself—Alexandria. The Greeks revered Egypt's glorious history and carefully copied its writing, art, architecture, religion, clothing, and foods. While ruling Egypt, the Greeks built on North African science and thereby contributed immensely to world civilization. Perhaps their most significant contribution was the great library they assembled in Alexandria, with six hundred and fifty thousand papyrus scrolls recording the most advanced science, literature, mathematics, astronomy, navigation, and medicine in the world. Sadly, this treasure was largely destroyed during later Roman invasions. Other notable Graeco-Egyptian contributions were the lighthouse at Pharos and the profoundly important trilingual text on the Rosetta Stone, which later enabled Egyptologists to decipher hieroglyphic texts. Some Greek influence spread into the upper Nile Valley, although the region remained independent of their political control.

The expansion of Roman rule in the Mediterranean in the first century B.C. led to wars with Carthage and the eventual collapse of Carthaginian influence. Within two centuries Roman settlers and traders occupied choice sites in North Africa and took over Carthaginian trade routes into the Sahara and East Africa. They never succeeded in controlling the Garamante nomads, however, whose adoption of the Assyrian camel gave them mobility and prevented total Roman domination. These nomads traded with sub-Saharan peoples for ivory, gems, skins, gold, and feathers and then exchanged them for salt and Roman goods.

The Romans conquered Egypt in 30 B.C. and reigned four centuries there. As with the Greeks before them, the Romans did not consolidate control over Nubia in the upper Nile Valley, although their influence spread there. Roman policy was built around strong military rule along the coast and indirect government in surrounding regions where ancient states (like Kush and its successors) and nomads could thwart or ignore their orders.

During the centuries of Greek and Roman domination in North Africa, goods and culture continued to move back and forth across the Mediterranean Sea. The exchange was unequal, however, because the military control exercised by the Europeans allowed them to appropriate taxes and maintain a balance of trade in their favor. This unequal relationship persisted until the arrival of a more powerful force throughout North Africa in A.D. 640 when the Islamic religion and its political alliances spread everywhere. As Islamic regions became united, North African (Afro-Semitic) peoples again came to dominate Iberia and many parts of southern Europe and ruled for about seven centuries.

Christian influence along the Nile Valley remained scant until the Roman emperor Constantine converted to Christianity in the early fourth century A.D. After that, Christianity became the official religion of Egypt, and its missionaries penetrated into the upper Nile and the Sudan in large numbers. When the bishop of Alexandria broke with the pope in Rome, however, North African Christians followed the so-called Eastern branch. This attachment became even stronger when Justinian came to rule Byzantium (527–565). During subsequent centuries the elites of the Sudan became adherents of Coptic (or Eastern) Christianity, whose languages and cultures supplanted the older Kushite ones, which were built on ancient Egyptian religion and architecture.

◆ THE SPREAD OF ISLAM IN AFRICA

In about 610 the prophet Mohammed formed a new religion, known as Islam, whose devoted followers soon spread his message throughout the Arabian peninsula and beyond. Calling themselves Muslims, they quickly established a base in Egypt and then swept across North Africa, con-

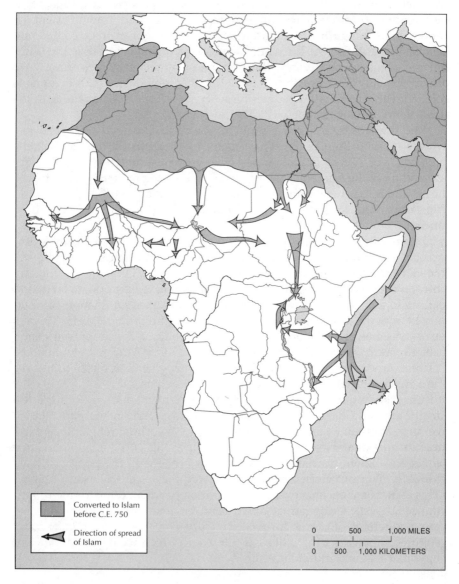

Map 1–2   Expansion of Islam in Africa to 1500

quering the old Greek capital at Alexandria and Carthage. Advancing southward into upper Egypt, they were blocked by Christian Nubia for seven centuries, and they failed to take the Christian kingdom of Axum (now in modern Ethiopia).

To the west, Arab followers of Islam consolidated their control over all of North Africa, sweeping aside Christians and others. (See Map 1–2.) From this stronghold they reaped great profits from the trans-Saharan trade originating in Ghana and the savanna states in West Africa. Arab Moors also crossed the Straits of Gibraltar in 711 and conquered Spain, Portugal, and southern France. In addition, they took over southern Italy and the Balkans. Introducing Arabic writing, modern science, government, trade, architecture, and agriculture to these lands, the Arabs brought tremendous progress to Iberia and eastern Europe. Under the Arabs Spain enjoyed a golden age in science, navigation, astronomy, and cartography, which aided its later establishment of an overseas Spanish empire.

Thus, under the unifying influence of Islam, Arab states, loosely joined by religious and ethnic interests, came to control most of the Mediterranean Basin for seven centuries. This was a time of unprecedented growth and prosperity for the region, yet it engendered the classic enmity between the Muslim world and Christian Europe. North Africans, Muslims, and even Jews became the economic and religious competitors of the Europeans.

The historical, political, and religious legacies of Islam in Africa are exceedingly complex and have great continuity over time. Islam has been a tremendous force for building multiethnic national unity, yet like Christianity it has also caused deep divisions. In the modern United States, many people of African descent have achieved personal and religious satisfaction by accepting Islam. In some contexts, both religions have been remarkably free of racial typing and intolerance, yet in other contexts they justified centuries of ethnic violence and systematic slaving.

Thus, some thirteen hundred years ago, Islam spread throughout much of Africa, both by peaceful conversion and by forceful conquest, and in the process, it won over both orthodox and folk followers and became partially Africanized. A major strength of Islam in Africa was its remarkably adaptive and syncretic character. Despite its vast and rich body of law and theology, the core ritual aspects of Islam were quite simple and did not demand elaborate training for conversion. Unlike Christianity, an individual could practice Islamic rites by simply praying in the desert, without the intervention of an elaborate hierarchy of religious officials. Like Christianity, Islam was universalistic and inclusive.

♦ **ANCIENT GHANA**

Archaeologists speculate that the oldest West African savanna kingdoms arose because of their strategic location above the northern curve of the

Niger River, deep in the Sahara region. (See Map 1–3.) Proto-Ghanaians probably supplied goods for the trans-Saharan commerce between Gara-mante nomads, Carthaginians, and Romans. This trade, making use of routes served by wells and oases, expanded rapidly after the arrival of camels and ironworking in West Africa some two thousand years ago. Millet and sesame agriculture in the Sahel grasslands was also critical to early Ghanaian expansion.

The empire of ancient Ghana emerged in about the fourth century, and its earliest formal rulers probably belonged to a Mande language group such as the Soninke. Ghana was not the only organized state during this period: Early Wolof, Tekrur, and Serer kingdoms also arose about this time in the Guinea highlands. Ghana's merchants probably traded with Jewish or Christian counterparts across the Sahara.

Ghana's ruling elite seems to have been concentrated in ancestral groups who claimed semidivine descent. The structure of the state in-cluded a standing army, centralized lawmaking and taxation, and ap-pointed officials with awesome powers. The kings had enormous powers, and upon their deaths, the early monarchs were accorded elaborate funeral ceremonies. Like the kings of Kerma, they were placed on beds with their weapons, ornaments, and utensils, and were buried under huge earthen domes.

Ghana's main trade routes stretched across the Sahara to the Mediterra-nean, and its principal trade goods going north included gold, slaves, kola

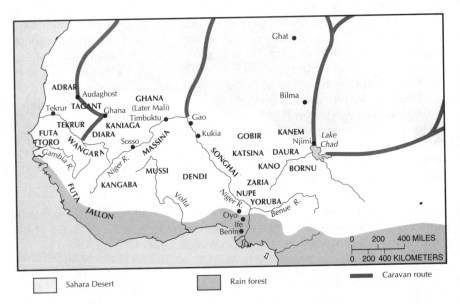

Map 1–3 Kingdom of Ghana, Mali, Songhai, and Assorted Cities

nuts, gum arabic, and other regional produce, which were exchanged for weapons, cloth and other manufactures, copper, and salt.

By the ninth century, Islamic culture began to arrive in Ghana, carried by Muslim converts who had followed the trade routes. Even the earliest Arab geographers already knew of Ghana because of its lucrative commerce across the Sahel. Several generations passed, however, before Ghana's rulers converted to Islam. The process of Islamization in the African savanna was parallel to that of the militant Moroccan Muslims in Spain and Portugal, who channeled their resources to carry on the Jihad, or religious war. A later independent Ghanaian dynasty, now Islamic, was restored to office, yet it was not able to rebuild the powerful government it had once commanded. By the twelfth century, it had faded in importance.

◆ MALI

The kingdom of Mali appears to have evolved from the small state of Kangaba in about 1235, east of ancient Ghana. Under the influence of northern trader-conquerors, Mali was converted to Islam. Some eight hundred years ago King Sumanguru, of the Mande people, extended his rule over Ghana and lands to the south and east, consolidating the second major savanna empire. Unlike Arabs, whose lineage was patrilineal, the rulers took their legitimacy from matrilineal descent. Mali was administered by a well-organized bureaucracy and a standing army. Its territory and wealth vastly exceeded those of Ghana, for it took control of distant gold fields and rich cities like Gao and Timbuktu.

Mali's most famous ruler was Mansa Musa, who came to the throne in 1312 during the "Golden Era." One of his most remarkable achievements was the pilgrimage he led to Mecca in 1324–1325, in the middle of his reign. He crossed the Sahara to North Africa and continued to Cairo. His awesome entourage, which included thousands of noblemen, retainers, and slaves, and a weighty cargo of gold, inspired the wonder of Egyptians, Asians, and Europeans. It is said that this infusion of gold inflated the Egyptian economy for a decade.

Besides its extensive exports of slaves, gold, and merchandise, Mali also boasted internationally renowned mosques. Its universities at Timbuktu and Sankore attracted students and scholars from across North Africa and the Middle East to study under its acclaimed Muslim teachers.

Some fascinating reports have suggested that African sailors from Mali traveled to the Americas before Columbus. According to the Arab historian Umari, a royal prince later known as Bakary II crossed the Atlantic during the rule of Mansa's predecessor (1312–1337). He was reported to have sent some two hundred vessels with men and two hundred with gold, water, and supplies. When only one vessel returned, another fleet of two thousand vessels with men and supplies was purportedly dispatched.

Mansa Musa, a fourteenth-century ruler of Mali, became famous after his pilgrimage to Mecca. Bibliothèque Nationale.

Such reports were still current among fifteenth-century European navigators, so that in the 1480s and 1490s the Portuguese and Spanish kings asked their sailors to look into the possibility that oceangoing African boats had traveled anywhere west of Cape Verde. Columbus did so but did not report evidence of any such traffic, and the reports were forgotten in the excitement of the larger discoveries of the era.

Meanwhile, some of Mali's secondary kingdoms began to assert their independence and rebelled against taxes and outside rule. When the Portuguese arrived in the region in the fifteenth century, Mali's rulers appealed to them for military aid against attacks by former subsidiary states. With no aid forthcoming, Mali fell to the armies of a rival empire, Songhai.

The case of Gabu, a secondary state of Mali, illustrates both the inner workings of the empire and its eventual demise. Gabu lay along the forested coastal area which today is occupied by Guinea-Bissau. It had existed well before the first European sailors explored the region and had prevented the Portuguese from penetrating the interior until the late nineteenth century. Gabu was founded about eight hundred years ago as a tributary kingdom of Mali. Administered by local Mandingo chieftains, Gabu was well situated to secure the trade in salt, gold, and slaves on the coastal river estuaries. After the arrival of Portuguese traders, Gabu served as an intermediary for exports. The central authority in Gabu derived from the mansa, or emperor, of Mali. Provincial farim, or governors, selected from the eldest of the provincial leaders, exercised considerable local control and were accorded their own administrative councils, symbolic war drums, and personal armies. Major towns were fortified and had a standing militia; some of these armed forces could be supplied to Mali in time of war.

After Mali was conquered by Songhai, Gabu, like many other tributary states, gained full autonomy and could maintain and even expand its own territory during three centuries. Gabu's power was based largely on military operations, which also produced many captives of war for the slave trade. In the sixteenth and seventeenth centuries, perhaps as many as half of all slaves on the Upper Guinea coast were generated from Gabu's wars.

◆ WOMEN IN TRADITIONAL
SUB-SAHARAN SOCIETIES

The history of women in sub-Saharan Africa must take into account the tremendous diversity of societies in the region. Although women generally exercised less power than men, they did not suffer complete subjugation or debasement. Male domination was indeed the rule, but it was tempered by varying degrees of female autonomy and influence. Thus, women's history there is neither one of total victimization or deprivation, nor one of complete equality with men.

Throughout much of sub-Saharan Africa, a division of labor based on sex prevailed, and this tradition was carried to New World societies as well. In Africa, men generally cleared the land and planted staple or "men's" crops that could be sold in the market. They also hunted, fished, and tended herds of domesticated animals. Women provided most of the labor on noncommercial farms, raising food for subsistence. In addition, they labored in the home, taking care of all domestic responsibilities— tending children, fetching water, collecting firewood, preparing food, cleaning house, and raising small livestock to supplement the diet. They also dressed out meat, which had to be cleaned, salted, smoked, and dried. Finally, if the family tended cattle, the women usually milked them.

This division of labor between the sexes also carried over into nonagricultural endeavors. Men defended their homes and villages when necessary, and they also wove cloth, made drums, and carved stools that were highly revered. Women practiced more domestic crafts, spinning and weaving cloth for family use and making pottery. They also gathered salt, a scarce and highly prized commodity. Such differences in sex roles varied by region, however. Tasks considered men's work in one culture might be open to women in another. For example, Oyo women made cloth, while Akan men monopolized the weaving of kente cloth, a colorful and valuable textile.

Both men and women participated in trading activities, but again with separate and unequal roles. The more profitable long-distance trade— between African markets, across the Sahara to the Mediterranean, or via the oceans—was conducted by men. Women in turn controlled the local trade and markets. Thus, in sub-Saharan Africa women primarily handled the sale of foodstuffs and craft goods on the local market.

Gender played a critical role in deciding the fate of slaves in sub-Saharan Africa. Domestic slave buyers favored women because of their reproductive and profit-making abilities. Whether the owner was from a patrilineal, matrilineal, or Muslim society, he could incorporate slave women into his family as servants, wives, concubines, and mothers. Slave women did not enjoy the protection of their original families, thus sparing their master-husbands the need to deal with interfering kinsmen. Children born to slave women belonged to their masters, which gave men the opportunity to obtain complete custodial rights to their own children in both matrilineal and patrilineal societies.

The kind of agricultural and domestic labor performed by slave women accounted in part for the high demand for their services in sub-Saharan Africa. While both African men and women labored on farms, it was the labor of women that produced the necessities of the daily diet. The cultivation of basic foods such as cocoyams, cassava, vegetables, and fruits, was considered women's work. Thus, the labor of slave women would ensure their owners a supply of the basic food.

The slave owner typically established the type of labor performed and the length of the workday, but in some areas, tradition and custom decided the regime of slaves, including female slaves. Domestic slaves in the Senegambia region, for example, were expected to work for their owners from sunrise until 2 P.M. five days a week; afterward they could farm for themselves. Because of the large demand for female slaves in Africa, they were priced higher on the domestic market. Certain slave markets like Winneba on the Gold Coast catered to the demand by specializing in the sale of female slaves.

Not all African women were victimized by enslavement. By having slaves, wealthy women were released from the drudgery of farm and domestic labor. A few women, usually of racially mixed parentage, even profited from the trade in the coastal fort towns, serving as intermediaries between European agents and African slave traders.

While men controlled the exercise of public power in sub-Saharan Africa, their domination was not absolute. Power in the state was closely tied to military service. Since women were excluded from the military, it reduced their potential for political power. Yet women could often play significant political roles. Among the Asante, for example, menopausal women served in the army, and the Dahomey placed no restrictions on women enlisting in the military.

Even when women were denied roles in the army, they could still influence politics in sub-Saharan Africa. The queen mothers, the royal women, and the women caretakers of the rulers wielded remarkable power, even controlling access to audiences with the ruler. Moreover, since they were responsible for the daily care of the kings, they were usually the first to know of the monarch's death. By withholding information on the king's death, they could often sway the choice of his successor. In several societies, particularly matrilineal systems, the queen mothers were invested with the power of making and deposing ("destooling") the king.

Social stratification existed among African women, just as it did among women in other societies. Three broad classes could be identified: members of the royal family, commoners, and slaves. Royal women held far more political, social, and economic power, of course, but commoners also enjoyed certain privileges. Slaves had little or no influence over their own lives.

In theory, a wide chasm existed between royal and slave women, but the practice of keeping slave women as wives and concubines easily blurred the lines of stratification. Slave wives and concubines could achieve power and prestige through their lovers or husbands, and even through the children born to such unions. African tradition did not prevent children born to slave mothers from ascending to political leadership. Children who succeeded would usually reward their slave mothers by elevating them to royal status. For example, many of the *askias*, or rulers, of Songhai were children of slave mothers.

A parent's slave status did not automatically pass on to the child. In matrilineal societies, the child's status was determined by that of the mother. When a free woman in a matrilineal society bore a child by a slave father, the child's status was decided by the mother's status, not the father's. But in a matrilineal society where the child was conceived by a slave mother and a free father, it was the father's option to elevate the child's status to that of a free person. In both patrilineal and Muslim societies, the child assumed the status of the father. Thus, in acknowledging paternity, the father also granted the child full citizenship. Generally, African society did not attach a stigma to children born of a slave parent, but it is true that children born of free parents must have felt superior.

Marriage was an alliance between families, not a contract between two individuals. Polygamy was widely accepted, though the financial burden associated with maintaining separate households limited the practice mostly to the wealthy. The Islamic religion allowed men to have up to four wives, and traditional African society, an unlimited number. Although the Europeans believed polygamy was demeaning to women, African women thought that it allowed a measure of economic and social independence unknown in monogamous marriages. It permitted separate households, separate farms, separate businesses, and the privileged positions enjoyed by senior wives.

Marriage did not undermine the sociopolitical power that women held in matrilineal societies. Women owned the custodial rights to their children and continued to retain all rights and privileges enjoyed by their original family.

As in other aspects of African life, men's roles in traditional religion ranked higher but did not totally bar women from active participation. Most traditional medical practitioners were men, but women still made up a large segment of the profession. Mediums—intermediaries between humans and the spirit world—were generally women, for example. Women also became priestesses of religious groups, especially those concerned with fertility, childbirth, healing, love, and marriage. Finally, women performed the religious rites associated with puberty, marriage, and childbirth.

Islam greatly affected the status of women in sub-Saharan Africa. Conversion meant following Islamic law and practices, including switching from the matrilineal to the Muslim patrilineal system. As a consequence, women converts lost the sociopolitical power they had held in their matrilineal societies. In particular, the Islamic practice of purdah, or seclusion, sharpened the gender restrictions on women. However, Islam provided certain compensations, such as legal rights in marriage and divorce, protection against enslavement, and the recommendation of freedom for slave women who bore their owners' children.

♦ PORTUGUESE VOYAGES AND TRADE IN WEST AFRICA

By the fifteenth century, the Portuguese and Spanish kings had partially regained their kingdoms from the Moorish forces that had invaded five hundred years before. They were eager to assert their economic, political, and religious power through the struggle they called the Reconquest, which itself was part of the larger campaigns known as the Crusades. (See Map 1–4.)

Long envious of the North Africans' access to rich trade in ivory, gold, hides, and slaves across the Sahara, the Portuguese promoted navigation along the west coast to bypass the thriving Moroccan ports. They and other European kings also wanted to find alternate routes to Asia so that they could bypass Arab emporiums in the eastern Mediterranean. Such routes would immediately reward their discoverer with vast profits from trading spices, porcelains, silks, and other exotic products. The Iberian kings also

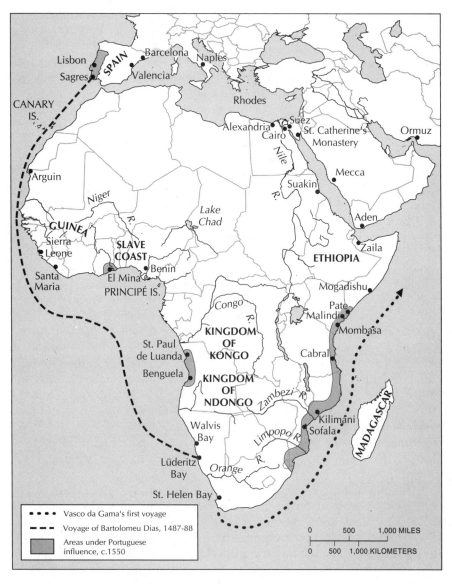

Map 1–4   Voyages of Exploration

wanted access to the fertile regions of Africa that produced cattle, sugar, fruit, grain, ivory, and cotton. Finally, they were motivated by religious factors as well. The battles against the Moors in Spain had weakened the entire forces of Islam in the East and had helped revitalize Christianity. Both Christians and Muslims believed they were fighting for the true religion, thereby pitting the Crusades against the Jihad.

During the first half of the fifteenth century, Portugal's royal house organized an ambitious program of maritime exploration, conquest, and colonization. Portuguese ships crossed to northern Morocco in 1415 and took the port of Ceuta to probe sub-Saharan Africa. They cautiously sailed down the west coast seeking a sea route that would bypass Muslim traders in North Africa. By midcentury they traded regularly on the Upper Guinea coast and brought back ivory, hides, beeswax, gold, and slaves.

Planning further explorations, Portugal requested and received exclusive authority from the pope to continue its African exploration. In turn, the Crown issued trade monopolies to wealthy merchants, who pushed down the coast and shared their profits with the kings. In this way Portuguese traders established bases at São Jorge El Mina (Almina in modern Ghana) and Fernando Po in the Bight of Biafra. Through several fortresses and small garrisons, the Portuguese managed to protect their coastal trading rights and merchants for about fifty years.

Africa also played a role in Columbus's enterprise in the Americas. In the 1480s, while working with his brother, a cartographer in the service of the Portuguese government, Columbus visited Almina on the Guinea coast at least once. It is quite likely that on these voyages he also stopped in the Cape Verde Islands off the coast of modern Senegal where he would have become acquainted with the trade practices of the African kingdoms. Columbus soon became obsessed with the dream of finding a route to India, which was also the driving force of the Portuguese explorations in Africa.

After his historic voyage to the West Indies in 1492, Columbus gained full Spanish support for further explorations. On his third expedition in 1498, he visited the Cape Verde Islands. No longer concerned with the Portuguese coastal monopoly in Africa, he planned to sail down to the latitude of Sierra Leone and then travel due west. He spent eight days in the archipelago but, becoming discouraged by the dry Saharan winds, he decided to sail directly west for the Indies.

◆ SONGHAI

Songhai, another powerful and brilliant West African empire, bordered on Ghana and Mali and largely subsumed them by the sixteenth century. Songhai was located on the middle Niger to the east of Mali. Its towns originated in fishing and farming villages that were gradually drawn into long-distance trade out of its major city, Gao. The elites of Songhai, converted to Islam by their rulers after the 1490s, came to dominate central Sahelian trade, especially in slaves. Relentless attacks from most of its neighbors, who were intent on plundering Songhai's wealth, caused its rulers to fortify the cities and form a large army. Despite a period of subjugation to Mali, Songhai regained its independence and began to build a true empire in the late fifteenth century.

As in other savanna kingdoms, elite families in Songhai chose their leaders according to their distinguished ancestry and then endowed them with semidivine powers. Songhai's huge territory, an amalgam of smaller states, required a complex bureaucracy, a council of ministers, and hundreds of district-level appointees. The trade networks of Songhai stretched to southern Algeria in the north and briefly to the Atlantic in the west. Songhai traders also operated complex feeder routes into the coastal forest regions. East-west routes linked Songhai with other savanna kingdoms across the Sahel. It was among the largest and most advanced states in the world at the time.

The most prominent leader of Songhai was Askia the Great, who came to power in 1493. He soon led a celebrated pilgrimage to Mecca, just as Mansa Musa had a century and a half earlier. Following his return, Askia spent two decades conquering neighboring states and bringing them into his expansive empire. His power grew steadily through deployment of a centralized administration, which among other things instituted Islamic law. Songhai amassed a far greater territory and army than any of its predecessor states. Askia's descendants were unable to maintain control, however, and Songhai began a long decline. Its principal enemies were Moorish forces to the north, who wielded more effective firearms than the Songhai lancers.

◆ CENTRAL AFRICAN CITY-STATES

In the tenth century, several merchant city-states arose in western Sahel, especially those of the Hausa and Fulani in what is now northern Nigeria. Each city controlled trade in its region, particularly in the goods it produced, such as leather, metalware, and dyed textiles. Still further east lay the kingdom of Bornu, organized at least twelve hundred years ago. As it began to control the trade of the central Sahel, Bornu took on aspects of other empires in the region, especially Ghana, Mali, and Songhai. Bornu imposed taxes on both east-west and north-south routes, the north-south routes extending to modern Tunisia and Libya. Bornu's King Houme converted to Islam in 1086, and at its peak four hundred years later, Bornu controlled the region from the Hausa and Fulani city-states in northern Nigeria to the Sudan.

◆ ISLAMIC KINGDOMS OF THE EASTERN SAVANNA

Darfur lay in the western part of modern-day Sudan. By the fifteenth century, its people were Muslims who descended from a variety of ethnic groups and who spoke a distinct language blended from Nilotic and Saharan languages. Their strategic position at the southern end of the trans-Saharan trail from the Selima Oasis in Egypt gave them considerable influence over east-west trade in the Sahel. They also controlled the north-ward export of ivory, honey, ostrich feathers and eggs, gum arabic, slaves, and camels. Darfur caravan routes went to Sennar in the east and to Chad and Nigeria in the west, and brought back gold, silks, and manufactured items. The sultan's personal wealth derived from this trade, for which he levied a 10 percent tax.

◆ EAST AND CENTRAL AFRICA

The cultural history of East and Central Africa is ancient and complex. Egyptian writers made early references to the Red Sea and Horn regions, whereas Roman historians reported on trade with East African cities on the Red Sea. (Archaeologists have discovered Roman coins in the area.) For several centuries the Persians purchased East African slaves for use in their armies. Finally, Red Sea traders exchanged goods with their Chinese counterparts during the period. Clearly, then, East Africa had active economies that produced surpluses that were traded for foreign goods.

To the best of our knowledge, before the Bantu expansion East Africa was originally inhabited by hunting and gathering peoples similar to the Click-language people of today's Kalahari Desert. Other early East Africans were the Cushite people who raised cattle and camels and grew millet and seem to be related to the Christian and Jewish people of Ethiopia. Around 1000 B.C. some of these Cushites also moved down to the East African grasslands and intermarried with local inhabitants.

The Bantu (literally "The People") make up another major group in East and Central Africa. They originated in the northwestern parts of the Congo Basin, and some two thousand years ago they began migrations into the south that continued for centuries. Their adaptation to new ecological zones was facilitated by the production and use of iron tools, such as hoes, axes, knives, and spears. They also transplanted important food crops that had originally been brought from Asia and cattle from the northeast. Within a few hundred years, they established towns on the eastern side of the Congo Basin and then pushed on down the east coast. Around the Lakes Region, they formed many small but powerful states with absolutist kings who claimed divine authority. As a result of their advanced tools, food crops, and sociopolitical organizations, the Bantu peoples were able to dominate or displace the traditional hunters and gatherers of the regions into which they migrated.

The Bantu migrations also caused fragmentation of what was likely a common culture and language. Today their descendants display a wide range of political, social, and economic lifestyles and often must communicate with each other through interpreters.

A fourth major East African people, the Nilotics ("Those of the Nile"), entered the region in the tenth or eleventh century, establishing advanced cattle economies where they settled. Some penetrated into the southern Sudan, and others intermixed with the Bantu in the Lakes Region of modern Uganda and Rwanda. The Nilotics contributed to cultural and economic diversification throughout East Africa.

East-Central Africa also served as a platform for extensive migrations and exchanges with Arabia. First, Muslims from the Arabian peninsula arrived at least by the ninth century, and they became increasingly involved in trading slaves, gold, ivory, copper, hardwoods, and spices. The intermingling of coastal Bantu with Arabs through the thirteenth century created still another linguistic and cultural group, the Swahili. This people borrowed about one-quarter of its vocabulary from Arabic. By the fourteenth century, as reported by the Arab traveler Ibn Battuta, Islam was well established on the coast. Both Arabs and Swahili speakers were found predominantly in the fortified coastal city-states of Pemba, Malindi, Mafia, Mogadishu, Mombasa, Kilwa, and Zanzibar. During that same period migrants and traders from Persia added to the cultural development of East Africa and were especially strong in the south. Eventually, Arab, Swahili, and Bantu migrants established Sofala, in modern Mozambique, to trade for slaves and other products with interior African kingdoms.

Extensive state formation also occurred in Central Africa, spurred by the arrival of Bantu settlers and Arab traders from the north and east. For example, in the tenth and eleventh centuries Bantu migrants moved south and established agricultural and ranching villages that later became federated into kingdoms.

Farther south, powerful families of Bantu descendants, the Shonas, organized the empire of Zimbabwe after the eleventh century. These rulers controlled most trade in copper, gold, ivory, and slaves in southeastern Africa. Zimbabwe's Great Enclosure and Acropolis of elaborate stone walls was so formidable that many Europeans found it difficult to accept it as an African achievement.

Most of the coastal and interior states of East and Central Africa had been deeply affected by Arab and Persian immigrant traders who settled along the seaboard in the fifteenth century. Their most lasting impact was the spread of Islam throughout the region. At this time, however, new foreigners entered the region. A Portuguese fleet commanded by Vasco da Gama rounded the Cape of Good Hope in 1497 in search of a trade route to India that would flank the Arab-controlled eastern Mediterranean. Portugal, which had established relations with Mali decades before, soon forged close ties with the large Bakongo kingdom in modern-day Angola and Zaire. The southern half of Africa would never be the same again.

The Portuguese received a much cooler reception in East Africa, however, where Islam and modern Arab warfare had already been established. The Arab towns and cities all along the coast resisted the Portuguese, whose only friendly contact was with the Ethiopian Christians farther north. The inland states all along the lakes and Rift Valley maintained their autonomy. They continued to sell goods to their earlier customers, the Arabs, who in turn sold them to the Europeans. The main trade items were slaves, gold, and ivory. The partnership role for the inland peoples, however, gradually transferred surplus, as profits, to the coastal intermediaries and to foreign buyers.

The Bantu migrations extended still farther south and east, into the superb savannas of South Africa, where their techniques of metalworking and animal husbandry allowed them to flourish. By the fifteenth and sixteenth centuries, their descendants had settled in modern-day Malawi and Mozambique. Within several generations others had pushed into southern Africa, just before the Europeans began migrating northward from the Cape.

♦ CONCLUSION

At their height, the African savanna kingdoms were equal or superior to contemporary European states in terms of their territory, bureaucratic effectiveness, wealth, and military power. Africa also had vast wealth in primary commodities (mineral, forest, and animal products) and sophisticated means of processing and shipping them. The very success of these societies led to population expansion and a growing trade in human slaves. In hindsight, we can see that an unequal exchange developed, by which Africans exported the permanent wealth of gold and the valuable labor of slaves, while importing manufactured items, such as metalware, cloth, rum, and firearms.

The great extent and antiquity of the slave system, both domestic and for export, may have foreshadowed the terrible inequality of modern relations between Europe and Africa. The long-term exportation of young, able-bodied men, women, and children to the Arab world, Europe, and the Americas had a negative effect on demography, accumulation of wealth, and development of human skills and helped keep Africa in the position of primary producer rather than manufacturer. Even the ancient technologies of iron smelting and smithing, weaving, arts and crafts, and weaponry were eclipsed by outsiders from Greece, Rome, Arabia, Asia, and Europe. Europe took many of its scientific ideas from Africa. Africa's loss, however, contributed heavily to the development of other lands, especially the Americas.

Chapter 2
AFRICA AND EUROPE BEFORE 1700

1434	Portuguese reach Cape Bojador in West Africa.
1456–61	West Africans accept peaceful trade with Portuguese.
1479	Alcaçovas Treaty allows Portuguese to import African slaves into Spain.
1491	Kingdom of Kongo converts to Christianity.
1575	Portuguese invade Angola and establish colony.
1680s	Gunpowder revolution in Africa.

European sailors, who had begun exploring the African coast beyond the Mediterranean Sea in the early fourteenth century, would take nearly two more centuries to sail around the continent. The Phoenicians had probably done so some two thousand years earlier. Between 1312, when the Genoese merchant Lanzarotto Malocello first visited the Canary Islands, and 1497, when Vasco da Gama managed to round the Cape of Good Hope, Europeans became familiar with the west coast of Africa.

Private exploration of the West African coast by Portuguese sailors began in the early fifteenth century, and soon it gained both royal permission and financial support. By 1434 the first Portuguese caravel had rounded Cape Bojador, which had previously been a barrier to southward navigation. After 1444 Portuguese sailors regularly visited the mouth of the Senegal River, and by 1460 they were trading gold in Sierra Leone. Portuguese ships visited the Gold Coast in 1471 and Benin a few years later. In 1483 the Portuguese Crown dispatched Diogo Cao on an official expedition to circumnavigate Africa. While Cao's caravels failed in this task, they did explore the whole coast of Central Africa down to the northern reaches of modern South Africa. Finally, in 1497, a Portuguese fleet under Vasco da

Gama rounded the Cape of Good Hope and sailed on to India. This feat allowed the Portuguese to complete their maps of Atlantic Africa and to establish trade depots, known as *feitorias,* or factories, along the coast.

During their early explorations, the Portuguese encountered people whose rulers and intellectuals were familiar with Europeans, although they were surprised to see them arrive by ship. Africans living in the swath of lands running from the coast of Senegal south to the beginnings of the tropical rain forests and east to the Nile had long had contacts with the Mediterranean world through the trans-Saharan camel trade. This commerce, dating to perhaps the sixth century, had led to the conversion of many African societies to the Islamic religion.

The average West African knew little about the Middle Eastern and Mediterranean lands in which Islam originated, but political, intellectual, and commercial elites were very knowledgeable. Many rulers, for example, had made the pilgrimage to Mecca required of Muslims. Several, like the celebrated fourteenth-century emperor of Mali, Mansa Musa, carried hundreds or even thousands of followers with them. Smaller numbers of wealthy commoners and intellectuals had also traveled to the heartlands of Islam. These religious pilgrims brought back valuable geographical knowledge, including information about the lands of the Christians, who also frequented the eastern Mediterranean.

The trans-Saharan trade occasionally brought Europeans to Africa. Since the fourteenth century, Italian and Spanish firms had had substantial businesses in North Africa, with their agents often giving detailed information about the western Sudan to the commercial and intellectual communities of Europe. Some of these agents also crossed the desert to Central Africa, but they left little beyond stories of trans-Saharan travel. Such visitors, and the more frequent North African merchants, also provided African elites with information about the Christian states of the northern Mediterranean and Europe.

Africans who lived in the forest zone farther south along the coast of Africa had far less information about Europe, probably less than Europeans knew about them. Archaeologists have shown clearly that the elites of this area did have outside commercial contacts. Goods from Europe and North Africa found their way to the most developed states of the Gold Coast (modern Ghana) and to the Yoruba and Edo societies in the south of what is today Nigeria. But such goods surely arrived by way of intermediaries to the north, and what stories they may have heard of Europeans were probably unreliable.

The inhabitants of Central Africa, in the forests of modern Gabon and Congo-Brazzaville or the savannas of Zaire and Angola, had no contact with Europe or the Mediterranean at all. Thus, when Europeans reached their shores in 1483, they discovered that the world was larger and more complex than they had imagined.

◆ THE PORTUGUESE PRESENCE AND COLONIES, 1445–1600

Portuguese sailors, and those from other parts of Europe who followed shortly, came to Africa with expectations of profit and new experiences. Their ideas were rooted in older traditions of interaction with foreigners, such as in the Mediterranean trade and earlier contact with Atlantic island societies. If they believed themselves to be strong enough, they would not hesitate to attack the foreigners. They seized any valuables that could be carried away, including the people themselves, who were later sold in Mediterranean slave markets. The warrior ethos of late medieval society, which rewarded raids against innocent and even unarmed people as feats of bravery, made such forays socially acceptable and potentially profitable. They might even result in conquest and colonization.

If the victims of outside attacks mounted effective defenses, however, Europeans were willing to trade peacefully. In these cases, they established diplomatic relations, exchanged ambassadors, and even set up courts to adjudicate trade disputes. Often only a thin line separated the two strategies, and ships usually traveled equipped both to raid and to trade. When opportunities to plunder arose, merchants became pirates and sailors became soldiers.

The first Portuguese contacts with West Africa were made between 1444 and 1455 and involved considerable pillage. Several young Portuguese squires were knighted for what amounted to attacks on unarmed fishermen and their families. But this phase did not last long. Soon the African authorities responsible for coastal areas organized military and naval defenses, and Portuguese raiders met with stiff and increasingly successful resistance. After a series of disastrous forays in the early 1450s left Portuguese casualties, the Crown decided that it would be more profitable to approach West Africans peacefully. In 1456, therefore, the king dispatched Diogo Gomes to the Senegalese and Gambian coast to meet with rulers and conclude treaties of peace and commerce.

This political approach prevailed in the years that followed. Even farther south, Portuguese captains sought to meet with political authorities from the very beginning and to offer peaceful trade proposals. African leaders were invited to visit Portugal, and those who did later returned to their homes laden with many gifts and sometimes converted to Christianity. Many also studied in Portugal, learned to read and write, and provided useful intercultural services. The most dramatic of these exchanges took place in Kongo between 1483 and 1491 and led to the conversion of King Nzinga Nkuwu to Christianity. This event paved the way for his son Afonso I to create a Christian, literate ruling stratum in Central Africa.

Once commerce was established, Portuguese traders built trading posts along the coast. In many African societies, merchants enjoyed special privileges, including the right to found small towns in which to live and to conduct their businesses. Often these towns were self-governing, although they always answered ultimately to officials of the host state. African rulers in West Africa, for example, typically allowed local merchants, called variously *juula* or *wangara*, to found free towns in their domains. By 1500 these towns formed extensive networks for foreign trade.

African rulers extended the same privileges to European merchants, who then founded posts in Senegambia, the area of the Rivers (modern Guinea-Bissau), Sierra Leone, the Gold Coast, Benin, and Kongo. Many of these posts were controlled by the king of Portugal, who gave them laws and sent officials to govern them. Others were not recognized by the Portuguese Crown, however, but were supported by African rulers instead. Sometimes, such as in Kongo, the African rulers gave the merchants at these posts lavish gifts and salaries and even treated them as their own officials to prevent Portugal from controlling them. In other cases, such as at São Jorge da Mina (Almina) on the Gold Coast, the Crown maintained jurisdiction over the post virtually to the exclusion of authority by its African hosts.

To gain a little more independence from the African states, the Portuguese set up regular colonies on the uninhabited offshore islands. Soon after 1460, the first Portuguese colonists arrived in the arid Cape Verde Islands and converted the area to a base and station for further exploration and commerce with Upper Guinea (the coast between Senegambia and Sierra Leone). In the 1480s they also colonized the islands of São Tomé and Príncipe. These served as a trading station for Central Africa and Lower Guinea (from modern Ivory Coast to Cameroon).

Portugal managed to establish one mainland colony, Angola, under its exclusive control. Originally, Portuguese affairs in Central Africa were handled through the factories established in Kongo; one factory was at the port of Mpinda, and the other at the capital of Mbanza Kongo, also known as São Salvador from the name of its principal church. Difficulties arose, however, when King Diogo I supported the merchants of the factory at Mbanza Kongo against royal agents sent from Portugal. In 1553 Portugal ceded authority to Kongo. In addition, merchants from São Tomé began trading in the kingdom of Ndongo, Kongo's southern neighbor and rival, without Portuguese permission.

To tax this trade, King Sebastião I of Portugal ordered Paulo Dias de Novais to establish a colony at Luanda on the sparsely inhabited coast south of Kongo. Dias de Novais arrived with a body of soldiers in 1575, which he offered as mercenaries to the expanding kingdom of Ndongo, the African state that controlled the interior beyond Luanda. King Ivaro I of Kongo initially supported the effort, hoping that it would allow him to control trade at the coast. When the ruler of Ndongo became suspicious of Dias de Novais's intentions and sought to eliminate the mercenary force, a

Kongo army intervened and rescued the Portuguese commander. Kongo's army was unable to overcome that of Ndongo, however, and a stalemate ensued. Dias de Novais, who soon received troops from Portugal and São Tomé, was then able to establish a permanent colony around the original Portuguese base at Luanda. From here they managed to attract disaffected nobles who had once been loyal to Ndongo and, using the expanded army, won a number of victories against Ndongo.

Dias de Novais's success against Ndongo alarmed Kongo, which then decided to switch sides. Kongo forces fought alongside Ndongo's at the battle of Lukala in 1590, which stopped Portuguese advances in Angola but still left the colony intact. New Portuguese alliances in later years, especially with a group of mercenary soldiers known as the Imbangala, allowed the Portuguese to annex more territory that had once belonged to Ndongo. Thanks to the defensive actions of Ndongo's Queen Njinga, however, the Portuguese were unable to conquer completely Ndongo or any other major Central African state.

Angola, Europe's first and only colony on mainland Atlantic Africa, was really little more than a base and trading station, much like Portugal's colony at Mozambique, which was developed simultaneously. Angola included some settlements along the Kwanza and Bengo rivers extending inland for about 100 kilometers. Much of the land under Portuguese control was lightly inhabited and of poor quality, however, and for nearly a century the Portuguese did not even occupy the main island offshore Luanda.

◆ AFRO-EUROPEAN TRADE

The nature of trade between Africans and Europeans was influenced by the relative economic strengths of the partners. Since modern Africa is economically weak and engages in unequal trade with Europe, some mistakenly believe this condition was always so. During the sixteenth century, little difference existed between the economic capacities of Africa and Europe. Only after the coming of modern industry in the early nineteenth century did Europe and Africa develop strikingly different levels of economic performance. The patterns of trade and development extant today date mostly from the colonial era, which began a little over a century ago.

During the sixteenth and seventeenth centuries, Africa had substantial industrial production. Several regions contained major textile centers, for example. The upper Senegal Valley, the middle Niger, and the towns of Yoruba-speaking people in what is today Nigeria, produced great quantities of cotton textiles of high quality. The last region alone exported over 10,000 meters per year in the seventeenth century—much of it carried to the Americas.

Central Africa also had important textile centers, producing cloth made from fibers found in bark. The largest centers were located in the forested region around Loango, in the eastern Kongo (known as Momboares), and in the Kuba region farther inland. Early–seventeenth-century customs statistics from Luanda show that the Portuguese factory there bought about 100,000 meters of Kongo cloth annually, besides tens of thousands of meters from Loango. Since these figures do not include local sales or regional exports, total production must have been much larger, comparable to the great European and Asian textile centers.

Dramatic archaeological discoveries also reveal the importance of African steel production. Researchers have only recently learned the antiquity and quality of this metal, which dates from about 500 B.C. African metallurgists smelted some of the highest quality steel in the world. West African sites were located in the middle Senegal Valley, Sierra Leone, and a broad band stretching from northern Ghana to Cameroons along the edge of the forest. In Central Africa, steel was made along the southern Zaire River and in the valley of the Nkisi. Finally, Ndongo and Ndulu (in the central highlands) were famous for their steel production.

The fact that Africans imported ironware, steel, and textiles from Europe created confusion among earlier economic historians, who assumed that this meant Africans did not produce their own. Recent research confirms that such imports did not displace native production but rather complemented it, for production was never large enough to satisfy the internal market. Also, linens and cottons were imported into West and Central Africa because those fibers were not available locally. Weavers in Allada (modern Benin) used the threads from imported textiles to manufacture a hybrid cloth that was sometimes reexported to Europeans and was consumed in Barbados. Besides the advantages of new fiber types, imported cloth appealed to some Africans simply because it was foreign. Demand for exotic textiles sometimes reflected wishes to display wealth or status.

It is unclear why Africans imported iron and steel, for native production rose steadily during the period of European commerce and peaked in the early nineteenth century. Some items, like swords and pans, were probably valued as foreign imports, just as cloth was.

At the time of European contact Africa possessed a substantial commercial economy, with most societies trading surpluses with other regions, often thousands of kilometers distant. African commerce began with local markets. Many travelers' accounts mentioned the large amount of goods offered for sale in local and regional markets. For example, on the Upper Guinea coast, many towns exchanged their agricultural surpluses for other commodities. Salt, fish, ceramics, textiles, and metalware produced by traders were also sold in local and regional markets. Thousands and even tens of thousands of people traded in these markets weekly. The volume

Smiths working a forge in Angola. Although Africans worked with simple forges, they produced high-quality iron and steel. Giovanni Antonio Cavazzi, *Historica descrizione de' tre regne Congo Matamba et Angola*, Bologne, 1687, ed. Passaro.

and types of goods exchanged in these markets depended on adequate transportation, especially along rivers and on lakes. Regional trade was most developed in Upper Guinea, the lagoon and river system of southern Ghana, Togo, Benin, Nigeria, and the Loango coast.

Extensive long-distance trade, managed by professional merchants, complemented the local and regional markets. Sometimes these lines were connected to local trade, and some merchants engaged simultaneously in both kinds. For example, boatmen transporting slaves on the Zaire River would use additional cargo space to carry local products, thus servicing both international and local markets.

Merchants operating beyond the borders of individual states formed a class unto themselves, comparable to the bourgeoisie of Western Europe. For example, several such merchant groups existed in West Africa: the Soninke, based in the area just south of the Sahara; the Jakhanke, originally from the town of Jakha on the upper Senegal River; and the Juula, to their south. Membership in these associations was determined by occupation rather than by language and custom, though most of these merchants were Muslims. Each group controlled chains of settlements under its collective leadership and negotiated with local political authorities for rights to operate. The associations developed currencies, credit, and exchange instruments. Members settled with their slaves and dependents in selected towns, which then might become major centers of agricultural production and manufacturing.

Similar trading networks operated all over Africa. The Hausas in today's Nigeria, for example, ran one network in the northern parts of Ghana, Togo, Benin, and Nigeria. In the seventeenth century, the Gold Coast had a smaller one in the hands of the Akan. In Central Africa, networks were established by the Vili from Loango, the Zombo in eastern Kongo, and the Imbangala of the state of Kasanje on the Kwango River. Taken as a whole, these merchant associations formed a substantial interconnected system whose organizations and methods were similar to those of merchants elsewhere.

The rulers of African states, like their counterparts in Europe, were often deeply involved in commerce. Many conducted trade themselves, exchanging surplus goods collected from their own subjects or operating estates engaged in production for the ruler. State officials also dabbled in commerce, using their authority to control labor and raise capital through taxes. In addition, most African rulers recognized that international trade provided new sources of revenue. They exercised the right to tax and participate in commerce. For example, European merchants usually had to pay various customs duties and met state officials or rulers to decide when, where, and at what prices their goods could be sold. African rulers also insisted that they get first choice of imported merchandise at special prices, while demanding that their own goods had to be sold first, also at special prices. Only after the rulers had conducted their deals were private citizens and merchants free to deal with the foreigners.

Few African states were large and powerful enough to exercise sufficient sovereignty to monopolize commerce over an entire region. Therefore, competition prevented closed economic systems of the sort that existed in Asia. Both African and European merchants redirected trade to induce African states into rivalry with each other, promoting more reasonable commercial behavior.

◆ AFRO-EUROPEAN WARFARE

Economic competition rarely led to warfare against African states. In most armed conflicts, Africans had defeated Europeans in direct action, and even when Europeans prevailed, the costs were so high that they preferred to trade peaceably. The survival of the Portuguese colony of Angola, for example, depended on alliances with other African states and recruitment of local mercenaries who fought by African rules and under native commanders. European tactics and technology were not especially effective in

Africa. Even in naval engagements, Africans enjoyed certain advantages: Their canoes and longboats were specifically designed to operate in lagoons, creeks, and estuaries, and so easily outmaneuvered European ships. Indeed, African pirates operating from various parts of the coast, in the Rivers Region of Guinea-Bissau and around Fernando Po off the Nigerian coast, often preyed on European ships.

Generalization about African warfare after 1500 is difficult. Armies in every region had different styles of combat, which influenced the way European weapons and tactics were accepted. In Senegambia, for example, the cavalry reigned supreme. Highly skilled horsemen, recruited from the elite, used missile tactics and horsemanship. They attacked their enemies with showers of arrows and light javelins, after which they closed in using sabers and lances. The infantry, recruited from the lower classes, then moved forward in disciplined formations. These tactics proved effective against the Europeans.

In the Upper Guinea area, cavalry was less important, for much of their fighting was conducted from boats on rivers and lagoons. In Sierra Leone and the Gold Coast, large phalanxes of highly skilled professional soldiers formed the main fighting forces. In Angola, too, professional soldiers, well trained in martial arts and hand-to-hand combat, were the norm. Some of these professionals were free, but many were conscripted as slaves. The Imbangala, professional mercenaries of seventeenth-century Angola, formed their units by enslaving young males and training them solely for warfare.

Most African infantry relied on shock tactics and hand-to-hand combat with swords, axes, and lances. While they rarely used armor, African soldiers were skilled at dodging and parrying in close combat. When not facing cavalry attacks, infantry generals deliberately kept troops in open or dispersed order to capitalize on individuals' skills rather than on mass discipline. Missile weapons were usually reserved for the cavalry and used in the initial stages of battle to soften up enemy formations for decisive infantry charges.

European technology was designed for different kinds of combat. Medieval armies, which depended mostly on cavalry, were heavily armored and used shock tactics. Their missile weapons, especially crossbows, longbows, and firearms, were designed to pierce armor. Speed of fire and accuracy were sacrificed for penetrating power, which was largely irrelevant in Africa. And since few African armies used cavalry, there was little need for massed infantry formations. Thus, medieval European warfare was usually ineffectual in Africa.

After 1625, occasional musketeers fought in the Gold Coast and Angola, usually as skirmishers taking advantage of the range (but not accuracy) of gunpowder weapons. Most armies, however, continued to rely on arrows and javelins for missile weapons. The development of the flintlock musket around 1680, however, made firearms more attractive to Africans. The flintlocks had a faster rate of fire than the earlier matchlocks and were more reliable, especially in rainy or windy conditions. As a result, many African armies began to rearm with these weapons, creating a gunpowder revolution by the eighteenth century. European armies also switched from pikes and close combat weapons to muskets, and they adapted the musket for hand-to-hand fighting by affixing a bayonet to the barrel. Thus, the bayonet charge became as decisive in European battles after 1700 as the advance of pikemen had been earlier.

African armies underwent deeper tactical changes in the seventeenth century, even before the gunpowder revolution. On the Gold Coast, for example, they adopted looser but larger armies of militia. They advanced in broad fronts, relying almost entirely on missile tactics against deep, dense columns of skilled professional soldiers. In the kingdoms of Denkyra, Akwamu, and Asante, such massed armies, originally equipped with bows and arrows, later changed over to muskets, when the new technology proved useful.

Similar changes also took place in Central Africa in the early eighteenth century. Armies in Kongo and Angola began to abandon professional armies specialized in close combat in favor of larger units equipped with muskets. These new armies, like their counterparts in the Gold Coast, dispersed their soldiers over a wide front and fought largely with missile tactics.

The adoption of firearms did not occur everywhere, however, for inland states like the kingdom of Oyo found muskets too expensive and so stuck with cavalry. Dahomey, its coastal neighbor, converted part of its army to musketeers who, in combination with tight infantry formations, were quite effective against cavalry. In Central Africa, the Lunda empire eschewed muskets as cowards' weapons, although price and scarcity may have been as important in the decision as tactical considerations. Perhaps for this reason, Lunda's armies were halted at the Kwango by the musketeers of Kasanje and its allies. In Senegambia, infantry began carrying muskets in the eighteenth century, and in the nineteenth century peasants armed with muskets prevailed over the aristocratic cavalry.

The gunpowder revolution played a significant role in the slave trade and in overall relations between Africa and Europe. European shippers found ready markets in Africa for guns and powder, which boosted the coercive powers of states there. Merchants who wished to operate in Africa were virtually obliged to supply munitions to stay in business. The larger armies made possible by the gunpowder revolution, especially in the Gold Coast and Angola, may well have increased the total number of people captured as slaves. This in turn lowered the prices of slaves.

◆ SLAVE TRADING AND AFRICAN SLAVERY

Europeans along the Mediterranean coast had long employed unfree laborers, including Jews, Turks, Muslims, sub-Saharan Africans, and even other Europeans. Slavery had been present in both the Roman and Islamic sociopolitical systems in the previous millennium and a half. Sub-Saharan slaves, however, had been scarce in the region until the Portuguese began importing them in the midfifteenth century.

African slaves had originally been brought to Spain by merchants who acquired them during their trans-Saharan trading expeditions. It was not until the fifteenth century that Portuguese explorations and trading missions to the African coast led to an expansion and formalization of the slave trade between sub-Saharan Africa and Europe. In 1479, for example, the Spaniards signed the Treaty of Alcaçovas, which granted to Portuguese shippers the right to supply Spain with all the African slaves that were needed. Based on this trade, by 1500 Seville had developed into a principal trading center for African slaves in Europe.

Most of the African slaves in Spain were located in the south, in the provinces of Cádiz, Seville, Málaga, Cartagena, and Granada. Sixteenthcentury censuses provide an idea of their numbers: In 1565 there were 6,327 slaves in Seville out of a total population of 85,538. Most of the slaves were probably sub-Saharan Africans, although the census also included Moors and Moriscos. Since agricultural plantations did not exist in Spain, most slaves were employed as miners, as oarsmen in galleys, and as porters, nursemaids, garbage collectors, and domestics.

After 1500, European merchants increased their imports of commodities from Africa, and slaves were among the most valuable from the very beginning. Soon slaves were also shipped across the Atlantic to the Americas, in what was called the Middle Passage. This trade, amounting to about five thousand people in the early sixteenth century, grew steadily until it reached average annual exports of nearly sixty thousand by the eighteenth century. African exports of people were possible in some measure because most societies there possessed slaves on a large scale. Although we cannot know precisely the percentage of people held in bondage, the available descriptions suggest a very extensive system. Since Africa had the legal, institutional, commercial, and logistical systems necessary to maintain slaves, it was possible for an outsider with trade goods to buy slaves in internal markets. Portuguese merchants began doing just that when raiding ended and commercial agreements were reached with the rulers of the West African coast.

Slavery had become widespread in Africa as a method by which individuals could create and accumulate wealth. African legal systems, unlike those of Europe and Asia, did not permit land ownership as a means of generating wealth. Thus, Africans who wished to profit through farming or ranching had to own or have rights to the labor of people in order to do so. Unlike Europeans, who owned land and then worked it with tenants, Africans owned slaves and acquired as much land as was needed to set them to work.

In Africa, the two main avenues to acquiring wealth were receiving a high government salary, usually drawn from tax revenues, or owning slaves who generated income. Since elite groups often monopolized state positions, ambitious persons of lesser status found slaveholding to be the better of the two alternatives. African slaves were treated as hired, indentured, and tenant workers were in Europe; thus, they were better off than slaves in Europe. In many African societies, masters purchased slaves and then allowed them to establish their own villages, raise families, and live almost as free peasants. Like peasants elsewhere, they had to pay fees and rents to the slaveholder, who was analogous to a European lord. Many observers have viewed African slavery as far more benign than the chattel slavery that developed in the Americas.

Because African masters bought and sold slaves to extend their holdings and replace losses, an extensive slave-marketing system existed within Africa. Slaves tended to be placed in the most dynamic sectors of the economy, especially where mercantile wealth was concentrated, either to expand operations or simply as an investment. For example, all the long-distance trading groups of West Africa established networks of villages populated by their slaves, who produced trade goods, fed their caravans, and served as porters.

In addition to their roles as revenue producers, slaves were also valued as dependents by private individuals and officials. Men used slaves to extend their immediate families, and kings developed administrations and armies of slaves that afforded them independence from powerful social groups. The great Sudanese empires, for example, all had extensive plantations cultivated by slaves, armies of slave soldiers, and administrations composed of slaves. Such dependents provided raw power with which to confront rival elites and territorial challengers. The Senegambian states of the eighteenth century also relied on slave soldiers and officials known as *ceddo* to buttress their authority. The kings of Kongo had slave plantations around their capital and used slaves as soldiers. Their neighbors in Ndongo used slaves as government officials who were an important part of the centralized state.

These two roles of slavery predisposed some people in Africa to own and sell slaves to anyone who could buy them. Another implication was that most slaves were in the hands of state officials and the merchants who were engaged in long-distance trade—the social groups most likely to deal with Europeans.

Methods of enslavement varied so much that we cannot easily state which was the most common three centuries ago. Eyewitness testimony, however, emphasizes capture in warfare, which may have been a usual way to take slaves. Launching a war merely to capture slaves, however, was probably an infrequent occurrence. Instead, slavery seems to have been a byproduct—a profitable one, to be sure—primarily of religious, political, territorial, or economic conflicts. For example, the kingdom of Dahomey attacked neighboring states virtually every year in the late eighteenth century, behavior that often labeled it a slave-raiding state. Yet these armies were not particularly successful: Fully one-third of the wars resulted in serious defeats, and another third ended indecisively, with no slaves being captured. Many of these wars followed upon the Dahomey rulers' attempts to force their neighbors, the Mahi, to consolidate power under a king who would be subservient to Dahomey.

Thousands of slaves were captured in eighteenth-century Kongo as a result of a complicated civil war, in which rival factions of the royal family fought for control of the capital city of São Salvador. Even the Portuguese army in Angola frequently lost wars or captured few slaves in operations that were otherwise successful. Portuguese defeats were particularly hard to accept, at least in the seventeenth century, because many resulted in the deaths of nearly all the Portuguese soldiers. Clearly, such patterns of war are better explained by diplomatic and political factors than simply as slave raids.

Other slaves were seized by bandits or army units operating informally. In the swampy areas of the Niger Delta and the Upper Guinea coast, for example, pirates often raided villages at night, advancing swiftly and silently in their boats and surprising defenders. Villagers responded to this threat by concentrating in larger fortified towns. Those forced to leave these secure places to farm, wash clothes, and fish exposed themselves to capture by pirates.

Soldiers on furlough often operated as brigands and informal slavers. The ceddo in the Senegambian states raided villages when not fighting wars, sometimes traveling several days on horseback to surprise their victims. Private raids by off-duty cavalrymen, common in the western Sudan, account for the export of many slaves through local ports. In Angola, too, soldiers on leave often harassed the population living in areas under Portuguese and African control. Civilians often avoided living near military posts because of brigandage.

Elsewhere in Africa, civil wars and the related breakdown of authority allowed soldier-slavers to become a serious problem. The Imbangala mercenaries pillaged many regions of Angola in the seventeenth century, unimpeded by the states weakened by war. The kingdom of Kongo, facing endemic warfare in the late seventeenth and eighteenth centuries, lost control of forests where bandits terrorized travelers and nearby villages. The kingdom of Benin suffered a similar problem of disorder in the early eighteenth century, as did the great Oyo empire in the early nineteenth century.

Another steady, though small, supply of slaves came from deportations ordered by African courts. Judges, seeking to collect a reward from slavers, may have favored such sentences. European missionaries in Upper Guinea and Angola accused the courts of sentencing innocent persons and even their families to collect fees from slave traders.

Africans who found themselves in debt or incapacitated often pawned (that is, entered bondage for a set period) themselves or members of their families. Normally, a pawn would work for the debtor during a fixed period or until able to fend for him or herself. Not all pawns entered bondage voluntarily, and some never redeemed themselves or their family members. In such cases, pawns simply became permanently enslaved. Climate changes that caused famines, droughts, and epidemics could occasionally induce people to pawn or even sell themselves or dependents as slaves, and they might also find themselves resold to foreigners and transported to America.

Other kinds of enslavement produced wide fluctuations in the number of slaves offered at West African ports. A ship's master might find that no slaves were available for sale one year, and a veritable flood in another. Most fluctuations were caused by conditions in the hinterland serving the ports. Wars might produce slaves, but they also closed down trade routes. European factors sometimes reported that no slaves were available because of a war but that many would be when it finished.

Some ports, especially those that served large and commercially integrated hinterlands, had constant supplies of slaves, since conditions were never completely unfavorable. Even at these ports, however, surges of recently enslaved people occurred, due to wars, droughts, and epidemics.

Patterns of capture and enslavement tended to concentrate people of similar language and culture on the same slave ships. Wars, for example, resulted in the enslavement of thousands of people from a small region that supplied the soldiers. Captives, sold to merchants within a year, could fill several ships in a short time. This tendency was reinforced by the preferences of ships' captains to buy as many slaves as possible at the same port to shorten the time spent in Africa. Often, then, slave ships carried people who knew each other or spoke the same language.

Although the slave trade started on a small scale, compared to total population, it soon exploded and compromised Africa's chances for long-term development. An examination of population loss by region shows that in some areas demographic decline or stagnation occurred. Just as important, it also left a gender imbalance and distorted the ratio of working adults to dependent children. Africans sold almost twice as many males as females into the trade. Researchers are uncertain as to whether this was due to American demand for male laborers, to the fact that most military captives were male, or to the African propensity to retain females. In any case, serious distortions did occur. An Angolan census of 1778–1779, for example, showed that among persons over the age of fifteen, women outnumbered men by more than two to one. Since similar imbalances did not occur among children, they may be attributed to the slave trade. Angola was probably an extreme case, but significant imbalances occurred elsewhere as well.

Gender imbalance in slave-exporting regions probably increased rates of polygamy. Travelers in Angola and in other areas reported that many men took two or more wives. The skewed sex ratio also altered labor systems, for women were obliged to perform the men's work. Sometimes imports substituted for goods usually produced by men. Finally, the sexual imbalance probably worsened the dependency ratio, forcing producing adults to support many more unproductive persons, mostly children. Travelers to Africa remarked that females worked very hard and that children had less parental attention.

Many researchers have debated the larger consequences of the slave trade in Africa, speculating on such issues as demography, slave treatment, long-term economic development, and environmental impact. Consensus on this matter is still in the future, for evidence is still being gathered on these important questions.

♦ CONCLUSION

During the period 1450–1700, Africans and Europeans engaged in complex and many-sided interactions, including many cultural exchanges and a major shift of population from Africa to the Americas. Given the relative equality of the two partners in these exchanges, and the fact that African leaders and economic elites were willing participants in them, historians have been puzzled by Africa's continued participation. These exchanges had very negative demographic and social effects.

The explanation probably lies in how decisions about foreign interaction were made—especially about the slave trade. African leaders were not elected nor were they held responsible to their subjects, any more than were the European traders and kings who organized the trade and settled the Americas. Yet those same leaders helped to supply slaves for the trade by allowing ambition, greed, and jealous rivalries to pull them into transactions with European merchants.

In the long view of history, Europe left a lasting imprint on Africa, and for the most part a negative one. Nonetheless, the earliest relations between Europe and Africa were as between equals. Europeans brought oceangoing ships, Christianity, the territorial nation-state, and certain technologies to Africa. In turn, Africa had a major influence on the colonies and peoples of the Americas.

Chapter 3

EARLY AFRICAN EXPERIENCES
IN THE AMERICAS

T he Middle Passage connected Africa and the Americas after 1500. The shorter routes ran from West Africa to eastern South America, whereas the longest ran from southeast Africa to southern North America. The route handling the most traffic linked Angola in south-central Africa with Brazil in eastern South America and usually required a five-week journey. (See Map 3–1.)

The voyage proved harsh and dangerous, killing many and leaving survivors weak and sick. In normal sailing it lasted from two weeks to more than five months. Conditions varied, though even the better ships were cramped and overcrowded. Food was sparse and poor. No real sanitation existed, and there was only limited opportunity for exercise. When disease invaded such circumstances, there was little to bar its epidemic spread. The close quarters and the filth simply cultivated it, and the result usually became a sickness unto death.

The longer the voyage, the worse the conditions to be endured and the greater the rise in injury and death. Mortality rates, which ran near zero for shorter trips from West Africa to Brazil, reached 15 percent during longer voyages from Angola to Cartagena in the western Caribbean. But the rate on any single voyage was a matter of fate. Relatively few voyages eluded death altogether; other voyages ended with half or more of the cargo of slaves and crew dead.

Depression combined with disease as the Middle Passage attacked the mind with psychological tensions and the body with physiological stress. Captured Africans torn from kith and kin and dragged across a vast expanse, unaware of their destination, feared all manner of fate. Some were afraid the passage was the product of witchcraft; others envisioned being eaten by cannibals; and still others anticipated being sacrificed to strange gods. But whatever they imagined, the reality they experienced was dismal, too. The abuse by people who treated them as cattle initiated strong bonds of common suffering among them, and, as a consequence, many became lifelong friends, "mates" from the experience, if they found themselves together after the voyage was over.

Survival of the Middle Passage stripped the Africans of their identities and served as a prelude to lifelong exploitation. Yet even in their naked-

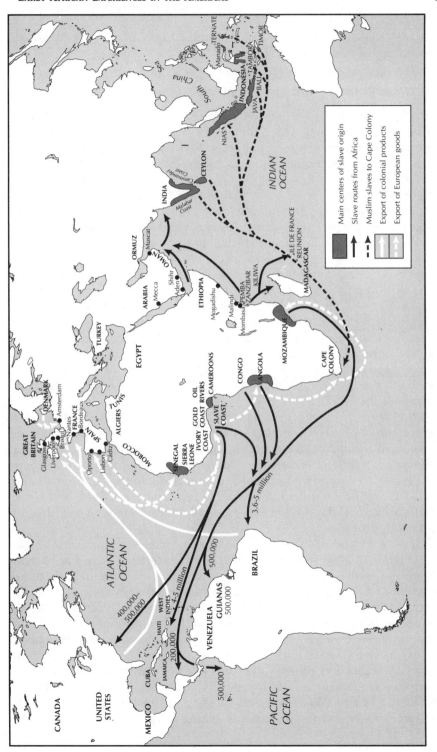

Map 3–1 Slave Trade Routes in the Atlantic

ness, they refused to succumb, so that in their new lives in the Americas they struggled and managed to forge their own way.

◆ WORK ROUTINES AND LIFE POTENTIALS

The Africans who crossed the Atlantic together shared similar experiences in the Middle Passage. Once they were purchased by masters in the Americas, they were put to continuous labor and were exposed to living conditions that varied from colony to colony, enterprise to enterprise, and master to master.

Most slaves were employed on the main lines of production in the American economies, which usually meant labor in sugar mills and mines or on smaller farms and ranches. Alternatively, it might mean domestic service, construction, or craft production in a city. Because of the variety of working and living arrangements in the several branches of production, slaves experienced dramatic differences in life expectancy and satisfaction. Their work conditions probably had a greater effect on their quality of life than either their physical location or their masters' nationality or religion. Many work arrangements actually permitted the slaves some social and family life, enabling them to establish permanent relationships with spouses, raise children, have friends, and enjoy community life. In some degree these compensated for the material deprivations of slave life. Such social and family life could mitigate somewhat the stress, duration, and hazards of the work.

Most slaves worked on plantations and smaller estates. Some of the large enterprises, such as sugar estates, had as many as two hundred slaves, and even the smaller farms that grew sugar had several score. While sugar mills and estates were found throughout the Americas, they were largely concentrated in Brazil and, after 1680, in the Caribbean. Less intensive production units were found in coastal Mexico, Peru, and New Granada (modern-day Colombia), especially during the seventeenth and eighteenth centuries.

Slaves were also used on tobacco farms, which were prominent in the early French and British settlements of North America and the Caribbean. Cacao and indigo were grown with slave labor in Venezuela, Central America, and the Caribbean islands. Slaves also raised cattle on ranches in Brazil, Mexico, Venezuela, and the Caribbean islands. Brazil produced lumber, which slaves gathered and cut and then shipped out to be sold in Europe. These secondary branches of production employed much smaller groups of slaves than did the large estates. In general, owners preferred to use free workers and Native Americans in risky and low-profit activities.

African slaves also worked in the silver-producing regions of Mexico and Peru. Native Americans and mestizos performed the heavy and dangerous tasks, leaving to Africans skilled work in refining, transport, construction, and supervision. In New Granada and Venezuela, from the late sixteenth century on, African slaves were the predominant sources of labor in gold, copper, and emerald mines. When the Brazilian mines of Minas Gerais began producing in the late seventeenth century, African slaves also supplied the manual labor. There, slaves usually worked in smaller gangs, rarely of more than eight or ten.

The labor involved in all these industries was very difficult and sometimes dangerous as well. Most masters expected slaves to work long days, and during peak seasons—such as cane harvest and milling—the shift might extend to twenty hours. A substantial proportion of slave mortality in the productive sector was attributable to accidents. Sugar-milling machinery was unusually treacherous, because slaves who worked long hours processing cane often grew sleepy or careless. Mining accidents frequently were fatal, since the primitive technology led to cave-ins and pick injuries.

From the slaves' point of view, the method of production adopted in the various enterprises largely decided their chances for social and family life. Sugar mills and mines, for example, were often worked by gang labor, which required total dedication to production. Gang labor was the most demanding and least rewarding of all labor regimes for slaves. Employers using this system, either in mines or mills, or in estates like the early Chesapeake tobacco plantations, sought to buy the maximum number of adult male slaves, thereby severely limiting prospects for family life. This meant fewer children could replace the many who died, making it hard to sustain any sort of community. These estates allowed only a few slaves—usually domestic servants or skilled workers—to marry, have children, and live in their own communities.

Gang slaves slept in barracks at night and worked all day. Their food and clothing requirements were largely the master's responsibility, so that all their time was devoted to producing an export commodity. These slaves, cut off from most social activity, unable to marry or establish families, underfed on a monotonous diet, and continuously overworked, had little to live for or to enjoy. Such estates often flourished in areas where ancillary jobs (food growing, construction, transport) were in the hands of other social groups, such as indentured European servants or Native Americans.

The other major form of slave labor organization was the so-called peasant system. Smaller, isolated, and nonexport enterprises usually favored this regime, yet some sugar estates and mines also adopted it. These operated in a more flexible fashion, similar to peasant societies in Europe and Africa. In this regime, slaves produced crops or minerals by a quota system, or they were required to labor for a stipulated time on the main crop. Once the quota was filled, or the task completed, they were free to tend their own grounds, and they could use this free time for social activities or family life. Each system had a radically different effect on the social dimension of slave life. Under this arrangement, masters afforded slaves a greater degree of autonomy in their private lives, in scheduling work, and in property ownership. As a result, it tended to promote fertility among women and stability in the slave communities. From the slaves' point of view, this was a far better form of existence than gang labor.

The peasant system was often found where nonslave labor was scarce or missing, so that slaves had to perform support activities in addition to their main duties. These systems were found in seventeenth-century Jamaica, for example, and became common throughout the Caribbean in the eighteenth century. Under the peasant system, planters typically purchased equal numbers of male and female slaves and encouraged them to marry and form families. In the French Caribbean they even allowed slaves to select mates from within their African group or nation. These new families then built their own homes in villages located on the estates and were given time to grow their own crops.

The peasant system's benevolent impact on slave life cannot be exaggerated. The slaves' resulting ability to form family units led to raising children and to the appearance of new generations of African Americans. In addition, their production of food not only improved their diets, but also enabled many of them to market surplus crops in town or on the estate, so that they could earn discretionary income. They could also dress themselves better and produce some items for adornment and personal use. Archaeologists excavating slave quarters on plantations in recent years have been surprised at the range and quality of goods that the slaves produced for their own use. Thus, slaves living on estates using the peasant system often developed a sense of community and enjoyed greater satisfaction than field laborers elsewhere, even if the work was equally hard and dangerous.

In the most liberal peasant regimes, masters granted slaves legal manumission but required their continued residence on the estates and payment of land rents. For example, in Dutch New York before 1664 many slaves were granted "half-freedom." That is, their masters freed them but collected land rents and reserved the power to reenslave their children. English planters in the Chesapeake lowlands sometimes granted even more legal freedom in exchange for either cash payments or rents and fees. Manumission in Latin America also followed these patterns, especially in the areas around towns where provisions were grown.

◆ URBAN SLAVE LIFE

Some slaves brought to the Americas were brought to urban areas, where they worked in a variety of enterprises: shop and manufacturing production, transportation, retailing, construction trades, and domestic service in large households. Urban employment typically allowed slaves more freedom of movement and even of residence than on rural estates. Thus, if the owner of a Mexican *obraje* (textile mill) had one or two male slaves, these men might not be forced to live in isolation, as gang slaves on a plantation would. Urban slaves therefore had greater prospects for social interaction, family life, and raising children.

The greater freedom slaves enjoyed in the city did not necessarily mean that their physical quality of life was better. Health, sanitation, nutrition, and housing were often of lower quality in urban than in rural areas. The Jesuit priest Alonso de Sandoval's description of Cartagena in the early seventeenth century, for example, suggests that slaves seldom married, were as exploited as rural slaves, and suffered the diseases and stresses of poverty: malnutrition, illness, and unhealthy living quarters. Living conditions for slaves in Rio de Janeiro one hundred and fifty years later were just as bleak. In all likelihood, only those who served as domestics in wealthy households, where higher standards of sanitation and nutrition mattered, enjoyed decent lives.

Skilled European craftspeople came to the Americas to found their own businesses, and many brought slaves to carry out work that hired workers and apprentices had done in Europe. But the American apprentices, since they were slaves, rarely became independent workers. Nevertheless, they learned trades and practiced them for their masters, who typically retired from productive activity when profits permitted. This pattern created a large skilled slave group in all American cities. Such slaves often exercised considerable control over their work and in many respects lived like craft workers in other societies. Still, sadistic and insecure masters could make workers' lives very difficult.

Slaves for hire led less fortunate lives since they were rented out by their owners to whoever needed casual labor. Typical jobs were loading and unloading goods, transporting commodities, or outdoor cleaning and maintenance. Also, public authorities often hired or commandeered slaves from this group for building and maintaining fortifications, roads, temples, harbors, and public buildings. Such employment was less satisfying and provided less freedom of movement than craft trades. It was also more dangerous, since those who hired slaves had little incentive to treat them well or protect them from job accidents.

Female slaves were especially important in retail business. Every city in the Americas had its slave vendors, hawkers, prostitutes, and keepers of small shops and taverns. Slave women in this line of work enjoyed considerable freedom, because masters rarely supervised them daily. Their masters claimed all proceeds except a subsistence allowance for the slave. Because of this freedom, however, disputes often arose over how much money slaves collected and sometimes led to beatings and flight.

A large group of urban slaves in the Americas did domestic services, including cooking, laundry, ironing, cleaning, nursing children, and performing personal services for their masters. Living in close proximity with their masters, these slaves usually had better living conditions than others employed outside the home. Many travelers commented on the well-dressed and elegant personal slaves of wealthy businesspeople and government officials. Still, the majority were probably poorly kept, mistreated, and overworked. Attractive females might be used sexually by their male masters, bear their children, and perhaps even win their freedom. Yet, if some women and a few men used their physical beauty to win favors, many were simply sexually exploited by men who faced few social or legal restraints in dealing with their slave partners.

◆ FAMILY LIFE AND CREOLIZATION

The most important aspect of all work situations for the slave was the ability to maintain a family. Realizing this, masters made family formation a reward for their best workers, even in gang systems. Often the peasant system was explicitly defended on the grounds that slaves were less likely to run away or rebel. Family life ensured that, no matter how hard the labor, slaves could go home to someone who would welcome them and have the satisfaction of raising children. The presence of families on estates also produced an atmosphere that resembled the rural villages where many Africans had lived.

Slaves in peasant labor regimes obviously had better demographic experiences than their counterparts in the gang systems. Through their natural reproduction, they could partially replace losses by death. For example, on sugar mills run by this system, as many as two-thirds of the slaves were born there after only one generation of operation. From fragmentary evidence found in estate inventories, it appears that better nutrition and child care in some areas produced newborn survival rates that were roughly equivalent to those of eighteenth-century Africa and Europe. No matter how they were organized, American slaves often experienced adult mortality rates above those of true peasant communities in Africa and Europe. Often high adult mortality made it difficult for slaves to maintain their numbers through natural reproduction. Under the best conditions, such as the peasant system estates and in North America, self-reproducing slave labor forces did appear.

Whenever slave families could produce new generations, American societies developed *creole* populations—that is, people of African descent born and raised in the Americas. This creole population was crucial for developing African American culture and for creating a community with historical continuity.

Where slaves were unable to raise new generations, especially on gang-worked estates, fresh African laborers arrived regularly. The imported African culture was constantly reinforced by the new arrivals, which made it difficult for African American culture to emerge. Even there, however, the skilled slaves usually created families and could reproduce themselves, thereby establishing their positions as a hereditary creole elite. The emergence of such families gradually led to a social division between creoles, who were often privileged and frequently provided labor supervision, and the African-born slaves, generally called *bozales*.

◆ SOCIAL ORGANIZATION—ESTATES AND NATIONS

Despite the hardships of slave life, many American slaves developed families and communities. Although masters shaped slave lives through work demands, importation patterns, and labor organization, slaves created their own social organizations. For the most part, masters allowed slaves to assemble and structure their private activities and leisure, as long as they did not threaten to undermine security or labor discipline.

One important organization of the slaves was, of course, the estate on which they lived. The estate was often quite large, and the slaves quickly formed social and economic communities within its confines. Where peasant-type labor management prevailed, the estate was very much like a village, in both social organization and physical setting. Under gang management, slaves bonded to one another closely but could not develop independent associations. Besides the constant interaction that members of the same estate had with each other through work, many social activities on the estate engaged them after work hours. Information on marriages reveals that the slaves married people from the same estate, especially if the estate was large.

After a few years, estates often developed complex social organizations. Typically, skilled slaves, house servants, and supervisors formed an elite whose powers over the other slaves were frequently reinforced by the owners or overseers. Over time, this elite became creolized and often, through intermixture with the masters or overseers, racially blended.

Just as the estate was a creation of the masters, the nation was a social organization formed entirely by the slaves themselves. The term *nation* (the English cognate of *nación* [Sp.] and *nação* [Port.]) referred to slaves from the same linguistic group in Africa. They shared common languages and cultures that helped them to survive in an unfamiliar and hostile setting. Nation gave a sense of identity in the confusing multilingual and multicultural world that Africans experienced in the Americas. Observers of slave life often commented on the slaves' propensity to associate with others of their same nation. *Country people*—the English term for the nation—often met for social events and funerals and even ran away together. French masters noted that slaves frequently visited others from their same *terre*, the French term for nation.

Slave trade patterns made a few nations very important in America. In Brazil, for example, the two most prominent nations were the Angola and

Mina or Nago (from modern Nigeria and Benin), whereas in eighteenth-century Haiti the most important nations were Nagos and Congos. Jamaica and other English colonies, on the other hand, saw a predominance of the Coromanti (Ghana) nation. Senegambians were prominent in the early Spanish American colonies and for a time in South Carolina.

Nations differed from estates in that they could arise both on individual units and on many estates. Nations were also a critical element of social structure in towns, where the kind of community defined by an estate was obviously lacking. Thus, when they participated in larger social events, slaves often met by nation, whether in towns or on occasions involving people from more than one estate in rural areas. Such events included Holy Day parades and Lenten carnivals (typical of Catholic countries), Pinkster black festivities in New York, and Negro Election Day in New England, when blacks could choose their local leaders.

The requirements of the slave trade itself deeply influenced the formation of nations in the Americas. Because of the distance between different African coasts, the prevailing trading patterns, and the dangers of retaining slaves on board for extended periods of time, most slaves were purchased at one port. As noted earlier, the typical ship carried slaves from one or two nations who had extensive contact before their capture. Because the slaves formed special bonds with others in their "cargo" (in Spanish *armazón*), their common nationality or African background helped to strengthen it.

Since the pattern of sale usually dispersed the members of a cargo, however, shipboard associations were rare in the Americas. Only the more vague loyalty to members of the same nation remained. In common with immigrants in many other times and places, slaves first sought comfort and support from others who spoke their language, understood and respected their customs, and shared their worldview.

Ethnolinguistic nations in America did not, however, always exactly replicate their counterparts in Africa. After all, African localities and states were political organizations with the powers to tax, conscript, and coerce in other ways. In the Americas, nations were loose ethnolinguistic associations without such powers. Such flexibility in the American setting had an advantage in that persons who might previously have been divided by political allegiances could now find common ground. Old state hostilities faded or remained behind when Africans were carried to the Americas.

Not all masters were willing to allow nations to develop, since nations cut across plantation boundaries and could serve to organize potentially large numbers of people. In some parts of the Americas, masters were nervous about concentrating slaves from the same nation on the same estate. Those in the English Caribbean, for example, made a special point of trying to mix slaves of different origins. This was not true everywhere, however. In the French Caribbean, for instance, masters sought to concentrate slaves from the same nation in the belief that the resulting homogeneous community would give slaves a stake in the system and discourage rebellions and flight.

Even when masters tried to break up national concentrations, they were never fully successful. Slaves came from about two dozen nations, and the systems of supply to each particular colony further limited the sources. Inventories and estate records show that some had great national diversity. (In extreme cases as many as twenty nations were found in one colony.) Yet, most estates of any size showed substantial concentrations of single nations.

Shipping records show that people of huge nations like the Akan (Coromanti), Fon (Mina, Arara), and Angola (or Congo) were so numerous that owners of large estates could not have avoided purchasing large numbers of them. For example, Angolans made up as much as 70 percent of the Africans imported into Brazil in the seventeenth century, and Fons became the predominant imports in the eighteenth century. Angolans also made up some 60 percent of early imports into South Carolina and were probably predominant in the early Chesapeake and New York areas. For most of the seventeenth and eighteenth centuries, Akans (followed by Angolans) predominated in imports to the Caribbean islands under English control.

The influence of the nation as a social force is suggested by the frequency with which slaves married others of their same nation. People from the Fon (and the related Yoruba) nation had the highest propensity to intermarry. Data from Brazil in the eighteenth century, where the ethnicity of slaves was routinely recorded, show that two-thirds of Fon marriages included Fons as both partners. The rates for persons from other nations tended to run at the 50 percent level. Considering that slaves were not absolutely free to pick their marriage partners, this propensity was surely significant.

The Remire estate in French Guiana illustrates the role of nations in American estates. An inventory conducted there in 1690 revealed a large number of nations and a propensity for the peoples to congregate. Remire was run on the peasant system, and each of the nations had its own home ground in one part of the estate. Even though the estate had persons from throughout Africa, half of the twenty-four married couples recorded in the inventory came from the same nation. The six slaves from Kalabar were particularly close, having intermarried and being constantly together. Two others, from the Allada nation, had been born in the same village in Africa, although they had arrived on different ships. The patterns of intermarriage persisted through creolization, for Philippe, an Allada man, married a creole named Marie Doré, whose parents were from Allada.

In urban settings, away from the restrictions of the plantation, nations often developed beyond loose identification based on ethnic background and took on characteristics of formal organizations. This was often achieved by the selection of kings and queens, and occasionally by the development of permanent administrations to look after the affairs of the

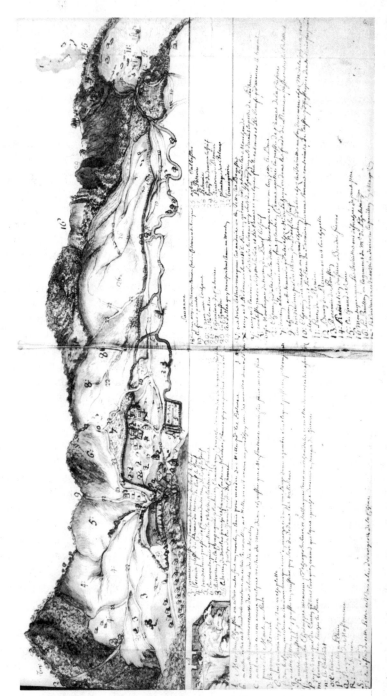

The Remire plantation in French Guiana, as drawn in 1690 inventory. Such plantations were among the largest capital-intensive enterprises of the period. Bibliothèque municipal de Roven, Montbret 125.

nation. By the end of the eighteenth century, most African American societies had ritual royalty elections called *congadas* (from Kongo). Spanish documents as early as the seventeenth century note such elections. Typically, the choice was made by the nation as a whole in a particular region, according to one or another method of voting and selection. Often these kings and queens were served by a host of other officials, who would meet as councils to decide various matters pertaining to the nation as a whole.

Although the kings were mostly symbolic figures, some evidence suggests that they did perform charitable and policing activities. In places like New England, they formed a shadow government, which the larger society used as a liaison with the slave community (and eventually the community of all persons of African descent). Colonial authorities elsewhere were suspicious of these royal courts, which they sometimes accused of creating racial tensions or, worse, fomenting major plots. Such suspicions were based on the great influence that nations exercised in the social organization of the slaves.

African American national organizations bore striking resemblances to the secret societies of Atlantic (West and Central) Africa. The African societies functioned something like Masonic lodges, in which members were initiated into organizations whose formal purposes were social, religious, and charitable. In exceptional times, however, they might take on labor, military, or political roles as well. The societies operated outside the kinship structure, and often they even overlapped state borders. Prominent examples are the Poro society of the Sierra Leone–Guinea region from the late fifteenth century; merchants' societies in the Gold Coast (modern Ghana) during the seventeenth century; various groups in the Igbo region of southern Nigeria; and the cults devoted to various territorial deities in the Kongo and Angola in the seventeenth century. These societies often played major political roles besides their formal religious, mercantile, or military functions. Membership was typically by internal selection, and members achieved rank only by paying large sums of money to the society. Although they were called secret societies because initiation gave the new member access to various secret information not available to the general population, in most respects they operated openly.

American national societies, as already noted, were quite similar. For example, holding office seems to have required displays of wealth, much as was required in the African societies. Still, the American groups tended to welcome members of diverse backgrounds, which would have been more difficult in Africa. In Haiti, and perhaps in other parts of the French Caribbean, these secret societies were the shadowy voodoo associations that were already formed in the eighteenth century. Many scholars have stressed their role in leading rebellions and poisoning plots (and ultimately the Haitian Revolution of 1791–1804), but the societies also performed more routine, self-help services.

In Spanish and Portuguese America, lay brotherhoods organized by the Catholic church took over many senior leadership functions of the nation in an effort to improve the deportment of the slaves. Lay brotherhoods had emerged in medieval times, and most elite members of society belonged to them. In the Americas, special brotherhoods for slaves and free African Americans sprang up as well. They frequently organized along national lines, and studies of their rules show that they performed many charitable and self-help functions. They played a prominent role in the activities of the nation and dominated the selection of kings and officials.

♦ CULTURAL TRANSFERS

The emergence of independent social organizations under their own con-trol gave African Americans opportunities to transplant aspects of African culture to their new homes. When families, nations, and other social groups gathered, members could play music and dance, exhibit clothing, and practice their religions. In this way, they preserved linguistic, religious, and aesthetic principles from extinction despite the rigors of the trans-Atlantic trade. The slaves also tended to mix traditions from various origins—Africa, Europe, America, and Asia—into hybrid cultures with dynamic principles of their own.

African cultures and their derivatives in the Americas changed con-stantly through their own internal mechanisms and their borrowing from other cultures. Language tended to change very slowly, almost impercepti-bly, from generation to generation. Religion and philosophy evolved even more slowly, for tradition had great significance in both. Aesthetics (art, music, dance, fashion, cuisine), however, shifted as rapidly as tastes change.

As was seen in Chapter 2, Africa possessed extensive commercial net-works long before the sixteenth century, and some Africans traveled wide-ly for religious and other reasons. (See Map 3–2.) In these ways, African societies developed regional cultures that changed internally even as they interacted with each other. From the midfifteenth century on, European contact added new elements to this mixture: languages, technology, and ideas. When Africans were uprooted and were taken to the Americas as slaves, where they came into intense contact with people from other parts of Africa, Native Americans, and still more Europeans, cultural change necessarily accelerated.

The conditions of slavery also caused radical alterations in the social and cultural environment in which transplanted Africans lived. In their new world they confronted new plants, soil types, animals, and climates. Wrenched from their traditional social structures and forced into alien ones, they survived by accepting the strange and novel. They were not

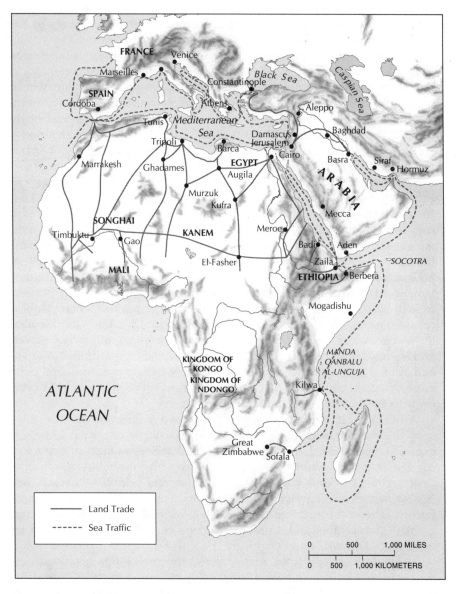

Map 3–2 African Centers of Production and Trade Routes

alone, of course: European immigrants, too, experienced intensive and fruitful cultural contacts.

Africans came to America speaking their home language or languages. Those who came from coastal or commercial districts also often spoke Creole or modified forms of European languages, especially Portuguese. For a generation or so, these nation and Creole languages persisted in the Americas, probably being essential for the psychological survival of the original immigrants. Most Africans who came to America soon learned to speak a Creole version of the European language of the colony, and their children typically became primary speakers of this language.

Although newly arrived Africans could usually find persons who spoke their home languages—members of national gatherings or spouses from their home area—they also had to learn the language of the colony so that they could communicate with Europeans, Native Americans, and even Africans from other nations. The logical choice was the European tongue of the colony, which some slaves would already have known from Africa. As long as new slaves came, the incentive for continuing to speak the nation language remained. As imports became less important, however, the European-based Creole language took over completely, except in special circumstances. For example, in Cuba, Puerto Rico, Trinidad, and Jamaica, the last group of Africans came as indentured servants rather than slaves, and so they tended to form their own homogeneous communities in towns and rural areas. These communities preserved the ritual and sometimes more extended use of national languages (especially Kikongo and Yoruba) even to the present.

While African languages generally dropped from everyday use, they survived in other ways. For example, the Creole forms of various European expressions contained African elements, and their grammars incorporated African structures, borrowing mostly European vocabulary. Such constructs could be understood by Europeans and Africans alike. A few African words also survived in Creole and even made their way back to Europe when no equivalent forms existed; examples are okra and gombo (plants) and zombie and voodoo (religious concepts). Such borrowings were quite limited, however.

Aesthetic survivals from Africa were more numerous and vigorous, because they did not require a long, concentrated study and they richly rewarded those who made the effort. We do not necessarily have to learn anything to appreciate beauty, nor do we need to abandon our own idea of beauty to appreciate another's. It is therefore easy to exchange and to adapt artistic tastes, which helps to explain the tremendous impact of African aesthetics on American culture. Aesthetics includes the obvious forms, music and dance, as well as patterns of decoration—even bodily decoration like hairstyles and fashion—and cuisine.

African music and dance were quickly transferred to the Americas; early observers noted the presence of performers at national gatherings. When these occasions brought together several nations to play simultaneously, performers recombined styles and instruments in imaginative ways. At the same time, Africans came into sustained contact with European music, which had begun to arrive in some areas even before the rise of the slave trade. American slaves often learned to play European musical instruments, even as they impressed their owners and neighbors with their own traditions and instruments. This naturally enough led to the mixing of traditions. Many masters, appreciating the contributions of musicians to the well-being of their slaves, allowed them to practice and create new material, thereby promoting African music's major legacy to cultural pluralism in the Americas. Other aesthetic elements underwent a similar process: reproduction in African form, followed by admixture with other African and European forms, finally resulting in new syntheses. African American cuisine is widely recognized in some areas—Brazil, Cuba, and Louisiana, for example—although most research is based on present-day recipes.

African religions became transformed in the Americas through a long, complex, and undocumented process, creating peculiarly African forms of Christianity that in outlook and ritual were sometimes more African than European. The Euro-African religious encounter had begun in Africa long before the slave trade to the Americas. All of Egypt and the upper Nile had once been Christian, and Ethiopia remains mostly Christian to the present day. In the fifteenth century Europeans sought to convert other Africans as they established their many commercial settlements along the African coast. Slaves or the African wives of Europeans at these settlements usually converted to Christianity, and their influence often extended to neighboring peoples. More dramatic were the conversions of whole African countries. The kingdom of Kongo was converted in 1491 and is still Christian today. Other conversions took place in southern Nigeria and Sierra Leone but proved less enduring.

Religious conversions in Africa affected American slaves in two ways. First, the Christians among the newly arrived Africans were often chosen to be instructors for the other slaves. This was especially true of Catholic masters, who tried to convert slaves as soon as possible. Since European priests did not know the languages of the slaves, they chose African Christians who often came from literate or from commercial families. Second, the Christianity they practiced had already incorporated African culture and become syncretic, or blended.

In Africa many conversions took place when the new religion was seen to contain elements in common with their beliefs, especially about the powerful idea of the Other World, or abode of ancestors and gods. Kongo's first Christian king, for example, dreamed about the Virgin Mary, which both he and European clergy accepted as a revelation from the Other

World. Later, his son Afonso miraculously won a battle after some of his soldiers saw Saint James in the sky. Njinga, a famous queen of the Central African state of Matamba, converted after several of her mediums, possessed with the spirits of her ancestors, told her to become a Christian and cease devotions to her ancestors.

Such conversions occurred in the Americas also. Costa Rican slaves, for example, revered a dark-skinned Virgin Mary who had appeared to a slave woman. European clergy occasionally performed miracles in the slaves' presence to convince them, as did the Jesuit priest (later Saint) Pedro Claver, who worked among slaves in Cartagena. Christian saints sometimes appeared to Africans in dreams, possession states, or communications with the Other World, resulting in an eclecticism of ideas. Such revelations often identified European saints as the same persons that Africans had worshiped. Accordingly, in many parts of America, the new Christianity included simultaneous representation of African gods as Christian saints.

Conversions generally took place later in Protestant, and especially English-speaking areas, than in Catholic zones. One reason was that in Protestant areas the authorities were reluctant to allow slaves to worship as Christians for fear that biblical injunctions against enslaving Christians might force them to release their captives. The fact that African Christians were usually Catholic complicated matters. For example, in the 1739 Stono Rebellion in South Carolina, Kongo Catholics revolted and sought to escape to Spanish Florida, where they hoped to improve their situation.

In Protestant North America and the British Caribbean colonies, slaves in the eighteenth century experienced the Great Awakening, a series of spiritual occurrences similar to the miracles that induced earlier Africans to accept Catholicism. The theology of this movement stressed personal contact with the Christian God through states of possession which occurred when a deity temporarily took over a believer's consciousness, a mechanism familiar to Africans.

◆ SLAVE RUNAWAYS, REVOLTS, AND REBELLIONS

Slavery on American estates and in cities involved considerable exploitation which many slaves sought to evade, resist, or eliminate. Sometimes they showed their resistance merely by working more slowly on their masters' tasks than on their own affairs. Many, however, deserted their workplaces entirely, usually for only a day or two, a practice the French designated as *petit marronage*. Such slaves were designated runaways, even though they often left to protest or merely to rest, visit friends, or pursue other interests. These temporary absences sometimes followed the separation of a slave from his or her family, an unfair punishment, or an argument. Runaway advertisements and court records suggest that many such

people only went a short distance from their estates
areas or among other slaves or kin. Most returned
soon caught. In intensively settled areas, substanti
might be absent and wandering about at times. Oth
roons (a cognate of the French "marronage"), fled
never returning. They usually sought refuge in *paleng*
[Port.], communities founded by runaways in hills, ιυιсλιο, anu υιιει
inaccessible areas. Occasionally, they found refuge with nearby Amerindians. Maroon communities were usually small villages, but under military
pressure by slave owners, some formed larger, fortified settlements.

Most colonies had large runaway communities in remote areas. Among
the most notable were Brazil's Palmares, which numbered tens of
thousands in the midseventeenth century, and those around the mines of
Minas Gerais. By 1650 Cartagena was surrounded by dozens of these
communities, and the densely forested coast between Panama and Cartagena held many of them. Maroon communities also arose in Mexico and
Peru and in the densely wooded hinterlands of the French, British, and
Dutch Guianas. Even the Caribbean islands had several: Jamaica's maroons sued for freedom and land, while Haiti's lived permanently in the
hills before the 1790s.

Many slave revolts in the Americas were large-scale, armed, and violent
attempts to flee servitude, rather than conspiracies to overthrow the colonial systems. Such risings often resulted in the founding of free communities, such as those of the Venezuelan maroons in the 1550s and the
Suriname slaves in the 1680s and 1690s. Jamaican maroons, in danger of
recapture, received a big boost when hundreds of Akan slaves revolted
and joined them in the late seventeenth century. The largest and deadliest
North American slave revolt, the Stono Rebellion of 1739, was, as noted
earlier, largely an attempt by South Carolina slaves to escape to Florida.

Once they decided to break with authority, maroon groups carried out a
variety of attacks on their oppressors, sometimes raiding nearby estates for
provisions and hostages and even stealing other slaves to serve as bonds-
men. In the eastern Caribbean the maroons entered into alliances with
Carib natives to attack colonists. They also helped pirates and foreign
raiders to attack colonial settlements, as, for example, when Sir Francis
Drake raided Panama City in the late sixteenth century. Worst of all, from
the planters' point of view, the very existence of maroon communities
encouraged slaves to run away by providing refuges. As a result, colonial
authorities went to great lengths to disperse maroon communities and
round up the runaways.

Fighting between colonial forces and maroons usually led to militariza-
tion of the runaway communities. Maroon officers and soldiers were not
hard to find, because many Africans who had served in African armies
were sold as slaves after capture. We have evidence of trained military

p in the 1522 revolt in Spanish Hispaniola, the Jamaican uprisings late seventeenth century, the Stono Rebellion, and the Haitian olution. Military leadership often made the communities' redoubtable rces capable of conquering other areas. At its height, Palmares allied dozens of maroon settlements under a single military leader. The Jamaican maroons developed a small state by conquering nearby runaway settlements and imposing order on the vicinity.

Many maroon communities escaped the threat of arms by winning autonomy from colonial authorities. They usually gained this status when they agreed to help round up other runaways, neutralize dangerous maroons, or defend the colony against outsiders. Spanish authorities often granted municipal status to runaway communities, while the British executed formal treaties with several (e.g., Jamaican maroons in 1729). Thus, thousands of Africans and their descendants gained their freedom through arms.

The slaves' ultimate defiance was to assault the entire system of colonial oppression, an effort the authorities countered by running spies and informants among the slave populations. Africans organized extensive conspiracies in Barbados (1692), New York (1712 and 1741), Antigua (1736), and Jamaica (1760), but the only one they carried to fruition was the Haitian Revolution of 1791. Colonial police often noted that plots involved members of the same nation, who used African languages and religious authority to win converts. This was especially noticeable in the great slave revolt of 1760 in Jamaica. Led by Coromanti (Akan) slaves, it mobilized thousands of slaves for years. The British had to ship regular troops to the island to reinforce the colonial militia and maroon allies.

♦ CONCLUSION

The conditions of slavery and forced labor placed strict limits on the lives and opportunities of Africans who came to America after 1500, but did not prevent the formation of African American communities. Where conditions allowed, Africans married, raised families, and socialized their children. In many parts of the Americas, they managed many of their own affairs, built homes, fed and clothed themselves, and modified their religious customs. In addition to the social organization the estates imposed, African Americans also had their own organizations. They followed national lines at first and racial lines later. The creation of a strong cultural setting gave Africans and their descendants the psychological, spiritual, economic, and cultural resources they needed to face the challenges of the emancipation era and beyond.

PART II

The Slave Trade and Slavery in the Americas

O nce established by Europeans, the slave-based economies of the Americas expanded rapidly, demanding ever larger numbers of African laborers. As the tropical regions generated more and more goods for export, the Americas were incorporated into worldwide trading networks. Sugar, tobacco, cacao, precious metals, rice, coffee, and cotton—the biggest money-makers in American trade—required millions of workers and created fortunes for merchants and shippers. The very advance of international capitalism depended in part on the smooth production of the American economies.

The societies that emerged in the Americas proved to be completely new experiments. Several million Europeans and over ten million Africans flooded the American continents and islands, partially replacing the declining numbers of Amerindians. Never before had such large numbers of people relocated in such a short time, nor had as diverse peoples intermingled so intimately, as in the so-called New World. Most of these emerging societies were multiracial, with small white governing elites and large numbers of subordinate persons who were Amerindian, African, or of mixed ancestry. Nonwhites worked and provided services for the elites through many coercive arrangements similar to those used in other parts of the world. Slavery was but one kind of forced labor used in the period of European expansion. Africans, usually the most valuable and productive members of the work forces, lived under the most restricted and abusive conditions. Nevertheless, in a matter of only a few decades, some Africans

won their freedom, others intermarried, and the community of African Americans became more complex.

The absolute number of Africans imported into American societies most affected the extent and nature of African influence there. In the tropical lowlands, where few Amerindians remained due to migration and disease, Europeans imported large numbers of Africans to clear, plant, tend, harvest, and process crops. In these areas the Africans revived society and culture and left their imprint on nearly all aspects of life. This process can be called *Africanization*. In contrast, in areas where fewer Africans arrived (owing sometimes to large Amerindian survivals), the slaves gradually gave up much of their cultural legacy and autonomy. Such was the case in highland Spanish America, in the Amazon, and in Central America. Even without a major Amerindian presence, if whites were the majority, the African heritage tended to fade in time as the European heritage became superimposed. This occurred in the British colonies of North America, the Dominican Republic, Puerto Rico, and southern South America.

The Caribbean islands and coastal Brazil imported over three-quarters of all Africans who came to the Americas, financing the dense slave trade from the profits from sugar and tobacco. As a result, African genetic and cultural influence was heaviest in these regions, some of which became deeply Africanized. The slave trade brought children as well as men and women of all ages, so that some family, clan, ethnic, and even national groups became reconstituted. Plants and technology also flowed across the Atlantic, enriching the transactions often called the Columbian Exchange. At the center of these African American societies was the sugar estate, called the *ingenio* in Spanish and *engenho* in Portuguese. But many other institutions, in small towns, ports, mines, runaway camps, and cities, sprang up across the lowlands of America and incorporated African elements. These social organizations served to mediate between the different ethnic groups and to legitimize and maintain the new arrangements.

Spain's mainland colonies imported fewer slaves from Africa, mainly because of higher costs (Spain did not trade in Africa and distances were longer) and lower profits from their employment. For reasons discussed in Chapter 6, Spanish American slaves tended to ally themselves more with whites than with Amerindians. Interaction and marriage occurred among all groups, so that larger sectors of mixed ancestry, called mestizos, zambos, and mulattoes, or simply *castas,* arose as intermediate strata. Cultural interaction and manumission led to a process called *creolization,* by which Africans and their descendants adopted local and European customs to substitute for African traditions. A variety of local African American cultures arose that today have largely been subsumed into the modern societies of Spanish America.

A variety of slave regimes developed in mainland British North America as black bondage infiltrated every colony from the northern reaches of

Massachusetts Bay, which would become Maine, down to the southern border where Georgia stood as a buffer against the Spanish in Florida. Product, place, and the pace of settlement marked the major differences among the patterns of slavery as evolving regional economies developed different labor needs and demographic draws.

Four major regional patterns emerged. The earliest and largest operated in the Chesapeake, where Virginia pioneered tobacco production before 1620 and Maryland joined in after 1635. What became the so-called Middle Colonies formed a second pattern from a legacy that began in the 1620s when the Dutch imported enslaved Africans into the colony of New Netherland, which later became New York, New Jersey, and Pennsylvania. This second pattern featured mixed use of blacks for domestic, farm, and general-purpose labor. The New England region represented a third pattern, distinguished from the second not so much by type of labor used as by location, proportion, and population mix. Blacks were more localized in New England than in the Middle Colonies, and they formed a significantly smaller portion of the regional population. The last of the regimes developed in the so-called low country of the Carolinas and Georgia, where rice came to dominate.

Even within regions, differences were often great. In the low country, for example, the Carolinas had two generations of experience before the English settlement of Georgia ever began in the 1730s. And it was not until the 1750s that Georgia adopted slavery, for its initial plan of settlement prohibited slavery. Also within regions, urban and rural patterns diverged. Colonial cities such as Charleston, New York City, and Philadelphia cast slave practice in somewhat different shapes distinguished by higher proportions of blacks in artisanal and domestic work. The density of blacks was higher, of course, and the interaction among blacks and also between blacks and whites, was broader.

Two watersheds marked the general patterns everywhere. The first occurred between 1680 and 1720 as enslaved Africans surpassed indentured Europeans as the primary bound labor force. While the shift developed primarily in the Chesapeake, the regional experience reflected the aggregate trend and its size influenced the composite result, which increasingly isolated African peoples as the only bound labor in the colonies. More clearly than ever, color became the measure of bondage.

The second watershed flowed with and from the U.S. War of Independence (1775–1783). It produced the so-called first emancipation, which ended the chattel status of blacks from Pennsylvania northward during the half-century from 1777 to 1827. Thus, it also settled slavery in its position to become the so-called Peculiar Institution of the U.S. South. That development became a cardinal element of the U.S. antebellum period, which served as prelude to the Civil War (1861–1865).·

African-Americans in urban settings lived differently than those in isolated locales, and they sometimes had more opportunities to improve their status and living conditions. In Latin American cities especially, creolization occurred more rapidly, and manumission was more frequent. Religious brotherhoods and neighborhood associations allowed some slaves to pursue their own interests in organized ways. More modern labor arrangements, like slave renting, apprenticing, militia service, street vending, and provision of services, taught slaves valuable skills and could lead to self-purchase. Urban slave regimes could be brutal, as in the sweatshops called *obrajes*, and they could prevent slaves from gathering to preserve their identity. Nonetheless, cities usually offered a greater variety of experiences and options than plantation life.

In a few regions, African influence, while substantial in colonial times, tended to disappear during the nineteenth and twentieth centuries. Highland Mexico and Peru, for example, had large black populations to sustain their cities and mining communities, but later they faded from view. Southern South America also had substantial numbers of slaves—up to half in Argentina's interior in the eighteenth century. Yet their descendants either emigrated or intermarried so thoroughly that little genetic trace of them remains.

Economic, spatial, and ecological factors played important roles in the Africans' arrival and habituation in the Americas. The huge profits to be derived from plantation agriculture fueled a booming trade in the Atlantic. Extensive humid lowlands, where sugar and other tropical crops grew well, pulled the largest numbers of Africans to Brazil and the Caribbean Basin. The closer the colony lay to the equator, the more Africans were brought, because transport costs were low and profitability in agriculture high. And sheer proximity to slave-exporting regions favored Brazil and the Caribbean.

These same factors tended to diminish the slaves' quality of life: Endemic illnesses in the tropics and ease of replacement led planters to pay less attention to survival and reproduction. In addition, the profits to be made in export agriculture led planters to neglect food production, so that slave diets in the tropics were usually skimpy. Finally, the tropical staples—manioc, yams, rice, and derivatives of sugar—had far less protein and vitamins than temperate-zone crops. To these disadvantages could be added the overcrowding and rigid discipline that were usual in regions where Africans far outnumbered whites.

Not all of the Americas within the tropics were hot and humid, of course. South-central Brazil, the Andes, and much of meso-America were medium- and high-altitude zones that usually employed Africans for mining operations, for overseeing Amerindian workers, and for food, transport, and maintenance work. By the eighteenth century, many blacks also served in urban services and defense. The alien geography of these highlands further allied African and Spaniard, both of whom were outsiders in

Native American heartlands. Few persons of African descent remain in such areas today.

Geography affected the paths by which Africans arrived in the Americas. Apart from the direct trade of the Middle Passage, dangerous as it was, many arrived by circuitous and even more perilous routes. For example, slaves bound for the agricultural valleys of Peru or for the mining cities of Bolivia had to land at Portobelo, Panama. From there they crossed the Isthmus on foot and in chains and then reembarked in Panama for their final destination. This trek took months, during which time poor nutrition and sanitation heightened the incidence of disease and death.

In another common transshipment experience, especially between the 1660s and 1730s, slaves who had worked for several years in the Caribbean would sometimes be sold to ship captains sailing to the Chesapeake or other North American colonies. Also, a transshipment route developed in the eighteenth century, in which English and Brazilian slavers landed Africans in the Rio de la Plata estuary and then marched them inland to Argentina's northwestern cities and up to the Bolivian highlands. The psychological and physiological traumas of these routes were devastating to Africans.

Topography and vegetation influenced the feasibility of establishing successful maroon communities in the Americas. Generally, colonies on the continent or major islands experienced the largest number of maroon camps; those on small islands with little forest cover had the fewest.

Finally, Africans in the Americas experienced psychological distance from their homelands. They often worked in radically different climates and physical conditions than they had known in Africa. Occasionally, slaves were literally transported halfway around the world, for example, from Mozambique to Louisiana. They underwent anguish at being out of touch with their ancestral burial grounds, which was so important for their religious and spiritual well-being. And most suffered separation from living family members as well.

Part II presents a detailed view of four different regions of the hemisphere where Africans were taken and settled. Each area had particular cultural, political, geographical, and demographic characteristics that distinguished it from the others. These regional flows of Africans may be considered currents of the diaspora. It is also essential to remember that, while the period from the seventeenth to the nineteenth centuries witnessed the high tide of the slave trade and crest of the economies it sustained, many Africans won their freedom or at least much control over their lives. Finally, the most deplorable legacy from the era of slavery—the racism that became firmly entrenched in Euro-American attitudes and behavior—evolved differently in each region.

Chapter 4
AFRICANS IN THE CARIBBEAN

1479	Spanish permit Portuguese to supply slaves under Treaty of Alcaçovas.
1494	Treaty of Tordesillas makes Africa a Portuguese sphere, after which the Portuguese dominate slave trade.
1494	Spanish establish settlements on Hispaniola.
1502	First slaves introduced into Caribbean islands.
1516	First Caribbean sugar mill erected in Hispaniola.
1522	First slave revolt in the Americas occurs in Hispaniola.
1600	Natives of islands largely disappear.
1630s	British begin sugar industry on Barbados.
1655	British take over Jamaica from Spanish.
1685	*Code Noir* promulgated in France to regulate Caribbean slavery.
1739	British sign the first treaty with the Jamaican maroons.
1791	Slave revolt begins in Haiti; independence declared in 1804.

The long arc of islands that stretches from Cuba in the northwest Caribbean down to Trinidad near the Venezuelan coast became home to several million Africans. (See Map 4–1.) Using slave labor, Euro-American planters and businesspeople created the most profitable enterprises of the day in these islands, plantations that produced

71

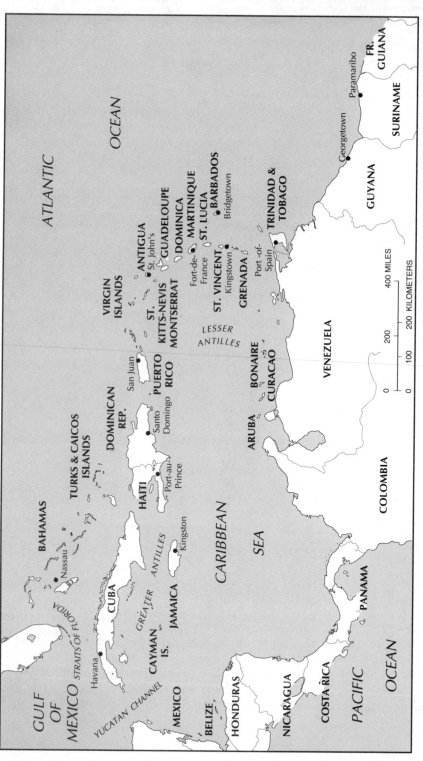

Map 4–1 The Caribbean with Principal Cities

tropical goods for export. Because of their sheer numbers, Africans and their descendants converted many islands into little replicas of Africa. Yet so few of the Caribbean slaves' babies survived that they could not sustain their numbers. Instead, their ranks were replenished yearly with new slaves from Africa. These and other factors created particularly intensive, severe, and challenging experiences for Africans and their descendants.

All these islands lay within the tropics and therefore were suitable for producing crops valued in European markets. They ranged in size from the Greater Antilles (Cuba, Hispaniola, Puerto Rico, and Jamaica) down to mere coral reefs. They varied greatly in topography, and many possessed high mountains, usually volcanic in origin; others were remnants of ancient mountains and upward-thrust sedimentary rock. Nearly all received enough rainfall to support the original forests and, later, European-style agriculture. When properly managed, the islands sustained enormous populations capable of producing huge crop surpluses.

For three and a half centuries, coerced black labor in sugar plantations provided the foundation on which the economies of the Caribbean rested. Sugar gradually spread through the islands until it became king during the eighteenth century. The Spanish had planted cane almost immediately, replicating their experiences in the Canary Islands. The first shipment of African slaves arrived in 1502. The following century, the British began to cultivate sugar in Barbados and later Jamaica with imported labor. During the second half of the seventeenth century, the earlier indentured laborers were replaced by African slaves. At the height of their imperial expansion, the Dutch also began cultivating sugar in their islands and South American colonies. The French followed suit in their colony of St. Domingue and in the smaller islands in the eighteenth century. Finally, the Spanish stimulated production in Cuba and Puerto Rico in the nineteenth century. This last economic surge crested in the midnineteenth century and became a tidal wave. For over a century the Caribbean Basin was considered the "sugar bowl of the world."

* * *

Spanish colonization of the Caribbean had begun in 1494, when Christopher Columbus established his first settlement on the island of Hispaniola (modern Haiti and the Dominican Republic). Residents of this fledgling colony supported themselves by exploiting the indigenous inhabitants. Amerindians were almost immediately forced to work for their new masters, but as a result of warfare, mistreatment, and epidemic diseases, their numbers began to decline rapidly. The indigenous populations of the entire region probably numbered several million in Columbus's time, with the largest concentrations on the islands of Hispaniola, Cuba, and Jamaica. A series of devastating epidemics struck the islands during the sixteenth century, however, and almost wiped them out. Particularly savage were the epidemics of smallpox in 1518–1519 and measles in 1529. By 1600 the indigenous peoples had largely perished.

The disappearance of the Amerindian population and the absence of a servile class of Europeans led the colonists to clamor for the importation of African slaves. Spaniards had long known slavery in their land, having been enslaved by the Romans, and in turn had enslaved Jews, Turks, Muslims, black Africans, and even each other. Sub-Saharan African slaves, however, did not form an important part of Spanish society until the decades just preceding Columbus's voyage.

African slaves had originally been brought to Spain by merchants who acquired them from trans-Saharan traders. Toward the end of the fifteenth century, Portuguese ships began bringing slaves from the Senegambia coast, thereby formalizing a larger trade. In the 1479 Treaty of Alcaçovas, Spain authorized Portuguese ships to sell slaves. By 1500 Seville had developed into one of the principal trading centers for African slaves throughout Europe. Sub-Saharan slaves in Spain were concentrated in Cádiz, Seville, Málaga, Cartagena, and Granada, that is, the productive trading cities of the South. Most were employed in the mines and galleys, or served as porters, nursemaids, garbage collectors, and domestics.

The decision to introduce African slavery into the Caribbean was not based solely on existing practice and economic need. There was nothing inevitable about employing African peoples on the islands, for the Europeans had several other options available. To suggest that the Caribbean could not have developed without slave labor would lend unwarranted justification for and legitimacy to the institution.

♦ THE NATURE OF SLAVERY IN THE CARIBBEAN

Beginning in 1502, the Spanish Crown sanctioned the shipment of African slaves to Hispaniola; by 1530 the institution had spread to Cuba, Puerto Rico, and Jamaica. Both Spanish opinion and law legitimized the practice of ownership of other persons in the Caribbean. The *Siete Partidas*, the foundation of Spanish jurisprudence, acknowledged the legality of the institution of slavery even while declaring it "contrary to natural law." The Siete Partidas protected enslaved persons from serious abuse by their masters and granted them the right to marry, inherit property, and be manumitted. Scholars doubt, however, the extent to which these laws were enforced in the Caribbean. A wide gulf separated law and practice.

The French, unlike the Spanish, had no slave laws on the books in the mother country, so they eventually enacted the *Code Noir*, a 1685 compilation designed to regulate slavery in the French Caribbean. This code resembled the Siete Partidas in that it accorded the slaves basic rights such as marriage, manumission, and judicial recourse in cases of mistreatment.

These laws—along with those adopted by the Danes and the Dutch—conferred legitimacy on the institution in the Caribbean and ensured its survival for several centuries.

The English, with no tradition of slavery in their land, lacked any laws to define the nature of master-slave relationships, therefore leaving English slaveholders in the Caribbean essentially to their own devices. Consequently, they developed local codes in the 1680s that gave virtually unlimited powers to the master.

Recent research has shed more light on how many Africans and their descendants served as slaves in the Caribbean islands between the sixteenth and nineteenth centuries. For example, studies of shipping show the numbers of slaves brought to the Americas, their ethnic origins, and the nature of the trans-Atlantic passage. We also know that the trade was a carefully organized business that attracted the Portuguese, English, French, Dutch, and others. The Portuguese were the major traders during the sixteenth and early seventeenth centuries. As party to the Treaty of Tordesillas of 1494, Spain had relinquished the right to participate in the slave trade on the African coast in favor of the Portuguese. Consequently, Spain had to rely on the citizens of other nations to obtain and transport slaves to its colonies. This dependence caused certain difficulties, among them unreliable supply.

During the early years of the trade, the Spanish government issued licenses to individual traders to deliver specified numbers of slaves to the colonists in the Caribbean. This method of supply was not particularly effective, because many licensees failed to meet their obligations. In 1595 that system was replaced by *Asientos,* or monopoly contracts, which granted individuals or joint stock companies the sole rights to supply specified Spanish colonies with slaves for given periods. By the mid-eighteenth century, however, the age of the contract and trading company had run its course, and private merchants became the dominant suppliers of slaves in the Caribbean. Among these, traders who flew the English flag predominated, but the French and the Dutch proved to be strong competitors.

We do not fully know the ethnic origins of the slaves taken to the Caribbean inasmuch as the information left by the traders always referred to the port from which the slaves were dispatched rather than to their ethnic identities. Other evidence, however, shows that most of the slaves came from the area bounded by the Senegal River to the north and modern-day Angola and Zaire to the south. The slaving frontier kept shifting according to supply patterns, but the principal areas included the Senegambia coast, Sierra Leone, the Gold Coast, the Bight of Benin, the Bight of Biafra, and Central Africa. Ethnic groups that lived in these regions included the Ibo, Ewe, Ga, Ashanti, Fanti, Wolof, Yoruba, and Bakongo.

The Caribbean islands received about four million slaves, slightly fewer than those who arrived in Brazil, the other main region of importation. During the sixteenth century, about two thousand slaves arrived in the Caribbean annually. A century later, annual importation jumped to some thirteen thousand. The supply to the Caribbean reached its height in the eighteenth century, with average annual importations of about sixty thousand. The numbers remained high until the 1840s and then dropped off in the 1860s. Over time, these African slaves and their progeny played a fundamental role in remaking the Caribbean. In the early decades of the sixteenth century, Spaniards used slave labor in the gold mines of Hispaniola, Cuba, and Puerto Rico. Once the mining economy collapsed, the colonists were forced to turn to a variety of other economic ventures, all of which relied to some degree on slave labor.

♦ THE ROLE OF AGRICULTURE

Sugarcane was one of the first crops to be planted widely by the early colonists. The first sugar mill (ingenio) in the Caribbean was erected on the island of Hispaniola in 1516, and the colony began to export sugar in 1522. By 1527 the island had twenty-five working mills. The settlers on the islands of Puerto Rico, Cuba, and Jamaica soon entered the sugar business as well. In addition, colonists developed flourishing cattle industries that shipped hides and tallow to Spain. Finally, planters on the islands of Hispaniola and Puerto Rico began to invest heavily in ginger cultivation. Black slaves provided the labor power to support these new agrarian and pastoral economies. By 1530 Puerto Rico, for example, had 2,292 slaves and only 327 whites. As many as 30,000 slaves may have been imported into Hispaniola by 1565.

The demand for slave labor accelerated in the seventeenth century, particularly after the English and the French acquired islands in the area and began to grow sugarcane for their protected home markets. Starting in the 1630s, the English in Barbados obtained from the Dutch the requisite capital and technology to grow sugar. After Barbadian tobacco got a bad reputation in European markets, planters shifted their resources to sugarcane cultivation.

The Barbadian growers quickly recognized that sugarcane could be most profitably grown on large plantations where economies of scale obtained. Consequently, they began to consolidate their farms into plantations and purchased large numbers of slaves from Dutch traders. This process of land consolidation would, in time, eliminate the small landholders. Thus, by 1680, 7 percent of the planters owned more than half the arable land and 60 percent of the slaves. The age of the Caribbean plantocracy had arrived, and the alliance between sugar, slavery, and the plantation system had been sealed.

The same pattern of land consolidation and the use of large numbers of slaves developed in the other islands. In Jamaica, for example, 467 persons owned more than 77 percent of the acreage in 1754. In addition to these dramatic changes in land ownership, sugarcane cultivation also produced a major transformation in the demographic structure of the islands. Population figures for Barbados in 1645, before the great shift to sugar, show that there were 5,680 black slaves and 37,000 whites, most of the whites being indentured servants. Within forty years the process of land consolidation and emigration of poor whites had reduced the European population to 17,187, while the black component rose to 46,602. By 1750 there were four slaves for every white person on the island.

This pattern of black demographic supremacy was most pronounced in the British, Dutch, and French islands. In general, wherever black slaves were imported in large numbers, poor whites virtually disappeared. For example, black slaves accounted for 80 percent of the Antigua population in 1724 and 90 percent in 1756. The island of Montserrat had 8,853 black slaves and 1,117 whites in 1745. In the Danish colony of St. Thomas, the black population reached 4,504 in 1720, while whites numbered only 524. Finally, the French island of Guadeloupe had 80,000 slaves and only 12,000 whites in 1770.

The Spanish islands never displayed such radical polarization between blacks and whites. Their white inhabitants often abandoned their farms and went to the mainland colonies, where opportunities beckoned. Those who remained behind settled into subsistence patterns of production, working alongside Africans and their descendants. During this lull in sugar cultivation, many farms evolved into the peasant type of organization, discussed in Chapter 3.

Cuba developed a unique form of labor and race relations. Work there was not as regimented as on the mainland, where productivity ruled all else. Among the first islands to be taken over by Europeans, Cuba was the last to be converted to wholesale sugar production. As late as the 1760s, Cuban landowners mostly raised cattle and tobacco commercially, using few slaves and loose supervision. Shortly afterward, however, the Cuban economy underwent a radical transformation to plantation agriculture based on African slavery. The causes were largely external, among them imperial reforms in Spain, growing markets in the United States and Europe, the Haitian Revolution, and free importation of Africans. Within a half-century Cuba became the world's foremost sugar producer and Spain's most valuable colony.

With slave imports running nearly twenty thousand a year by the 1810s, Cuba multiplied its production and wealth. Regional differentiation emerged in the nineteenth century: Sugar dominated the central lowlands, tobacco the western provinces, and coffee the eastern mountains. So although Cuba was a late arrival to plantation agriculture, it soon became the leader in the area. Spain encouraged this trend by adopting policies favorable to landowners, including duty-free imports of British machinery. Refining equipment, railroads, steam engines, powerful grinders, and, of course, hundreds of thousands of Africans revolutionized the Cuban economy. By 1841 slaves slightly outnumbered whites and constituted 43 percent of the population. They helped Cuba to resurrect and modernize the sugar ingenio.

After 1750, Africans had a clear demographic supremacy in the Caribbean. Perhaps as many as three million slaves had been imported by then, and the rate of importation would increase during the latter part of the century, in response to the growing demand for labor. Virtually every large sugar estate employed at least a hundred slaves, with Jamaican plantations averaging two hundred. A typical plantation on the larger islands consisted of two hundred acres of land and scores of slaves. In general, the larger the plantation, the more slaves were required and the higher the productivity of the land. For the period 1741–1745, for example, the colonies of Jamaica and St. Domingue, with huge concentrations of slaves, accounted for 97 percent of the sugar produced by the four largest islands.

Black slaves were used in many other enterprises besides the sugar industry. They were widely employed as domestic servants, accounting for one-fourth of the servant population. Slaves also cultivated coffee, indigo, tobacco, cotton, and cacao in St. Domingue; ginger and cotton in Barbados; coffee in Martinique and Hispaniola; and bananas, manioc, yams, and other staples throughout the islands.

The slaves in the urban areas performed every imaginable skilled task, from construction and drayage to barbering and retail sales. As the region's economies matured, a new form of slave employment evolved, called hiring-out. Masters allowed their more skilled and trusted slaves to work for others on short- or medium-term projects. Masters collected the rental fees but usually gave some to the slave to encourage continued good service and loyalty. Eventually, some slaves hired themselves out (on wharves, street corners, in warehouse districts, etc.) and gave set amounts to their masters at the end of the week. This labor arrangement probably contributed to more racial mixing in urban areas but did not increase manumissions, as it did in Brazil.

◆ AFRO-CARIBBEAN SOCIETY

The quality of slave life in the Caribbean does not lend itself easily to generalization. First, it is nearly impossible to imagine today what it felt like to be the property of another person or to experience the physical and spiritual impact of that condition. The emergence of racial slavery—that is, a form of servitude in which the masters were white and the slaves were black—must also have exacted a psychological price from the unfree.

African-born slaves probably experienced the greatest difficulty in adjusting to servitude in these new lands. Creoles, that is, slaves born in the islands, were socialized into the institution from birth and probably experienced other psychological costs; they had known no other life and had been subjected to the psychological and physical exploitation of slavery from birth. Yet it is also clear that slaves, as persons, were never totally vanquished by the system that held them in thrall. They had to struggle to define themselves as persons and to preserve, as best they could, a sense of self.

Even on the voyage to the Americas, Africans forged deep and occasionally enduring bonds as shipmates. The term *shipmate*, in fact, had a profoundly emotional resonance because of the danger and fear of the crossing. Once on land, Africans had to struggle to define themselves and to preserve as much as possible a sense of self. Throughout the Caribbean, slaves expanded on their shipmate linkages and established networks of relationships with one another to help meet everyday challenges and to add humanity to their lives.

Both African and creole slaves faced enormous problems of physical survival in the Caribbean. Many who disembarked from the ships were ill with various maladies. Smallpox, yellow fever, dysentery, and ophthalmia had taken a grim toll during the Atlantic passage, and those who managed to survive were often in poor health. Some of the recent arrivals died before they were sold or shortly after. The disease environment of the Caribbean was particularly inhospitable. Poorly fed and overworked, slaves were prey to a number of diseases, including typhus, typhoid, tuberculosis, dysentery, and various gastrointestinal disorders. Nowhere in the region could slave owners rely on natural births to replenish the ranks of their slaves. It was not until the nineteenth century, when the slave trade ended and material conditions and medical knowledge improved, that some Afro-Caribbean societies began to experience small natural increases, that is, excesses of births over deaths.

Notwithstanding the physical risks Caribbean slaves faced, as soon as they became demographically significant they created rich creole cultures. These complex and dynamic cultures reflected the slaves' African heritages as well as their Caribbean lives. With variations conditioned by the local milieux, the core of these cultures, their internal rhythms and voices, remained essentially African. The music, stories, dances, styles of food preparation, ways of socializing children, and family life in general drew on African roots.

Slave women in the Caribbean and the other societies of the Americas shared similar experiences. The type of work they performed, in addition to being defined by traditional gender roles was also determined by physical capacities and skills. Performing domestic chores for members of the Big House as well as for their own families, slave women also worked on the plantations alongside the men, often performing the same jobs. Men dominated the artisan trades, already possessing such skills when they arrived in the Caribbean, and more likely to be selected for such training.

Within the quarters of African-born slaves, domestic arrangements were determined by cultural heritage to the degree possible. Although both men and women shared child-rearing responsibilities in the quarters, domestic duties were primarily female. And, when possible, both men and women raised crops to supplement their rations and sold their surpluses at popular Sunday markets.

Slave birth rates in the Caribbean were much lower than in North American colonies, especially after the mid-eighteenth century. This resulted from disproportionate sex ratios, physical abuse and overwork, malnutrition, and disease. Some women may have practiced contraception and abortion but existing evidence only permits generalizations to be made. Most African cultures would not have endorsed abortion, affirming childbirth as a time of special joys and an event that strengthens ties of kith and kin. Many slave children died in infancy. However, we cannot attribute this to a widespread practice of infanticide, as some earlier historians concluded. In fact, Sudden Infant Death Syndrome (SIDS), the cause of many deaths, is believed to be the result of certain mineral deficiencies.

African slaves had been taken from societies where kinship stood at the center of all relationships. Ties of kinship defined the individual's place within the ethnic group and formed the core of the community. In the Caribbean, slaves recreated these ties as much as possible. Some owners allowed family and social activities as a means of encouraging stability and higher productivity.

Family Arrangements

Marriage was, of course, central to any society, especially one that had been uprooted from a distant homeland and placed in a hostile environment. Formal matrimony among slaves was called for in virtually all European legal codes, yet in fact it was extremely rare. Even the Protestant English did not encourage formal unions among their slaves until the 1820s. Therefore, very few legal marriages were performed among slaves. This low rate of Christian marriages did not, however, signify an absence of kin or family among the slaves. Evidence from all the slave societies indicates that many male and female slaves lived in settled unions—often for long periods of time—without the formal sanction of church or state. The African-born slaves, particularly in the early years, experienced greater difficulty finding partners because of the disproportionate ratio of males to females. With the emergence of a creole population, however, a more equal sexual ratio favored the formation of families.

Slave marriages were precarious everywhere and could be broken up with impunity by masters, despite the protective legislation on the books. Masters exercised an imperious control over their property, so that husbands could be separated from wives, and children from parents, without any moral compunction. In instances where masters respected their slaves' settled relationships, however, as in the case of Worthy Park estate in Jamaica, slaves were less likely to run off and may even have been more productive workers.

Miscegenation was a fairly common feature of Caribbean societies. African slaves mated with whites, and soon a mixed mulatto population emerged. African women often became the mistresses of their owners and bore their children, adding to the ranks of mulattoes. Children inherited their mothers' legal status, and because sexual encounters usually occurred between white males and black females, most mulattoes were born slave. If the mother was not a slave or the father granted manumission before the birth, the children were born free. Slaves of mixed racial heritage increased in number over time and became a major proportion of the slave population by the nineteenth century. In the British Caribbean islands, for example, persons of mixed race constituted about 12 percent of the slave populations alone. In Cuba, where manumission was more common, mulattoes constituted 4 percent of the slaves in 1846 and a much larger portion of the free population.

Religion

If slaves drew some solace from their family arrangements, whether legal or informal, they also obtained psychic rewards from their religious beliefs and practices. African peoples came from intensely religious societies, and not surprisingly they struggled to maintain their faiths in these hostile islands. The Europeans, however, made some effort to convert them to Christianity. The Spanish made sporadic attempts at proselytizing recently arrived Africans, whereas the Dutch, French, and English (at least in the early years) demonstrated little interest in the spiritual lives of their human chattel. Such seeming neglect or lack of interest was probably a blessing in disguise for the slaves, for it allowed them to retain their own beliefs and practices while incorporating selected traditions of other ethnic groups. Most Caribbean slaves had not embraced Christianity or even been exposed to it in any systematic fashion before the nineteenth century.

Only later did missionaries from the home countries establish religious contact with slaves. In the early nineteenth century Protestant masters began to attempt the conversion of their slaves. They began to see Christianity as an agency for the so-called civilization of the slaves, by which they meant Europeanization. The English planters, in particular, stated that Christian principles would improve the slaves' moral characters. In practice, such ethno- and Eurocentric views required that the Africans and their descendants divest themselves of their African identities. When the British Parliament in 1823 debated the amelioration of slavery in the West Indies, Parliament maintained that the adoption of Christianity by the slaves was "an indispensable necessity . . . the foundation of every beneficial change in their character and future conditions."

Christian instruction—whether in its Catholic or Protestant variants—was intended to accomplish more than just the substitution of one set of religious beliefs for another. Religion was to be a powerful agency for the cultural remaking of the Africans and their children, imparting to them European values and worldviews. Religious instruction would also make the slaves more tractable. In the early eighteenth century, for example, the French missionary Charle Voix remarked that the colonists of St. Domingue believed that "the most efficacious means of ensuring" the fidelity of the slaves was "to try to make them good Christians." Given the strength of their beliefs, it is not surprising that the slaves clung to their religions and refused to embrace Christianity. Instead, many incorporated Christian concepts into their existing cosmologies in very dynamic and complex ways. The syncretic Caribbean faiths that emerged possessed a distinctly African flavor.

Some slaves, however, employed Christianity as a way to fight the institution of slavery itself. This strategy was evident in Jamaica in 1831, for example, when the slaves invoked the Bible to give legitimacy to their assault on the system. In part, they followed the examples of North American counterparts like Nat Turner, who equated their conditions with those of the Israelites in Egypt and used Christianity to justify violent measures.

◆ RESISTANCE

Slaves in the Caribbean had a long tradition of opposition to their enslavement, and resistance took complex, multidimensional, and ever-shifting forms. (See Map 4–2.) Slaves were not always on the barricades, however, and long periods elapsed during which they remained quiescent. Moreover, slaves used a variety of nonviolent ways to manifest their opposition to their conditions. One of the most important elements of this struggle was simply preserving their sense of self and dignity despite crushing personal hardships.

Escape constituted one of the most effective means of resistance and occurred in all slave societies. These slaves began to desert their masters shortly after the introduction of slavery. Mountainous terrain on islands like Jamaica, Hispaniola, and Cuba was topographically amenable to flight by the slaves. There they could establish sanctuaries in inaccessible areas and defend themselves against efforts at recapture by masters and public

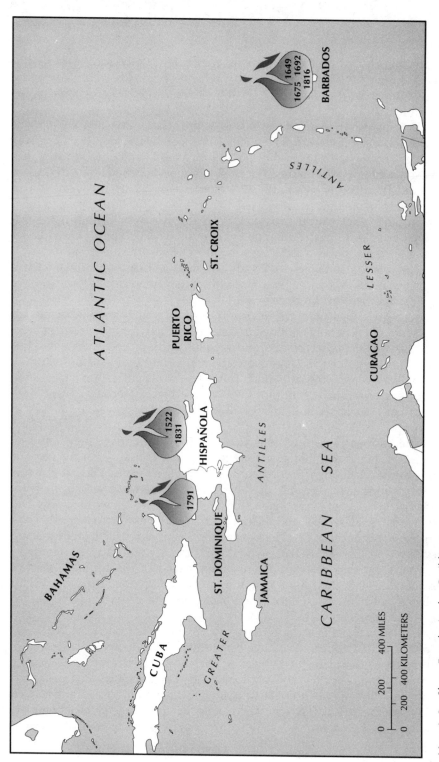

Map 4–2 Slave Revolts in the Caribbean

authorities. The Jamaican maroons were particularly successful in this regard, and by the mid-seventeenth century they had established secure settlements in the mountains of the eastern and western parts of the island.

The Spanish tried unsuccessfully to destroy these settlements, a struggle the English continued after they took control of the island in 1655. Far from being contained, however, the maroons increased in number and kept up a steady series of raids on the English plantations. A general state of warfare prevailed, and it was not until 1739 that a peace treaty was signed. This momentous document recognized the freedom of the maroons, granted them land, and waived their obligation to pay taxes. In return, the maroons promised not to harbor any future runaways. Similar peace treaties were signed with escaped slaves in Cuba, Hispaniola, and Suriname.

The maroon settlements gave the Africans a chance to maintain a free but precarious existence. The communities they established appear to have been patterned on the African societies they had known, but we do not know a great deal about the interior lives of these persons because outsiders were not generally admitted to the sanctuaries. Even new recruits were not exposed to the secrets and remained in isolation. New Cuban maroons were not permitted to leave the settlements until they had proven their reliability over a two-year period. The new recruits in western Jamaica had to take a sacred oath, and those who refused were executed. These were essentially societies under siege that could be destroyed by lapses in security.

The various slave rebellions that occurred throughout the Caribbean area certainly had more dramatic impact than maroon settlements. The first slave rebellion on record occurred in Hispaniola in 1522, and it was easily suppressed. In time, as the slave populations increased, violence against the system became a fact of life for owners. Jamaican society had the most restless slave population, and rebellions occurred with great frequency after the 1670s. The last and most serious rebellion on that island occurred at Christmas 1831, when about twenty thousand slaves in the western parishes rose up against their masters. The terrified planters responded with their full might and managed to reestablish control. This bloody rebellion is credited with hastening the passage of the British Emancipation Act of 1833.

Barbados experienced a series of abortive rebellions in 1649, 1675, and 1692. The first appeared to have been quite minor in scope, while that of 1675 led to the arrest of 110 slaves, of whom 11 were beheaded and 6 burned alive. The 1692 conspiracy demonstrated sophisticated planning, with the formation of a military command three months before the revolt was scheduled to break out. The slaves' objective was to take complete control of the island. After the conspiracy was discovered, authorities arrested between two and three hundred slaves and executed nineteen, including the leaders Sampson, Ben, Hammon, and Sambo.

Barbados experienced no slave revolts or conspiracies during the eighteenth century, perhaps because the overwhelming military strength of the authorities may have served as a deterrent. Some evidence suggests, however, that the slaves' energies were channeled into nonviolent protests aimed at improving their working conditions. The period of apparent quiescence was shattered in April 1816, when the slaves rose up to claim their freedom. Known as Bussa's Rebellion after its leader, the revolt lasted three days before it was quelled. About fifty whites were killed, and probably as many as a thousand slaves either died in the fighting or were executed.

◆ THE HAITIAN REVOLUTION

The most spectacular slave rebellion ever in the Caribbean, and indeed the world, occurred in St. Domingue (modern Haiti) in the 1790s. Present among the half-million slaves on that island by 1790 were many who had a long tradition of opposing slavery. *Marronage,* the French term for escape, had been widespread there, leading to the formation of several runaway communities in the mountains. But the occasional raids by these groups paled in comparison to the violence that engulfed the island when the slaves rebelled in 1791.

Another possibly explosive ingredient was added in the 1780s, when tens of thousands of prisoners of civil wars in the Kongo were sold to planters in St. Domingue. Many were battle-hardened soldiers willing to risk death rather than suffer the humiliations of slavery. Sullen, proud, and easily mobilized by their own former officers, these fresh slaves would defeat many times their own number of European soldiers sent to subdue them in the 1790s and 1800s. This process went on elsewhere, too, but only in St. Domingue did it lead to total victory by the slaves.

The slave revolt occurred in the context of a conflict between the French colonists and the French Assembly in Paris. Two years earlier, the French Revolution had broken out, inducing vicious fighting in St. Domingue between the white planter elite and the emerging and increasingly aggressive free mulattoes, many of whom were managers or even owners of sugar plantations. The free mulattoes demanded equality with the whites, who were unwilling to share power, profits, and status. As time passed and the fighting intensified, the leaders and slaves increased their demands on the planters. After two years of intermittent fighting between the two groups, the slaves realized that they could take advantage of this disunity to gain their freedom. The first leader of the slaves was Boukman, a maroon reputed to have come from Jamaica. He plotted their revolt and contacted conspirators using African languages. Choosing to launch the uprising after planters arbitrarily cut the three-day rest period decreed by the authorities, Boukman and his forces went on the attack on August 22, 1791. Outnumbering the whites by a ratio of about fourteen to one, the slaves set fire to the plantations, particularly those in the fertile north. Boukman died shortly after the fighting began, but by then many other creole slaves and freedmen, many of whom were from the managerial ranks of the plantations, recruited officers and soldiers to take over lands and buildings.

The leaders' objectives were not revolutionary in the Parisian sense. Instead, they demanded freedom for Africans as well as better jobs, pay, and status for themselves. When the white planters rejected all such demands, the struggle went on for a dozen bloody years. Thus, what began as a revolt with limited objectives soon became a full-fledged revolution.

Eventually, a former plantation overseer, Toussaint L'Ouverture, emerged as leader of the various rebel units and became one of the most extraordinary figures in Caribbean history. Displaying enormous leadership capability, Toussaint fended off both British and French expeditionary forces, and by 1797 he and the former slaves controlled the island. Within a few more years they even annexed the Spanish portion of the island. A British officer later reported of the fighting, "The Negroes . . . are infinitely the most formidable enemy the British arms have to encounter." Toussaint assumed control over the remnants of the island government in 1798, introduced a modified system of coerced labor, and sought to revive the sugar industry. Most of his efforts in this period were devoted to rebuilding the economy and mending the wounds in society. He ruled with authority and even severity, yet his goals were honorable and attainable. He promulgated a constitution in 1801 that gave persons of all races full equality and citizenship, and he appointed himself governor general for life and kept a standing army for defense. Toussaint did not declare independence, however, hoping to finesse the inevitable French response to such a move.

Unfortunately for the Haitians, in 1802 Napoleon Bonaparte dispatched twenty thousand fresh troops to remove Toussaint and return the island to French rule. Unwilling to be reenslaved, the blacks fought valiantly and doggedly in defense of their liberty. Toussaint laid down his arms and attempted to mediate, but the French commander had him arrested and sent to France in chains. Toussaint's lieutenant, Jean Jacques Dessalines, took up the banner of freedom and soon drove out the French. In 1804 he declared independence and renamed the island Haiti, thereby founding the second republic in the Americas. Toussaint, meanwhile, had died in prison, unaware that his people had once again defeated the French invaders.

Toussaint L'ouverture emerged as the leader of 1790's slave revolution in St. Domingue. Culver Picturers, Inc.

The Haitians' achievements proved inspiring to other slaves in the Americas, but they also struck fear into slave owners and whites everywhere. When it became clear that resistance could lead to revolt, the planter class everywhere mounted strong, well-organized, and effective movements to preserve slavery. Haiti became a bogey that rallied whites to their own defense. Yet the Haitian success was never duplicated. The Haitian struggle was unique only in the sense that the slaves succeeded; everywhere else slave resistance continued but led to concessions by the masters and eventually freedom.

* * *

The institution of African slavery in the Caribbean, then, lasted almost four centuries. It spanned the years from 1502, when the slaves were first introduced, until 1886, when the last slaves in Cuba were freed. The African presence had changed the human landscape of the Caribbean in profound and irreversible ways. These forced migrants had brought Africa with them, and they and their children laid the foundations of the contemporary Caribbean, with all its cultural and genetic richness and complexity.

Chapter 5
AFRICANS IN BRAZIL

1500	Portuguese fleet encounters and claims Brazil.
1530s	Portuguese create captaincies to promote settlement.
1549	Portuguese establish Salvador as colonial capital.
1580s	Brazilian sugar *fazendas* begin shifting to African field labor.
1580–1640	Spain annexes Portugal and its colonies.
1610s–1694	Palmares, an African state in Brazil, maintains its independence against Portuguese and Dutch attacks.
1680s	Gold discovered in Brazil.
1750s	Mining declines in Brazil.
1770s	Coffee and other new crops introduced to promote exports.
1822	Brazilian independence declared.
1831	Law to end slave trade proves unenforceable.
1850	Queiroz Law effectively ends slave trade.
1850–1880s	Internal slave trade of some two hundred thousand from Brazil's northeast to the coffee zone in the south.

Many millions of years ago, before the continents began to drift apart, Brazil and Africa were joined. A glance at a geological world map shows how the "hump" of Brazil used to fill the Gulf of Guinea. (See Map 5–1.) This ancient connection left common legacies:

The two continents have similarities in geology, vegetation, climate, and fauna. Nevertheless, divergent development on the two continents led to sharp contrasts as well. Africans, in touch with Asia and southern Europe, possessed iron technology, beasts of burden, and political states; the Amerindians of Brazil had none of these.

New links were forged in modern history, especially during the period of the African slave trade, from the 1530s to the 1850s. The forced migration of about five million Africans was complemented by the transfer of technology, culture, microorganisms, plants, animals, and social structures. Because of these new connections, Brazil became Africanized to a greater degree than any other part of the Americas except Haiti. In this sense, human history reversed geological history by reuniting two regions that had split apart through continental drift.

Humans evolved in Africa after the continents separated, and until recent times the Americas lay isolated from and unknown to our species. Then, between thirty and forty thousand years ago, small numbers migrated to the Americas by way of the Bering Strait ice bridge that temporarily connected the two continents. Their descendants in Brazil, called Amerindians, lived seminomadic lives, establishing villages and cultivating cleared lands for several years and then moving on to new sites. Their culture and society were analogous to those of sub-Saharan Africa, from which many slaves were brought. Women managed the homes, cultivated simple crops, raised children, and passed on simple accumulations of goods. Men hunted, fished, built timber-and-thatch structures, conducted warfare, and, when elders, formed councils for public discussions and decision making. Like most sub-Saharan Africans, the Amerindians of Brazil did not recognize individual property rights to land. They worshiped naturalistic gods, with whom they communicated through older men or women called *shamans*.

Portugal claimed Brazil as its territory after its chance discovery by a merchant fleet in 1500. The claim was based on a 1494 treaty with Spain granting jurisdiction over Africa and the South Atlantic islands where its merchants had established settlements. At first the Portuguese believed Brazil to be another island, and even when they learned that it was part of a new continent, they treated it as an extension of their African territories. Fearing that a rival European power might attempt to take over Brazil, the Portuguese undertook to colonize it in the 1530s. They took much from Africa to South America: artisans, soldiers, and agricultural workers; cash crops; capital; and institutions. Soon they began importing slaves as well. In exchange, Brazil supplied trade goods, money, and services of many sorts to West Africa. For over three centuries Africa and Brazil were intimately linked together as Portuguese colonies. Brazil became the more profitable of the colonies, but Africa supplied the people and cultures that

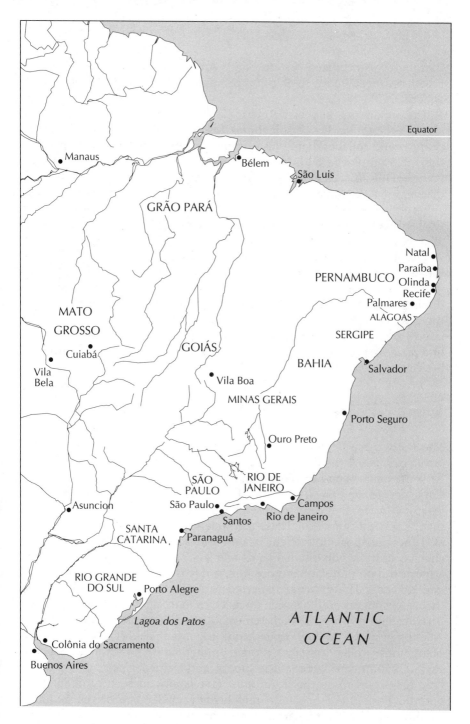

Map 5–1 Brazil with Principal Cities

thoroughly Africanized eastern South America. Thus, for three centuries Brazil belonged more to the South Atlantic than to the North Atlantic sphere.

The similarities between Amerindian cultures and those of the many slaves brought to Brazil sometimes fostered African-native cultural exchanges and collaboration. This occurred in runaway camps and on plantations that employed both peoples as workers. Nevertheless, planters and government officials did everything they could to separate the two and to discourage Amerindians from harboring fugitive slaves. In addition, mixed Amerindian-white Brazilians, called *Mamelucos,* served as native slavers, while mulattoes were hired to recapture runaway Africans. Thus, no major alliances ever formed between Amerindians and slaves.

The Africanization of Brazil reached its height in the decades between the late eighteenth and the midnineteenth centuries, when Brazil's slave imports and commodity exports were immense. Since then contacts have diminished, yet the African legacy in Brazil remains strong, visible today in the physical appearance of the people and in their culture. Brazil has the largest population of African descent outside of Africa. The Africanization of Brazil—a prolonged, complex, multi-directional process—contributed heavily to the creation of a distinctive African American civilization.

◆ THE SUGAR BOOM

The Portuguese Crown chose to establish permanent settlements, called *captaincies,* along the Brazilian coast in the 1530s, using the same methods earlier colonizers had employed on the islands of Madeira, the Azores, the Cape Verdes, and São Tomé. Brazil was divided into fifteen huge territories (captaincies) that were awarded to twelve court favorites, mostly noblemen, known as grantees. These men financed the recruitment of colonists and the transportation of the goods and supplies they would need to survive, and they distributed lands and jobs. Their broad powers included administration of justice and taxation to pay the costs of local government and defense. The grantees expected to make enough profits to recover their investments and to enrich themselves too. Sugar was the only known product that could yield such returns, as had been proven on Portugal's Atlantic islands. Moved there from the Mediterranean shores, sugar plantations—called *engenhos* [Port.] or *ingenios* [Sp.]—brought together capital, equipment, labor, sugar shoots, and technology to produce a cash crop for export to northern Europe. Slave labor had been used all along, but the Portuguese began to rely heavily on African slaves for sugar production. The fateful marriage of sugar and Africans in the late fifteenth century would produce the lowland sugar societies of the Americas.

Sugarcane is a perennial grass that yields a sucrose juice that can be refined into granular sugar. After becoming established, the plants can be harvested annually for about ten years. In a typical ingenio, the cane was cut and stripped of its leafy foliage, transported to the mill, squeezed between rollers to extract the juice, and then discarded or dried for later uses. The juice had to be boiled down and refined in huge caldrons to separate impurities from the syrup that would become sugar. This latter operation, requiring great skill, close timing, and persistent attention, usually took place in steamy rooms next to the grinding mills. At the last stage, the thickened syrup was allowed to stand in clay molds until it dried into the classic sugarloaf shape. These loaves were crated and transported to Europe for sale. At the time, sugar production was one of the most complex and capital-intensive enterprises anywhere in the world.

Africans were essential to the transfer of sugar to Brazil and hence to the survival of the early captaincies themselves. The grantees and most colonists imported African slaves to serve as workers, soldiers, and overseers, providing skilled services and acting as auxiliaries to the settlers. Many of them possessed valuable trades, such as ironworking, carpentry, soldiering, and animal husbandry, and they learned Portuguese and understood European ways. Even the few Muslims among them got along with the Portuguese, whose ancestors had coexisted with followers of Islam during the Moorish domination of Iberia.

The early Africans formed a technical backbone of the new Brazilian colony, much as they did in other parts of the Americas. Most important, many Africans were experienced in the sugar business as then conducted on the Atlantic islands, and so they were able to help lay out fields, construct buildings and machinery, and set up refining operations. Because these Africans represented heavy investments of money, training, and acculturation, planters avoided overworking or exposing them to great danger. Africans also helped build and maintain the cities, ports, churches, and ranches, and made other improvements that the Portuguese considered essential for their survival in the Americas.

Most of the early sugar plantations in Brazil employed Amerindian slaves for the intensive labor of clearing, planting, weeding, harvesting, and transporting cane. The Portuguese regarded the Amerindians as expendable, for they were numerous and could be captured easily. Typically, a slaving party, commanded by a European but made up mostly of mestizo and African soldiers, would strike out into the forests, raid native villages, and take their prisoners back to the plantations in chains. A later variety of enslavement was the *resgate* (or rescue), by which the Portuguese would incite intertribal wars so that they could purchase captives from the victor. During the sixteenth century, Amerindian slaves were far more numerous than Africans in Brazil.

In the 1580s a fateful change began in the sugar industry, one that would alter the Brazil-Africa relationship and condemn millions more Africans to a terrible existence. Planters gradually replaced their Amerindian field slaves with Africans, who henceforth did the heaviest labor. This shift had several causes. First, as sugar became a staple in the European diet profits rose rapidly, allowing planters to purchase more Africans. Second, government policy during Portugal's annexation to Spain (1580–1640) provided greater protection for natives and indirectly encouraged the African slave trade. Third, the Amerindian men resisted field work for cultural reasons, whereas Africans had long practiced agriculture. Finally, the Amerindians' susceptibility to European diseases reduced their ability to withstand the rigors of harvest work. So for some fifty years after 1580, plantations in the most productive regions along the Brazilian coast (especially between Pernambuco and Bahia) abandoned using Amerindians in field work and replaced them with Africans.

The growing demand for African laborers in Brazil increased slaving activities in parts of Africa where the Portuguese were active and led to more regular voyages across the South Atlantic. Typically, a ship sailed from Portugal laden with goods and money that could be exchanged for slaves in Africa. The ship then took on a cargo of slaves and sailed for Brazil. The final leg was the return to Europe with sugar, tobacco, and other tropical products. The entire triangular voyage took about a year.

Higher profits and increased use of Africans in the sugar industry raised productivity but led to heavier demands on the laborers, causing the work regime to become regimented and impersonal. The earlier collaborative relationship between masters and slaves now grew antagonistic, and field slaves were treated as chattel. The drive for increased productivity led to overwork, maltreatment, rationed food, nocturnal lock-ups, and corporal punishment. Under these conditions, the average field slave did not live many years. Moreover, Africans could be replaced more easily since the trade had become more efficient. A terrible calculus was used to justify the purchase of more African slaves: In the years they would survive on the plantation regime, they could produce enough to yield high profits for the slaveholder or planter.

Although Amerindians continued to work on sugar plantations after the 1580s, they moved into ancillary activities. Typically, they lived in separate villages on the margins of the plantations, and they performed tasks that were more in keeping with the Tupi-Guaraní culture. The men hunted and fished to provide food for the plantation, and some tended cattle on nearby pastures. Others cut and transported firewood for the refining mill. Finally, Amerindian men operated canoes, rafts, and oxcarts that transported food, wood, raw cane, sugar, and other supplies throughout the plantation and to and from market. Women raised corn, manioc, and other staples, and they also prepared food for the field hands. In the seventeenth century, these Amerindians enjoyed a degree of autonomy in the plantation regime and were often paid on a piecework basis.

Slave traders altered their routes in the seventeenth century. Brazilian merchants had now taken over more of the trade and tended to sail directly to Africa, abandoning the Portuguese leg of the route. They exchanged chewing tobacco and rum for slaves along the west coast of Africa, and they often took on Asian goods for resale in Brazil as well. A fast slaver could make several trips a year. Increasingly, the traders bought Bantu-speaking and Kongo people in west-central African ports. Adult men predominated in the trade; women and children made up a minority of the slaves shipped. These people were thought by the Brazilians to be more adaptable to plantation labor and less inclined to create resistance. Many had little prior experience dealing with Europeans, and captivity proved to be highly destructive of their cultures and societies. Therefore, as the slave regime became harsher, the Africans' psychic abilities to resist diminished.

In the first half of the seventeenth century, sugar production reached its apogee in Brazil, and at the same time the Africans experienced their heaviest labor demands in the New World. Sugar exports peaked in the 1640s, when profits were at their highest. At this point Brazil earned almost as much revenue as Mexico and Peru combined, and it surpassed Portuguese India as the chief colony in the empire. The African slave population of Brazil reached several hundred thousand, and some five to seven thousand Africans were brought every year to the main ports of Recife and Salvador. Sugar was king by the midseventeenth century, and it drove the Africanization process.

The plantation compound at the peak of sugar prosperity resembled a miniature township. The *casa grande,* or manor house, accommodated the planter/mill owner as well as his extended family—sometimes dozens of relatives—and many household slaves. Nearby lay the *senzala,* or slave quarters, a low structure with small, poorly ventilated rooms. The mill itself was located near the casa grande, where the planter could supervise the most critical tasks, milling and refining sugar. The quadrangle was completed by a chapel, where the slaves often received the sacraments. (The owner's family worshiped separately or in a private chapel in the manor house.) The yard itself served to muster slaves in the mornings and evenings and often witnessed infliction of punishment. This seventeenth-century sugar plantation complex became a paradigm for slave-based plantation agriculture in many tropical areas of the Americas and was replicated in later phases of Brazil's history. Under development for a century, the plantation would survive as an institution for another two hundred years. Even in regions that were not suitable for sugar, slaveholders employed African labor to produce ground crops, livestock, tobacco, forage, fowl, and crafts.

Africans also supplied labor for myriad other businesses besides sugar. The coastal cities, where African slaves made up at least half the population, could not have existed without them. Africans performed most manual and skilled trades, carrying out most construction, haulage, manufacturing, vending, provisioning, sanitation, and peace keeping. They also supplied nearly all domestic and personal services. Finally, the entire shipping industry depended heavily on Africans, both free and slave, for shipwrights and crewmen. In the sense of labor power, then, coastal Brazil was largely Africanized by the midseventeenth century.

The Decline of Sugar

Sugar prices began to fall after midcentury, provoking complex readjustments in coastal Brazilian societies and economies. When planters could no longer afford to hire skilled artisans from the towns to carry out specialized jobs, they began to rely more on talented slaves who had been apprenticed to masters. In this way, a range of artisan positions in the plantation complex again became the slaves' domain. Skilled slaves enjoyed better treatment, more rations, and shorter hours. They could begin families, and some even bought their freedom. Generally, in the last decades of the sugar cycle conditions improved for skilled African and Brazilian-born slaves.

With the decline of profits in sugar, the plantations became more self-sufficient. Planters, who could no longer afford to purchase all the food needed by their slaves, began giving them time to raise their own provisions. Those slaves who did so undoubtedly ate better, and some managed to sell small surpluses in nearby towns and plantations. Some planters, no longer driven by high sugar prices, began honoring the church rule that slaves rest on Sundays. Some replaced expensive luxury imports (liquors, silks, porcelain, jewelry, religious icons, and paintings) with substitutes made locally by their slaves. Finally, planters began to reassign slaves to household service when their labor was no longer critical in the fields. It was in this period that the manor house, with its masters and slaves, became the crucible of racial and cultural mixing in which modern Brazilian society was created.

Because slaves in Brazil (and elsewhere in Latin America) did not have enough children to reproduce their numbers, their ranks had to be constantly replenished from the African trade. The reasons for their low birth rate suggest something of their poor quality of life. First, women as well as men worked long hours at physically exhausting tasks, which left them vulnerable to illness and miscarriage. Second, their diets contained mostly carbohydrates and fat, laced with amounts of salt that caused heart disease in Africans. Third, disruption of their religious, social, political, and economic life reduced their psychic defenses against despair and depression, leading to malaise and suicide. Fourth, the sexual imbalance among the African imports lowered the general reproduction rate. This was aggravated by greater manumission rates among women. Fifth, celibacy and abortion reduced women's fertility, and infant mortality took a high toll among those babies carried to term. For these reasons, the Afro-Brazilian population in the seventeenth century, excluding the effects of imports, declined at a rate of about 5 percent a year, a rate far higher than that for healthy groups.

Africans employed in the Brazilian sugar cycle did not, however, exist as automatons, for they possessed many means for self-expression and fulfillment. For example, many could begin families and raise children. What is more, Catholic and legal traditions defended their rights to some extent, allowing them to form kin networks and brotherhoods and even to be heard in court. The Africans reconstituted their religions in Brazil during this era, though never with official approval. Finally, persons assigned to the plantation house blended African and European cuisine and child-raising methods, a new form of cultural expression. Thus, most could at least hope to improve their lives.

The tens of thousands of Africans living in cities enjoyed freedoms and rights that were unusual on plantations. They worked finite hours or had set tasks, after which they were able to rest, socialize, work for themselves, or hire out their services to others. Religious brotherhoods for Afro-Brazilians became meeting grounds for community organization and even political expression. Gradually during the seventeenth century, a new class of Afro-Brazilians, both slave and free, appeared in the cities, whose status was many notches above that of the plantation slaves. Some learned to read and write and assumed leadership roles in the black brotherhoods and trade groups.

Manumission and Runaways

Far greater self-expression came with slaves' manumission, which was common in Brazilian cities but sporadic on plantations. Based on scholarly analyses of letters of freedom (*alforria*), we know a good deal about who gained liberty and how. Most of the manumitted lived in cities, because there they found greater opportunities to earn money and to live in freedom. In addition, most were female and were born in Brazil. Children and adolescents made up a substantial minority of freed persons. Nearly half the manumitted purchased their freedom by themselves or with relatives' help. Compliant behavior and close relations (sexual or caretaking) with the masters were mentioned in many letters. Usually, manumission was unconditional and irrevocable, but occasionally, it was given upon the masters' death, provided for in their wills.

From the earliest days of the sugar economy in Brazil, some Africans gained their freedom by running away from the plantations and towns. Thousands of runaway camps, called *quilombos* and *mocambos* in Brazil, sprang up between the sixteenth and nineteenth centuries. At first, many Africans who fled into Amerindian territory were captured and killed, but eventually some were accepted and lived permanently among the Amerindians, leading to some cultural mixing. More usual was the founding of independent camps, more or less permanent and defensive, within a day's travel from Portuguese settlements. These Africans raised their own food and sometimes preyed on travelers. They also raided plantations for provisions and encouraged others to flee. Slave owners naturally regarded their existence as threatening to the plantation system. Brazil's quilombos were analogous to the maroon and cimarrón settlements in other parts of the Americas.

Palmares, the largest and most famous quilombo in Brazilian history, was formed at the turn of the seventeenth century in the backlands of Pernambuco and lasted nearly a century, until its destruction in 1694 by irregular soldiers from São Paulo. Zumbi, the king of Palmares at its peak, ruled over thousands of subjects and commanded a guard reported to number five thousand. Portuguese attempts to overrun the settlement failed because of the fine fortifications and disciplined troops, especially during Zumbi's time. (The 1984 movie *Quilombo* by Brazilian filmmaker Carlos Diegues idealized Palmares as an Afro-Brazilian society and suggested the extent to which Brazilians trace their cultural roots back to Africa.)

Most quilombos existed in constant jeopardy because of special deputies known as *capitães do mato,* or bushwhacking captains, men who attacked the camps and returned runaways to their owners or resold them. By the late nineteenth century, however, in the heat of the abolition campaign, quilombos swelled with fleeing slaves and the authorities largely ignored them.

The sugar industry in Brazil, which led colonial employers to depend almost exclusively on African slaves for laborpower, never recovered the sustained profitability it enjoyed in the midseventeenth century. Sugar's long-term importance lay in financing the import of more than a million Africans, who left their imprint on virtually every aspect of life. The patterns of labor, social control, and race relations laid down in Brazil, especially in the sugar plantations, were adopted in other European colonies in the Americas and continue to influence society today.

◆ THE MINING ERA

In the 1680s the discovery of gold in the Brazilian highlands set off the world's first gold rush. Tens of thousands of Portuguese flocked to Brazil to make their fortunes, and over a million Africans were taken as slaves to labor in the mines and towns. The mining boom also spurred colonization and economic growth from the Amazon to the far south, causing more slave imports. The mining industry differed sharply from the sugar economy, and Africans contributed more to the broad development of the mining regions. The eighteenth century saw the accelerating Africanization of Brazil.

Most of the Europeans who settled in the mining districts of Minas Gerais, Mato Grosso, and Goiás were of northern Portuguese stock and tended to be hard-working, pious, frugal, and family-oriented people. They generally had little experience with Africans. The immigrants invested what capital they had in slaves, tools, provisions, and livestock, and took them into the camps. Since life in these isolated districts was extremely difficult in the early years, few Portuguese women migrated to the region. Many Brazilians also flocked to the mining districts, principally from the northeast coast and from São Paulo. They were used to employing African slaves, and many took with them slaves they had used in other businesses. They also left behind their wives because of the hardships in the mines.

The prices of slaves increased sharply at the turn of the eighteenth century because of the inland migrations produced by the discovery of gold. During the gold rush importations from Africa more than doubled—from about seven to fifteen thousand per year. At first, the Crown attempted to require that slavers buy only at Angolan ports, but the miners preferred Africans from the Costa da Mina region (between the Bight of Biafra and the Windward Coast), because they knew or readily learned mining techniques. The king finally acquiesced, and huge numbers of Mina slaves arrived.

Eventually, shipments of Angolan slaves—favored for general labor—surpassed those from Costa da Mina. The mining boom created a tremendous demand for livestock, tools, food, transport, ships, construction materials, and manufactures. Indeed, the mining boom generated capital and laborpower for later development efforts in the Amazon and along the north and southeastern coasts as well. During the eighteenth century, almost two million slaves were shipped from Africa to Brazil, deepening the process of Africanization.

In Minas Gerais, the numbers of Mina and Angolan slaves remained about equal, and ecological factors limited the total district population to about two hundred thousand. Several censuses provided information on mining slave owners and their slaves. The most frequent occupations among the slave owners were military officer and priest. Most owners had two slaves, whom they used to work mining claims, carry on other business, and do household duties. A few entrepreneurs possessed dozens of slaves each. In the early days male slaveholders outnumbered females thirty to one, but by the end of the eighteenth century the ratio had fallen to about five to two. At first nearly all slaves were African-born, but by the end of the century the majority (59 percent) were native-born. Female slaves, who made up only 14 percent in the gold rush days, later made up about 42 percent, owing to the rising numbers born in Brazil. The age structure of slaves, highly skewed toward youth at first, became more normal by the end of the century.

Manumissions were at least as frequent in Minas Gerais as in the rest of Brazil, because slaves could hide nuggets and gems with which to buy their freedom. They also had many opportunities to work for themselves and to save money for self-purchase. Women and children more often gained their freedom through grants, because many were concubines or illegitimate children of masters. Some freed persons (especially women) later purchased slaves themselves whom they used in mining, business, or personal service. One of the most famous freedmen was the African prince Chico Rei, whose followers purchased his freedom, elected him king, and then worked in his mine in the town of Ouro Prêto.

Because of the scarcity of white women during the gold rush, many miners formed conjugal unions with their female slaves or patronized African prostitutes. Within a few years a generation of children of mixed race arose, some with substantial Amerindian heritage as well. Thus, Minas society was far more racially blended than that of the coastal sugar zone.

Life and work in the mines exposed slaves to more severe risks than they had faced in the sugar fields. Most labored in placer deposits, where they were continuously wet and cold due to the altitude. Pick and shovel mining was as exhausting as plantation work. Nutritious food was not as abundant as on the coast. The greatest scourges for whites and blacks alike were pneumonia, intestinal parasites, and dysentery, for which no effective treatments existed. The slaves' existence in Minas remained as "nasty, brutish, and short" as it had been in the sugar industry. Still, the age distributions and sex ratios revealed in censuses suggest that life expectancy for slaves in Minas Gerais was at least as long as in the plantations. Several causes may be postulated. The small number of slaves owned by most miners might have led to a more familial existence than on plantations, where slaves lived in crowded quarters and ate inferior rations. Closer personal relations between masters and slaves led to high rates of miscegenation, recognition of illegitimate children, and manumission, which could have improved their quality of life. Perhaps the urban residence of most slaves (the mining camps had become towns and cities) improved their chances for survival.

Well-to-do slave owners in Minas provided more education for their sons, white and mulatto, and even underwrote advanced schooling for some in Europe. Their patronage of the church and the arts created jobs for talented artisans, writers, painters, musicians, architects, jewelers, sculptors, and designers. Africans and their descendants, both slave and free, were very active in the flowering of the first truly Brazilian artistic age, the baroque. One of the most famous Afro-Brazilian artists of all time—the master Aleijadinho—left an exquisite legacy of statuary, religious artifacts, furniture, and churches in Minas Gerais. Such educated and skilled mulattoes formed a racial middle class in Minas Gerais.

Most of what has been said about the African experience in the gold mines was also true of life in the adjoining diamond district after 1730. The work was hard and discipline rigorous. Nevertheless, slaves were often rewarded for finding large stones, and thousands managed to save enough money to buy their freedom. The exclusion of outsiders by Portuguese administrators led to even closer relations between masters and slaves. One of the most extraordinary Afro-Brazilian persons of this era was Xica da Silva, a beautiful and canny African princess, who won her freedom and was lavished with favors by the area's chief diamond contractor, an enormously wealthy man who had fallen in love with her. Her story was made into a film in the 1970s.

With depletion of the ores, the mining cycle went into decline in the 1750s. This change tended to lighten the work demands on the slave population and encouraged economic diversification. Many miners' sons and grandsons took a slave or two and struck out to farm or ranch. Slavery continued to be practiced in the mining region until late in the nineteenth century but in an unusual manner. Operators of small and medium-sized farms and ranches possessed several slaves, who worked as hands and were to some degree members of the owners' extended families. This type of production was profitable and apparently allowed for a natural increase among the slaves, for the first time in Brazil's history. Nowhere else was slavery adapted profitably to agriculture on small holdings.

◆ AFRO-BRAZILIAN CULTURES

By the early nineteenth century, distinctive Afro-Brazilian cultures had arisen, shaped by regional origins in Africa and by the dominant industries in Brazil. The Northeast was dominated by Yoruba influence from the Mina coast. Tens of thousands of Minas remained in the highland region after the decline of mining exports. They had longstanding contacts with Muslims, Europeans, and other Africans, better enabling them to adapt and preserve their culture. Also, they came late and in large numbers, so their culture remained active in the community experience. In particular, some freedmen visited Africa to reestablish contact with ancestral spirits, important in their religion, called *Candomblé*. In this way they became the interpreters of a new, adaptive African faith in Brazil.

Throughout the time Brazil was a Portuguese colony (1500–1822), most of its population was black and Amerindian. The Amerindians continued to be enslaved for work in regions with low-profit industries, but Africans and their descendants predominated in lucrative branches like sugar, tobacco, mining, urban crafts, and coffee.

Because large numbers of slaves arrived from abroad, one of the sharpest social distinctions among the workers was African versus local birth. A recently arrived African was called a *boçal* (*bozal* in Spanish). This designation implied limited knowledge of European culture, lack of familiarity with local conditions, and greater attachment to his or her nation. Boçais might be guarded more closely and kept isolated from native-born slaves who, in turn, were called creoles (*crioulo* in Portuguese, *criollo* or *ladino* in Spanish). Creoles tended to look down on the boçais as ignorant and inferior. This social gap probably impeded efforts to organize resistance and filtered out some African culture that creoles regarded as backward, pagan, or primitive.

In addition, large intermediate groups of mulattoes, mestizos, and other mixtures continued to grow. Racial boundaries blurred, while other criteria—family, education, occupation, physical appearance, income, place of birth, dress, and so on—took on more importance for assigning status. According to an old saying that simplified a complicated situation, *dinheiro embranquece*, or money whitens. Persons of color residing outside the plantation environment came to be judged and categorized by several attributes, producing the myth that slavery was less harsh and race relations more peaceful in Brazil.

Race still mattered, of course, for nonwhites filled out the lower tiers of the social pyramid, while the whites and mulattoes dominated the upper levels. A racial hierarchy emerged that operated like a self-fulfilling prophecy. Light mulattoes tended to experience upward mobility and rose in social standing, whereas darker persons found opportunities scarce and movement difficult. Blacks, whether slave or free, rarely escaped from the drudgery and suffering of manual labor and low remuneration. The racial terms for these mixes, *moreno, pardo,* and *negro,* fully conveyed society's estimate of and expectations for each group. The ability of lighter colored persons to elude the full opprobrium of racial discrimination in Brazil (and to some extent in Spanish America) has been called the "mulatto escape hatch." Those who eschewed identification with African origins could pass as pseudowhite, and society would recognize such behavior with better treatment. The widespread passing of light-skinned persons distinguished these societies from those founded by northern Europeans, where rigid race lines were observed and enforced. Some critics, however, argue that such behavior merely postponed any discussion of racism as a societal ill.

◆ THE COFFEE BOOM

After a recession in the 1770s, the Brazilian economy (except mining) recovered and grew rapidly for the next one hundred and fifty years, driven by exports of agricultural products from the coastal regions. Although Brazilian producers continued to use Amerindian slaves in marginal areas, they preferred African slaves wherever profits allowed. They were employed in cattle ranching, extraction of forest products, and production of rice, tobacco, cotton, cacao, indigo, sugar, and—the latest boom crop—coffee. In addition, the rising profits from export agriculture caused cities to grow, and most relied on African slaves to sustain their activities. Most Brazilians assumed that civilized life would be impossible without Africans.

Owing to freer navigation, rising agricultural exports, and the growth of cities, slave imports into Brazil grew after the 1770s. British diplomatic pressure on Portugal (and on independent Brazil after 1822) did little to reduce the trade. Faster and larger ships brought slaves from many parts of Africa. A shift in the African sources of slaves occurred in the late eighteenth century. Now many more came from below the equator, from the west-central coast, and from southeastern Africa. Although all Brazilian regions imported slaves, Rio de Janeiro was the principal slave market in the nineteenth century due to the surge in coffee planting in its hinterland. The African trade peaked in the 1840s, when it reached about thirty-eight thousand slaves per year, and then ended shortly after the Brazilian government abolished it with the 1850 Queiroz Law. After the end of the trade, African slaves were supplied to the coffee plantations by means of an interprovincial slave trade, originating in the depressed sugar areas of the Northeast. Between 1850 and 1881, as many as two hundred thousand slaves were transported in this way. While slavery persisted, planters met with little success in recruiting European workers.

Labor on the coffee plantations was as demanding as that in the sugar fields and mines in previous centuries. The hardest work, done by men, was clearing land. Most of the region suitable for coffee (Rio's Paraíba Valley, the high plain of São Paulo, and Triângulo of Minas Gerais) had been heavily forested. Slaves cut down smaller trees and brush, which was allowed to dry before burning. They cut rings in the bark of larger trees to kill them. Seedling coffee trees had to be protected during the six years it took for them to reach producing age. Once the groves were established, they required weeding, pruning, and harvesting, done by men and women. Processing the beans involved hulling, drying, and sacking, tasks usually done by women. Until the coming of the railroad after the 1860s, sacked coffee was loaded by men and transported by mules down from the mountains to the ports of Rio and Santos.

The coffee barons, attempting to recreate the seigneurial life that had prevailed in the heyday of sugar, built manor houses, senzalas, mills, and chapels in the quadrangular fashion of seventeenth-century plantations. They purchased titles of nobility, arranged financially advantageous marriages for their children, and consumed conspicuously while the money lasted. Some used large numbers of slaves in domestic chores. So here, too, the manor house encouraged the mingling of cultures and genes as in a melting pot. In the end, the dream of a coffee aristocracy faded, due to erosion of the land, the decline and aging of the slaves, and limits to the world demand for coffee. Coffee, it turned out, was Brazil's last cycle of tropical enterprise based on African labor.

Africans brought to Brazil during the nineteenth century helped create new subcultures, which drew on the ethnic heritages of their homelands. In Rio, in particular, a unique culture arose, with its own languages, dress, food, manners, art, music, dance, and calendar of celebrations. The Afro-Brazilian religion called *Umbanda* blended deities and rites from Africa with the relaxed Catholicism practiced by those of European descent. It won converts through private ceremonies *(terreios)*, the black brotherhoods, family worship, and word of mouth. By this time the Africanization of Brazil was a self-sustaining, irreversible process.

These African cultures spread throughout Brazilian society in the nineteenth century. A folklore of African origin was passed on to white children by black nannies. Music—instruments, harmonics, melody, and rhythm—also became Africanized, and Brazil's samba is surpassed only by jazz as an Afro-American invention. Dance, speech inflection, food preparation, dress, family relations, work habits, and many other intimate aspects of life in Brazil also showed the effects of Africa, and, obviously, Africa's genetic contribution was very evident in the Brazilian physiognomy. The melting pot did not homogenize its contents, however; thus, the white, European elements remained on the surface, and African culture was officially discouraged. Even today these African elements are more identified with the working class and the *povo* (people) than with the elite.

♦ MULTIRACIAL SOCIETY IN THE TROPICS

From the 1830s on, groups of freed slaves returned to Africa because they were not entirely secure in their rights as freedmen in Brazil. There they created small Brazilian communities out of nostalgia for their adopted homeland. Most of the returned Africans engaged in commerce with Brazil, even the slave trade. Once this trade ended in the 1850s, they moved into other activities: merchandise exports, ranching and farming, and various trades. The Brazilian communities of Lagos and Dahomey, in particular, numbered in the thousands and were quite prosperous for the remainder of the century. Eventually, however, the connections with Brazil faded, because only scant family, economic, religious, and cultural links remained. The African colonies, like Brazil, became engaged with (and were eventually conquered by) European colonizers and no longer shared mutual interests.

The Africanization process per se ended in the nineteenth century, and what followed was the evolution of a distinctive Afro-Brazilian culture, with its own institutions, language, and behavior. Africanization has not turned Brazil into a replica of Africa, of course. The legacy of three hundred years of slave imports, trade, and development was more complex. In its broad structure Brazil's was a multiracial society led by a white elite, and its dominant culture and institutions were derived from Europe. This meant that European families—some descended from Portuguese nobility—monopolized power, wealth, and prestige and therefore commanded the course of history. They were the least affected by Africanization.

The strata beneath the elite were truly multiracial, composed of the masses of black, Amerindian, and mixed persons. The elite commingled with and yet remained distant from these masses. Members of the elite lived, worked, procreated, worshiped, and took leisure with the masses, yet they were always aware of the racial and cultural differences between them. The elite needed the masses to do society's work, and this required sustained contact. But the elite had to keep the masses in a subordinate position lest it lose its right to command. In the nineteenth century the elite developed an elaborate system of rewards and sanctions designed to preserve the socioeconomic system inherited from colonial times. It required that persons who wished to enjoy the major benefits of society—money, leisure, respect, travel, family—had to behave European, which in essence meant to behave white. This option was only available to persons in positions intermediate between the elite and the masses. Oddly, even racially mixed persons who behaved white passed as white, a process called *branqueamento*.

◆ Conclusion

By the midnineteenth century, Brazil had become more Africanized than any other area in the Americas except Haiti. Its religion, mores, language, folklore, music, and social structure clearly revealed the influence of the four million Africans imported in the preceding three hundred years. Africanization most affected the workplace—due to continued slavery— but it also penetrated the bedroom, chapel, kitchen, and drawing room. In subtle ways even the elite was Africanized, despite a tenacious desire to remain European. The nanny who nursed and nurtured the master's children in the plantation house imparted to them her culture. Gilberto Freyre believed that this nexus between two races was what destined Brazil to become a unique and successful civilization in the tropics.

Since the midnineteenth century, the African influence has abated. For one thing, Brazil's relations with Africa have changed markedly. Ties with former Portuguese colonies are now more political and cultural than economic. Brazil's trade has shifted from sub-Saharan to northeast Africa. And recent immigrant populations in Brazil have led to a diversification of its international linkages, especially with northern Europe, the Middle East, and Japan. Brazil has become a multiracial, multicultural society to which Africans, Europeans, and Native Americans have all contributed.

Chapter 6

AFRICANS IN MAINLAND SPANISH AMERICA

1513	Balboa crosses Panama and claims Pacific Ocean for Spain.
1550s	Mexico and Peru begin producing large quantities of silver for export to Spain.
1570–1610	Peak imports of African slaves to Mexico.
1573	Acapulco becomes sole port for Pacific trade with the Philippines.
1767	Spain expels from its American colonies the Jesuit order, whose slaves pass to government ownership.
1810–1826	Era of Latin American independence.

fricans and their descendants in the mainland Spanish American colonies experienced different lives than their counterparts in the Caribbean, Brazil, and British North America. (See Map 6–1.) While some crops produced and social institutions were analogous, labor and enterprise were more diversified and organized on a smaller scale in Spanish America than elsewhere. This led to closer relations between blacks, whites, and often Amerindians.

Throughout Spanish America, Africans interacted with large numbers of Spaniards and Amerindians. They found themselves surrounded by two dominant ways of life—those of the European settlers and the indigenous Amerindians. The existence of larger numbers of Native Americans on the mainland often put African Americans in positions intermediate between Europeans and Amerindians. Moreover, the continental landmass allowed runaway slaves to establish safer settlements than on the islands, thereby gaining their freedom. Finally, in a general way, Africans and their de-

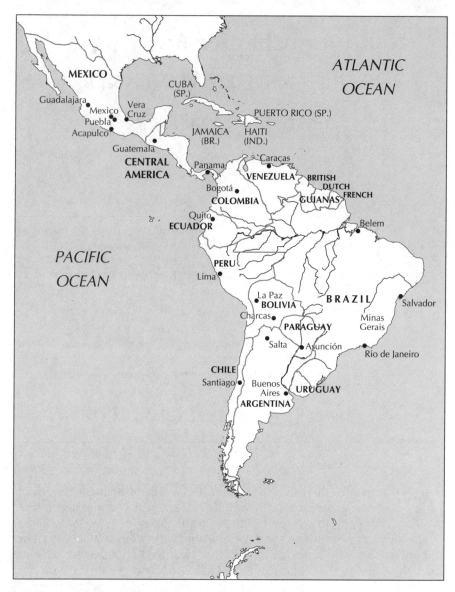

Map 6–1   Central and South America with Principal Cities, circa 1800

scendants could take part more fully in colonial life because their numbers were smaller than in Brazil, the Caribbean, and North America.

Racism and ethnocentrism permeated the African American experience in this region, as they did elsewhere. Spanish immigrants and their white and near-white descendants (called Spanish creoles) defined race principally by means of physical characteristics, especially skin color, hair, and facial features. The less Caucasian a person, the lower the rank in status. Colonial whites judged ethnicity, on the other hand, by sets of acquired characteristics such as language, customs, lifestyle, and religion—in a word, culture. Here too, the less European a person, the lower he or she was ranked. Newly arrived Africans, then, faced oppression for both their race and ethnicity. Yet by becoming acculturated, they could improve their social and even racial standing. Thus, the African Americans' status depended on physical and cultural attributes that affected one another. White European colonizers, a demographic minority almost everywhere, used racial and ethnic differences to divide and control African American and Native American peoples. The Amerindians' distrust of outsiders made it easier for the Spanish to divide subject peoples; so did the growing identification of slavery with dark skin color.

The heaviest African presence in Spanish America came during the colonial period (except in Panama, which later attracted a huge influx of Afro-Antilleans). Spanish colonists opted to import African slaves when they perceived an absence or shortage of local labor. They also had the means to generate enough wealth through agriculture, mining, or commerce to pay for the expense of buying African slaves. Black slaves proved especially costly in the Pacific rim colonies, owing to high transportation costs and mortality during long ocean and overland voyages.

The slave trade directed the greatest number of Africans to three mainland locales: Mexico (called New Spain at the time), Panama, and Peru. In Panama, Amerindians virtually disappeared after the European contact, thereby creating a need for additional laborers to handle trade across the Isthmus, Spain's principal link between the Atlantic and the Pacific oceans. Peru and Mexico began producing large amounts of silver and some agricultural products for European markets after 1550. This lucrative export trade coincided with crises in local labor markets caused by the catastrophic decline of Amerindian populations. The Spaniards imported large numbers of African slaves into all three colonies to increase production levels.

◆ MEXICO

Mexico was the first mainland Spanish American colonial area to receive large numbers of African slaves. Between about 1528 and 1620 it served as the principal American market in the Atlantic slave trade. An average of as many as one thousand Africans in bondage disembarked at Veracruz each year during this entire period, with the heaviest flow occurring from about 1570 to 1610. Upward of one hundred thousand Africans were relocated as slaves in New Spain before the end of the colonial period. Most of these individuals were destined for work in one of three sectors of the post–1550 Mexican economy.

Many Africans went to northern regions where they labored in the growing silver industry from the midsixteenth century on. Amerindians and free casta (mixed race) workers did most of the actual mining. The Spaniards often used black slaves in the refining process that required some of the highest skill levels in the industry. Wage laborers proved too scarce and transient in the sixteenth and early seventeenth centuries to warrant training in these tasks. Local Amerindians were even more mobile, and they sometimes turned defiant when coerced to work in the mines. They either rebelled or simply fled into the countryside.

Although blacks also acted unruly at times, and their purchase represented a considerable capital outlay, they emerged as the most reliable work force, one that offered the greatest cost effectiveness when trained for refining tasks. Bishop Alonso de la Mota y Escobar typified Spanish feelings toward black slave and free laborers in the mines at the turn of the seventeenth century when he said, "Bad to have them, but much worse not to have them." Black slaves dominated refining positions through the seventeenth century.

Commercial ranches sprang up in northern New Spain to supply adjacent mines with much needed meat, hides, and mules. The mines consumed thousands of hides just to make pumps to clear water out of the mines and bellows to push fresh air down into them. Workers used cattle hides to make sacks for hauling ore to the surface. Mules provided virtually the only form of transport in the mountainous mining districts.

Colonial life in the north proved both harsh and tenuous. Northern Mexico received too little rainfall to support other forms of agriculture. Moreover, the nomadic Amerindians who roamed the region posed a constant threat to outsiders who tried to settle there. For that reason whites relied heavily on blacks and mulattoes to staff the sprawling livestock haciendas in the region. There, both slaves and free blacks accepted the hardships and dangers of frequent drought and hostile Amerindians in return for greater freedom of action.

In addition, Africans and Afro-Mexicans made a significant impact on life in Mexico's dynamic urban centers. Cities remained the hubs of Spanish colonial life throughout the Americas, where Europeans and their descendants attempted to re-create conditions similar to those at home. In the countryside, however, mines and haciendas represented islands of capitalism surrounded by the demographically dominant Amerindians. The viceroyalties of Mexico and Peru led the way in the development of this type of spatial, racial, and ethnic differentiation. And just as black slaves had accompanied whites into hinterland mines, they accompanied them into their masters' urban enclaves. In sites like Mexico City, Guadalajara, Querétaro, Valladolid, Antequera, and Puebla they served whites as domestic servants. They engaged in a host of urban trades, and they contributed to public work projects like the construction and maintenance of roads, bridges, aqueducts, and government buildings. They also provided much of the labor force in oppressive sweatshops that produced cheap textiles for consumption by the poor population.

In areas like Morelos, Puebla, and above all Veracruz, Africans and their descendants performed crucial tasks in the production of sugar. As in the mines, Amerindian workers outnumbered blacks, but Afro-Mexicans controlled the skilled positions and oversaw Amerindian field labor. African slaves, and later their black and mulatto descendants, supervised Amerindians in clearing, planting, cultivating, and harvesting cane fields. Blacks made most of the critical judgments and supplied most of the labor for grinding cane. They boiled the syrup and poured the purified liquid into clay cones, where it dried and crystallized into sugar. Mistakes could ruin a whole batch of syrup. Spaniards entrusted this responsibility to expensive but reliable slave labor. After the beginning of the eighteenth century, however, free persons of all racial mixtures became numerous enough to replace African and creole slaves in most roles.

Blacks' important functions in sugar production were also the most dangerous and physically demanding. Persons who ground cane stalks ran the risk of having their clothes or bodies caught in the rollers, costing them fingers, hands, and even limbs. Gerónima, a slave on the Almolonga plantation just outside of Jalapa, Veracruz, had to have her crushed arm amputated in 1700. Slivers from the splintering cane occasionally blinded slaves. This happened to María Cochichi, also an Almolonga slave at the turn of the eighteenth century. Those who worked in the boiling houses risked terrible burns from scalding sugar syrup that bubbled over cauldron edges. At times the temperature in the refining houses topped 120 degrees Fahrenheit. Work under such oppressive conditions proved debilitating. Diseases like lung infections and malaria were common, for the work environment simply stripped the body of its natural resistance.

Placing Amerindian workers in this work environment proved out of the question, because they died too easily. By the end of the sixteenth century the Crown outlawed the use of native labor in refining houses. The prohibition stuck, not so much out of respect for the law as for expediency. Owners did not wish to train Amerindians in skilled jobs whose conditions would probably kill them. Only coerced slave workers proved dependable and strong enough to fill these labor needs.

Mexico's southwestern coast offered few attractions to Spanish settlers. Its narrow plain butted up against the western mountain ranges, restricting agricultural uses. The first European settlers came to mine placer deposits of gold in the streams that flowed down from the foothills to the Pacific. To perform the most arduous tasks, they brought black slaves with them to supplement Amerindian workers. After the gold deposits played out in the 1550s, the Spaniards operated cacao plantations and cattle ranches there. Shipbuilding and coastal commerce complemented these enterprises. Agricultural commodities went primarily to Mexican markets in the highlands. Ships built at the ports of Acapulco, Guatulco (present-day Santa Cruz), and Tehuantepec plied the Pacific coast as far south as Peru in search of cargos. Acapulco eclipsed these other two ports after 1573, when it gained a royal monopoly on trade with the Philippines. Still, the limited economic activity along the Pacific coast restricted the number of African slaves imported to the area. Africans simply cost more than most producers could afford.

Despite the small number of slaves imported to the west coast of Mexico, Africans soon outnumbered Spaniards, who tended to emigrate. Because of its rugged topography and isolation from highland Mexico, the area also became a refuge for runaway slaves (cimarrones). Fugitives founded maroon camps that evolved into towns and eventually became incorporated under Spanish law. Royal authorities, tacitly admitting their inability to disband the runaway communities, tried to win them over through legalization.

A combination of circumstances—the presence of fugitive blacks, the scarcity of Spaniards, the rough nature of the terrain, and the poverty of the region—created an unusually fluid social environment for Pacific coast Afro-Mexicans. Spanish authority was too tenuous to enforce racism or divide and subordinate nonwhites, as was done elsewhere. Because the region did not hold great significance within the empire (except Acapulco), it afforded Afro-Mexicans an extraordinary degree of freedom and enhanced their impact on local economic and social development. Free blacks and slaves alike intermarried with Amerindians and persons of mixed race (pardos and castas), and Africans and their descendants became numerically dominant.

Throughout New Spain, Afro-Mexicans made important contributions to social development. Widespread racial miscegenation created a kind of buffer group that both whites and Amerindians found more acceptable than Africans. The intermediate group, related to both whites and Amerindians, tended to relieve racial tensions by serving as a mediating group. In most types of face-to-face relationships, like marriage and godparenting, Africans and mulattoes more often than whites or Amerindians crossed over racial and ethnic lines. (Mestizos also acted as interracial and interethnic agents of bonding.) In this sense, Afro-Mexicans contributed proportionately more than whites or Amerindians to the process of mestizaje that Mexicans proudly see as the foundation of their racially and culturally hybrid society.

◆ PANAMA

The most common route between the Atlantic and the Pacific oceans traversed Central America at Panama. Between 1531 and 1660, up to 60 percent of all the precious metals shipped from the New World to Spain passed through Panama. Most Spaniards who crossed to the Pacific during the sixteenth century took black slaves with them. African soldiers and aides accompanied Balboa when he first gazed on the Pacific in 1513; they helped staff the Pizarro expeditions into the Andean strongholds of the Inca empire; and they escorted Diego de Almagro and Pedro de Valdivia into present-day Bolivia and Chile. Africans served as auxiliaries for whites in the conquest and early settlement of South and Central America.

Panama served as the staging area for the exploration and conquest of the entire Pacific side of South America. Europeans and Africans, equipped with boats and arms, arrived at the Atlantic harbor of Portobelo. From there they moved across the narrow Isthmus and were organized into quasimilitary expeditions at the Pacific port of Panama.

During the first half of the sixteenth century most of the traffic in people and goods flowed one way, from Spain to the Pacific coast. After mid-century, however, American exports to Spain began to predominate, and Panama served as the transshipment point for both directions of this trade. Between 1531 and 1731 trade fairs that operated on the Atlantic side of the Isthmus handled an estimated 1.5 billion pesos in goods.

Panama's indigenous peoples, who had little resistance to European and African diseases that the newcomers brought with them, nearly died out in the early decades of contact. So the Spaniards replaced Amerindian tribute workers with African slaves, just as they had done on the Caribbean islands. As early as the 1520s Panama had a sizable population of African descent. Spanish merchants directed African slave workers in moving people and materials to and from ships on both sides of the Isthmus.

Portobelo on the Caribbean side hosted the oldest and biggest trade fair in the Americas. Slaves did most of the manual tasks that went into these fairs. Not only did they build and maintain the warehouses at the site, but they also drove and cared for the pack animals that hauled trade items. About twenty African slaves drove nearly fourteen hundred mules back and forth across the Isthmus from four to six times during each of the fairs, which lasted six to eight months. Muleteers had to cope with many dangers in their work: Poor roads injured animals, Amerindians and pirates occasionally assaulted them, and harsh weather stranded them in the mountains.

Africans attended to the personal and family needs of the whites, both Spanish and creole, who managed Panama's commerce. In addition, slaves built and repaired ships for the trade along the Pacific coast; they worked in furniture factories that produced goods for west coast Spanish settlements; and they mined gold in the region throughout the colonial period.

Because of the heavy reliance on slaves, the number of blacks in the region grew constantly. As early as 1625, an estimated twelve thousand blacks labored in Panama, and just five years later they outnumbered Spanish inhabitants by a ratio of ten to one. At the end of the colonial period, Afro-Panamanians made up over 60 percent of the population in the transit zone between Panama City and Portobelo.

Because of their status as slaves, Afro-Panamanians were relegated to the lower rungs of the social ladder; their bondage and dark color restricted social advancement. Moreover, the disappearance of the Amerindians created racial polarization, strengthening the color line between blacks and whites. As Amerindians became more scarce, white racism focused more on persons of African descent. Thus, both slaves and free persons of color experienced legal disenfranchisement to a greater degree than in most areas during the colonial period. The Afro-Panamanians' work regimen, social degradation, and large numbers made them and their descendants an explosive element in the Isthmian society. Black slaves often rebelled or ran away, further exacerbating strained racial relations between them and whites. All these physical, social, economic, and political conditions combined to create a harsh experience for Afro-Panamanians.

◆ PERU

As the Spaniards established their towns and fortifications in Panama in the 1520s, they heard tales of large and rich Amerindian kingdoms to the south. Adventurer Francisco Pizarro and his soldiers made continuous probes down the west coast of South America in search of riches, and in his expeditions he relied heavily on black slaves. Between 1529 and 1537 the Crown issued licenses for the importation of 363 slaves from Africa, nearly 70 percent of whom were sold to Pizarro. At the Inca stronghold of Cajamarca, he finally found what he sought. There he captured the Inca ruler and held him for ransom. The conquistadores accepted huge amounts of silver and gold for his release, and then killed him anyway.

Many other Spaniards, attracted by Pizarro's success, rushed in for a share of the spoils of conquest. When they, too, brought African slaves as auxiliaries, the number of blacks in the region grew. With the precious metals they plundered from the Incas, the Europeans could import even larger numbers of Africans. These slaves adapted to the highlands, the coast, and the outlying areas where advance expeditions were sent.

During the remainder of the 1530s and through the following decade, about two thousand black slaves fought in Amerindian conquests and civil wars between Spanish factions. Peru's heaviest concentration of blacks occurred in the lowlands, whose climate was especially unhealthy for whites and Amerindians. The Spaniards believed that blacks could survive in humid, disease-ridden environments better than Amerindians or whites. Because of this belief and because slaves were far more educable and dependable workers in European production systems, they became the preferred labor force in early colonial Peru.

Within two generations of initial contact, most of the native Amerindians had died or had fled from the coastal plain of Peru. African slaves, the mainstay of the labor force, established thriving wine, cereal, and sugar plantations producing primarily for Andean markets. By midcentury over three thousand African slaves labored in Peru, an area that stretched from present-day Bolivia, in the south, northward through Peru and Ecuador, and into southwestern Colombia.

Peruvian commercial agriculture proved more diverse than that practiced in most other parts of the Americas. On many Caribbean islands single crops tended to predominate, whereas the varied Andean climates produced a wider variety of products. Peruvian slaves performed the multiple tasks very well under difficult physical conditions. In this more complex regional economy, slave and free African Americans came to enjoy intermediate social status between Amerindians and whites. African slaves represented a more fixed and reliable labor force than Amerindians, and they often served as overseers for the large numbers of sedentary Amerindians.

Africans made only limited contributions to the huge silver mining industry in the Andes. Silver deposits were found in highland regions, where the altitude diminished the blacks' endurance for hard labor and undermined their health. Although many Africans did find their way into the highlands, they were overshadowed by the denser Amerindian and Spanish populations there. Large native gene pools and entrenched Hispanic and Amerindian cultures absorbed and overwhelmed blacks as a racial and ethnic group.

Disruptive forces in the Andes fostered greater interaction among ethnic and racial groups. Native mortality from disease, coupled with impositions by the Spanish, caused a high level of instability in village life. Disorder encouraged many Amerindians to detach themselves from villages and wander the countryside until, by the end of the seventeenth century, about 25 percent of them had become vagrants. They came into close and sustained contact with blacks on a more equal basis than whites did, leading to marital liaisons and social alliances. Similarly, heavy contact with Amerindians further diluted African cultural and racial characteristics.

Until as late as 1640, the number of African slaves probably equaled the number of Spaniards in the Andean region. The mixing of all three races created ever more nonwhite groups, whom the Spaniards called castas. In 1788 the province of Cochabamba had over 127,000 residents, only 16 percent of whom were white. Amerindians made up 45 percent, blacks had fallen to under 1 percent, and castas accounted for over 38 percent. Mestizos formed the largest element within this last group, and African mixes were scarce.

Estimates for the entire viceroyalty of Peru showed the population to be 60 percent Amerindian and 21 percent mestizo, with the remainder made up of Spaniards, mulattoes, other castas, and blacks. Europeans simply did not have the resources to control this racially and ethnically pluralistic society, especially in a region so distant from Spain. Two-way communication between Lima and Madrid normally required eight to twelve months, which meant that local whites had to rely on their own authority to maintain order.

Outnumbered Spaniards and creole whites tended to use indirect means to control nonwhites, and out of these circumstances grew a unique social order based on racism and ethnocentrism. The Spanish state and church cooperated in keeping the lower castas in their places. Peru, like Mexico, became a proving ground for a society in which whites enjoyed superiority over Amerindians and persons of African origin. Clerics did proselytize and helped to mitigate the sufferings of subject peoples, but they labored just as hard to strengthen the racist and ethnocentric social order.

By 1540 three core areas stood out in Spanish America, surrounded by vast peripheral regions: on the Atlantic side, Mexico, which became the northern pole of the mainland empire; on the Pacific rim, Peru, which served as the southern pole; and in between, Panama. The native populations in all three areas came under heavy stress, causing the death of tens of millions of Amerindians. The Spaniards sought to relieve pressure on indigenous peoples by supplementing or replacing their labor with African labor. As a result, the cores became the principal markets for African slaves.

The social system that emerged in Spanish America appeared to be more feudal than mercantile or capitalistic. White Hispanics, having either conquered or purchased Amerindians and blacks, enjoyed power far beyond the force of their numbers alone. From the whites' point of view, the natural order of things required that blacks, Amerindians, and castas be subordinated. Spaniards and creole whites also created a corporate system of estates based, in order of importance, on racial, ethnic, and economic distinctions. The resultant seigniorial authoritarianism proved more important than Spain's material technology, administrative efficiency, or military might.

◆ NORTHWESTERN SOUTH AMERICA

In the kingdoms of Quito and New Granada (present-day Ecuador and Colombia, respectively), Africans were concentrated in low-lying regions, where they labored in commercial agriculture, most notably on cacao estates. The port of Guayaquil and its environs became the locale of greatest African influence. In this important river port, Africans and their descendants served as stevedores, raft hands, and muleteers moving goods to port and onto ships working the Pacific coast. Free blacks and slaves practically monopolized skilled labor positions and became a labor elite in the shipyards, where most of Spain's Pacific fleet was built and maintained.

The coastal area in and around Guayaquil became so dependent on black slave labor that its economy went into crisis whenever the slave trade through Panama ebbed. The varied nature of Ecuador's economic activities affected blacks' lives. Cacao cultivation and logging brought slaves, Amerindians, and mestizos to work side by side. Because blacks often occupied skilled positions or supervised Amerindian laborers, they had elevated status over their Amerindian co-workers.

In 1621 the Spanish Crown outlawed direct trade between Guayaquil and New Spain, cutting off Guayaquil from its principal market for cacao. From that point on, the industry survived on contraband, mainly with Dutch traders who controlled commerce in the southern Atlantic at this time. These northern European interlopers regularly rounded Cape Horn and made their way to Guayaquil. Acapulco remained an important but illegal port of entry to the Mexican market. The respectable status of blacks and the dependence on contraband created a freewheeling atmosphere in coastal Ecuador that eased racial barriers.

In the Chocó region on the Pacific slopes of Colombia, gangs called *cuadrillas*, consisting of six to one hundred black slaves, scoured the streams and valleys for gold in alluvial sands and outcroppings. They produced the bulk of the gold exported from Spanish America after about 1650, and at times they did not even work under white overseers. The harsh living conditions of the wilderness paradoxically afforded slaves a great deal of independence of movement and action, enabling many to earn enough savings to purchase their freedom. They mingled and intermarried with free Amerindians and mulattoes, establishing hybrid populations and cultures in the coastal region.

At first, Africans in northwest South America ranked at the bottom of the social scale, for even Amerindians considered them racially inferior. In addition, Spanish law forbade blacks to bear arms (except as members of the colonial militias) and wear expensive clothing or jewelry appropriate to persons of higher socioeconomic status. Slaves could only travel at night in the company of their owners or overseers. Moreover, free blacks could not possess Amerindian slaves or hire servants. In practice, however, blacks enjoyed far greater social and economic opportunities than Spanish law granted them. This was especially true of the quasifree miners in the gold fields and the overseers of native workers on commercial agricultural estates. Their standing resulted from the Spaniards' dependence on them to manage their businesses and from occasional protests and resistance.

Blacks in this area were regarded as unruly and inclined to run away if they were mistreated. The many maroon retreats along the coast kept Spanish and Amerindian authorities on constant alert.

Esmeraldas, located west of the capital at Quito, was the best-known runaway community on the west coast and became a symbol of African slave resistance. In 1553, after a voyage in heavy weather, a Spanish ship laden with slaves and European goods anchored just beyond the Cape of San Francisco to take on provisions. Sailors took a company of seventeen African males and six females ashore to help forage for supplies. The slaves overpowered their captors, returned and seized control of the ship, freed the other slaves, and put all the whites ashore. The slaves then sailed south, beached the vessel, and escaped into the rugged foothills of the Andes. There they established their palenque, taking land, goods, and women from Amerindian villages in the vicinity. They also raided Spanish estates and robbed travelers. For nearly a century the cimarrones beat back Spanish attacks on their stronghold.

Generations later, colonial authorities finally overpowered the descendants of these runaways. By then, however, they found that the blacks had so integrated with the Amerindian and casta inhabitants of the region that they were nearly indistinguishable. In this sense, the residents of Esmeraldas mirrored the experience of most Afro-Ecuadorians, who with time blended racially and culturally into the area's mixed population.

◆ BOLIVIA

Bolivia, known as Upper Peru during colonial times, had a very light African presence. Spaniards took few blacks there, believing that they were ill suited to its high-altitude climate and rarefied air. Moreover, the region's large Amerindian population, even after the demographic catastrophe elsewhere, provided most of the labor needed in the silver mines and the haciendas that provisioned the mines. Some Africans were transported there to do specialized tasks in the silver refining processes and to oversee Amerindian workers on commercial estates. A few also worked as domestic servants for wealthy Spaniards. In these capacities blacks held authority over Amerindians, which led to a good deal of mixing between the two groups, eventually blurring color lines and providing a mobile social environment for Afro-Bolivians.

◆ CHILE

Chile was annexed to the Spanish empire during the conquest of Peru. In 1536 Diego de Almagro pushed southward beyond Inca territory into the land of the Araucanians, a loosely organized hunting and gathering people. Like other conquerors, Almagro depended on Africans to fill out the ranks of his unit. For example, Juan Valiente, a runaway slave from Mexico, enlisted and distinguished himself in fierce combat against the Amerindians. For his valor (and in violation of Spanish law) he was granted land and an *encomienda*, or rights to tribute Amerindian labor. Ironically, when Valiente died in battle a year later, his Mexican owner laid claims to Valiente's property and encomienda. Grateful local officials, however, confirmed Valiente's titles and passed them on to his free-born son.

While perhaps the most famous, Valiente was not the only African American to receive lands and tribute Amerindians for his exploits in the difficult conquest of the area. Juan Beltrán, Cristóbal Varela, Leonor Galiano, and Gómez de León won similar battlefield awards.

Once the Spaniards had consolidated their hold over Chile, they used black slaves in every important dimension of the local economy. When it proved difficult to secure Africans through the legitimate slave trade via Panama, local buyers purchased them from smugglers who traveled overland from Argentina. There, English and Portuguese-Brazilian merchants carried on a brisk commerce exchanging manufactured goods and slaves for Peruvian silver and Chilean gold.

With limited access to native workers, Chilean whites relied heavily on Africans throughout the colonial period. African laborers mined placer gold through the eighteenth century and herded livestock on estates that supplied meat, hides, and mules to Peru and Bolivia. Their involvement in commercial agriculture remained strong throughout the colonial period. For example, when the Spanish Crown expelled the Jesuits from its colonies in 1767, they possessed between twelve hundred and two thousand slaves on their many estates. Even in 1810, travelers noted many black servants laboring beside Amerindians and castas on estates throughout Chile.

African slaves played even larger roles in Chilean cities than in most other Andean areas, since the seminomadic native population did not take to urban life. Chile's chronic shortage of labor restricted economic growth, making the economy little more than an appendage of Peru's. Moreover, heavy reliance on black slaves where Spanish authority was menaced by Amerindian resistance created the potential for a combined Amerindian and black rebellion. Such an alliance never appeared, however, for from the earliest contact Amerindians identified blacks with whites and regarded both as enemies.

Although blacks' legal status in colonial Chile was inferior to that of Amerindians, they exercised greater de facto power than natives. For example, Afro-Chileans often supervised transient or coerced Amerindian laborers. This circumstance, coupled with the auxiliary role blacks played in the conquest of Amerindians, engendered in blacks an attitude of superiority over the natives. Amerindians, frequently complaining that slave and free blacks exploited and abused them, loathed them as much as they did Spaniards. In the end, despite legal stipulations regarding the races, slaves occupied an intermediate position between Spaniards and Amerindians.

In Chile, as in other colonial fringe areas with a moderate African presence, some Spaniards married blacks because of the shortage of white women. So blacks not only achieved freedom at times but could even approximate Spanish status as well. Socially, Chile proved a land of extremes for blacks—of brutal oppression and unusual opportunities.

◆ AREAS OF MODERATE AFRICAN PRESENCE

Spaniards accorded blacks a lower legal status than any other people in these regions. But laws written by bureaucrats in Spain often went unenforced by overseas administrators, who daily faced the realities of life. Officials sometimes invoked the formula, *obedezco pero no cumplo*, meaning, I comply with the spirit of the law but I do not carry it out to the letter. In settings of moderate African presence, royal authorities, clerics, and colonists often applied this principle by treating blacks better than Amerindians and sometimes even as equals.

African Americans along the west coast of South America had mixed experiences, determined in part by the size of their respective communities. Socially, they often found a lower degree of racism than in settings where blacks were more numerous. In Bolivia, where Amerindians represented a greater threat to Spanish authority, officials and colonists exhibited more racism and ethnocentrism toward Amerindians than blacks. In the highlands of the Andes, whites needed blacks as allies to subordinate Amerindians and to exploit the natural resources of the land. For these reasons, Spaniards tended to accord blacks higher social status in practice than provided by law. Economically, blacks possessed greater occupational skills and supervisory authority over Amerindian workers.

◆ AREAS OF LITTLE AFRICAN PRESENCE

After founding Panama City, Spanish adventurers pushed on to Central America. While the Pacific coast held little attraction for Europeans, some settled with their African slaves in present-day El Salvador and Costa Rica, especially in Guanacaste and Punta Arenas, engaging in gold mining, ranching, and farming. Africans also served as domestic servants for their Spanish masters. The African presence in this area remained scarce, because Guatemala and Honduras had large native populations to meet the Spaniards' labor needs. In addition, the rudimentary economies of the region would not support the high costs of numerous African laborers.

The underdevelopment of Central America contributed to lax record-keeping, so that the African American experience there is difficult to reconstruct. Moreover, the African presence became diluted in the gene pool. It is likely, however, that the weak Spanish occupation allowed blacks greater freedom. Moreover, in areas like Guatemala and Honduras, blacks were the principal allies of the Spaniards and white creoles and thus enjoyed higher status than the more numerous Amerindians. Finally, as partners with Spaniards in economic enterprises, Afro–Central Americans received greater economic benefits than they did in many other areas.

♦ CONCLUSION

During the sixteenth and seventeenth centuries, a combination of forces molded the African American experience in the Spanish colonies. Between 1500 and about 1630, most of Spanish America suffered extreme demographic stress, as Amerindians died in large numbers and raised the specter of annihilation of the indigenous peoples. The Spaniards reacted by importing large numbers of African slaves to relieve natives of the most demanding labor tasks. The key to survival in many areas was generating enough surplus wealth to import expensive African slaves. Peru, Colombia, Mexico, and Panama satisfied this requirement—the first three because of precious metal and sugar production and Panama because of its commercial importance. Chile, Bolivia, Ecuador, Nicaragua, El Salvador, and Costa Rica did not develop enough surplus to pay for many Africans.

Several additional conditions affected the lives of African Americans in the Spanish colonies. One, climate, played an important role, since the Spaniards usually assigned blacks to unhealthy tropical lowland areas where health risks proved great for all persons regardless of race. Second, many other African Americans found themselves in frontier regions exposed to hostile Amerindians and unsettled living conditions.

Chapter 7

AFRICANS IN THE THIRTEEN BRITISH COLONIES

1607	Jamestown, Virginia, founded as first permanent English settlement in North America.
1610s–1620s	Dutch bring enslaved Africans to Virginia and to New Netherland.
1670s–1720s	Enslaved Africans displace indentured Europeans as mainstay of colonial bound laborforce.
1712	Slave uprising in New York City.
1739	Stono Rebellion in South Carolina.
1741	Great Negro Plot in New York City.
1763–1767	Mason-Dixon line drawn between Pennsylvania and Maryland.
1775–1783	U.S. War of Independence.
1777	Vermont constitution first to outlaw slavery.
1780	Pennsylvania passes first U.S. gradual emancipation statute.
1787	Northwest Ordinance designates slave and nonslave territories.
1787	U.S. Constitution recognizes and protects slavery.
1793	U.S. Fugitive Slave Act.
1793	Improved cotton gin spurs plantation production.
1795	Point Coupée Conspiracy in Louisiana.
1799	New York law begins gradual emancipation, completed in 1827.

1800	Gabriel's Plot in Virginia.
1808	U.S. outlaws the importation of slaves.
1821	Denmark Vesey's Conspiracy in South Carolina.
1831	Nat Turner's Rebellion in Virginia.
1861–1865	U.S. Civil War.
1863	Emancipation Proclamation.
1865	Thirteenth Amendment to U.S. Constitution outlaws slavery in the United States.

African Americans in the English colonies of North America stood on the periphery of the Atlantic community's great plantation regimes. Introduced as captive labor into England's first permanent mainland settlement—Jamestown, Virginia, founded in 1607—blacks became a presence north and south. They served from the far reaches of the Massachusetts Bay colony, later to become Maine, to Georgia's border with Spanish-held Florida. Although they became integral to the developing culture, in many ways they remained on the fringe of the dominant New World patterns of slavery and race relations.

◆ SUGAR AND THE SLAVE TRADE

Sugar dominated plantations and slavery elsewhere in the colonial Americas, but the sweet crystals offered no sustenance for slavery in England's thirteen North American colonies. Consequently, they received only about one in twenty of the Africans landed in the Americas during the trans-Atlantic slave trade. The torrents of captive humanity freighted as cargo from Africa to the Americas flowed to the tall and slender tropical grass of jointed and flexible stems called sugarcane. They poured into the Caribbean and Brazil. Tiny Barbados—an island of only 166 square miles, about one-seventh the size of Rhode Island—received almost as many Africans as all thirteen colonies combined.

As an indication of where the thirteen colonies stood in the scheme of the Atlantic slave trade, they received only 45 of every 1,000 Africans landed in the Americas. Barbados received only slightly less: Its 387,000 imports represented about 40 of every 1,000 Africans landed in the Americas. Other small West Indian islands received many more Africans than what became the United States. The French islands of Martinique in the Windwards and Guadaloupe in the Leewards received a total of 657,000—about 68 per 1,000, or one and a half times as many as the United States.

Cuba—the largest of the West Indies but only slightly smaller than New York State in area—imported 702,000 Africans; that was about 73 per 1,000 of all Africans landed in the Americas. Jamaica—an island about the size of Connecticut—imported 748,000 Africans; that nearly doubled the U.S. total. Hispaniola, which was more than half Cuba's size, imported 864,000 Africans—roughly 90 of every 1,000 landed; that was more than double the imports into the British colonial precursors of the United States.

The mainland colonies simply posed no significant competition with sugar sites for slaves. They lacked the means to bid away cargoes from the Caribbean and Brazil, areas of much richer revenues. The population ratios revealed the result: In 1650 blacks made up a mere 4 percent of the population in English North America but 25 percent of the population in the English Caribbean.

◆ POPULATION DIFFERENCE

As a result of the imbalance in profits and production, the thirteen colonies not only received fewer slaves but also a different mix than the sugar regions. The intensive and ponderous work of the ingenios demanded robust and rugged laborers. The rigors put a premium on males age fourteen to twenty-five years and made a small market for females of any age. As prices reflected demand, the richer regions skimmed off prime-age males. Females were relegated to the mainland colonies where necessity drew less distinction between male and female slaves.

The long-term result of the disparate regional demand was a strikingly different sex ratio among African peoples in the Americas. Whereas in the sugar regions males consistently outnumbered females, sometimes by ten to one, in the English mainland colonies a fairly even sex ratio developed. The more balanced sex ratio produced notable consequences: It generated a significantly higher birth rate than in the Caribbean; and it quickly transformed the mainland black population into creoles, as Africans born in the Americas were called.

By 1740 most blacks in the thirteen colonies were American-born. In contrast, creoles did not form the majority in the Afro-Brazilian or Afro-Caribbean population until about 1840, owing to continued importations and lower birth rates. The difference meant that Afro-Americans were among the earliest American-born populations. The difference also resulted in what North American planters sometimes called a "prolifick people." The regions that became the United States received only 5 percent of the Africans in the slave trade, yet they came to have the largest population of African descent in the Americas.

◆ THE SLAVE TRADE AMONG THE THIRTEEN COLONIES

Among the thirteen mainland colonies, the tobacco plantations that dominated the Chesapeake region—principally, Virginia and Maryland—and the rice plantations of South Carolina and Georgia employed the most Africans. But throughout the colonies Africans were in the work force, growing as a presence from 1675 onward. Virginia led the way. The oft-mentioned group in 1619 that tobacco planter John Rolfe noted with his comment—"about the last of August came in a dutch man of warre what sold us twenty Negars"—reflected less the initiation of a presence than its growth.

In the 1620s the Dutch supplied captive Africans not only to Virginia but also to their own mainland colony of New Netherland—from which English New York and New Jersey, primarily, were later carved. Dutch traders provided the main supply of Africans to the colonies before the 1660s. After the English seized New Netherland, they also displaced the Dutch as slave traders to the mainland. Most of their trade was conducted by the Company of Royal Adventurers, chartered in 1663, and then the Royal African Company, chartered in 1672.

The Chesapeake proved the most lucrative early market for Africans; yet the numbers were meager there until the late 1670s. In 1680 the English mainland had only about seven thousand blacks, but then they poured into the bay area with a gush until 1720. In those forty years the annual importation rates reached the thousands. As that stream developed, importations also picked up in South Carolina. Particularly after 1700 the Charleston slave market expanded to overtake the Chesapeake as the primary market for slaves. By the 1730s Charleston handled an average of two thousand Africans annually. Georgia, founded in 1732 as the last of the mainland colonies, added to the demand for slaves after forsaking its founders' initial ban on African labor. By the late 1750s Georgia was importing shiploads of slaves, but primarily from the West Indies in a reexport trade. Yet by 1766 when Savannah received its first black cargo directly from Africa, Georgia still had fewer African peoples in its population than New York.

Georgia made up for lost time after the 1760s by taking cargoes directly from Africa rather than accepting so-called seasoned slaves from the West Indies—the usual practice for most of the 1600s. As the West Indian imports frequently proved particularly troublesome and as they were more expensive, because of the seasoning experience, the continental colonies in the early 1700s shifted their preference to blacks directly from Africa, who were called "outlandish." The shift was especially apparent after the 1720s

Table 7-1
Black and Total Population of the Thirteen British Colonies of North
America, 1750

Colony	Black	Total	Percentage of Blacks
Virginia	101,452	231,033	43.9
Maryland	43,450	141,073	30.8
South Carolina	39,000	64,000	60.9
North Carolina	19,800	72,984	27.1
New York	11,014	76,696	14.4
New Jersey	5,354	71,393	7.5
Massachusetts	4,047	187,972	2.2
Rhode Island	3,347	33,226	10.1
Connecticut	3,013	111,283	2.7
Pennsylvania	2,872	119,666	2.4
Delaware	1,496	28,704	5.2
Georgia	1,000	5,200	19.2
New Hampshire	550	27,505	2.0
TOTAL	236,395	934,340	20.2

Source: U.S. Department of Commerce, Historical Statistics of the United States: Colonial Times to 1970 (Washington, D.C., 1975), 2:1168.

when about four of every five blacks introduced into the Chesapeake and Carolinas came directly from Africa.

Slavery reached into all the thirteen colonies, and the slave trade also became a significant commercial enterprise, particularly among New England merchants. Rhode Island slavers led the way, averaging eighteen cargoes and 2,133 Africans annually through ports between 1760 and 1775. Throughout the 1700s slavers from New York City, Philadelphia, Baltimore, and Boston joined the Newport and Providence shippers in the trade. Indeed, ships from the colonies carried about one-third of the Africans that the British slavers brought to the Americas between 1750 and 1775. (See Table 7-1.)

◆ Beginnings of Slavery

Virginia colonists officially listed captive Africans as "servants," but such an appellation should confuse no one about the slave status of the Africans in the colonies. English-language usage in the 1600s conceived of slave as a category of servant. So the use of the word "servant" in documents such as the Virginia censuses of 1623 and 1624 in no way denied the slave status of

Africans. Nothing could deny the reality of their slavery. Africans in bondage in Virginia were captives, coerced in presence and in effort. They were bought and sold as chattel, made by law movable property; they occupied a heritable status; and they were liable to service for an indefinite term extending to life. The fact that some Africans served less than their natural lives in the slave status did not indicate that they had not been slaves; it showed only that they had not been slaves their entire lives. Being released from slavery short of death hardly denied the existence of slavery.

Nothing could rationally support any conclusion other than that the captive Africans were slaves from the first. They occupied no status as indentured servants who had entered contracts voluntarily. Africans had no contracts for service, and for sure they had not entered service voluntarily. As it was in Virginia, so it was elsewhere in the thirteen colonies. Captivity enslaved Africans, coercion kept them enslaved, and social controls held them and their descendants separate as slaves and as nonslaves. The dominant society put them in a position distinct from all others. Specifically, the slave was salable, and no other persons were. An indentured servant's contract and, thus, labor was salable, but the person was not. Slavery was heritable, and no other personal labor obligation was. No others were marked from birth as unfree labor. Even recognition at birth marked Africans apart. Among settlers in the dominant society, heritability followed the father's line; among captive Africans, in contrast, heritability followed the mother's line. So a person was a slave if his or her mother was a slave, despite the father's status. In every crucial feature, settler stood apart from slave.

◆ SLAVERY AND LAW

As a relationship between the African and the European colonists, slavery did not depend for its existence on legal recognition. It needed no law to be reality. Law did not create slavery; law merely recognized slavery. It sought to add clarity to the implications of the relationship and to move it formally into the sphere of explicit public policy.

The Chesapeake colonies initiated the law of slavery in the 1650s as they moved from a labor force of mostly white servants to one of mostly black slaves. The transition saw Africans in Virginia multiply from about 300 in 1650 to 12,000 in 1708, when blacks formed about 40 percent of the colony's 30,000 residents. By 1756 Virginia had 120,156 blacks, ten times as many as in 1708. But the percentage changed little: Blacks in 1740 made up 40.9 percent of the colony's total population. By 1750 Maryland, too, had a substantial black population numbering about 43,000 and forming 30.8 percent of its population. The increased numbers themselves suggested a need for a more formal structure within the slavery relationship. (See Table 7–1.)

Virginia exhibited its sense of distinction between blacks and whites in service in a 1661 statute that provided differing punishments for fugitive white servants and black slaves. The law referred to "negroes who are incapable of making satisfaction by addition of time." Such a difference in tenure of service formed a cornerstone of the practice of slavery, as it would also for the legal institution of slavery. In 1662 Virginia enacted a law to recognize the heritable slave status through the mother. Maryland more than Virginia revealed the pervasive colonial presumption equating African-ness with slavery when in 1663 it enacted a statute defining all blacks as slaves at birth whatever the status of their mothers. In 1681 the colony revised the act to accord with practice elsewhere that mandated a child's following his or her mother's status.

◆ RACIAL SEPARATION

The initial legal recognition of slavery in both Chesapeake colonies revealed the preexisting discrimination that formed the basis of the practice. Virginia showed an extending basis in 1667 when it provided that baptism had no effect on slave status. In 1671 Maryland likewise declared conversion irrelevant to slavery. Similar declarations made their way to other colonies. By 1706 the Carolinas, New York, and New Jersey had enacted the rule that Christianity in no way affected slave status. Such laws recognized a shift in the sanction for slavery from moral and spiritual concerns to material and mundane justifications.

Christians long used paganism to justify slavery as a means of conversion. Thus, Christian Europeans claimed that wrenching Africans from their homeland and enslaving them in the Americas served to advance Christianity. They defended the slave trade and slavery as the means of removing millions from idolatry, paganism, and superstition. The rationale lay in the feeble but long lineage of distortions that sought to excuse white savagery as a black civilizing school. Like most proslavery apologies, the slavery-for-conversion rationale contradicted reality. It also encouraged a schizophrenia that characterized slavery and white supremacy. Slavery-for-conversion would have meant catechizing and baptizing captive Africans and would have suggested a real theology of liberation, for it would have meant that conversion led to manumission. The logical conclusion was simple: If being a non-Christian meant being a slave, then being a Christian meant not being a slave.

Both settlers and slaves saw the unsettled ground and rushed to different judgments as the colonial slave codes took shape during the years 1660 to 1710. Slaves grasped the liberation that Christian baptism proclaimed and reached for the freedom Christianity preached. Settlers, however, hastened to sever any connection that allowed slaves to lay claim to European entitlements. The developing idea was simple: what separated slave and settler was not Christianity but color and culture. Maryland legislators made this point in 1664 when they suggested that slaves could only pretend to be Christians. And, indeed, the Europeans debated the Africans' capacity for conversion. Settlers pondered perplexing questions: If baptized, would a black be as Christian as a white? If so, would a baptized black stand on the same footing as a baptized white? The codified answer was that if faced with a black Christian and a white Christian, the law saw a black and a white, not two Christians.

Race, not religion, mattered most as color prejudice permeated not merely slavery but colonial society. The result, however, was no monolith. Massive though the burden of race was, and grow as the oppression did, neither slavery nor black-white relations was single or uniform. Circumstances and conditions mattered. Time and place and, of course, individual persons themselves made a difference. Innumerable variations existed, and yet the fact was always merely that, variation.

The reality of black-white relations had a sordid similarity. The society imbued each group with stereotyped characteristics of its own, setting each apart. Not every black nor every white experienced the same effect of race. Not every black in the thirteen colonies or in the later U.S. nation was a slave, of course, but every black and every white experienced the effect of race and slavery.

Social insistence on the supremacy of whites and the subordination of blacks created the tenacious context of American life. Whether enslaved or unenslaved, people of African descent felt the social forces of supremacy and subordination. During the early period of fluid racial relations before the 1670s and the slave code, unenslaved blacks enjoyed only limited conditions of liberty. It was to become much worse afterward.

◆ A FEW UNENSLAVED

A notable number of unenslaved blacks carved out a niche in the developing colonial structure from the 1630s through the 1660s. In the Chesapeake, particularly on Virginia's Eastern Shore, and in Dutch New Netherland, they worked free from the shackles of slavery. They owed their free status to one of four reasons: They purchased their own release; others, usually kin, purchased their release; they secured release for good service; or they were born of nonslave mothers. Emanuel Driggus, Anthony Johnson, John Johnson, and Francis Payne were examples in Northampton County on Virginia's Eastern Shore.

Driggus, the Johnsons, and Afro-Americans like them could call themselves planters because they owned land and livestock and laborers. They also wielded legal rights in court—suing and being sued, giving testimony and making testaments, and winning and losing cases. In many regards they stood like any small planters. In addition, some blacks had lesser holdings and thus made up a black peasantry that farmed their own land and sometimes hired out their own labor.

On Manhattan Island in New Netherland, blacks also worked tracts they owned or rented in what was known as the "Negroes' Land." The parcels lay near Fresh Water Pond, the later site of the infamous Tombs prison. As early as the 1640s, Domingo Antony, Anthony Portuguese, Peter Van Campen, and other blacks held title to small tracts. Claes Emanuels and John DeVries II became yeomen farmers in northern Manhattan, supporting themselves and their families by land and labor.

Each of the thirteen colonies had its unenslaved blacks who enjoyed notable success. Their relative good fortune was notable, because it was exceptional for blacks, but the level of achievement was less extraordinary in the society as a whole. Among blacks, however, the success of the few as the exception proved the rule, the rule being that most blacks were slaves and that those who were unenslaved eked out paltry existences. Moreover, the rule was that economic success was reserved for whites and the few. Thus, while some unenslaved blacks enjoyed a higher degree of success in colonial America, they merely reached the sustaining middle. They had little more than a tenuous hold on meager fortune, always remaining only a stone's throw from hardship. Success allowed them liberties, but it never set them free: Rich or poor, they were black.

◆ A Hardening Line

Two roughly simultaneous trends that became apparent from 1660 to 1760 helped formalize the rules and principles of black-white relations in general and of the emerging institution of slavery in particular. First, wealth and power increasingly became concentrated in fewer hands. As a consequence, opportunities diminished, social lines hardened, and status differences based on race sharpened. Second, the multiplying number of slaves heightened the need to prescribe and enforce public policy as to who was allowed to do what and incur what penalty.

Until the 1660s most unfree labor was white; by 1690, 80 percent of all unfree labor was black. Slavery spread in size and strength from the 1680s onward as the number and percentage of blacks soared. In 1680 the English mainland had only about seven thousand blacks; then about three thousand entered the Chesapeake alone between 1680 and 1699. As a reflection of the increased demand, another three thousand Africans entered Virginia and Maryland in 1700 alone. Imports increased almost annually until about 1750 when unfree labor was virtually synonymous with slavery, and blacks alone had that status.

By 1750 freedom in the colonial context had been colored white and slavery black, and complexion cast a sharp separation between the two. The cracks through which blacks slipped from slavery with its social sanctions narrowed, with the result that the proportion of blacks holding lands or living outside slavery dwindled, and the legal lines between black and white hardened. Thus, the settling framework of race and slavery in the English mainland colonies further aggravated the conditions of black life.

◆ A LONELY MINORITY

Black life in the English mainland colonies remained distinct from the experience of African peoples elsewhere in the Americas. Even as the number of blacks proliferated between 1650 and 1750, the thirteen colonies remained on the fringe of the predominant demographic structures in the Americas. In 1650 blacks formed merely 4 percent of the English colonial mainland population, but 25 percent of the English Caribbean population and significantly more than that in the French and Spanish Caribbean. Even the southern mainland colonies paled in comparison to the Caribbean. In 1650 the southern colonies were only 3 percent black—less than the mainland colonies as a whole. But blacks averaged more than ten times that level in the developing plantation islands in the West Indies, as Barbados and Jamaica illustrated.

Barbados epitomized the African population explosion that in the mid-1600s rapidly distinguished the West Indies from the thirteen colonies. The tiny island absorbed a tenfold increase in blacks between 1640 and 1645, as it moved from several hundred blacks to more than six thousand. Africans there topped twenty thousand in the 1650s. By 1700 the island had eighty thousand blacks; that meant about as many blacks per square mile (482) as had lived on the entire island two generations earlier.

Jamaica further illustrated the consequences of such growth for the ratio of blacks to whites. By the time Spain formally ceded the island to England in 1670, after English Admiral William Penn (the father of Pennsylvania's founder) had captured it in 1655, blacks outnumbered whites there about five to four. By the 1720s the ratio was more than two to one, as blacks comprised 69.6 percent of all Jamaicans.

Clear demographic differences increasingly separated the mainland's northern and southern English colonies and distinguished them from the Caribbean colonies. By the eve of the U.S. War for Independence (1775–1783), the percentage of blacks in the thirteen colonies had surged, now reaching 22 percent. And showing the growing North-South difference, it rose to 40 percent in the southern colonies. Yet the percentage lagged far behind the West Indian standards. Elsewhere in the colonial Americas, Africans often formed a majority of the nonindigenous population. They overwhelmingly dominated the Caribbean labor force, for example. Yet they remained a minority in the thirteen colonies. Only in the middle 1700s did a few counties in the thirteen colonies have more blacks than whites. South Carolina alone had a black majority in 1750, and even there geographic concentration limited black dominance to a small area.

The racial configuration of what became the United States was atypical of the Americas. Only in the thirteen British colonies did African peoples stand as a minority in the colonial Americas. Even at their peak in 1770, blacks formed only 22 percent of the population in the thirteen colonies. The increasing concentration of slavery in the southern colonies changed local demographic mixes in the 1800s, and a so-called Black Belt of counties with black majorities emerged. Nothing, however, altered the controlling reality of a white majority and a black minority. Such dimensions were uncommon elsewhere in the Americas.

Although black majorities became a local or regional anomaly in the United States, they were the rule in the Caribbean. Blacks formed at least 91 percent of the population in the British, French, and Spanish Caribbean by 1800, and some islands had ratios of twenty blacks to one white. The difference was growing, as Cuba showed most dramatically by importing via Havana alone about three hundred thousand Africans between 1791 and 1825.

◆ BORN IN AMERICA

The blacks' experience in the thirteen colonies was also extraordinary in its early shift to a creole majority. By 1720 more blacks were being born in the colonies than were being imported there, and by 1740 most blacks there were American-born. Contrast this picture to Brazil and the Caribbean where most blacks were African-born as late as the 1820s. Thus, the U.S. black population was American-born long before the black population elsewhere. In fact, as mentioned earlier, Afro-Americans as a group formed one of the oldest American-born populations.

The more rapid transition to a creole population further distinguished Afro-Americans from other Africans in the Americas. It pushed their acculturation at a faster pace than elsewhere, for it more quickly shifted the mix away from those who had lived and learned traditional ways in Africa. With the smaller flow of African-born peoples to refresh the memories and practices of the ancestral homeland, new attenuated patterns developed. African origins remained apparent, but new influences and departures also became clear.

Even the flood of Africans in the Atlantic slave trade after the War for Independence failed to alter the predominance of American-born blacks in the United States. President Lincoln would speak of the "new nation conceived in liberty and dedicated to the proposition that all men are created equal" during the American Civil War (1861–1865). Yet the country imported almost as many Africans during its first thirty years after 1776 as entered the thirteen colonies in the 156 years from 1620 to 1776. Still, in 1800 fewer than one in seven blacks in the United States was African-born. In contrast, not only were most blacks in Jamaica in 1800 African-born, but also one in four had arrived from Africa since 1790. And in Cuba, ninety-four hundred Africans annually entered Havana alone between 1791 and 1825.

◆ SLAVE RESISTANCE

Contrasts between the thirteen colonies and other significant slaveholding areas in the Americas did not develop only in their demographic profiles. Differences in population composition, geography, and political structure shaped divergent patterns of resistance. In the colonies from which the United States sprang, slave insurgency tended more to individual varieties than to communal forms. When group action occurred, it was usually of smaller dimension and shorter duration than that in the Caribbean and South America. But throughout the Americas the enslaved exhibited characteristic recalcitrance.

The record of African rebellion against slavery in the Americas began with the first slave gangs that arrived in the 1500s. The form of resistance varied, as did the frequency. The most daring and dramatic manifestation of black defiance in the contemporary and historical imagination was open, organized, armed attack on slaveholders and their social, political, and economic structures. The Haitian Revolution that abolished slavery and established the Americas' second independent republic in 1804 epitomized the form. In no other place, however, did African Americans succeed in overthrowing the government that maintained slavery. Unique was the success on Hispaniola, the Caribbean's second largest island, encompassing an area about the size of South Carolina.

Uprisings occurred in many areas. Hispaniola had notable revolts in 1679, 1691, and 1704; New York had a slave uprising on Manhattan Island in 1712; the Danish-held Virgin Islands of St. Thomas and St. John faced rebellions in 1726 and 1733; and South Carolina had the bloody Stono Rebellion of 1739. Perhaps foreshadowing the Haitian revolutionary hero Toussaint L'Ouverture, the charismatic Macandal led an uprising in 1758 at Le Cap, a major port on St. Domingue, as the French called their colony on Hispaniola. Louisiana's Point Coupée Conspiracy in 1795, eight years before the United States acquired the territory, reflected on the mainland the unrest roiling the Caribbean during the French Revolution in the 1790s.

At least four waves of slave unrest swept the thirteen colonies during the 1700s. One wave hit during the 1710s, encompassing Sebastian's band in South Carolina in 1711 and New York City's 1712 uprising. A second hit during the 1730s and reached into the 1740s, including the bloodiest of

North American colonial incidents in South Carolina's famed Stono Rebellion of 1739 and New York City's so-called Great Negro Plot of 1741. A third flowed with the unrest of the American Revolution, beginning about the time of the Stamp Act crisis in 1765 and ending close to the British surrender at Yorktown, Virginia, in 1781. A last wave swelled in the 1790s with the agitation of the French and Haitian revolutions. Gabriel's Rebellion in Virginia during 1800 offered an example.

In dimension, the third wave washed deeper and farther than any other as the War for Independence offered blacks an opportunity to bear arms for their own liberty. More than ten thousand blacks seized the moment. Five thousand, mostly from the northern colonies, served the patriots; at least that number, mostly from the southern colonies, served in the royal forces.

States such as New Hampshire and New York offered promises of freedom to slaves who shouldered arms for the patriot cause. Others won freedom fighting against the patriots. Indeed, the royal forces were the first to make formal offers to slaves. Virginia royal governor Lord Dunmore issued his renowned proclamation of 5 November 1775 that declared "all indentured servants, Negroes, or others (appertaining to rebels) free, that are able and willing to bear arms, they joining his Majesty's troops." Given the chance to rise up for their freedom, African Americans throughout the thirteen colonies showed themselves willing, ready, and able to fight in open, organized, armed fashion. Those who were interested in seeing slaves in North America violently join in revolution needed to look no farther. And it was again the case during the American Civil War that African Americans took arms for their own freedom: More than two hundred thousand fought in the federal land and naval forces in the war that resulted in the blacks' general emancipation from slavery.

◆ SUPPRESSION

Everywhere in the Americas harsh suppression was the response to slave rebellion, and everywhere slaveholders used exemplary punishment as a deterrent. The whip served as their symbol and tool. Slaveholders ruled by terror, cutting off slaves' fingers and hands, toes and feet, ears, and arms; branding recalcitrants; and if hot irons searing a slave's flesh failed to soften resistance, sometimes consuming the person completely in fire. In 1712 New York City burned two black rebels at the stake in response to slave uprisings and roasted another over a slow fire for about nine hours. In response to the Stono Rebellion in South Carolina in 1739, slaveholders decapitated recalcitrants and displayed their heads on pikes at mile posts. Again in New York City, in 1741 officials burned thirteen blacks at the stake in response to the Great Negro Plot. At other times and places, recalcitrants were broken on the wheel, drowned, hanged, shot, and starved to death. The executions aimed not merely to dispatch troublemakers but also to humiliate them and, most of all, to discourage others.

Focusing on mass uprisings, however, gives us a distorted perspective on slave resistance, for although it was much idealized, open, and organized, armed rebellion was neither the primary nor preferred form of African American resistance. Nor was it a common form of slave resistance anywhere in the history of slavery. Of all slaves anywhere, African Americans proved the most rebellious. Rebellions occurred more frequently in the Caribbean than in the continental colonies, and more often in South America than in North America, but uprisings were atypical throughout the Americas. Indeed, almost every area that had any significant enslaved population experienced some uprising episode as the enslaved sought to subvert the ultimate coercion that maintained slavery, but uprisings were flashes. They were desperate bursts sparked spontaneously and fueled by unusual conditions.

◆ A PERSPECTIVE ON REVOLTS

Under usual conditions slave revolt was suicidal. The odds were heavily against the possibility that insurrection would succeed in the grand aim of overthrowing slavery and all its works. Wretched outcomes were particularly likely in the thirteen colonies and in the later United States where whites always outnumbered blacks on average by at least four to one. Unlike the absentee holders who characterized the Caribbean and South America, there slaveholders were on hand with their squads of overseers. Holdings of slaves were smaller—usually fewer than twenty—in contrast to the common holdings in the hundreds in the Caribbean and South America. The critical mass of a relatively large concentration was less likely, except in cities or heavily trafficked market areas such as Charleston or Stono, South Carolina, or New York City, where slave massings did in fact occur. Yet even in cities the dispersal pattern of small holdings diluted the concentration.

In sum, Afro-Americans in what became the United States seldom had favorable opportunities for large-scale operations requiring the maneuvering of many slaves to attack the society holding them. As black participation in the War for Independence and the U.S. Civil War showed, when favorable opportunities did appear, armed blacks stormed the ramparts for freedom.

◆ PRACTICAL RESISTANCE

The red-hot insurgency that most undermined slavery everywhere and sapped the structures of oppression was actually subtle, stealthy, and insidious. The usual forms were less sensational than uprisings and consisted in attempts to secure tangible liberties rather than to overthrow the social system that was slavery. They subverted the captive labor system by attacking not the ultimate coercion that maintained slavery but by interfering with the immediate concerns of daily life. Slaves frustrated slaveholders' desires to deprive them of their own selves, to seize their bodies, to strip their choices, and to steal the products of their labor. They thwarted those ends, blocking the slaveholders' drive to dominate their lives.

Enslaved African Americans fought every aspect of being captive labor. They sabotaged the work process at every point of performance and operation, and by consciously working poorly, they wasted time and inputs. They also destroyed tools and hobbled draft animals, they ruined output, and they let crops rot. Sometimes they balked completely and refused to work, or they shirked and stayed away as truants. Others pretended illness and injury or even feigned stupidity, avoiding work by pretending tasks were beyond their abilities. They reclaimed part of their expropriated labor by taking a share of goods for themselves. They defied authority, taking liberties to violate curfew, meet in groups, or entertain themselves.

Day-to-day resistance against slavery reduced slaveholders to continual carping that slaves were disobedient, headstrong, idle, incompetent, lazy, stupid, surly, and recalcitrant. Perhaps the most notable sign of the slaves' unmanageability was their running away, which removed more African Americans from slavery than any other form of resistance. Those known as fugitives and runaways in the United States, or cimarrones, mocambos, maroons, or quilombos in Brazil and the Caribbean, overthrew slavery individually and in small groups, though not systemwide.

◆ RUNAWAYS

Fugitives by the tens of thousands generated such recurrent political problems in the United States that they received a reference in the U.S. Constitution of 1787. The third paragraph of the second section of its Article 4 provided that

> No person held to service or labor in one State, under the laws thereof, escaping into another, shall, in consequence of any law or regulation therein, be discharged from such service or labor, but shall be delivered up on claim of the party to whom such service or labor may be due.

In 1793 Congress provided for enforcing the provision in the so-called Fugitive Slave Act. Another such act passed in 1850 as a desperate attempt to staunch the black flood spilling out of the South. Newspapers from the colonial period through the 1850s ran repeated columns filled with runaway notices that described fugitives of all dimensions.

No single type of Afro-American fled slavery. Those who could run apparently did, and those who couldn't didn't. Clearly, some were more capable than others. Not surprisingly, the young but mature made up the majority of reported runaways; most were in their twenties. Males fled more frequently than females, at least in part reflecting the male's greater opportunities to travel alone and get work. Teenage and young adult males appeared to run alone, whereas women fled with young children and families fled together. Unrelated groups banded for flight. No exclusive pattern developed.

Time necessarily influenced the mixture. After the colonial period, reported fugitives were overwhelmingly creoles—that is, blacks born in the Americas. In North Carolina during 1775–1835, African-born blacks comprised less than 2 percent of about twenty-five hundred reported fugitives. This small percentage has two possible explanations. First, the African-born were noted for standing and fighting rather than running. Second, and more likely, this low number reflected their diminishing proportion among the Afro-American population in the United States. During the colonial period no large, significant statistical difference appeared in the rates at which creoles and outlanders fled slavery.

◆ ECONOMICS AND SLAVERY

Demographics and economics continued to separate the Afro-American and African experience elsewhere in the Americas. For example, the crop mix that dictated the tempo of slave life differed almost from the beginning as the thirteen colonies tried to copy Caribbean patterns. Caribbean planters pioneered the plantation crops that sustained the Americas. Sugar led their list, followed by tobacco. While the continental colonies proved inhospitable to sugar, they found conditions for growing tobacco favorable. Spanish explorers had introduced the product to their Iberian homeland in the mid-1500s, and had named the indigenous tropical American plant after tabaco, the pipe Carib people used to smoke it. A market for the product for snuffing, smoking, and chewing then spread throughout Europe and to Asia and Africa. Caribbean planters met the early demand, but English settlers in North America followed close on their heels.

Chesapeake production rose rapidly in the 1610s to claim the European tobacco market, after Virginia began shipping its relatively mild-flavored, fast-burning variety to England. By the 1630s Caribbean tobacco growers felt the pinch of Chesapeake competition, with their profit margins declining as prices fell under the pressure of proliferating Virginia and Maryland crops. The mainland colonies had found a plantation crop suited to generating cash, and they pushed it as hard as they could—and that meant pushing more and more enslaved black labor.

Squeezed from the tobacco market, Caribbean planters tried indigo and cotton, but neither panned out as West Indian growers had hoped. Like tobacco, the deep blue-violet dye from pea-family plants entered Europe from the Americas in the 1500s. It superseded the mustard-family dye called woad as the most important blue dyestuff for woolens. Its real future lay in cotton, but cotton's time had not yet come. It awaited the Industrial Revolution, which began its march in Great Britain in the 1760s. Textiles formed the first rank in the revolutionary move to large-scale machine production. And cotton became its mainstay.

Eli Whitney's improved gin of 1793 secured cotton's rise by overcoming a production bottleneck—the laborious tasks of separating fiber from seed. Prior to the saw gin that twenty-nine-year-old Whitney patented in 1794, the quantity of cotton available for weaving depended more on the amount of fiber separated than on the amount grown. Thus, although English settlers sought to grow cotton even before tobacco in Virginia, it had not been practicable on a scale large enough to profit from high-level production. The problem was that no separating device worked well enough with the rugged short- and medium-staple cotton textile manufacturers preferred. Long-staple cotton, with its thin fiber, presented fewer ginning problems. Ancient devices such as the charkha of India worked well enough at stripping the seeds from slender strands by drawing the lint through two revolving wooden rollers, leaving the seeds to fall away. However, the shorter the staple, the coarser the fiber surrounding the seed, and the harder to separate seed and fiber.

The seeds in short- and medium-staple cotton tended to hold fast to the fiber rather than be pushed off in a charkha-type device. Whitney's saw gin solved the problem in stages, revealing his genius for fitting together parts, each of which performed a specialized operation. Whitney used a revolving, toothed cylinder to catch the fibers, a grate to screen out the seeds, and then a revolving brush to remove the seed-free, captured fiber.

Whitney's solution made American cotton king, thereby giving new prominence to the so-called Peculiar Institution in the four decades before the Civil War. The antebellum era (1820–1860) witnessed the rise of the United States to the ranks of the world's foremost slaveholding nations as the U.S. South came to dominate world cotton production. In 1860 the South produced 5.4 million bales of cotton. Four of the fifteen southern states—Mississippi, Alabama, Louisiana, and Georgia—accounted for about 60 percent of production and, in that order, also led the way in number of holdings with more than twenty slaves. Cotton clearly changed what the majority of Afro-Americans did and where they did it. In 1800 the crop had claimed eleven in every hundred slaves in the United States; in 1850 it claimed sixty-four, while tobacco took twelve, sugar five, and rice four.

Nevertheless the United States remained on the periphery of the largest

plantation societies. The average size of U.S. slaveholding units was minis-
cule compared to the typical holding elsewhere in the Americas. Before
national independence, when tobacco plantations held most slaves in the
thirteen colonies, a unit with twenty slaves was relatively large. After
independence, U.S. tobacco plantations increased only slightly as the
median size remained about twenty slaves. U.S. cotton plantations were
moderately larger, reaching a median of thirty-five slaves in 1860. Rice and
sugar produced the biggest U.S. plantations; Louisiana had the largest,
with a typical sugar plantation of about one hundred slaves in 1860. Yet
even Louisiana's plantations were dwarfed by the plantations in Brazil and
the Caribbean.

Indeed, compared to others in the Americas, the United States maintained "a peculiar institution" in its slave system. Yet by the 1820s the slave
experience in the United States was becoming the dominant African American experience in the Americas, for the United States—and more particularly the South—had become home to the largest black population in the
Americas. By 1825 the 1.75 million Afro-Americans in the United States
represented 36 percent of all African peoples in the Americas.

◆ ACCULTURATION

Before the Civil War, at least ninety-five of every one hundred Afro-
Americans were slaves. During the antebellum years, most worked on
southern plantations and lived within a physically separate area or quarter
that was a society within a society. They shared a culture of their own, and
their attitudes, knowledge, skills, sensibilities, and values reflected a historical experience filled with adjustment and assimilation. The acculturation was not all theirs, however. The give-and-take in slavery was not
one-sided, nor did it flow in only one direction. Afro-Americans formed a
core of common experiences in field and factory, as domestics and as
artisans. They created and controlled much of their own arrangements, for
their beliefs and mode of behavior outside of work and white supervision
were dictated by their own community. The dictates of that community
created cultural themes that whites were forced to tolerate—whether in
ways of cooking, eating, talking, or working.

A material culture emerged among slaves that was neither purely African nor European nor Native American. It was particularly apparent in
plantation communities. In urban areas slaves also produced distinctive
modes that usually became evident only after work hours in the grog shops
and other illegal entertainment centers that formed something of an underground alternative culture. A few public holiday celebrations such as
the Pinkster in New York and New Jersey or Negro Election Day in New
England or Mardi Gras in Louisiana offered a glimpse into an African

American culture that was distinct in its mockery of Euro-American forms and its retention of African forms.

Neither planters and overseers nor slaveholders, in any time or place, had complete control over enslaved blacks. True, holders had power over life and death and controlled all manner of decisions between living and dying, but the slaveholders never were able to encompass every moment of every day or every action in any slave's life. They had slaves for work, and when the slaves satisfied that central concern holders usually left them to themselves, as long as their activity showed no sign of overt subversion.

◆ SLAVERY BY SECTION

Distinct from other slave systems in the Americas, the U.S. slave system became even more so within its own boundaries. After national independence, slavery increasingly defined major U.S. sections. Prior to the War for Independence (1775–1783) both North and South maintained some slave presence, but after the war it momentarily waned everywhere. Then an accelerating distinction appeared that would separate the two sections. In the states north of the boundary line that surveyors Charles Mason and Jeremiah Dixon laid out in the 1760s between Pennsylvania and Maryland, political pressure pushed slavery on a road to extinction, while economic developments south of the line pushed slavery along a road to expansion.

Although shouldering arms in the war emancipated thousands of African Americans, their reward remained individual. It was a personal victory, not a group triumph; therefore, some slaves were freed, but slavery persisted. Political ideology and demographic composition, however, shifted slavery's position during the war era.

Afro-Americans early noted the telling issues when they confronted those who asserted that "We hold these Truths to be self-evident, that all Men are created equal, that they are endowed by their Creator with certain unalienable Rights, that among these are Life, Liberty, and the Pursuit of Happiness." One group of blacks declared during the war that they had "in Common with all other men a Natural and Unaliable Right to that freedom which the Grat Parent of the Unavers hath Bestowed equalley on all menkind and which they have Never forfuted by any Compact or agreement whatever." The contradictions between the new American nation's avowed principles and its actual practices were plain. Establishing the hallmark of what became historic protest, black Americans highlighted the incongruity and inconsistency of their position in the United States. For example, a group of blacks in Massachusetts in 1777 made the point in expressing "their Astonishment that It have Never Bin considered that Every Principle from which Amarica has Acted in the Cours of their unhappy Dificulties with Great Briton Pleads Songer than A thousand arguments in favours of" freeing enslaved blacks.

◆ THE FIRST EMANCIPATION

The last quarter of the eighteenth century marked the beginning of a movement against the slave trade and against slavery which became known as the first emancipation. It started in Vermont in 1777 and moved onward until 1827, when New York announced general emancipation, culminating in the decision of all states north of the Mason-Dixon line to end slavery within their borders. Political pressure from male white workers unwilling to compete with slave labor propelled the movement, particularly in New York, which with its twenty-one thousand slaves was the chief northern slave state holding more than all its northern sister states combined in 1790.

Humanitarian-based antislavery societies also contributed to the cause. The first emerged in Pennsylvania in 1775. The New York Society for Promoting the Manumission of Slaves, formed in 1785, was also important; among its leaders were the soon-to-be chief justice of the United States, John Jay, and secretary of the treasury, Alexander Hamilton. These societies were not confined to the North. By 1792 every state from Massachusetts to Virginia had an active manumission or antislavery society.

◆ INITIATIVES FOR SELF-IDENTITY

African Americans immediately seized the initiatives prompted by the momentary swell of emancipation in the North and sought to throw off the vestiges of bondage to make emancipation real freedom. Establishing their self-identity was a high priority. Former slaves shunned the classical, whimsical, and diminutive names slaveholders had called them. Scipio, Pompey, Caesar, Tickle, and Fortune gave way, and rather than a single name or possessive from a slaveholder, such as Roosevelt's Quack, blacks took on surnames. Through their new naming patterns they were able to merge into the larger population, and for the most part they were no longer immediately separable by name.

Along with individual self-identity, Afro-Americans organized for group self-identity, coming together in common cause. The African Union Society, formed at Newport, Rhode Island, in November 1780, was the first such documented group, followed by others such as the Free African Society in Philadelphia, Pennsylvania, the African Lodge No. 459 of Masons, and then the Negro Grand Lodge in Boston in the 1780s and 1790s. They all acted as mutual aid and benefit societies, for blacks understood that self-help and racial solidarity were the primary engines of their collective advancement.

Black Christian churches also laid their organizational foundations during the independence era. Southern Baptists became the first visible assembly, establishing churches in Virginia and Georgia. They organized congregations in Petersburg, Virginia, in 1776, in Savannah in 1779, in Richmond in 1780, and in Williamsburg in 1785. Later, in 1809, they established themselves in the North with the First African Baptist Church in Philadelphia, the African Baptist Church in Boston, and the Abyssinian Baptist Church in New York City.

The Methodists initiated development in the North with the Bethel Church in Philadelphia in 1794, renamed in 1799 the Bethel African Methodist Episcopal (AME) Church. The AME expanded into Maryland, Delaware, and New Jersey and formed a conference in 1816. New York's Methodists formed the African Methodist Episcopal Zion Church in 1796. All these sects built independent bases of black leadership, initiative, and support, and the individual churches themselves usually acted as community centers servicing the blacks' temporal and spiritual needs. Indeed, black churches became the institutional centers of black communities.

◆ CREDITS TO THEIR RACE

Between the developing personal identities and institutional identities emerging in Afro-American churches, another sort of identity developed: the celebrity black elevated by public attention as a credit to the race. The poets Jupiter Hammon and Phillis Wheatley stood as early examples, celebrated as demonstrations of literacy and literary ability among African Americans. Both Hammon and Wheatley wrote inspirational verse. Hammon's first noted work was a 1761 poem titled "An Evening Thought: Salvation by Christ, with Penitential Cries." Not far from where Hammon slaved on New York's Long Island, Wheatley emerged in Boston. She became known in 1770, when she was about seventeen years old, with her poem "On the Death of the Reverend George Whitefield." Eulogizing one of the leading figures of the trans-Atlantic religious revival of the 1730s and 1740s known as the Great Awakening, Wheatley herself became a trans-Atlantic figure. Manumitted in 1773, she traveled to England where her celebrity spread and her first book, *Poems on Various Subjects, Religious and Moral*, appeared.

As Hammon and Wheatley worked to perfect their hands at established forms, so too did other blacks labor on the literary side. In the process, there developed a singular type of narrative literature that came to be associated with blacks. It was a subgenre of autobiography, something of a life and times story. The form resembled the tradition of the autobiography of confession and exaltation prominent in the Mediterranean world and illustrated by the African St. Augustine's *Confessions*, published about A.D. 400. The confession was not, however, an acknowledgment of wrong the person had done; rather, it was a declaration of wrong done to the person. And the exaltation was rejoicing in being set free. The form focused on what it was like to be a slave and was later extended to depictions of what it was like to be black.

An early example of the form appeared in 1789 in the two-volume work: *The Interesting Narrative of the Life of Oloudah Equiano, or Gustavus Vassa.* Written by a Benin-born man who called himself Oloudah Equiano, the narrative had a clear political purpose. It excoriated the slave trade and slavery as it carried Equiano from his birth in 1745 in the West African kingdom on the Gulf of Guinea to his kidnapping in 1755 and his Middle Passage, his sale in the Americas, his slavery in Virginia and Pennsylvania, and his ultimate freedom. Like the Afro-American petitions of the War of Independence era, which pilloried the contradiction between the patriot's pronounced principles and actual practice, the narrative ridiculed the contradiction between Christian principles and the practices of slave trading and slavery. Equiano addressed those who partook in or merely tolerated the slave trade and slavery as "nominal Christians." His central refrain was the biblical injunction, "Do unto all men as you would men should do unto you."

The clear political cast of Equiano's writing separated him from Wheatley and Hammon. His setting explained some of the difference. Equiano wrote from England, where an antislavery movement was stirring popular agitation to force Parliament to suppress the slave trade.

Wheatley always eschewed racial themes in her work. Focus fell not so much on the content of her work as on its style, demonstrating to those who needed such proof that Afro-Americans possessed intellects capable of mastering the higher arts and letters. Hammon was similarly renowned, but his pen was pressed into political uses. His 1787 "Address to the Negroes of the State of New York" spoke directly to the question of emancipation that was then being hotly debated in the state. Counseling patience and fidelity, Hammon's conservative note no doubt sounded sensible to slaveholders and to other whites worried that freeing slaves en masse would create chaos. Hammon himself died in slavery in 1800.

◆ GRADUAL EMANCIPATION

Hammon lived long enough to see New York begin a process of gradual emancipation. The state adapted the plan Pennsylvania had begun in 1780, as the first statutory scheme to free slaves. The concept embodied an essential compromise that first and foremost recognized the fundamental legal fiction on which slavery rested: the notion that one person could hold a property interest in another person. The Pennsylvania act negated the fiction by declaring that all persons thereafter born in the state were born free. However, the act also admitted a property claim in the newly born of mothers held as slaves. Those holding such mothers were due compensation for being deprived of property, the law declared, and it directed that the newly born pay the compensation by working for their mothers' holder until they were age twenty-eight. The plan thus required the emancipated to pay for their own emancipation.

New York adopted the plan in 1799, declaring that those born after 4 July 1799 were free at birth but liable for labor until age twenty-five if female or twenty-eight if male. Neither the Pennsylvania nor New York plan provided for freeing those born before the enabling date; both states later supplemented their acts for that purpose. New York proclaimed emancipation complete on July 4, 1827, the reputed fifty-first anniversary of U.S. independence.

Neither the New York nor the Pennsylvania plan abolished slavery in the sense of declaring the institution's legal base null and void. In that regard, the gradual emancipation plan illustrated the contrast in the two basic approaches that Afro-Americans themselves had recognized and used in seizing their own freedom. One approach was to free slaves, with the corollary that if all slaves were freed then there would effectively be no slavery. The other approach was to abolish slavery, with the corollary that if there were no slavery then all who had been slaves would be free. So, runaways freed themselves even while slavery remained.

The contrast between emancipation and manumission further illustrated the divergence. The private act of a slaveholder in relinquishing legal property rights and investing the rights in the manumitted person reiterated slavery's premises. Manumission legally conveyed to the former slave the property rights in himself or herself. It in no way affected slavery's standing, only the individual slave's standing.

Emancipation did much the same. Rather than being a private act, emancipation was a public act: The government declared that some class of slaves, whether small or large, was free. Thus, emancipation might be partial, as with slaves who shouldered arms during the War for Independence, or it might be general, as with slaves throughout a jurisdiction, as in Pennsylvania or New York. Neither partial nor general emancipation necessarily abolished slavery, for neither necessarily attacked slavery's legal basis. Thus, in northern states such as New York, New Jersey, and Pennsylvania it was not state action but the Thirteenth Amendment to the U.S. Constitution that in 1865 abolished the legal basis of slavery. Furthermore, the gradual emancipation that New York and Pennsylvania adopted initially freed no person who was a slave. At birth, the acts declared, a person could not be considered a slave. Thus, legally the person never was a slave, and if never a slave, then never emancipated.

◆ AFTER EMANCIPATION

The aftermath of the first emancipation presaged what was to come after the Civil War following both general emancipation and abolition. One clear similarity was in the press for education. Schooling slaves was long a sore subject. The British Society for the Propagation of the Gospel in Foreign Parts, known simply as the SPG, tried some early education. During colonial times, it taught slaves the principles of religion by instructing them to read the Christian gospel. The effort usually met with a cold reception among slaveholders who saw literacy as loosening the linchpin of slavery.

Illiteracy was an element of the segregation on which slavery and racial caste rested. Thus, in grasping for effective freedom, Afro-Americans immediately reached for schooling. In the early national era, such a reach extended to grammar schools, which were usually sponsored by manumission societies. For example, the New York Manumission Society's African Free School, started in Manhattan in 1787, was among the most prominent, but as with the statutory movement to emancipation, Pennsylvania was the most active state. Philadelphia Quakers established a school for black children in 1774; philanthropists enlarged the effort in 1787; and by 1797 Philadelphia boasted at least seven schools for blacks. New Jersey also entered the effort, opening schools for black children in 1777 and starting at least short-lived schools in such principal cities as Trenton, Burlington, and Salem. Southern states such as Delaware, Maryland, and Virginia also made efforts to school the slaves, but the unrest of the Haitian Revolution in the 1790s and Gabriel's Plot in Virginia in 1800 dampened the movement.

Display of the Afro-American capacity for learning remained ever controversial. The credit-to-their-race phenomenon became an entrenched element in U.S. culture. The literary aspect that Hammon and Wheatley illustrated was important, but the science aspect was often stressed. James Derham was an example. Born into slavery in Philadelphia in 1762, Derham became a noted physician—reputedly the first Afro-American physician—after purchasing his own freedom.

The most renowned black in the sciences in the early American republic was easily Benjamin Banneker, who trained himself in mathematics and mastered astronomy, engineering, mechanics, and surveying. Born free in Maryland in 1731, Banneker became one of the foremost almanac producers of the 1790s. His astronomical data, forecasts, and tables, issued from 1791 to 1802, proved to be models of accuracy and dependability, garnering him comparison to the famous early American publisher and statesman Benjamin Franklin, whose *Poor Richard's Almanack*, issued from 1732 to 1757, set a standard for the genre. Some referred to Banneker as the "Black Poor Richard." Banneker also earned distinction as a member of the commission that surveyed and platted the new national capital of Washington, D.C.

◆ SLAVERY AND SEGREGATION

For many, the Afro-American's achievement outside of slavery served as a measure of the degradation slavery imposed. The comparisons often lay on the faulty premise that the problem with slavery was merely the way slaves were mistreated. Physical and psychological abuse without question deserved wholehearted condemnation. Yet the essential problem with slavery was its basic deprivation and denial of liberty.

Two interconnected elements exacerbated the essential problem: (1) the deprivation and denial rested on racial contrast, and (2) the contrast existed in a nation that pronounced "all men created equal." The result was that slavery alone was neither the problem nor the root of the problem. Rather, it was a mere manifestation of the problem, being an antagonism and feeling of difference based on physical characteristics that spawned beliefs of group inferiority and superiority and propagated the practices of discrimination, domination, and segregation.

Slavery was not the sum but only a part of a context of race relations within the United States in which both an Afro-American who was not a slave and an Afro-American who achieved economic success were anomalies. Thus, throughout the early national and antebellum eras, very few Afro-Americans who lived outside the status of slave succeeded in acquiring material success, being far overshadowed by the mass of slaves and the majority of too often impoverished free blacks who by race and status were excluded from economic opportunity.

Nowhere was hostility absent; its presence was merely a matter of degree. Even as slavery disappeared from the North, acceptance of blacks there also receded. Much of the antislavery movement in the North was also an antiNegro movement. While usually portrayed as a place of refuge for free blacks, the North was a place of considerable anguish. Throughout the slavery period that ended in 1865, more free blacks lived in the South than in the North.

◆ ANTEBELLUM FREE BLACKS

Free blacks concentrated in two types of areas: in rural areas where they had a long settled tradition and were somewhat isolated from new settlement pressures, and in urban areas where their density formed something of a critical mass to sustain a solid community. Thus, in 1790, the eastern areas of Maryland and Virginia, known as the "tidewater," which had the oldest African American presence in the original United States, became the foremost area of free black population. The western mountain areas of Virginia and North Carolina followed as the chief rural sites. (See Table 7-2.) Maryland stood as the consummate border state or middle ground between what became known as the slave states and the free states. It led the nation with free black population during the antebellum era, and in 1860 it ranked first among states in free black population with 83,900. Virginia ranked second with 58,000, and Pennsylvania was third with 56,000.

The South's major cities were also free black centers. Chief among them during the antebellum years were Baltimore, Charleston, Mobile, New Orleans, and the national capital at Washington, D.C. Nonsouthern cities also served as centers for free blacks, particularly Philadelphia, New York City, Cincinnati, and Boston.

Everywhere the free blacks' status was tenuous, especially during the antebellum era. During the independence era unenslaved Afro-Americans appeared to suffer few explicit proscriptions; perhaps there were few enough free blacks that informal patterns could handle their situation. By the 1820s, however, distinct lines in the law separated unenslaved Afro-Americans from other Americans, just as the law set apart slaves.

TABLE 7-2
Afro-Americans by Status in U.S. States, 1790

State	Status	
	Slave	Free
Virginia	292,627	12,866
South Carolina	107,094	1,801
Maryland	103,036	8,043
North Carolina	100,783	5,041
Georgia	29,264	398
New York	21,193	4,682
Kentucky	12,430	114
New Jersey	11,423	2,762
Delaware	8,887	3,899
Pennsylvania	3,707	6,531
Tennessee	3,417	361
Connecticut	2,648	2,771
Rhode Island	958	3,484
New Hampshire	157	630
Massachusetts	—	5,369
Maine	—	536
Vermont	—	269

Source: U.S. Department of Commerce, *Historical Statistics of the United States: Colonial Times to 1970* (Washington, D.C., 1975), vol. 2, 1168.

◆ RIGHTS DENIED

States abridged or denied Afro-Americans all the rights and privileges enumerated in the U.S. Constitution's Bill of Rights. Almost every southern state prohibited blacks' free exercise of religion; therefore, to assemble in most places in the antebellum South, a black congregation required a licensed white minister. Nor were free blacks allowed otherwise peaceably to assemble. They also lacked the right of free association, for the law forbade their forming even benevolent societies. For example, Maryland barred blacks from forming "lyceums, lodges, fire companies, or literary, dramatic, social, moral, or charitable societies." For the most part, they had no standing. They had no right to keep and bear arms, nor any right to compel a trial with an impartial jury to protect themselves against lack of due process or cruel and unusual punishment. Indeed, in most of the United States the law held Afro-Americans incompetent to testify in court.

Afro-Americans certainly were not secure in their persons against search and seizure. Indeed, the dread of enslavement perennially hung over free blacks as a Damoclean sword, only a hair holding it from falling and crushing all happiness. Slave-snatchers lurked everywhere and reached into communities far-and-wide, even into Canada, to enslave blacks. Statutes throughout the antebellum South required a free black to carry a pass at all times. The certificate was essentially the blacks' only ticket to continue unenslaved. Without it the free black had no ready defense against the presumption of being a slave. Some states supplemented the pass requirement with additional registration that put a free black's name on a central roster. If his or her pass were lost or taken, there was a record to which to appeal—if he or she found some white person to take such an appeal.

Some states barred free blacks' entry. Virginia led the movement, beginning in 1793. Similar prohibitions existed in almost every southern state by 1835. Nor was the South alone in barring free blacks' immigration. At an early date Ohio, Indiana, and Illinois enacted black exclusion laws; Michigan and Iowa also had discriminatory measures to discourage black migrants. In an 1857 referendum Oregon voters demonstrated the no-slavery-and-no-blacks position of nonsouthern states. By a vote of 7,727 to 2,646, they rejected permitting slavery and by 8,640 to 1,081, they rejected permitting free blacks. They wanted no blacks at all, and free blacks were most unwelcome.

Segregation relegated Afro-Americans to a separate and unequal position throughout the society and economy—north, south, east, and west. Antebellum New Yorkers, for example, consistently denied blacks equal privileges of law, including the right to vote. By 1860 only Maine, Massachusetts, New Hampshire, Rhode Island, and Vermont permitted blacks to vote on the same basis as whites. Massachusetts, too, succumbed to segregation, with Boston instituting a separate school system for blacks in

the 1840s. When blacks challenged the practice, the Bay State's Supreme
Judicial Court in 1849 presaged a national ruling nearly one half-century
away by declaring that, as long as black children had access to schools that
provided an education equivalent to that available to whites, the constitutional guarantee of equality was met. That separate-but-equal public
school policy differed from practices in Baltimore and Pensacola, Florida,
which levied school taxes on free blacks but refused them admission to
public schools.

♦ ACHIEVING DESPITE THE ODDS

Yet Afro-Americans achieved despite nearly insuperable obstacles. Both
outside and within slavery, Afro-Americans did all manner of work; almost
no skill was without an Afro-American practitioner somewhere. The federal census lists of occupations and city directories during the antebellum era
indicate the broad diversity ranging from professionals such as dentists,
lawyers, pharmacists, doctors, and ministers to artisans such as bakers,
barbers, brick-masons, cabinetmakers, carpenters, confectioners, engrav-
ers, jewelers, launderers, paper-handlers, photographers, pilots, quarry-
men, sailors, seamstresses, and tailors. Never and nowhere was the real
issue that of what Afro-Americans had the talent to do; rather, the issue
was what the society *allowed* Afro-Americans to do. From colonial times
onward, white workers protested bitterly and successfully against competing against black workers. In many places the law reflected that protest in
prohibitions. Code and custom thus restricted the blacks' efforts and in the
process limited their opportunity and security.

In a society in which ultimate economic success depended on property
rights, Afro-Americans usually stood beyond the pale. The operation of
law, through statutory code or legally enforced restrictive covenants between and among individuals, denied or abridged what Afro-Americans
could acquire. Such a restriction determined their patterns of wealth-
holding and intergenerational wealth development. Deterred from
possessing most economic valuables, or even competing to possess them,
Afro-Americans had little opportunity to accumulate wealth for their own
use or for future distribution. Even if not poor themselves, in that they
were able to earn incomes sufficient to satisfy their needs, they were
relegated to having only their immediate earnings with no prospect of
substantial improvement.

Yet some succeeded to wealth. During the antebellum years hundreds,
even thousands, of Afro-Americans did accumulate significant real estate
and other property holdings. Particularly in major cities, North and South,
free blacks took title to property. Afro-Americans owned $2.3 million in
real estate in New Orleans in 1850, and they owned hundreds of

thousands of dollars in real estate in Baltimore, Brooklyn, Charleston, Cincinnati, Philadelphia, New York City, and Washington, D.C.

The few thousand Afro-American propertyholders were hardly typical; they were the exceptions who proved the rule. Moreover, particularly in Louisiana and South Carolina, they were mixed-race "persons of color," as they were often called, who inherited property, position, or privilege from their white parent. Paternalism and patronage put the so-called mulatto elite in place and promoted distinctions of color that suggested that success depended on complexion: The whiter a person, the better the person and the better off the person. The distinction rang in the words of the oft-repeated aphorism: "If you are white, you are right; if you are brown, stick around; if you are black, get back."

Individual achievement distinguished many Afro-Americans. Paul Cuffe became a leading shipbuilder and shipping magnate in Massachusetts. James Forten made his fortune rising from shopboy to a magnate in the sailmaking industry in Philadelphia. Solomon Humphries became the leading grocer in Macon, Georgia. Jehu Jones became a leading hosteler in Charleston. But with most blacks, as with most whites, holding property and having money in the bank went beyond the individual: It reflected at least in part family and friendship networks.

Where Afro-Americans lived largely determined their economic position; the more prosperous the place, the better off materially the free blacks there were likely to be. For free blacks to maintain any significant economic standing usually depended on their not posing a threat to whites. The better whites did, the better blacks were allowed to do. Rarely were blacks permitted to surpass whites without specific patronage and protection, and in such a case, a dual separation usually appeared. Prosperous blacks were set off, not only from whites, but also from less fortunate blacks as the multiple edges of class, color, and race made their marks.

During the antebellum period, most free blacks, as most whites, lived in a noncash, rural economy. If they held property, it was usually a small plot that produced their subsistence. Barter, rather than commerce, supplemented their living, and at the center of that living—no less than for prosperous blacks—stood family and friendship. In major cities blacks banded together in benevolent, fraternal, self-help groups. In rural areas the church, where it was allowed to exist, served as the omnibus social center. But the church itself was an association of family and friends.

◆ FAMILY

The emancipation movement north of the Mason-Dixon line that followed the War for Independence reflected in microcosm what the post–Civil War years showed large: the Afro-American devotion to family. Being legally free from the bonds of slavery allowed separated black mates to search out each other; mothers and fathers to seek separated children; children to find their parents; and siblings to find each other. It allowed them all to come together and live as a family, enjoying and sharing a household.

The natural strength of family relations vibrated with vitality even during slavery. Kinship, after all, was the cement of traditional African interpersonal relationships, and kinship was no less the core of intimate Afro-American interaction. Slavery never displaced the core; rather, slavery blocked the radiance through which the core's warmth reached, gratified, and embraced kin. For the fragmentation that slavery wrought on family among Afro-Americans was a physical separation, not the quashing of feeling.

Affection was not at issue. The intensity and depth of Afro-Americans' love, tenderness, and warmth remained legend, as did their attachment to the domestic arrangements that provided for mates and for parents and children to live together. It was those domestic arrangements, not familial love and affection, that slavery made tenuous. Slavery imposed on blacks an environment that restricted and denied their power of domestic association, attenuating their family choice by physically confining their household relationships. Slave mates lacked the ultimate, independent power to live together or to have their children live with them or, in some cases, even to have children or the intimacy that creates children.

The assertion of independent familial choice marked both the first emancipation that followed the War for Independence and the general emancipation that followed the Civil War. Former slaves sought to regularize their domestic arrangements. They longed for what they were denied as slaves—the formal, legal recognition of familial status. They wanted marriage licenses and public church ceremonies to legitimate their union and offspring, which only their own community had informally sanctioned earlier.

The familial pattern of mother-headed household that slavery often imposed on African Americans, particularly in urban settings, gave way to two-parent households. The law of slavery dictated that a child born to a slave woman was born a slave, the property of the mother's holder. Thus it was that the mother-headed household emerged. Mother and infant were a unit, much as the law of property in cattle determined. While the mother's mate who fathered her children was not physically resident in the same household, he was known and recognized. A relationship existed. Slavery may have forced physical separation, but bondage lacked the power to destroy the bonds of birth and blood.

Emancipated families reconstructed the domestic arrangements that centered on the nuclear family as the basic element of African American society. However, the pressures against that nucleus remained strong. The chronically uneven sex ratio with more black females than black males, in a society in which the norm was more males than females, strained a pattern of lifelong mating. Economic and legal pressures also pushed black males from households either for work or other benefits or as penalties.

The plight of the black family in slavery and freedom again displayed the decisive barrier to the African Americans' life, liberty, and pursuit of happiness in the United States. In a land that announced its dedication to individual achievement, segregation—both within slavery and outside slavery—barred blacks from their own full self-realization. The nation's cultural, economic, political, and social systems denied blacks the self-determination that even the most recent white immigrants experienced.

♦ WORK LIFE

If the intimate personal life of African Americans revolved around family, their public life centered on work; what they did and where they did it dictated the rhythm of their lives. Mind and body moved with the accent and beat of the exertion, pain, and stress of their labor. Setting the tempo for most slaves at almost all times was agriculture of some sort—clearing and cultivating the soil and producing crops usually engaged about eight of every ten slaves.

While sharing certain basic features, life for slaves in agriculture varied with the crop they tended. Tobacco set a distinct tempo with its large, lance-shaped leaves. Rice measured its own course as its cereal grass of starchy seed grains clustered on separate stalks that reached a height of two to six feet. The pea-family plant yielding the blue dye indigo forced its separate concessions. The tall, noded stalks of the perennial tropical grass called sugarcane bent workers to its own demands. And the seeded fiber of the shrubby cotton plant also had its own cadence. Each crop had its peculiarities, and the strong individuality along with the environment distinguished slaves' lives.

The way slaves went about their toil changed over time and differed by place, so that the technologies of the 1600s became rudimentary by the 1800s as the pace of knowledge about seed, soil, and conditions increased. Afro-Americans applied their own know-how to shape various farming techniques. Their skill at rice-growing proved particularly crucial in colonial Carolina, for example. In the process of producing in the new environment, they adopted both European and Native American technology. The result was a new American technology—a product of Africa, the Americas, and Europe.

Among the distinct modes of production that particularly shaped the slaves' lives was the gang labor system that came to dominate antebellum plantations. The system represented an application of organizational efficiency to agricultural tasks, and at its core lay a strategy of task specialization. It operated on the principle of detailed division of labor and approached the plantation as a complex production enterprise requiring systematic work. Specifically, to get that work done, the gang system separated complex tasks into stages of relatively simple tasks, which it then directed slaves to attack intensively. The system was thus able to predict an expected quantity and quality of labor inputs and outputs.

The gang labor system further robbed slaves of individuality in labor as it pressed them into the fields to work in units of ten to twenty closely monitored by a driver. The system usually made tasks brutally monotonous and tedious and tended to reduce the range of slaves' skills, the degree of reduction depending on the specific crop and the size of the plantation. The system was designed to set the slaves in motion and to organize their movements so as to maximize their production over time, which varied by season in work hours but averaged about sixty per week.

The gang system first emerged on colonial Caribbean sugar plantations, and with its economic success it began to be applied to most other areas of slave agricultural production, spreading to rice, coffee, and cotton. The peculiarities of tending tobacco limited the system's use for that crop since tobacco offered only limited opportunities for division of labor. Nevertheless, the gang system became central to antebellum slave life. Most Afro-American males and females over sixteen labored in gangs, and their work was rated by ability, age, and gender. Every able hand played a part in the system with the aim of maximizing production per worker. By 1850 most slaves on U.S. cotton plantations toiled in the gang system, and they alone accounted for sixty-four of every hundred slaves in the nation.

The work life of the minority of slaves outside the gang system varied, though in general most of these slaves operated on a task system with assigned pieces of work demanded, usually on an individual basis with little direct supervision. The largest group worked in general farming in nonplantation settings. Another group worked in domestic service, which employed mostly—but not exclusively—women. Artisans constituted a significant proportion of the group. Afro-American men in urban settings were especially likely to work in skilled tasks such as smithing or closely related semiskilled areas. Relatively self-sufficient plantations also housed significant proportions of slave artisans to make and repair metalwork and to do carpentry and other building work.

Nonfarm occupations always engaged only a minority of Afro-Americans before the Civil War. Perhaps one in five men and one in six women worked exclusively at something other than field labor. The human capital such workers amassed often placed them in something of an occupational elite among Afro-Americans and, sometimes, in the labor market as a whole.

The pace of technological development in farm mechanization, particularly during the mid-1800s, combined with the restrictive effects of the gang labor system to marginalize the skills of field laborers in most areas. The pace had less general effect on black artisans and semiskilled workers, but what technology may not have done, white attitudes often succeeded in accomplishing. Refusing to compete with black labor, whether slave or free, whites worked to squeeze blacks out of skilled areas. And in the absence of any sizeable black community with resources sufficient to sustain its own skilled workers, they usually succeeded. For that reason, black artisans tended to survive after slavery primarily in predominantly black rural areas or in cities with considerable black populations.

♦ THE COLOR LINE

In work as in all else in the United States, whether or not in the District of Columbia or the fifteen slave states that alone maintained legal chattel slavery in 1860, whether slave or free, Afro-Americans stood apart in U.S. society. They stood separate by law. Slavery was the central and controlling form of segregation in the United States until 1865, after which legal bondage gave way to other forms of social domination over blacks.

Afro-Americans stood apart, separated by attitudes, behavior, demeanor, and expectations. They stood in contrast to whites, answering to separate standards. Their emotional security and personal identity sprang from separate sources. Intimacies such as sleeping in the same house, or the same room, or even sharing a bed; providing a personal service or even acting as companions or playmates—none was enough to deny the reality of the black-white separation.

Segregation both within slavery and outside of slavery stamped the tenor of U.S. race relations. No century of postemancipation was required to produce two nations clearly separate and clearly unequal. The separation existed within and without slavery, and it would persist.

PART III

Ending the Slave Trade and Slavery

T he struggles of African Americans for freedom and human dignity constituted an integral and dramatic part of the larger phenomenon called the Age of Revolution. From the mideighteenth to the mid-nineteenth centuries, discontented and oppressed peoples fought to free themselves from inherited intellectual, religious, social, political, and economic restraints. Although European radicals and their American associates were at the center of these movements in their respective countries, the African slaves and freedmen, among the most oppressed of New World populations, took full part in them. Unable to write impassioned texts or even to organize political parties, they increased the level of resistance to slavery, fled to freedom, and, when possible, assumed leadership of emancipation campaigns. After all, a large proportion of the slaves transported to the Americas were prisoners of war. They usually began by joining the white elites' forces as soldiers and then maneuvered to advance their own interests. In this era African and creole slaves forged a powerful fellowship of purpose.

The Age of Revolution began with the revolt of the thirteen American colonies against England. Early on, many slaves offered to join the British army in exchange for their freedom, based on a proclamation by General Dunmore in November 1775. When fighting broke out, British commanders recruited thousands of black soldiers and auxiliaries on this basis. When the rebellious colonies also offered the blacks liberty in exchange for

military service, many slaves joined them, although few bore arms. Some northern slave owners allowed their slaves to serve in exchange for manumission. During the American Revolution, as many as five thousand former slaves fought on the patriot side; one-fifth of the sailors in fact were former slaves. By all accounts, slave recruits were motivated primarily by their desire for liberty. In the main, they believed the British were more likely to honor their pledges than the patriots. Although the slaves' military service was not critical to the outcome of the war, they greatly advanced their people's cause.

During the American Revolution, an even larger number of slaves, men and women, took advantage of the warfare and pillage to strike out for towns and regions where they would be safe, and in this way freed themselves. Perhaps a fifth of the slaves in the thirteen colonies gained their freedom during the war, making it the largest slave rebellion in North America prior to the Civil War. Clearly, the precedents set in this era would reverberate among African Americans for generations afterward. From then on, all U.S. military campaigns would rely increasingly on troops and officers of African descent.

In Latin America, colonial authorities had long recruited and trained free blacks for territorial defense and police duty in the militias. Called *pardos y morenos*, these units had traditionally been segregated and inferior to their white counterparts and to the regular army. During and after the Seven Years' War (1757–1763), however, the black militias grew in size, privileges *(fueros)*, and influence, owing to threats from rival colonial powers. When black militias were mustered with regular units, the troops received training with firearms and artillery, while officers became eligible for additional privileges. Soldiers were exempted from civil courts and jails and enjoyed retirement pay and burial costs. In a general sense, military service conferred a higher social rank on persons of African descent, which was manifest in the right to wear uniforms and other marks of distinction.

Because of their shared creole culture, black officers often proved more effective than whites at commanding racially mixed soldiers in the Americas, and some rose rapidly through the ranks. In the Spanish American wars for independence, at least a third of the officers and a great segment of the troops were of African descent. Both Latin American liberators, Simón Bolívar (1783–1830) and José de San Martín (1778–1850), manumitted slaves who enlisted. Down to contemporary times, the military has always been an attractive avenue of upward mobility for talented nonwhites in the hemisphere.

In addition, the Spanish government commissioned two regular companies of blacks to fight against the British in Florida and Alabama during the U.S. War of Independence, under General Bernardo Gálvez's command. These troops acquitted themselves well and were garrisoned in New Orleans until Spain withdrew in favor of France in 1800. Veterans of these black units probably participated in defeating the British in the battle of New Orleans (1812), where two black West Indies regiments fought opposite them.

The British had long recruited some black freedmen into their colonial police forces. After their deployment against African rebels in St. Domingue in the 1790s, the British government began forming slave regiments in Jamaica, buying slaves directly off ships from Africa and offering pay, better treatment, and eventual freedom in exchange for military service. These forces were charged with repelling attacks by other powers and putting down local rebellions, such as the Trelawney Town Maroon rising. For the remainder of the Napoleonic Wars, the British actually utilized black regiments in several parts of the Caribbean. From all accounts, the experiment proved successful, for the Africans' very effective skirmish tactics nicely complemented European set-piece battles and logistics. From then on, black constabulary units and occasional expeditionary forces became traditional in the British West Indies and elsewhere. Upon mustering out, these men were resettled in Sierra Leone, West Africa.

African American soldiers and officers distinguished themselves in other regions—notably Brazil and the French Caribbean—and constituted major elements of the military throughout the hemisphere during the nineteenth century. Chapter 11 discusses the Brazilian government's policy of granting freedom to slaves who served in the Paraguayan War in the 1860s. Hopefully, future research will further reveal the African Americans' contributions to the Age of Revolution. Meanwhile, the military skills and experience gained in the wars of independence unquestionably prepared African Americans to play more decisive roles in the later struggles for emancipation, political citizenship, and social equality.

The long and complex fight to abolish the African slave trade is recounted in Chapter 8. Launched by European liberals in lands where slavery had not existed, the campaign took over a century before finally ending the iniquitous traffic. Three main patterns emerged from these events. Where colonial governments committed themselves to abolition, it was accomplished early in the nineteenth century. In newly independent nations, where authorities succumbed to pressure to outlaw the trade, the results were mixed. U.S. traders smuggled slaves for some years before finally giving up. In Brazil, powerful labor demands fueled a huge contraband trade until midcentury. Where European governments did not especially care, colonial authorities allowed the trade to continue even longer. These three different outcomes deeply influenced the parallel efforts to abolish slavery itself, as well as the abilities of freed men and women to adjust to their new status.

Emancipation itself did not sweep the hemisphere for another half-century and constituted one of the most dramatic and wrenching episodes in the history of the Americas. The first full emancipation, of course, came in Haiti, where independence under Jean-Jacques Dessalines (1758?–1806) in 1804 confirmed the demise of slavery. Most Spanish American nations made emancipation a feature of their early constitutions, reflecting the reality of escape and recruitment of soldiers during the wars. Yet in a few regions slavery lingered until the 1850s. In any case, voluntary manumission and economic depression in the 1830s and 1840s led to rapid declines in slave populations throughout Spanish America.

The British Parliament began the process among the European colonial powers during the 1830s by passing a law granting gradual release to slaves in its colonies. The French and Danes followed suit in the 1840s. The Europeans' motives were complex, at once combining humane, religious, bourgeois, and ideological sentiments. But whatever the mix of causes, the powerful economic reasons for sustaining slavery had collapsed, and only weak resistance remained.

In three American locations—two independent nations and one colony—slavery had to be terminated by violence. In the United States abolition had swept quickly through the North after the War of Independence, by individual action, constitutional edict, laws of free birth, and court decisions. Southerners, however, clung tenaciously to servitude, which they increasingly believed sustained their entire way of life. The issue split the states and in large measure caused the Civil War, during which President Lincoln signed the Emancipation Proclamation.

In addition to freeing slaves in areas in rebellion, the Emancipation Proclamation provided for the enlistment of black men in the U.S. armed forces. By war's end, some two hundred thousand Afro-Americans had served, most of them in segregated army units known collectively as the United States Colored Troops. A majority of these soldiers had been slaves who, consequently, had a special interest in transforming the war for union into a war against slavery. Their service greatly bolstered Union fighting power at the rebels' expense. Black troups also fired the spirit of freedom among southern slaves and the spirit of civic and political equality among northern Afro-Americans. Finally, their part in defeating the Confederacy helped undermine slave regimes elsewhere in the Americas.

In the Spanish colony of Cuba, the abolition of slavery became an issue during the Ten Years' War (1868–1878) and was finally decreed in 1886, more than a decade after Spain freed the slaves in Puerto Rico. Finally, Brazil became the last country in the hemisphere to end slavery, in 1888, as a result of widespread violence and a hard-fought, divisive, and emotional campaign launched by freedmen and urban reformers. These late and violent cases demonstrate that the interconnected struggles for freedom penetrated deeply and painfully into the social and economic structures of these young nations.

Formal emancipation in the nineteenth century, difficult as it proved, marked only one more step toward full citizenship and equality for African

Americans. In country after country, freed blacks were prevented from voting by property and literacy requirements, poll taxes, and intimidation. Some governments attempted to ameliorate tensions and poverty with social programs; others turned their backs on racial injustice. Economic systems kept blacks in subordinate, low-paying jobs, perpetuating an unequal distribution of income and opportunities. No society in the Americas has quickly or easily dealt with these questions, which are in part a legacy of flawed policies during the age of emancipation.

Chapter 8

ABOLITION OF THE ATLANTIC SLAVE TRADE

1780s	Peak of the trans-Atlantic slave trade.
1803	The Danes abolish the slave trade, the first ban by a modern nation.
1807	British and U.S. nationals barred from the slave trade.
1831	French slave trade finally suppressed.
1841	Quintuple Agreement (England, France, Russia, Prussia, and Austria) declares slave trading piracy and allows searches.
1845	Aberdeen Act permits the British to inspect Brazilian and flagless vessels suspected of carrying slaves.
1845	Spanish law forbids slave trading by nationals.
1850	Brazilian law forbids slave trading by nationals.
1856	Last documented arrival of slave ship in Brazil.
1862	Anglo-American antislave trade agreement.
1867	Arrival of last slave ship in Cuba marks end of Middle Passage.

The trans-Atlantic slave trade dominated migration to the New World for almost as long as the trade lasted. As late as the 1880s, more immigrants to the Americas had left Africa under duress than had left Europe voluntarily. The traffic brought death to hundreds of thousands in Africa long before slavers received their human cargo and ensured a short life for millions more in passage. By almost any standards,

This 1860 woodcut depicts the deck of a ship illegally transporting slaves to the Americas. The Bettman Archive.

it was probably the most appalling long-distance mass migration that ever occurred. Free migrants, indentured servants, and even transported convicts rarely faced the horrendous conditions, extended duration of travel, loss of life, and sheer human misery that were routine for Africans in the Middle Passage.

Like slavery itself, the slave trade did not simply wither away. It ended because of an arduous campaign that began in the 1780s as the traffic reached its peak, with over nine hundred thousand Africans shipped during the decade. Another eight hundred and fifty thousand or so embarked in the 1790s. In all, from 1780 to 1867, when the traffic was supposedly winding down, over five million persons—or about half of all those who landed in the traffic—began the Middle Passage. In the face of this enormous forced migration, with its economic importance, its longevity, and its indifference to humanity, explaining the purposeful abolition of the traffic in the 1800s challenges modern historians.

Ending the traffic was not easy. Despite restrictions and resultant high prices, slave trading expanded in two of the three major plantation economies in the Americas as late as the 1850s. Cuba continued to import slaves to grow its sugar. Brazil also continued the trade for its coffee regions. Only in the United States did expansion not feed on the traffic, as the South's cotton grew with only a domestic slave trade. Yet during the U.S. Civil War (1861–1865), the South itself came close to reopening the trade. Demand for Africans continued in the Americas, and access to them made a significant difference among plantation economies in the 1800s.

Ending the slave trade required abolition and suppression. The first was a formal prohibition, the second an actual cessation. By whichever means, a restructuring of the Atlantic economy was heralded, particularly in the plantation Americas, and the prospect of such drastic change raised the specter of widespread resistance. Force or the threat of force accompanied the process everywhere.

The timing proved crucial to the future complexion of the Americas. If the slave trade had not ended when it did, the transportation revolution might have transformed the traffic, as it did North Atlantic passenger shipping. A large share of the mass trans-Atlantic migration in the 1800s might then have been enslaved Africans rather than free Europeans. Employers probably would have found ready use for plentiful slaves in an ever-widening range of nonplantation occupations unless the ideological climate changed drastically from that of the 1700s. Thus, stopping the flow of coerced labor from Africa in the early 1800s ensured that the Americas would become predominantly white rather than predominantly black.

Like modern narcotics trafficking, slave trading was an international activity; yet international law never outlawed it, and so the force used to suppress slave trading sometimes violated international law. While force was necessary, it was not sufficient, for ending the traffic required international cooperation. As was demonstrated time and again, one nation acting alone might shift the traffic's course, but it would not stop the flow. Slavers simply chose other routes to evade the interdicting nation. They eluded its forces by smuggling, or they denied its authority by sailing under a different flag. Only nations acting together could effectively end the traffic.

Great Britain led the way. It initiated the first serious restriction on the traffic in 1787 when it ordered British slavers to reduce their slave-per-ton ratios. In 1792 Denmark became the first nation to abolish the trade, although its actual part in the traffic continued until 1803. Britain continued to show the strongest commitment to ending the traffic and outlawed it in 1807. As the world's foremost maritime power, its actions proved the most effective, although national trade rivalry also impeded cooperation.

Britain's act of 1807 outlawed slave traffic by its nationals and barred slave ships to and from any of its territories. In the next seventeen years Parliament added fourteen supplemental acts to close loopholes in enforcement. Liverpool, London, and Bristol traders, who ranked among the world's foremost slavers, quickly switched their vast fleets to other businesses.

Not all British hands abandoned the slave traffic so quickly. British bankers lent handsome sums that kept slavers thriving. They furnished mortgages for plantation owners to buy slaves in the traffic, and they advanced credit to outfit and sponsor slavers not flying the British flag. In addition, British merchants furnished goods and services to slavers. They sold ships to slavers and insured the voyages. In short, while no longer doing the actual hauling, some Britons willingly supplied the means to support the traffic long after 1807.

Getting Britons totally out of the traffic required more than statutes. Mercantile prowess, industrial development, and imperial reach made British business and financial interests nearly ubiquitous in the Atlantic economy of the 1800s. At some point British goods or services touched almost every significant series of Atlantic transactions. Thus, any continued traffic almost by necessity carried some British connection. However, it often proved difficult to ferret out the actual identity of the British firms or individuals involved. With enormous profits at stake, secrecy, misdirection, espionage, bribery, and worse thwarted law.

♦ Enforcement: The British Experience

Even when the Britons' activities seemed clearly contrary to law, successful prosecution proved difficult. Conviction required proof not merely of the illegal act but also of illegal intent. Showing that a British merchant sold goods or services used in slave trading was not enough. To convict the merchant required showing that he knew or should have known the customer's purpose to use the goods or services in the slave trade. Not surprisingly, prosecutors found the standard hard to meet, and so the British courts were not able to produce even a single conviction for the crime of supplying slavers.

While seeking to bring its own nationals into line, Britain also attempted to move other nations to eliminate the slave trade. Its efforts began with force during the Napoleonic Wars (1804–1815). Like other combatants, Britain claimed the right to search and seize ships at sea with contraband cargo, and so it directed its navy to seize slavers whenever and wherever it found them. In addition, in 1808 it dispatched a squadron to Africa with the sole purpose of interdicting the traffic. Thus began its sixty-year campaign against non-British slave traders.

The cover of war was incomplete and temporary. Taking their opponents' slavers or other ships as prizes was routine business; searching and seizing allied and neutral ships was not. So when Britain seized and sank Portuguese or Spanish slavers, it acted illegally. The same was true when it stopped U.S. ships. To uphold its right of freedom of the seas, the

United States went to war with Britain in 1812. The Iberian powers pursued damage claims and received large reparations. With the arrival of peace in 1815, British search and seizure became naked aggression. Britain persisted, however, and paid dearly. Attacks on French slavers provoked outrage and further expensive damage claims. Between 1808 and 1824, Britain paid millions of pounds sterling to settle claims for damages its ships inflicted on slavers.

Britain's direct and unilateral attack on traffickers proved expensive—and not only in monetary terms. It generated ill-will that threatened to drive rivals into a hostile alliance against Britain. The international balance of power was at stake. Neither custom nor international law backed Britain's position. For centuries Europeans had plied the slave trade as a business like any other. Not only had Christians of most sects sanctioned it, but also international law never banned it. Therefore, Britain stood alone in its initial campaign, and even with its enormous power was incapable of halting the traffic alone.

◆ MUTUAL RIGHTS PACTS

International cooperation was imperative. Because Britain needed to persuade other nations to join in suppressing the traffic, it launched diplomatic initiatives to accompany its naval campaign. Promoting a network of bilateral and multilateral treaties, Britain became a party to every international pact signed to suppress the slave trade. By the 1850s, when the campaign peaked, the British-backed network featured four types of agreements aimed at blocking the export of slaves at their sources and at barring the arrival of slaves at their destinations.

In the main, all the treaties dealt with problems of national sovereignty that international law posed for antislaving activities. The crux was that the international law never made slaving into an act of piracy. Had it done so, slavers would have been punished under the laws of whichever country seized them. Nationality would have furnished no protection. As it was, however, international law permitted seizing a slaver only on the high seas where no nation had sovereignty, and even then, it required the consent of the nation under whose flag the ship sailed. The treaty network conveyed consent for suppression to overcome sovereignty issues.

Britain tended to favor pacts that provided mutual rights of search. Any nation, of course, had the power to search any ship flying its flag. Signatories to mutual rights pacts were permitted to search each other's ships. If inspection uncovered evidence of slaving, the ship became subject to detention. Its fate then depended on courts of mixed commission which were empowered to act under the signatories' joint authority. These early agencies of international law brought together jurists of the participating countries to try shippers accused of violating antislave trade agreements.

Such courts exercised no jurisdiction over persons, for countries balked at subjecting their nationals to foreign laws. Thus, captains and crews were off limits. The mixed commission courts had jurisdiction only over property. The mutual rights pacts allowed them to dispose of ship and cargo, and under that guise they gained power over one class of persons—the human cargo paradoxically logged as property.

Britain signed mutual rights pacts with Spain, Portugal, and the Netherlands in 1817 and 1818; with Sweden in 1824; with Brazil in 1826; and, eventually, with the United States in 1862. The early pacts established mixed commissions at Freetown in the British West African colony of Sierra Leone; at Rio de Janeiro in Brazil; at Havana, Cuba; and at Paramaribo in Dutch Suriname. In time, the mixed commission courts ringed the Atlantic from New York City to Capetown, South Africa.

Mutual rights pacts gave Britain the authority to police shipping among the signatories, and the activity remained overwhelmingly British. The mixed commission in Sierra Leone adjudicated 80 percent of all captures under the mutual rights pacts. Elsewhere the pacts encountered serious problems. Judges often bickered and split along national lines, resulting in the release of seized ships. Moreover, the pacts laid narrow grounds for condemnation. Slavers initially had to be caught in the act with slaves on board to warrant condemnation. Yet the main problem was simply getting the pacts in place. Nations such as the United States long refused to agree and thus allowed their flags to shield slavers.

♦ **DETENTION AND SELF-POLICING PACTS**

Many nations refused to surrender jurisdiction of either persons or property under their flag. Thus, they shunned mutual rights pacts with mixed commission authority. Several countries, however, France, for example, were willing to join the suppression effort, and Britain developed a second type of treaty with them. The Anglo-French pacts signed in 1831 and 1833 illustrated the typical terms. Under these agreements, France permitted Britain to detain ships flying its flag, but the British had to release the suspected slaver to French domestic tribunals.

The so-called Quintuple Agreement of 1841 marked the acme of the detention pacts like the Anglo-French treaties of the 1830s. In all, Britain signed fourteen such agreements before 1850, but not all of them worked as well as the one with France. The treaty with Sardinia, for instance, became nearly worthless. The western Mediterranean island kingdom released most of its ships that the British detained. The law of states like Sardinia continued to shield slavers from ultimate condemnation; nevertheless, the pacts deterred the slave traffic by allowing British policing.

Before the Anglo-American mutual rights pact of 1862, the United States exemplified a third treaty approach to international suppression. The

United States denied any other nation's authority to detain or search and seize any ship flying its flag. It agreed only to maintain its own squadron on the African coast to interdict slavers flying the U.S. flag.

After its 1830s pacts expired, France switched to the self-policing form of agreement and at one time had twenty-eight ships, or about 15 percent of its total naval resources, stationed off West Africa. The measures worked well enough to remove the French flag from the traffic and to make the French a major force in suppression. At their peak in the 1840s, the suppression squadrons of Britain, France, Portugal, and the United States averaged over sixty ships on African duty.

The mutual rights, detention, and self-policing pacts wove a net that covered most of the Atlantic, but traffickers continued to find shelters. Brazil and Portugal, for example, continued to shield slavers, despite their mutual rights pacts. The British responded with two parliamentary acts named after foreign secretaries Lord Palmerston and Lord Aberdeen. The Palmerston Act applied to Portuguese ships between 1839 and 1842, and the Aberdeen Act applied to Brazilian ships after 1845. Both laws directed the British navy to detain Portuguese and Brazilian slavers for adjudication in British courts. As clear assaults on Portuguese and Brazilian sovereignty, these provocative acts offered cause for war and undoubtedly would have prompted fighting with stronger powers. The acts also authorized British naval ships to detain carriers with no papers and thus no flag to which to answer. They, too, were hauled into British courts.

♦ SUPPRESSION ACTIVITIES

With the sea lanes covered by the first three treaty types and parliamentary acts, the British turned to inland sources for the fourth treaty type—Anglo-African suppression pacts. Ultimately, Britain signed forty-five African powers to agreements that required the Africans to end the slave trade in their territories or suffer British incursions to suppress the trade. More than anything else, these pacts provided Britain with a pretext for the sequel to the slave trade in Africa—direct colonization. Under the guise of attacking slave trading, Britain landed expeditions that made inroads in the European scramble beginning in the 1880s.

To monitor and coordinate suppression activities, Britain maintained a foreign office section called the Slave Trade Department which surveyed and scrutinized domestic and foreign laws and diplomatic dealings with a bearing on slaving. With eyes, ears, and hands around the Atlantic, it was first and foremost an intelligence agency gleaning information everywhere it could. Then it disseminated the knowledge where it thought best to aid suppression.

Since the Foreign Office's Slave Trade Department acted as something of a brain, the Admiralty formed the backbone of suppression. At least ten ships and a thousand men were usually assigned specifically to antislaving duties. At peak strength in the mid-1840s, the commitment reached thirty-six ships and forty-four hundred men—about 20 percent of British naval resources. The Crimean War (1853–1856), the Indian Mutiny of 1857, and other events slashed the British commitment. Yet, between 1815 and 1865, Britain spent over 7 million pounds on naval antislaving activity.

Naval expenditures were only part of the cost Britain paid for suppression. It paid a host of other direct costs: damages for its illegal search and seizure of foreign shipping; financial inducements to get Spain and Portugal to sign early suppression pacts; maintenance of the mixed commission courts under the mutual rights treaties; and bounties for landing recaptured slaves alive. In sum, between 1807 and 1865, Britain paid at least 12 million pounds on suppression—an amount comparable to the total profits British slave traders earned between 1760 and 1807.

The full cost of suppression greatly exceeded the 19 million pounds Britain spent in its naval expenditures and other direct payments. Indirect costs abounded. For example, suppression meant higher prices to British consumers for sugar, cotton, coffee, and other slave-produced commodities. Even so, the total cost could have consumed only a small share of British national income.

Evaluating the success of suppression is more difficult than counting its monetary cost. Based on measures such as slavers captured and condemned, suppression appeared a greater failure than success. Between 1807 and 1867, for example, traffickers launched about 7,750 trans-Atlantic slaving expeditions. At least 1,635 of the ships—about one in five—were caught and condemned or otherwise disposed of at a loss to traffickers. British admiralty courts, rather than the courts of mixed commission, accounted for most of the loss. Still, for every one caught, four slavers eluded the international suppression effort.

Efforts to Elude Suppression

Traffickers accepted the risk of interception as a cost of doing business and devised artful dodges to minimize losses. The risks merely raised the rewards. The lucrative returns on a successful voyage induced slavers in the 1860s to send out ships in sections for assembly, loading, and launching in isolated inlets along Central Africa's Zaire River. Ships bearing such parts to Africa could pass inspection as freighters, for they carried no contraband. They sailed at liberty.

Slavers worked to decrease exposure to capture primarily by cutting sea time. Speedier voyages with quicker ships were significant aids in evasion. Slavers even entered steamships in the traffic. Most emphasis, however, fell not on time under sail but on time at anchor. The stress lay where most interception occurred—not out in the Atlantic but on the African coast. That pushed slavers to enter and exit quickly in loading their human cargo.

Before 1800, ships had commonly waited on the coast to load groups of slaves until the holds were full. After suppression began, slavers stopped lingering, and they usually loaded no slaves until they had assembled a full cargo. Then they loaded and left, all within a few hours. Quickly in and quickly out were the ways slavers usually tried to skirt even the tightest naval blockades.

In order to cope with the risk of capture, suppression era slavers pushed every voyage to the utmost margin of profitability. Thus, they tended to pack captives tightly. The *Minerva*, a 21-ton bark measuring 36.5 feet from stem to stern, offered an appalling illustration of the extremes to which this could be carried. In 1842 the *Minerva*, a little ship for little people with little space, carried slaves from Ambriz, Angola, to Salvador, Brazil. When intercepted, it held 126 children; half sat exposed on deck, while the other half lay below deck in a 14-inch crawl space. So close were the conditions on board that they could neither stand nor even shift position by rolling over. Although atypical, the *Minerva* episode revealed the effects of profit-taking in the later years of the trade.

While crowding did not increase shipboard deaths, mortality on the Middle Passage was higher in the nineteenth century than it had been earlier. The major causes were dysentery and other gastrointestinal diseases. The greater morbidity was probably associated with the increased time captives spent confined in shore-based barracoons. Slave ships spent less time at sea than in earlier times, but they carried people who had been subjected to greater epidemiological stress. The net result of suppression on shipboard mortality was to increase it.

As a result of suppression, traffickers altered their routes. Before 1800, the typical slaver sailed from Europe to Africa to the Americas and back to Europe; after 1800, the trip usually went from the Americas to Africa and then back to the port of origin. Thus, while England's Liverpool and France's Nantes dominated the early traffic, Cuba's Havana and Brazil's Rio de Janeiro became headquarters for the later traffic.

Suppression also exaggerated the slavers' profits. By increasing the risks, it pushed profits up during the illegal phase of the slave trade higher than during the legal era. Profits were probably never so high as in the 1850s and 1860s—the trade's last two decades. Traffickers suffered losses, of course, but the margins of return greatly favored their continuing business.

Bluntly put, suppression at sea was a woeful failure in its intent to destroy the traffic. At best it probably reduced the amount of slaving after 1807 by about 12 percent. Its greatest success was in driving up prices in slave markets in the Americas. It raised distribution costs almost everywhere in the receiving regions. Of every $1,000 paid in Brazil and Cuba for a newly arrived African in the 1860s, about $660 went for premiums due to suppression risks. The excess fattened slavers' profits and fed bribes that corrupted government officials throughout the Atlantic Basin.

◆ SUPPRESSION EFFORTS IN THE AMERICAS

Internal political pressure rather than external pressure in the form of naval suppression ended the trans-Atlantic slave trade. It died when importing regions in the Americas closed their shores to the traffic. In the colonies of the British Caribbean, the French Americas, and Dutch Suriname, the end came when popular sentiment demanded an end. The same was true in the United States where popular attitudes demanded a halt to slaving, as they did later to slavery. Brazil and Cuba proved different situations.

Brazil reflected most clearly the combination of internal and external pressure. British agents bribed Brazilian government ministers, infiltrated the Brazilian customs service, and covertly funded Brazilian newspaper campaigns against the traffic. Under the 1845 Aberdeen Act, Britain took captured Brazilian slavers into British courts for condemnation. Furthermore, in the mid-1850s, the British Royal Navy took advantage of a revolt in Pernambuco that occupied Brazilian forces in the north to sail into Brazil's southern waters and destroy every slaver found.

Brazilian public opinion, which was sympathetic owing in part to the secretly funded antislaving propaganda, applauded rather than condemned the British aggression. Before long, Brazil began to enforce and strengthen its own antitrafficking provisions. As a result, when an importing region's sovereign power finally stopped its people from buying slaves, importers stopped selling slaves there.

Cuba reflected a different mix of external and internal pressures for suppression. As Spain's main Caribbean colony, the island enjoyed protection that deterred the kind of action Britain used in Brazil. Moreover, direct British action would have provoked hostility not only with Spain but also with the United States, where the slaveholding South coveted the island. As the notorious Ostend Manifesto of 1854 showed, the South wanted to annex Cuba. And if it could not claim the island outright, the South wanted to keep Cuba as something of a slave auxiliary.

Only the outbreak of the U.S. Civil War in 1861 changed official U.S. thinking. Indeed, during the war the United States for the first time took an unequivocal stand for suppression. The South's defeat and the abolition of slavery in the United States in 1865 dealt a hard blow to Cuba's slave trade. The fall of the largest slaveholding regime suggested that slavery elsewhere in the Americas had little future. As a consequence, slave prices everywhere plummeted. Indeed, after 1865 prices were too low in Cuba to make slaving imports viable. In that context, genuine cooperation developed among Britain, Spain, and the United States to end the island's traffic.

Suppression and the Plantation System

In the 1760s almost all plantation produce in the Americas came from five sectors: the British Caribbean, the Dutch West Indies, the French West Indies, and the colonies of the two Iberian powers—Spain and Portugal. The rise of the United States added a sixth by the 1780s. Each sector attempted to produce a wide range of plantation products and aimed at self-sufficiency. The French and English led as the most developed and dominant sectors; the Portuguese and the Spanish, in particular, lagged as the least developed. All areas had open land frontiers and the capacity to absorb more labor from seemingly limitless Africa. Nothing then signaled any slackening of the slave traffic or any shift in rank among the plantation economies.

By 1860 the major features of the plantation system of the 1700s had largely disappeared. Neither Cuba, Brazil, nor the United States, the three dominant plantation regions in 1860, had been of more than marginal importance in the 1700s. Then they had all sat on the periphery of the core plantation zone in the French and British West Indies. Moreover, the three new regions each specialized in producing a single crop on an almost unprecedented scale. By 1850, 80 to 90 percent of the exports of Cuba, south-central Brazil, and the U.S. South were made up of sugar, coffee, and cotton, respectively. Although each dominated the world markets for its product, in 1760 none of these commodities was of much importance in these regions. Three new systems had emerged.

The pattern of rise and fall among the Americas' various plantation regions during the 1800s reflected the effects of suppression. Denmark ended the traffic to its colonies in 1803; Great Britain followed four years later; and the United States abolished the trade effective 1 January 1808. The French Revolution (1789–1799) and the Napoleonic Wars (1804–1815) curtailed the Dutch traffic. The Haitian Revolution (1791–1804) and other wars had the same effect on the French traffic, although it was revived again between 1814 and 1831. As the flow of fresh labor from Africa ended in most of these areas, their economies declined.

The British plantation colonies exemplified the fall. In 1800 the British Caribbean—led by Jamaica—stood atop plantation producers, producing nearly two-thirds of the world's sugar exports, half the coffee, and a third of the cotton exports. The abolition of the British slave trade in 1807 marked the start of a precipitous slide. The abolition of slavery itself in 1833 pushed the downturn further into stagnation. Only in the 1850s, when the flow of indentured workers from Asia became significant in Trinidad and British Guiana, did the British colonies see economic growth again.

After 1800 the Danish, Dutch, and French colonies also slipped relative to Cuba and Brazil, but the process was slower than in the British islands because each of these areas preserved slavery longer than did the British plantation colonies. The Dutch sugar-growing area of Suriname in northeastern South America never matched its dynamic performance during the 1700s when the slave trade was open. The loss of St. Domingue following Haitian independence crippled French Caribbean production. Only after the 1820s did the French islands again respond to expanding European demand.

Brazil and Cuba stood apart from their declining neighbors, with each boasting considerable natural advantages. Yet the signal difference between them and other nations was their access to labor from Africa. The continued Portuguese and Spanish trade drove the rapid expansion of coffee and sugar production after 1800; their chief competitors lacked that edge.

Only the United States managed to dominate a world market for a plantation product without access to fresh labor from Africa. It had an expanding domestic supply, and by 1860 it was producing over half the global exports of raw cotton. The United States was an exception that confirmed the general pattern. It joined Barbados and one or two smaller areas as the only regions in the Americas where the slave population experienced high rates of natural increase. Between 1800 and 1860, the U.S. slave population increased from about one million to about four million and had become a very effective substitute for the slave trade.

♦ IMPACT OF CHANGES IN THE SLAVE TRADE

Even in Brazil, Cuba, and the United States, the growing restrictions on the Atlantic slave trade triggered major changes. Indeed, the impact reverberated in all slave societies. The restrictions tightened the supply of slaves while demand for slave plantation produce soared. As a result, slave prices also soared after 1800. The increased cost and increased profit potential induced planters to move slaves into the most productive regions and tasks.

Thus, major new slave migrations occurred, as internal traffic replaced the old Middle Passage. In Brazil, for example, holders moved slaves from the older, northeast cotton and sugar provinces to the south-central Paraíba Valley coffee-growing areas. Cuba's western provinces, like Brazil's upper Paraíba Valley, acted as a magnet and drew slaves from the rest of the island. In the United States, slaves flowed from the older tobacco lands in Virginia, Maryland, and Kentucky to the frontier cotton lands in Alabama, Louisiana, and Mississippi.

Changes in occupation coincided with changes in location. As slaves became more expensive, they were increasingly concentrated in the highest earnings areas. Thus, Brazil, Cuba, and the United States claimed increasing shares of the hemispheric slave population, for they dominated the export sectors producing profits in the 1800s. Instead of the wide range of occupations at which slaves worked in the 1700s, they worked in an increasingly narrow range in the 1800s. They became specialized for the sake of efficiency, and their per capita output rose at a rate comparable to that of contemporary British textile factory workers.

With the ending of the slave trade, blacks throughout the Americas suffered more than changes in location and occupation. Their connections with Africa were disrupted, and they increasingly lost a sense of commonality with African societies. The result was that they became much more isolated from their old world than their white counterparts from Europe. Without fresh reminders from the motherland, customs, language, and religion became less African. Except among scattered and isolated maroon communities, distinctive African American forms emerged, and Euro-American influences also increased.

◆ THE EFFECT OF ABOLITION ON AFRICA

Abolition of the slave trade affected Africa, too, though the impact was probably smaller than in the Americas. Until the 1850s no drastic decline occurred. Contraband carriers offset much of the early Danish, Dutch, British, and United States withdrawal, but the results differed by region. Early suppression most affected areas north of the equator. In Senegambia, the most northerly of the provenance zones, the traffic was already a trickle before any formal abolition occurred. The traffic died in the Gold Coast by the 1820s and in the Bight of Biafra by the early 1840s. It lasted longest in the Bight of Benin and in southeast and west-central Africa. The Zaire River was the focal point of the traffic after 1850. Throughout the 1800s, then, the center of the slave trade steadily shifted southward.

Africa's political response to abolition of the trade also differed by region. North of the Slave Coast the infamous kingdom of Dahomey diminished in power as the slave trade declined, yet its capacity to export slaves did not apparently lessen. Down the coast near the Bight of Benin, the great Oyo empire of the Yoruba collapsed between 1800 and 1850, but the fall resulted from no drastic drop in traffic, because slave exports had been declining since the 1720s. Further south in the Angolan area, the abolition of the trade apparently triggered massive change. No clear common pattern emerged, however. In southern Africa, as in West Africa, diverse local conditions and developments mitigated the impact that ending the trade had on indigenous power bases and structures.

The economic impact of abolition was clearer and relatively smaller in Africa than in the Americas or Europe. The main reason was that the Atlantic trade, including the slave traffic, was tangential to the commerce and income of most African economies. Key slave-trading enclaves such as Cabinda, near the Zaire River, and Efik trader towns in the Niger and Cross River deltas, suffered lost incomes in the declining traffic. Outside such centers, however, few Africans lost income, for most never partook in, let alone profited from, the traffic. Indeed, the larger Atlantic trade hardly touched most Africans and was always of relatively small value to Africa in monetary terms. Among Atlantic Basin participants, Africa reaped the lowest per capita revenues from trade.

With fewer slavers to the Americas, fewer Africans were enslaved. The trans-Saharan slave trade increased to the east as slave prices declined on Africa's Atlantic coast during the 1800s, but the volume paled in comparison with the Atlantic flow. Domestic slavery made up for the smaller numbers being shipped to the Americas. As the trans-Atlantic traffic declined, however, total enslavement decreased, and with that decline came fresh economic development.

Africa enlarged its Atlantic trade in commodities as the traffic in human beings declined. Already by the end of the 1700s, for example, Senegal gum had risen to commercial importance. Between 1800 and 1850 palm oil and palm oil kernels became important in the Bight of Biafra. In the 1840s peanut cultivation for export developed rapidly in Upper Guinea. The products did not rapidly replace the slave trade; some involved slave labor, and in no sense did they squeeze out the slave trade. Neither the earlier Atlantic trade nor the later commodities absorbed more than a minuscule share of African resources.

Throughout the era of the slave traffic, Africans engaged overwhelmingly in domestic economic activities; Atlantic activity remained tangential. Africa's large population and sophisticated economies allowed it to supply its basic needs while producing substantial surpluses for trade and tribute. West Africa was especially self-reliant. The continent as a whole was self-sufficient in contrast to Europe and its colonies in the Americas; thus, the abolition of the slave trade disturbed Africa less than it did Europe and the Americas.

Chapter 9

EMANCIPATION IN THE CARIBBEAN AND SPANISH AMERICA

1780s	Antislavery campaigns begin in England and France.
1791	St. Domingue slave revolution; leads to Haitian independence in 1804.
1810s	Latin American independence movements begin enlisting slaves by promising freedom.
1815	Haitian president aids independence leader Bolívar.
1816	Barbados slave rebellion.
1833	Emancipation Act begins manumission in British colonies, completed in 1838.
1850s	Peru begins importing indentured Chinese coolies.
1868–1878	Ten Years' War in Cuba raises emancipation issue.
1870	Moret Law begins emancipation of newborns in Cuba.
1880	Spanish law for gradual emancipation in Cuba, completed in 1886.

I t took nearly a century, from the 1790s until the 1880s, to eliminate slavery from the Caribbean and Spanish America. Not only were these advances toward freedom spread over a long period overall, but in most individual places they took years to complete. The fact that the European homelands had themselves abolished slavery made it easier to extend the measure to the colonies, usually against the wishes of the planter and merchant elites. Slaves themselves played important roles through local bargaining, subtle resistance, occasional rebellions, and formal legal enactments. Once the African trade diminished and ended, in most places emancipation became inevitable, giving slaves, especially the creoles, increased leverage in their dealings with masters.

Except for the Haitian Revolution of 1791, the abolition struggles caused only modest bloodshed, but they left a legacy of racism, poverty, and ethnic divisions. In most places emancipation coincided with economic downturns caused in part by the ending of the trade. These recessions led elites to reinforce their grip on the lower social orders. The journey from slave to citizen only began with emancipation, then, and for millions it still has not ended.

The liberals who led the independence movements in Spanish America after 1808 began offering freedom for slaves who enlisted as patriot soldiers. In this way emancipation became identified with political freedom from Europe. By the 1820s most slaves on the Spanish American mainland were free. The British Parliament then liberated slaves in the West Indies, and soon the French, Danes, and Dutch followed suit. Another round of abolition laws in the 1850s freed the remaining slaves in the Spanish American republics. Finally, the Spanish government liberated the slaves in Puerto Rico and Cuba.

Emancipation in Haiti and the British colonies liberated the largest numbers of Africans and their descendants, about a half-million each. The effects of these two events continue to reverberate today. Haiti's example precipitated many rebellions and helped convince planters elsewhere not only to tighten security but also to grant concessions to slaves to avoid further upheavals. Haiti paid a heavy price for setting the example, however, for the colonial powers and even the newly independent republics shunned contact with the most Africanized territory in the hemisphere. The British experiment with gradual emancipation in the 1830s, though flawed, served as a model for other governments. No other developments in nineteenth-century Spanish America matched the importance of these emancipations.

◆ **EARLY ABOLITIONISM**

The first and most dramatic emancipation in the region occurred in St. Domingue, where slaves began a massive rebellion in late 1791. The local governor, inspired by the radicalism of the revolution in Paris and worried about the breakdown of order on the island, abolished slavery there in 1793. He soon lost command of events, for British and Spanish armies invaded in order to seize the territory and its former slaves. They failed, and Afro-Haitian leaders took control over the island after years of bitter fighting. Even the enormous French expedition of 1802 could not defeat the former slaves, who declared their independence in 1804. Although hundreds of thousands perished in the fighting, the results proved truly revolutionary to Afro-Haitians and African Americans in general.

During the 1790s and 1800s, word of the Haitian insurrection spread throughout the hemisphere, inspiring many to emulate the slaves and striking fear into the hearts of slaveholders. Black and mulatto sailors carried stories to their brethren in many ports, who in turn informed members of local brotherhoods and associations. Newspapers also circulated information about events in Haiti. Meanwhile, elites in other islands and in Spanish America regarded the moment as extremely dangerous, and most took measures to reinforce security and prevent uprisings.

The planter and merchant classes who had the most to lose from emancipation tried to ally with their colonial governments to protect their property and power. Many decided to grant certain concessions to their slaves, however, in the hopes of averting rebellions and/or imposed emancipation. Slaves gradually expanded their customary rights to possess property, farm garden plots, market their surplus, rest and socialize on Sundays, save money, and even buy their own freedom. Such privileges made the slaves a proto-peasantry long before formal emancipation. In many places slaves enjoyed greater autonomy and relaxed discipline, especially where the sugar industry was in decline.

Independence Movements and Emancipation

In 1808 imperial upheavals in Europe sparked independence movements in several Spanish American colonies, led by liberals who for the most part sympathized with freeing the slaves. Some of the leaders were of African descent themselves—José Maria Morelos and Vicente "El Negro" Guerrero in Mexico, for example—and many others were mestizos who had experienced racial prejudice. While they were philosophically committed to the Enlightenment ideals of liberty, equality, and fraternity, they also had personal reasons for wishing to end racially defined caste distinctions.

General José de San Martín, who eventually freed much of South America from Spanish rule, had suffered discrimination because of his birth in Paraguay (rather than Spain) and his swarthy complexion. In 1813 the Argentine legislature that had commissioned him for the independence wars decided to offer freedom to slaves who served in the military. Slaveholders were obliged to sell upon request. The Chilean rebel government did the same in 1814. Over the next decade San Martín and other patriot leaders in the region recruited and freed several thousand slaves, who contributed measurably to their successes. Many blacks rose to officer rank by 1820. In this way emancipation became intimately linked with political independence.

A most striking conversion to abolitionism occurred in 1815, when the Venezuelan leader Simón Bolívar arrived in Haiti after four years of fighting the Spanish on the mainland. Born into a wealthy family that owned many Africans, Bolívar did not give much thought to the issue of slavery. However, he condemned the Spanish policy of confiscating and conscripting slaves belonging to patriot sympathizers. When Bolívar requested refuge, arms, and supplies from Haitian President Alexandre Petion, Petion stipulated that Bolívar would have to promise to free the slaves in lands he liberated from Spanish control. Bolívar agreed and received the requested aid. Soon he began recruiting slaves into special units, and he conscripted and freed nearly five thousand during his campaign in Colombia. He also saw that free-birth articles were written into the constitutions he sponsored.

Patriot leaders in Spanish America, even those of African heritage, remained ambivalent about the masses of slaves, for they distrusted the ability of former slaves to participate in democratic government. Bolívar once remarked,

> I am convinced to the very marrow of my bones that America can only be ruled by an able despotism. . . . We are the vile offspring of the predatory Spaniards who came to America to bleed her white and to breed with their victims. Later the illegitimate offspring of these unions joined with the offspring of slaves transported from Africa. With such racial mixture and such a moral record, can we afford to place laws and principles above men?

And ever fearful of race war because of the Haitian example, these patriotic leaders occasionally executed black officers accused of inciting violence against whites.

So the outcome of these early emancipations in the 1810s and 1820s was mixed. On the one hand, tens of thousands who joined warring factions gained their freedom, and many thousands more simply ran away, as had occurred during the U.S. War for Independence. Most of the slaves became liberated during the wars of independence in Spanish America (excluding Cuba, which remained firmly under Spanish control). Some countries extended political rights to former slaves, but in most countries they remained marginal in public affairs. However, many mulatto officers rose in status and held high positions after independence, with several even becoming presidents.

On the other hand, many former slaves died in the fighting and epidemics, and those who survived often faced grave troubles owing to the destruction of property and equipment. Moreover, constitutional provisions of liberty and equality usually went unenforced, for new chieftains seized control of the independent nations and regimented workers by intimidation and force. In the Andean countries, slaves—African and

Amerindian—continued to labor as before, and in others emancipation decrees were rescinded. A prolonged depression in the 1830s and 1840s compounded their hardships. Even free blacks suffered discrimination because of their color and former servitude. Thus, Afro-Hispanic Americans slipped into a nebulous status in the nineteenth century. They were partially free yet hardly autonomous, as new mechanisms of labor coercion and social discrimination took hold.

◆ EMANCIPATION IN THE CARIBBEAN

Antislavery campaigns began in England and France in the 1780s, coincidental with movements to abolish the slave trade from Africa. As seen in Chapter 8, the latter movements gained strength after 1807 and triumphed in 1867, when the Spanish stopped imports to Cuba. The movements to end slavery itself, particularly in the Caribbean islands, followed different paths. (See Table 9-1.)

Reform and Rebellion

The British antislavery campaign in the 1790s and 1800s, led by William Wilberforce and others, concentrated on lobbying to improve conditions for slaves in the islands. Called *amelioration,* this effort sought to replace the draconian codes of the early days of slavery with more humane laws that would give slaves limited legal rights and protection against abuse. In addition, thousands of Africans liberated from illegal slavers settled as apprentices in the islands. (Most, however, were landed in Sierra Leone, an African colony.) West Indian assemblies, dominated by planters, resisted enactment of amelioration laws, arguing that they were either dangerously lenient (in the case of Jamaica) or unnecessary (as in Barbados). Abolitionists gradually became convinced that the only means to change slavery was to get Parliament to impose its will and to end the relative autonomy enjoyed by island planter elites.

A major slave rebellion in Barbados in 1816 undermined the planters' claims that the slaves were contented and that matters were under control. The well-constructed conspiracy, led by slaves in administrative positions, sought to eliminate all vestiges of the white population and to create an Afro-Caribbean republic in Barbados, as the slaves in Haiti had. The strength of the uprising, which very nearly succeeded, stunned planters and British observers alike. Over 1 percent of the Barbados slaves perished in the fighting and subsequent repression. In all likelihood, the 1816 revolt marked a turning point by showing that slavery could not continue indefinitely without exacting a price neither planters nor the imperial government was willing to pay.

TABLE 9-1
Years of Definitive Abolition of Slavery

Slavery Ended by Conflict

St. Domingue, 1793
United States, 1863

Slavery Ended by European Power

British Caribbean, 1838
French Caribbean, 1848
Danish Caribbean, 1848
Dutch Caribbean, 1863
Puerto Rico, 1873
Cuba, 1886

Slavery Ended after Independence

Chile, 1823
Central America, 1824
Mexico, 1829

Slavery Ended by Law

Colombia, 1851
Ecuador, 1852
Argentina, 1853
Uruguay, 1853
Peru, 1854
Venezuela, 1854
Bolivia, 1861
Paraguay, 1869
Brazil, 1888

Abolitionist sentiment gained strength in Parliament during the 1820s and led to a new round of amelioration laws. Reformers' plans now emphasized gradual progress toward ending slavery, as well as preparation of slaves for freedom through education and religious instruction. Barbados planters, hoping to avoid abolition, passed their own amelioration act in 1824 in which they expanded the rights of slaves but also increased punishment for violence against whites. Even then, many provisions remained unenforced, intended only to prevent imposition of more drastic measures from London.

Memories of the 1816 revolt in Barbados, insurrections in Demerara (modern Guyana) in 1823, and the bloody Christmas 1831 uprising in

Jamaica convinced many that slavery had to be eliminated immediately. The government itself, assailed with crises and faced with a reform-minded Parliament after 1832, sponsored the Emancipation Act of 1833. The law stipulated that the following year children under six would become free and that the remaining half-million slaves in British territories would become apprentices for their former masters during a four-year transition period, ending with complete freedom in 1838. Slaveholders were compensated with substantial cash payments and offered help in recruiting laborers from other colonies.

The Post-1838 Caribbean

Britain's gradual emancipation program envisioned some training for ex-slaves and adjudication of disputes between apprentices and planters by over a hundred specially appointed magistrates. It also made available funds for promoting literacy and elementary education, mostly carried out by missionaries and other religious agents. These efforts, poorly funded and supervised, tended to reinforce the planters' dominant roles in the colonies and did little to promote the welfare of the former slaves.

The planters faced a great deal of labor unrest in the 1830s, and most sought ways to secure workers outside the apprenticeship system even before its official closure. The main problem was that former slaves felt cheated because their lives and working conditions had changed little after 1834. Most had been aware for years that emancipation was coming, and they anticipated major improvements in their lives. Those who remained as laborers on plantations experienced the same oppression and deprivations as before, since planters' attitudes had not changed and conditions remained depressed throughout the region. Large numbers of former slaves simply left the plantations and settled in hills and remote locations, subsisting on ground crops, fishing, and hunting. Such free village settlements made up a new peasantry with a strong aversion to plantation labor because of its prior association with slavery.

Former slaves who became independent farmers found it difficult to support themselves and their families, because of the marginal quality of the lands they occupied. When land was unavailable, they were obliged to sharecrop plantation fields, a system called *metayage* in the British islands. This ordinarily meant splitting the harvest with the landowner. Most former slaves worked for others only for the minimum time required to subsist, preferring to invest more effort in their own provision grounds. They also displayed a heightened sense of personal independence in any employment.

Living and working conditions after 1838 necessarily adjusted to the former slaves' new status. Most laborers preferred to build modest homes for their families and to live in a town or away from their place of employment. Families grew closer, as women tended to remain at home to raise children. Gradually, women almost disappeared from field work, where they had once been extremely numerous. Planters, for their part, formed core work forces to reside on or near the estate and do year-round chores. These families had access to land, tools, credit, and other favors the owners could dispense at little cost. Beyond this permanent force, the planters relied on transient laborers to help the permanent staff at planting and harvest time. Because of the critical timing required in sugar processing, it was essential that the planters have enough people to cut and transport cane. Thus, they constantly attempted to expand the pool of cheap and subservient labor.

Another way landowners adapted to the freer labor market of the post–1838 Caribbean was to make wage advances to workers to keep them indebted and unable to move on to other employment. This system, called debt servitude in Latin America, worked the same way as a company store did in the United States and Canada. Upon their employment, workers received lines of credit to set up housekeeping. The company deducted small portions of these debts from wages and added on any new credit purchases. Often, the company (estate, business, ranch, factory) paid workers in chits that could be redeemed only at its own commissaries, for overpriced goods. This system was routinely abused, but most workers welcomed the credit and found ways to get out of past debt.

The British Colonial Office, collaborating with island elites, pursued two more policies that tended to keep former slaves in the vulnerable position of being neither peasants nor wage laborers. First, it priced vacant government lands out of the reach of poor farmers, so that only well-to-do whites could afford to put them into production. This "dear land" policy obliged most freedmen to sharecrop, rent, or seek wage employment with landowners, thereby perpetuating their subordination. Coincidentally, without land they could not qualify to vote.

Planters also won another concession from the government in exchange for emancipation: authorization to import outside labor to replace their slaves. The favorite source was India, where workers signed papers of indenture promising to work off the cost of their passage. About half a million arrived in the Caribbean in the eighty years following abolition. Large numbers of Chinese also arrived, followed by smaller influxes of immigrants from Africa, the Americas, and Europe. In some places, most of the original African American work force was replaced by newcomers, while the former slaves subsisted in freedom and poverty or emigrated.

After midcentury, landowners and urban elites in the Caribbean islands employed immigrant workers to divide labor along ethnic, racial, and national lines. They encouraged each group—Afro-Caribbean, Indian, Chinese, Spanish American—to compete and avoid cooperation with the others. In this way they managed to preserve their own reduced fortunes and to prevent collective action almost completely. The animosities bred by these policies flourished among the illiterate and hungry, and even today they divide Caribbean societies.

Meanwhile, the Afro-Caribbean population grew rapidly, overwhelming the meager resources and government services of the islands. Faced with crop failures, droughts, famines, and epidemics, many black West Indians opted to emigrate in search of better wages. Many of them went to the Greater Antilles to harvest sugar and coffee; others traveled to Central America to plant bananas and work on canal projects; and still others went to the Amazon to build railroads or struck out for the Gulf coast to work in the oil industry in the early 1900s. Afro-Caribbean emigration began as a trickle in the 1860s and 1870s but became a torrent by World War I.

Economic Changes in the Region

Meanwhile, the French and Danish governments, under the influence of the 1848 revolutions, abolished slavery in their dependencies that year, without gradualism but providing compensation for former owners. The Dutch colonists, who held few slaves, ended the institution in 1863. Having the advantage of the British experience as a guide, authorities in these colonies handled emancipation in a more perfunctory fashion. In island after island, the same patterns emerged: land consolidation, tenant farming, illiteracy, overpopulation, and emigration.

By this time, urban industrial problems and the rivalry among modern nation-states in northern Europe preoccupied colonial policymakers, who gave virtually no attention to colonial matters. Almost every island suffered contracting agricultural revenues, decapitalization, and overpopulation. No longer the "sugar bowl of the world," the Caribbean Basin had become a colonial backwater and a region of poverty and unrest by the early twentieth century.

In hindsight, the relative speed and efficiency of the abolition programs in the Caribbean clearly occurred because imperial governments could make decisions without undue concern over offending planters and other economic elites in the colonies. Throughout the period the elites remained opposed to altering the labor systems. The legislators' readiness to make other concessions—cash compensation, protected markets, and alternative labor supplies—also facilitated the process. Finally, slaves themselves contributed greatly to the process by subtle tactics and outright defiance that encouraged planters to accept the transition to wage labor.

It is also clear, however, that the progressive outcomes abolitionists expected to result from emancipation did not appear. They had optimistically forecast the emergence of stable, productive families of ex-slaves, able to earn their livelihood from farming and employment. They reasoned that education, job training, exposure to European manners and morals, religious instruction, the franchise, and the natural forces of society and economy would uplift these people. Ideally, freedmen would become bourgeois members of society. Virtually none of these things happened, because colonial authorities lost interest in pursuing them. In addition, colonial elites could prevent these changes in order to preserve cheap and available labor pools.

Of course, in those areas where colonial governments were weak (e.g., Spain) or had been eliminated (the United States, Brazil), slaveholding elites and their allies fought emancipation laws and provoked violent confrontations over the slavery question.

◆ LATE SPANISH AMERICAN AND SPANISH EMANCIPATIONS

Stimulated by the English reforms of the 1830s and the 1848 revolutions in continental Europe, a new wave of liberalism swept the Americas in the midnineteenth century. The most influential principles of the era were laissez-faire economics and representative democracy. In country after country, politicians and parties calling themselves liberal passed laws favoring freer trade, private property, individual enterprise, universal education, and foreign immigration. As an afterthought, most of these governments eliminated slavery, usually for the second time.

By the late 1840s, very few slaves remained in Spanish America as compared with earlier times. For one thing, importations had ended a generation earlier, and for another, most Africans and their descendants had managed to gain their liberty through flight, self-purchase, or manumission. Declining numbers of the remaining slaves worked in agriculture, and a substantial number provided domestic services for prominent families. Slavery would probably have died out on its own eventually.

Still, slavery was unfinished business for the liberals. In some places, the last contingents of slaves were freed in exchange for enlisting in civil wars; in others, the government used compensation payments to win support from wealthy or landowning families. The process was usually brief and peaceful. Also, little was done to ease the transition of slaves to freedom. In any case, large numbers of nominally free persons were subject to labor coercion, such as debt servitude, vagrancy laws, indentured service, and the mita (a periodic labor levy). The former slaves simply joined the ranks of other less-than-free workers.

In Peru, Venezuela, and Colombia (including Panama), where tens of thousands of slaves had arrived by the 1810s to work in coastal plantations and mines, their numbers had dwindled greatly. When final emancipation came, each country had about fifteen thousand slaves, employed mostly on large estates. A large number of slaves were already approaching middle age—for example, the average age of those freed in Panama in 1852 was thirty-eight. Therefore, their release was not a matter that caused widespread debate. The government bonds issued to indemnify the former owners proved far more controversial.

Peru was the only South American country to import large numbers of indentured Chinese after 1850, the way Caribbean planters did. Over a hundred thousand had landed there by the end of the century. While some Chinese worked alongside former slaves on plantations, most moved into new enterprises, such as road and railroad construction, guano shipping, and mining. Their living conditions were atrocious, by most accounts being worse than those of the Afro-Peruvians.

In Ecuador and Uruguay, the number of slaves had declined to around two thousand by the time of formal abolition. Former owners received some compensation.

In the southernmost republics, slavery had virtually ended on its own, so the laws passed in the early 1850s were largely symbolic gestures.

Emancipation in Cuba

The last Spanish American emancipations occurred in Puerto Rico and Cuba, the only remaining western territories of Spain's once vast empire. The Cuban sugar economy had exploded since the last years of the eighteenth century, so that by the midnineteenth century it was the world's largest supplier. Huge numbers of African slaves and extensive virgin soils, as well as imports of heavy machinery (such as steam crushers, trains, and conveyors) from Europe, rendered Cuban plantations far more efficient than the older British and French ones. Considering this new source of revenues and profits and its losses elsewhere, Spain fought tenaciously to hold on to Cuba and to expand its plantations. This meant resisting pressures to end the African trade and slavery itself.

Spain, under pressure from the British government, passed several laws during the 1830s and 1840s prohibiting the slave trade. Still, the voracious labor demand created by the sugar boom overcame the Spanish objections, and hundreds of thousands of Africans were smuggled in from 1835 to 1866. In addition, planters recruited over a hundred thousand Chinese indentured workers whose lives differed little from those of the slaves. Spain's reluctance to enforce the trade ban reflected its concern that Cuban planters, if cut off from labor sources, might secede from the empire and annex the island to the United States.

After the U.S. Civil War, Spain could no longer avoid dealing with the evils of servile labor in Cuba. European pressure mounted to end the importation of Africans, and groups of Cuban liberals extended the campaign to include gradual emancipation. The contraband slave trade question was resolved quickly; strict enforcement ended it after 1866. But abolition required reaching agreements among planters, Spaniards, Puerto Ricans, professionals, and others, and Spain was too weak and distracted by internal problems to deal forcefully with the issue. In view of the drifting policies, initiative shifted to Cuba itself.

The Ten Years' War (1868–1878) was fought over colonial relationships and difficulties, but it served to move abolition up on the political agenda. The junta that seized power in Spain in 1868, little concerned about the interests of Cuban planters, issued a decree freeing all children born to slave mothers after that date. The abolitionist leader Segismundo Moret, chosen as minister of colonies in 1870, pushed the Spanish legislature to enact the Moret Law that year. Its main effect was to reinforce the free-birth decree for Cuba. By that time, the independence insurrection in Cuba had been underway for two years, so the legislature offered freedom to slaves who enlisted or aided in the war effort. (It also imposed harsh treatment for slaves or masters who aided the rebellion.) Those slaves over sixty years of age or belonging to the state were also freed. The law created a form of tutelage similar to the British apprenticeship, by which persons born into freedom would remain in the care of their mothers' masters until age twenty-two. Finally, the Moret Law promised to end slavery completely once the fighting was over.

The rebels, for their part, began offering freedom to slaves who joined their ranks, and a few made emancipation a general goal of the movement. The rebels' commitment remained ambiguous, however, so as not to alienate slaveholders. As time went on, the rebels became isolated in the mountainous eastern end of the island, where wealthy slave owners were scarcer, and they recruited thousands of male slaves as soldiers. By then both sides in the struggle vied for the allegiance of Afro-Cubans by offering to abolish slavery gradually. The war ended without resolving the question but left the impression that the rebels more strongly favored emancipation. About sixteen thousand slaves, nearly a tenth of the total, had gained their freedom fighting on one side or the other.

The civil war and the Moret Law had an important spillover effect in Spain's other Caribbean colony, Puerto Rico, where they opened wide the door for total emancipation. Very few slaves remained on that island, and growers and merchants alike favored ending slavery. Responding to their pressure, the Spanish legislature freed the slaves in 1873 without compensation, more peaceably than anywhere else in the region.

The insurrection in Cuba finally ended in 1878, but it left a residue of hostility among the vanquished and the desire by the slaves to improve their situation. The Spanish government again took up the issue of gradual emancipation in Cuba and passed a law in 1880 providing for an eight-year phaseout of slavery. During this time, the former slaves remained under the tutelage (called *patronato*) of their former masters, who received their labor instead of indemnification. The law was hardly liberal in spirit: The government acted to eliminate pressure and to stem growing resistance and flight by the slaves themselves. Some feared a total breakdown of order if nothing were done.

As occurred in almost every other case of gradual emancipation, however, the Cuban law of 1880 merely accelerated the pace of events. Slaves resented working to indemnify their masters, and growing numbers balked or were shifted to wages. Within three years, half the slaves had won their freedom, and corporal punishment had been outlawed. Abolitionists increased their attacks on the system. Large numbers of planters freed their slaves in the hope of keeping them on as workers. Others stepped up recruitment of Chinese and other immigrants to offset the anticipated shortage of labor. The slave population continued to fall rapidly. Only twenty-five thousand remained on the eve of final abolition in 1886, two years ahead of schedule. The Caribbean was at last free of the hated institution.

◆ CONCLUSION

Generally, slaves who participated in military operations associated with the Age of Revolution won emancipation earlier than those who did not. Haiti was the most dramatic example, but the Spanish American colonies that broke away from Europe in the early 1800s began to free their slaves as a reward for armed service. By the 1820s the process was advanced, and the final wave of formal abolitions in the 1850s freed few persons.

Abolition in the British and French West Indies responded most to threats of disorder and revolt, a haunting specter ever since the Haitian Revolution. The colonial governments, pressured by reformers at home, took measures that gradually ended slavery by midcentury. Gradualism became the preferred method of emancipation throughout the region, down to the very last slaves in Cuba and Brazil. Supposedly designed to provide a constructive transition period into freedom, gradual procedures were often adopted to postpone emancipation and squeeze the maximum amount of labor from the slaves.

Economic factors helped determine the timing and character of emancipation. In areas experiencing growth and high profits, planters continued to import Africans and strenuously resisted efforts to end slavery. Where economic decay had set in or where slaves had never been very numerous, emancipation came more easily. There, businesses did not depend so heavily on them, and coerced labor had not become so closely identified with African origins.

Emancipation proved a shallow victory in most parts of Spanish America and the Caribbean. In some areas, former slaves found themselves competing with recent immigrants and were hard pressed to sustain their standards of living. In others, they drifted into low-wage jobs in towns, took up subsistence agriculture, or eventually had to emigrate in search of work. The other two emancipations—political and socioeconomic—would have to be fought for in the twentieth century.

Some legacies of emancipation in Spanish America and the Caribbean were similar. Nowhere in the region did people of African descent emerge with a strong awareness of their common origins, shared culture, and linked destiny. Instead, they ended up divided and poor, often competing with recent immigrants from Europe and Asia. With the sole exception of Haiti, white elites retained power in their nations and territories.

Only the Brazilian abolition (1888) occurred after the Cuban. The two followed similar trajectories. Among the major causes of these late emancipations were moral pressure from abroad, aging of the work forces, restiveness and violence among the slaves, and difficulty in attracting immigrants. In both cases, the planter elites retained most of their authority and property and emerged powerful from the process. Virtually nothing was done to promote citizenship or economic skills among ex-slaves, who were destined to become a labor reserve and marginal producers.

Two sharp differences, however, distinguished Cuba and Brazil. Cuba's abolition campaign was shorter and more violent, so that little regional shifting of slaves could occur. In Brazil, the campaign went on for decades, affording planters in the northeast the opportunity to sell some two hundred thousand slaves to coffee planters in the south, and thereby creating a vigorous domestic slave trade. In this respect, the Brazilian experience was closer to that in the U.S. South.

Chapter 10

EMANCIPATION IN THE UNITED STATES

1688	Quakers begin opposition to slavery in Pennsylvania.
1693	Quaker George Keith prints the first antislavery tract.
1758–1788	Quakers in Pennsylvania, Maryland, and Virginia free their slaves.
1777	Vermont abolishes slavery, followed by most other northern states.
1780s	Several states press to end slave trade.
1787	Northwest Ordinance.
1808	Slave trade banned.
1820	Missouri Compromise, pairing slave and free states for admission to the Union.
1827	First black newspaper, *Freedom's Journal,* in New York City.
1830s–1850s	Negro National Convention Movement.
1860	Election of Lincoln induces southern states to secede.
1861–1865	U.S. Civil War.
1863	Emancipation Proclamation decrees freedom for slaves in secessionist states.
1865	Thirteenth Amendment abolishes slavery.

Emancipation in the United States represented the culmination of an extended campaign, which the enslaved themselves had started and sustained with their own continual resistance. In grappling for liberation, however, the slaves had worked outside the legal lines to formally free themselves; it fell to others—to persons recognized within the legal bounds—to press emancipation as a factional or partisan cause.

◆ RELIGIOUS OPPOSITION TO SLAVERY

Members of the Society of Friends, a religious sect commonly called Quakers, delivered the first formal word against slavery in the English colonies that became the United States. Addressing a monthly meeting of their sect in Pennsylvania in 1688, four Quakers declared their opposition to the institution. They asked their fellows to "consider well this thing, if it is good or bad." If slavery was good, they asked rhetorically, "what can we say is . . . evil?" Their words became known as the Germantown Protest; these protestors proffered a simple principle: "There is a saying, that we should do to all men like as we will be done ourselves; making no difference of what generation, descent, or colour they are."

The campaign quickened in 1693 when Quaker George Keith printed the first antislavery tract in the English colonies, "An Exhortation and Caution to Friends Concerning Buying or Keeping of Negroes." Keith urged the Quakers to adopt a three-pronged protest: to free their own slaves, to work against slavery, and to help fugitive slaves. Quakers such as John Woolman also pressed hard, warning their fellows of divine wrath unless they abolished slavery immediately. But more than two generations would elapse after Keith's pamphlet before most of Pennsylvania's Friends took even the first step. Then, between 1758 and 1774, Pennsylvania Quakers severed all connections with the international slave trade and demanded that all members in good faith free their slaves; in 1788 Quakers in Maryland and Virginia also freed their slaves.

Quakers were hardly alone in the English colonies in asserting a religiously based opposition to slavery. Among colonial Pennsylvanians, the evangelical Protestant sect known as Mennonites also denounced slavery. In Massachusetts the Puritans, descendants of the English church reformers, added a notable antislavery word in Samuel Sewall's 1700 tract, "The Selling of Joseph." He argued that Africans were God's children descended from Adam and, as do all men, had "equal Right unto liberty." Sewall charged that any man who held another enslaved had "forfeited a great part of his own claim to Humanity."

◆ THE WAR FOR INDEPENDENCE AND ANTISLAVERY

The natural rights themes of antislavery flourished in the War for Independence, in which the colonies won independence from Great Britain. Virginia patriot Thomas Jefferson relied on the philosophy of natural rights in drafting the Declaration of Independence in 1776. Jefferson saw no apparent contradiction, however, between his own and his fellows' slaveholding and his assertions in the Declaration. Afro-Americans certainly noted those contradictions, however, and called whites to task for them. In the 1770's, for example, blacks in Massachusetts issued several open petitions pillorying whites for these inconsistencies. Meanwhile blacks played a huge military role in the actual fighting, as already noted in Chapter 7.

Many whites also took advantage of the war to confront slavery. Vermont made slavery a dead letter under its first state constitution in 1777, and in 1780 Pennsylvania enacted a so-called gradual emancipation plan, providing that Afro-Americans born thereafter would be free in status but held to labor only until they became twenty-eight years old. The Massachusetts constitution of 1780 became an instrument of freedom for slaves, beginning with judicial decisions in 1783.

After the war, a swell of antislavery sentiment washed north and south. Notable leaders of the new nation condemned slavery. For example, New York's Alexander Hamilton wrote antislavery tracts championing blacks' right to freedom and their natural equality with whites. He also became a member of the New York Society for the Manumission of Slaves, the first president of which was future U.S. Chief Justice John Jay. Similarly, Pennsylvania's Benjamin Franklin was a founder and president of the Pennsylvania Abolition Society.

Down the line, from Massachusetts to Virginia, every state had its antislavery society by 1792. Connecticut and Rhode Island adopted gradual emancipation plans in 1784. New York effectively joined the gradualists' ranks in 1799, and New Jersey in 1804. Moreover, the Continental Congress in 1787 laid an important national foundation for freedom by forbidding slavery in the territory of the Northwest Ordinance.

But antislavery forces failed in the great U.S. document of 1787—the Constitution. Rather than offer slaves succor, it explicitly sanctioned their bondage and shielded slavery with the full protection of federal law. In its notorious three-fifths provision, it declared slaves less than persons. Moreover, it made slaves who escaped their shackles forever fugitives, liable to be "delivered up on Claim of the Party to whom such Service or Labour may be due."

Nonetheless, the Constitution did contain one major antislavery element in closing the United States to the international slave trade in 1808. Several southern states had pressed for such a result. Maryland banned the trade in 1783; North Carolina limited it in 1786; and South Carolina prohibited it intermittently from 1787 to 1803. Even proslavery Southerners backed closing the trade, reasoning that a continued influx of slaves would produce a surplus that would diminish the value of their investments in slaves. Although outlawing the trade in 1808 reduced the numbers coming into the country, it did not end all importation. Nor did it do anything for emancipation.

Slavery tightened its grip on the country during the early national period. In the generation spanning the end of the colonial period and the first federal census, the number of slaves nearly tripled, increasing from 236,395 in 1750 to 697,897 in 1790. While ebbing in the North, it was swelling in the South. In 1750 about one of every eight (12.8 percent) of the slaves in the colonies lived above what would become the Mason-Dixon line. In contrast, in 1790 only about one in twenty (5.8 percent) lived above the line. The number of slaves in the North increased by one-third (34 percent), going from 30,197 to 40,370 between 1750 and 1790. The number of slaves in the South more than tripled (319 percent), rising from 206,198 to 657,527 between 1750 and 1790. Slavery was becoming an exclusively southern institution, with both the U.S. Constitution and the economy guaranteeing its entrenchment.

◆ THE BLACK ANTISLAVERY MOVEMENT

Yet the number of Afro-Americans free from formal slavery was also expanding. In 1790 the total was 59,466 largely because of the postindependence emancipation movement. Most of those called "free negroes" lived in the South, but the portion who lived in the North played prominent roles in pressing emancipation on the nation.

A black press emerged in 1827 with the appearance of the weekly newspaper *Freedom's Journal* in New York City. "Too long have others spoken for us," the Afro-American editors declared in their opening issue. Other organs followed, such as the *Mystery* published in Pittsburgh in 1843; the *Colored Man's Journal* in New York City in 1851; the *Mirror of the Times* in San Francisco in 1855; and the *Anglo-African* in New York City in 1859. Probably the most influential of the newspapers was the *North Star*, which the escaped slave Frederick Douglass edited and published beginning in 1847. In 1850 the name was changed to *Frederick Douglass's Paper*.

The Afro-American newspapers stood in the first ranks of the militant abolitionism that emerged in the 1830s to urge the immediate and total destruction of slavery. They put in print the words that outspoken Afro-Americans such as Frederick Douglass, Henry Highland Garnet, Robert Purvis, Harriet Tubman, Sojourner Truth, David Walker, and Peter Williams expressed at meetings held at home and abroad.

The unified aim of all these spokespersons and newspapers was to persuade public opinion to end slavery. An especially popular genre called the ex-slave narrative combined antislavery publishing with the personal story of a black spokesperson such as Frederick Douglass. The *Narrative of the Life of Frederick Douglass, An American Slave* became an almost instant best-seller upon its appearance in 1845. And it was not the only example.

Scores of narratives appeared between 1840 and 1860, among the more notable of which were William Wells Brown (1842), Lunsford Lane (1842), Moses Grandy (1844), Henry Bibb (1849), Nancy Prince (1850), J. W. C. Pennington (1850), Solomon Northup (1853), Austin Steward (1857), Sally Williams (1858), J. W. Loguen (1859), and William and Ellen Craft (1860).

Neither the printed nor the spoken word represented the most pointed activity of black antislavery. As Harriet Tubman exemplified, militant Afro-Americans also took a more direct hand in freeing their brethren by assisting fugitive slaves. Their advocacy of immediate emancipation was pivotal, becoming the primary thrust of the antislavery movement by 1850.

Free blacks pushed for emancipation not only from slavery but also from the racial oppression that relegated them to a lesser and uncertain status. Beginning in the 1830s, they created what became known as the Negro National Convention Movement, which brought Afro-Americans together in different cities to plan concerted action to improve their condition. They refused to accept less than equal status with whites.

The convention movement emphasized education at every level and of all kinds. The 1847 convention in Troy, New York, for example, pushed for blacks to gain admission to white colleges, which represented the only route to higher education. The call was not merely to college, and it was no solicitation of an elite. The 1850 convention in Columbus, Ohio, illustrated the breadth of educational promotion. It called for universal education—schooling for all, regardless of race, color, previous condition of servitude, age, or gender. It directed Afro-Americans to reach for the top by pursuing the learned professions—law, medicine, and theology—and by advancing through training in agricultural and mechanical occupations. The call echoed the notion that education addressed both personal and community needs. Hardworking black students would prepare themselves for life, while winning respect and converting opponents into friends.

Education was a means to attack oppression, and while touting education, the Columbus convention also insisted that Afro-Americans resist all forms of oppression. They particularly attacked prejudice as the basis of oppression, and the 1853 convention in Rochester, New York, continued with force. Except perhaps for the Jews, no people at any time in history were "pursued with a more relentless prejudice and persecution, than are the free colored people of the United States," the Rochester delegates declared.

The convention's protest against prejudice and the accompanying persecution of discrimination carried both charge and challenge. At every level the United States stood accused of allowing and even authorizing blatant and insidious attacks of such severity that they would "humble the proudest, crush the energies of the strongest, and retard the progress of the swiftest." Yet blacks had met the challenge. Standing unbent and unbowed, the Rochester delegates proclaimed that "In view of our circumstances, we can, without boasting, thank God, and take courage, having placed ourselves where we may fairly challenge comparison with more highly favored men."

◆ THE SLAVE TERRITORY ISSUE

Slavery intensified the nation's growing pains. Every step westward deepened the split, dividing the increasingly black, slave South from the increasingly white, free North. Two nations, separate and dissimilar, had developed, a trend that had appeared almost immediately upon independence. It showed in the Northwest Ordinance of 1787, which banned slavery from that federal territory. The 1787 Constitution fully displayed the strain between North and South, and it also showed the national policy of compromise to maintain the Union. The policy abandoned Afro-Americans to the perversity of slavery and racial prejudice. Meanwhile, the nation reaffirmed its commitment to the policies followed by two generations of antebellum leaders.

Each national acquisition of territory from the War of Independence to the Mexican-American War (1846–1848) tested the nation's resolve on slavery, and at each test the same answer echoed: In the balance of national interests Afro-Americans' rights of whatever dimension—natural, constitutional, statutory—carried little weight. The parties at interest were concerned almost exclusively with economic organization, and that was where slavery fit—not as a concern about humanity but as an institutional accommodation.

The first national action on the slavery-territory issue exemplified how the United States would decide its course. The Northwest Ordinance set the precedent of having the federal Congress decide the status of slavery in emerging states. Using the Ohio River as a line, the national lawmakers in 1787 decided where slavery would and would not be allowed as an institution. Above the line slavery was banned. Thus, the states that emerged from the Northwest Territory—Ohio (1813), Indiana (1816), Illinois (1819), Michigan (1837), and Wisconsin (1848)—did not permit slavery. Below the line slavery was allowed, and so the states that emerged there—Kentucky (1792), Tennessee (1796), Mississippi (1817), and Alabama (1819)— permitted slavery. The demarcation resembled the Mason-Dixon line, which in the popular mind came to separate North and South, nonslave and slave states.

As the lands annexed in the Louisiana Purchase of 1803 were considered for statehood during the antebellum era (1820–1860), Congress drew another line at 36'30" north latitude. It formed the southern border of Missouri, which entered the Union in 1821 as the only state permitted to maintain slavery above the line within the Louisiana Purchase territory. The slave status of Louisiana, which entered the Union in 1812, and later that of the new states of Arkansas (1836), Iowa (1846), and Minnesota (1858), was determined by their position above or below the line.

Congress's treatment of the Louisiana Purchase territory included more than a line. It provided for a rough pairing of emerging states that allowed North and South to maintain parity within the U.S. Senate, where each newly admitted state added two votes to a side. This pairing, which became known as the Missouri Compromise of 1820, coupled the admission of Missouri and Maine. As a result, North and South each had twelve states and, thus, twenty-four senators. The pair system worked until 1850. Under it Arkansas (1836) and Michigan (1837) entered the Union as a pair. Two slave states entered in 1845—Florida and Texas—but were offset by Iowa (1846) and Wisconsin (1848).

Texas did not emerge from the Louisiana Purchase territory, of course, but from its break from Mexico in 1836. It posed a significant problem for the old compromise pattern, as did the so-called Mexican Cession lands that the United States took after the war with Mexico (1846–1848). The vastness of the area worried the keepers of the balance. When it entered the Union, Texas had 390,143 square miles, representing 17.9 percent of U.S. territory; the cession lands offered another 529,017 square miles, representing 19.5 percent of U.S. territory. As Texas was already committed to slavery, a balance appeared to require banning slavery in the cession territory.

Antislavery representatives took the offensive. In 1846 the U.S. House of Representatives considered a $2 million, and then a $3 million, appropriation for negotiating a territorial acquisition from Mexico. Pennsylvania Congressman David Wilmot introduced an amendment that "neither slavery nor involuntary servitude shall ever exist in any part" of the territory the United States got from Mexico. The northern-dominated House accepted the amendment that became known as the Wilmot Proviso and passed the bill at successive sessions in 1846 and 1847.

The Senate balked. The South would not stand for a ban on slavery in what appeared to be the nation's last large land purchase. It would fight rather than submit to such an assault on its rights to share in national property, South Carolina Senator John C. Calhoun declared. Other southern senators agreed, and in their arguments they challenged a central principle of territorial adjustments since 1787: that Congress had authority to exclude slavery from any state. Because slave states outnumbered non-slave states fifteen to fourteen in the Senate until Wisconsin entered the Union on 29 May 1848, the Wilmot Proviso failed.

The status of slavery in the territory the United States formally acquired under the Treaty of Guadalupe Hidalgo in 1848 became a hot political issue. One compromise called for extending the 36'30" Missouri Compromise line to the Mexican cession, which would have divided California at a point between Santa Barbara and Los Angeles. This compromise had support, but not enough to carry. Having reached what appeared to be the end of the stick, both the antislavery and proslavery advocates were reluctant to surrender any handhold.

A workable compromise took nearly two years to emerge, and when it appeared it came in pieces, not together. It contained four major provisions concerning slavery: (1) the admission of California as a single, free state; (2) the organization of the remaining cession lands as the New Mexico and Utah territories without mentioning slavery; (3) the abolition of the slave trade in the District of Columbia; and (4) a stronger fugitive slave law to replace the original 1793 act. The parts became known in sum as the Compromise of 1850.

◆ Fugitive Slave Laws

The aftermath of the Mexican War showed how formidable slavery was as an issue in national politics; it also revealed how easily national politics dismissed Afro-Americans, for concern about slavery was not the same as concern for slaves. Property and profits were at issue, not the personal rights of blacks. That was clear in the Fugitive Slave Act of 1850, which laid blacks bare to slave-nappers operating with the full sanction and force of federal authority and power.

The act struck at the most effective and frequent form of black resistance to slavery: running away. By 1850 tens of thousands of blacks annually escaped slavery and left slaveholders screaming for greater security. Slaveholders demanded that the federal government make good on the Constitution's pledge of security in Article IV, Section 3. The Fugitive Slave Act of 1793 had sought to provide assurances of the return of what it called "Persons escaping from the Service of their Masters." The process proved insufficient, however, especially after the U.S. Supreme Court's ruling in *Prigg* v. *Pennsylvania* (1842).

While upholding the Fugitive Slave Act's constitutionality, the High Court in 1842 made returning escapees solely a federal matter. The law obligated no state or its officers to aid and assist in restoring a fugitive to the state from which he or she was accused of escaping, the Court said. "The right to seize and retake fugitive slaves and the duty to deliver them up" fell on Congress and its authorized federal officers. The ruling vindicated the rendition (return) principle, but in practice it left slaveholders unsatisfied. Northern states such as Pennsylvania and Massachusetts enacted so-called personal liberty laws that forbade state officers from aiding or assisting the capture or return of fugitive slaves.

So slaveholders pursuing fugitives before the 1850 act had the law on their side but scant means of enforcement. The new act sought to change that. It authorized new federal magistrates to handle fugitives. They now became federal slave-catchers, as did U.S. marshals and their deputies, whom the law ordered to help in capturing fugitives. President Millard Fillmore even ordered the U.S. Marines to pursue fugitives, and he sought in vain to extradite fugitives from Canada. Enforcing the law became a priority.

The act slapped not only at fugitives but also at every Afro-American and at reputed principles of U.S. law. For example, it disregarded habeas corpus. The slave-nappers did not bear the burden of proof that they acted legally in seizing and holding any Afro-American. The burden fell on the victim to controvert the process. The perpetrators needed no more than testimony from one white witness or an affidavit from a state court attesting to the victim's alleged status and ownership.

The law leaned further against freedom by providing federal commissioners the inducement of a $10 fee when they ruled in the slave-nappers' favor. They got only $5 if they ruled for the alleged fugitive. Moreover, the law brooked no dissent. It barred all state process such as habeas corpus proceedings, a hearing, or a jury trial on rendition. Anyone who assisted fugitives or interfered with the act stood liable for six months in prison, a criminal fine up to $1,000 and a civil damage award of $1,000. The stiff penalties were designed to show how serious the federal government was about protecting slaveholders' rights; they also showed the ease with which the federal government dismissed blacks from consideration.

Rather than calming contention, the Fugitive Slave Act of 1850 further incited emotions over slavery. People in the nonslave states argued that the act effectively extended slavery to their homes and that it attacked states' rights and basic civil liberties. Particularly in New England and western New York, people refused to accept the act without protest. Massachusetts pronounced its defiance in its 1855 Act to Protect the Rights and Liberties of the People of the Commonwealth. It extended its original personal liberty law of 1842 and provided explicitly that "every person imprisoned or restrained of his liberty is entitled, as of right and of course, to the writ of habeas corpus."

Michigan, Ohio, and Wisconsin joined the ranks of states with personal liberty laws that sought to protect basic legal process. People in the streets also got into the act. For example, bystanders sometimes carried out "rescues" to release alleged fugitives from the clutches of slave-nappers. Dozens of blacks benefited from such resistance, but such rescues were notable only because they were infrequent. For all the political huffing and puffing, however, the northern public sat largely unconcerned. On average, ninety-seven of every hundred alleged fugitives identified to federal judges and magistrates were turned over to claimants.

◆ NORTHERN ANTIBLACK SENTIMENTS

The major public concerns with the act, as in the national slavery controversy, were about economics and politics—not blacks as persons. The politics of many northerners were antiblack. They feared black competition and opposed slavery and slaves as rivals, linking blacks to lower wages and fewer jobs. What is more, they loathed having to associate with blacks in or out of work. Their antislavery sentiments were overwhelmingly sentiments for a white man's America.

The desire to rid the United States of slaves was part of the desire to rid the United States of blacks. Northerners clearly did not want blacks and dreaded any prospect of widespread black migration north. New states that emerged without significant black populations sought to remain white. Ohio, Indiana, and Illinois early enacted black exclusion laws, and Michigan and Iowa also had discriminatory measures to discourage black migrants. Oregon voters in an 1857 referendum displayed the no-slavery-and-no-blacks position of some states. They rejected permitting slavery by 7,727 to 2,646 and free blacks by 8,640 to 1,081. They wanted no blacks at all, and free blacks were the most unwelcome.

The North was becoming a white man's land throughout the antebellum era. The number of blacks did nearly double between 1820 and 1860, rising from 118,389 to 226,216, but the relative proportion of Afro-Americans in the North dropped by more than half. In 1820 about twenty-three in every thousand northerners were Afro-Americans; in 1860 less than twelve were. Throughout the antebellum years, more free blacks lived in the South than in the North.

Northern attitudes were homegrown—they were neither accidental nor derived from the South, as was demonstrated in Chapter 7.

Northern blacks fought segregated transportation too. Again foreshadowing later tactics, Boston blacks in the 1840s waged a sit-in campaign that blocked service on railway lines in the city. Insisting on first-come-first-served rules, blacks paid their fares and then occupied the cars reserved for whites and refused to leave. The disruption proved costly enough to get the rules changed. But separate cars for blacks and whites remained the rule elsewhere throughout the North.

In antebellum New York City, blacks had their choice of segregated public transportation: They could wait for an occasional Negro streetcar in which they could sit, or they could hop aboard the regular cars reserved for whites. But hop aboard was literally all they were allowed. Banned from entering, blacks could ride only on the outside platform. In 1854 a black woman named Elizabeth Jennings prefigured another courageous black woman a century later when she took a seat and refused to relinquish it. White passengers and railway employees snatched Jennings up bodily and threw her into the street. She sued and won a jury verdict for damages, but the public policy remained in place. Segregated facilities prevailed as the rule.

◆ DRED SCOTT DECISION

While relegating blacks to separate areas and services, segregation at least recognized the presence of the Afro-American personality. The U.S. Supreme Court came perilously close to declaring blacks to be nonpersons in its notorious *Dred Scott* ruling in 1857. The Court reached far beyond the issues of the effect of residence on slave status that lay at the core of Scott's argument. In brief, Scott contended that, although born a slave, he had been effectively emancipated by his having lived in Illinois and the Wisconsin territory, both of which barred slavery. The Court had settled the apparent issue in the 1851 case of *Strader* v. *Graham* when it declared that residence for a time in a nonslave state in no way affected a slave's status: The slave remained property.

Chief Justice Roger B. Taney, son of a wealthy slaveholding Maryland tobacco planter, pressed the decision in *Dred Scott* far beyond expectation. Insinuating issues that were not before the Court in the case, Taney unburdened himself on the slavery-related political questions of the day. He cast abolition as the crime, rather than slavery, and he championed the strictest enforcement of the Fugitive Slave Act of 1850.

Taney further declared that free blacks had no standing under the Constitution. Not only were they not U.S. citizens, but they could not become U.S. citizens, the chief justice declared. So, Scott could not have won his case no matter what his argument had been, for he had no standing to be heard or to make a federal case, Taney ruled. The sweep of that ruling ran second to Taney's ruling that Congress had no power under the Constitution to limit or bar slavery in any state. That tore open the political patchwork of a generation. Taney's decision cast the Constitution as not merely a compact protecting slavery but as a white man's covenant excluding blacks. The chief justice asserted that the nation's fundamental law showed that blacks had "no right which the white man was bound to respect."

The *Dred Scott* decision entrenched slavery's constitutional basis and affirmed the antislavery advocates' contention that only violence would end slavery. And violence did indeed come. The struggle over the status of slavery in the emerging state of Kansas played as a prelude for a national movement. Militant John Brown, a leader of abolitionist forces in Kansas, served notice of the spreading intensity of the struggle with his raid on Harpers Ferry, Virginia, in 1859.

◆ SECESSION, THE U.S. CIVIL WAR, AND EMANCIPATION

The clash that more immediately produced the U.S. Civil War occurred neither in Bleeding Kansas nor in Harpers Ferry but in national political caucuses. The dominant Democratic party split in choosing a presidential candidate for the 1860 election, rather than standing as a unified party behind a single standard-bearer. Stephen A. Douglas, the Democratic U.S. senator from Illinois, received the regular party nomination; defecting southern Democrats nominated incumbent Vice President John C. Breckenridge, a Democrat from Kentucky; and yet a third group formed the Constitutional Union party and backed John Bell, U.S. senator from Tennessee.

Bell, Breckenridge, and Douglas faced the fledgling Republican party's nominee Abraham Lincoln. Two years before, this fifty-one-year-old former U.S. representative from Illinois had lost the Illinois Senate race to Douglas. Six of every ten voters at the polls in November 1860 cast their ballot for a candidate other than Lincoln. In the U.S. electoral system, however, the split vote among Lincoln's rivals allowed him a plurality of votes that gave him the presidency.

A Republican president was more than many southerners could stomach, and cries for secession soon followed news of Lincoln's victory. On 20 December 1860, following a state convention to decide the issue, South Carolina announced its withdrawal from the United States. In turn, by 1 February 1861, Mississippi, Florida, Alabama, Georgia, Louisiana, and Texas had also announced their secession.

Constitutional questions, not slavery, framed the formal issues in the secession crisis. Lincoln himself sought repeatedly to assure slaveholders that he lacked the desire, intention, or power to interfere with slavery in any area where it existed. His position was the Republican party standard; the party was not abolitionist, and neither was Lincoln. The election had changed nothing about slavery's position in fact or law.

Republicans, like the new president, merely opposed any further extension of slavery and wanted to ensure the continuation of the territorial compromise that the *Dred Scott* decision had jeopardized. Republicans, like Lincoln, were not advocates for Afro-Americans. Like Lincoln, the party championed resettlement of free blacks in Africa, the Caribbean, and Central America. The president publicly stated his belief that whites were superior to blacks and that an unbridgeable gulf separated the two groups. He saw colonization as the most practical solution to what he viewed as the ineluctable social conflict the black presence engendered. Lincoln's dream and that of his party was a United States without blacks—and if the slaves could not legally be touched, the unenslaved could be and should be.

Had slavery been the issue, a deal might have been struck. But it was not, and no compromise appeared. North–South tensions were not to be soothed, and civil war resulted. The national government's consistent position, which President Lincoln repeatedly enunciated and Congress reaffirmed, was that the war was being fought solely to preserve the Union and not to abolish slavery or to infringe on state sovereignty. The African Methodist Episcopal Rev. J. P. Campbell, of Trenton, New Jersey, stated the idea bluntly in an October 1861 issue of the *Christian Recorder* (Philadelphia): "The President is not now, and never was, either an abolitionist, or an anti-slavery man. . . . He has no quarrel whatever with the south, upon the slavery question."

As the fighting intensified, positions shifted. Slave labor clearly strengthened the South. Frederick Douglass noted in July 1861 that slavery allowed the Confederacy "to send and sustain a stronger body of rebels to overthrow the Government than they could otherwise do if the whites were required to perform the labors of cultivation." Douglass thus urged abolition as a military measure that would allow the federal government "to turn this mighty element of strength into one of weakness." A year later Douglass's entreaties were embodied in a draft document that President Lincoln circulated for comment to his cabinet. On 22 September 1862

Frederick Douglass, an escaped slave and leader of the U.S. emancipation movement. UPI/Bettman.

Lincoln issued the document as the preliminary Emancipation Proclamation.

When it went into effect on 1 January 1863, however, the Emancipation Proclamation did not immediately free even one slave. The reason was that it was a war measure and not an abolition measure. It affected only those slaves under Confederate control and touched none of the slaves under federal jurisdiction—four hundred and fifty thousand in the border states and three hundred and fifty thousand in Union-occupied rebel zones.

Afro-Americans noted the proclamation's shortcomings but also rejoiced that it committed the federal government to "recognize and maintain the freedom" of specified slaves. "We shout for joy that we live to record this righteous decree," exulted Frederick Douglass. A Pennsylvania gathering declared that "we, the colored citizens of the city of Harrisburg, hail this 1st day of January, 1863, as a new era in our country's history—a day in which injustice and oppression were forced to flee and cower before the benign principles of justice and righteousness." The black Pennsylvanians further declared that "we would have preferred that the proclamation should have been general instead of partial; but we can only say to our brethren of the 'Border States,' be of good cheer—the day of your deliverance draweth nigh."

The Emancipation Proclamation heralded a new day, even if it was more symbolic than substantial. Yet even before it was issued, the federal government had begun to give substance to the goal of spreading emancipation. During the first seven months of 1862, Congress made several moves to abolish slavery in the nation. In March it endorsed a resolution for compensated, gradual emancipation, and it also counteracted the Fugitive Slave Act of 1850 by prohibiting federal military personnel from returning fugitive slaves to their holders; in April it abolished slavery in the District of Columbia and other federal territories; and in July, the Congress provided its own forerunner of the proclamation in the Confiscation Act of 17 July 1862, which emancipated slaves owned by Confederate supporters.

Although Afro-Americans quickly rallied to take up arms for the cause of emancipation, the government did not immediately accept their offers. Frederick Douglass bitterly lamented in August 1861 that "the Government continues to refuse the aid of colored men, thus alienating them from the national cause." The Union refused black enlistments for more than a year. Congress provided for black enlistments in July 1862, but the president continued to reject them. For example, in August 1862, he refused to accept two regiments of black soldiers from Indiana.

Military necessity soon brought blacks into the conflict. The first blacks on the battlefield were those in liberated South Carolina and Louisiana. As soon as U.S. Secretary of War Henry M. Stanton authorized black recruitment (August 1862), thousands of northern blacks answered the call to arms. The most famous of the black units was the Fifty-fourth Massachusetts Regiment. By the war's end, more than one hundred and eighty-six thousand Afro-American men had shouldered arms in federal forces.

The black presence helped the Union cause, but the blacks' battlefield experience proved little different from their experience elsewhere in the United States. As always, segregation ruled. Blacks served only in segregated units, and they got lower pay and heavier labor details. Nevertheless, their great aim was accomplished when the Confederacy collapsed and the South surrendered at Appomattox Courthouse in Virginia in April 1865.

Federal control over the areas declared to be in rebellion on 1 January 1863 meant that the slaves there were, in the words of the Emancipation Proclamation, "forever free." Yet hot questioning arose about the slaves' legal status as the issue concerning the Emancipation Proclamation's legal force persisted. In January 1865 Congress moved to quiet the questions by offering an amendment to the U.S. Constitution. It declared that "Neither slavery nor involuntary servitude, except as a punishment for crime whereof the party shall have been duly convicted, shall exist in the United States or any place subject to their jurisdiction." Declared ratified on 18 December 1865, the Thirteenth Amendment guaranteed legal emancipation for all Afro-Americans in the United States. With emancipation achieved in law, the task for African Americans then became that of achieving equality in fact.

Chapter 11

EMANCIPATION IN BRAZIL

1815	Treaty between Brazil and Great Britain pledges end to slave trade above the equator.
1830	Treaty between Brazil and Great Britain pledges Brazil to outlaw slave trade.
1831	Brazil bans slave trade but fails to enforce law.
1850	Queiroz Law abolishes slave trade and provides stiff sanctions.
1850s–1880s	Large internal slave trade from northeast to southeast Brazil.
1865–1870	Paraguayan War.
1871	Law of Free Birth.
1880	Resurgence of abolitionist movement.
1885	Sexagenarian Law frees persons over sixty-five.
1888	Golden Law frees all slaves.
1889	Military overthrow of Emperor Pedro II; republic is declared.

African and creole slaves in Brazil, by the imperial decree of 13 May 1888, gained their freedom just over a century ago. Princess Regent Isabel, occupying the throne in the absence of her father, Emperor Pedro II, helped break a political deadlock in Parliament by calling for immediate abolition. The so-called Golden Law ended slavery in one stroke, giving no compensation to masters and establishing no program to ease former slaves into their new lives. Thus ended a long, sometimes violent, and divisive era in Brazil's history. Abolition surely hastened the fall of the empire the following year, just as it produced a massive shift toward European immigration and industrial expansion in the south.

Many historians regard abolition as the most important event in the country's social history.

Forced African labor had been as much a part of life in Brazil as it had been in the U.S. South. Despite some similarities between their histories, the two nations followed very different paths to emancipation. Brazilian abolitionists waged a protracted campaign over decades without provoking a civil war, and in the background Brazilian slaves increasingly took direct action against their owners, raising fears of massive unrest and rebellion. Political leaders never forced a showdown on the issue, however, preferring gradual, incremental measures that would avert conflict between the elites. Finally, Brazil simply turned its back on slavery after abolition, thereby avoiding the problems caused by Reconstruction in the United States and yet failing to address the needs of millions of former slaves.

The fact that Brazil was the last country in the western hemisphere to free its slaves left a stain of guilt on the national conscience. The institution was more deeply entrenched in its economy and society than anywhere else in the hemisphere. The protracted struggle to end slavery set the stage for muted racial problems that have existed ever since. Unable to exorcise the demon of slavery, Brazilians have repressed its memory and denied its legacy.

◆ THE NINETEENTH-CENTURY SLAVE SYSTEM

Brazil's declaration of independence from Portugal in September 1822 coincided with an upsurge in sugar and coffee production. In the aftermath of the Haitian Revolution, growers and merchants began to sell sugar and tobacco to markets formerly supplied by the plantations of St. Domingue. They shipped valuable slave-grown commodities to consumers abroad and used the profits to purchase manufactured goods, land, and more slaves. The number of slaves arriving in Brazil during the first half of the century reached unprecedented levels. Although Brazil had signed an antitrade treaty with England in 1827 and passed a law abolishing slave imports in 1830, the trade continued to flourish until British intervention and an imperial law brought it to an end. (See Chapter 8.)

During the first half of the nineteenth century, Rio de Janeiro served as a beachhead for thousands of Africans each year. The African presence suffused every aspect of life in the city. Traders could be seen selling recently arrived slaves at public auctions, and countless slaves labored in the port unloading ships and transporting goods to destinations throughout the city and province. Affluent whites employed slaves to carry them in chairs through narrow and winding streets. Masters compelled African and creole slaves to do a variety of tasks, such as cooking, cleaning, caring for young children, and disposing of human waste on nearby beaches. In addition, skilled slaves constructed buildings and performed most urban occupations. African dress, music, and language could be seen and heard in all parts of the city. Afro-Brazilian culture infused religious ceremonies in honor of African and Amerindian gods, and also prevailed in brotherhoods organized by African tribal groups, or nations.

Slave labor relations were characterized by constant resistance. In January 1835 the largest urban slave revolt in the history of the Americas broke out in the northeastern coastal city of Salvador, and that same year, slaves joined a revolt by Indians and *caboclos* in the capital city of Belém which soon spread throughout the lower Amazon region. Other upheavals during the 1830s, in Rio Grande do Sul, Bahia, and Maranhão, created deep concern among provincial elites. Fears of peasant and slave rebellion led to the centralization of power in the hands of the young Emperor Pedro II, who was backed by the planter-merchant elite.

High world prices for sugar, cotton, tobacco, and coffee in the 1840s induced Brazilian planters to import some four hundred thousand slaves from West Africa, Angola, and Mozambique. To elude British squadrons patrolling the African and Brazilian coasts, ship captains often landed slaves at clandestine locations. North American shipbuilders, captains, crews, and investors played major roles in this contraband trade. British businesspeople also invested in these voyages, while manufacturers provided necessary goods to balance trade accounts. Brazilian planters and merchants viewed British antislave patrols as an infringement on their right to free trade.

Some individuals had spoken out against slavery before 1850. José Bonifácio de Andrada e Silva, a leader of the independence movement against Portugal, had adopted radical ideologies while studying in Europe. He regarded the exploitation of African slaves as the antithesis of enlightened ideals. Like other early patriots in the American colonies, however, Andrada e Silva could not unseat the landholding class that profited from slave production. Most abolitionists before 1850 focused on ending the trade, which they opposed on moral and philosophical grounds.

Until midcentury, few Brazilians questioned the legitimacy of slavery in their nation. The spread of Enlightenment ideals after the American, French, and Haitian revolutions had little impact on their attitudes and values. Any liberal impulses were countered by the long history of slavery in Brazil and the dependence of so many families on slave labor. Since less than one-third of Brazil's inhabitants were literate and concentrated in coastal cities, progressive ideas rarely spread to plantation regions.

The strength of Brazil's slave system and the weakness of abolitionism can best be understood within a hemispheric context. Like owners of slave plantations in the U.S. South and Cuba, planters and merchants looked to the future with optimism. Consumption and prices of tropical plantation commodities had been on a steady upswing, particularly in Europe and the United States. Brazil's elite had observed that the end of slave imports into the United States had not ended slavery in that nation. Thus, they did not view the end of the trade as antithetical to the slave regime itself.

♦ ABOLITIONISM AND WAR

A small group of persons who wanted to end slavery in their country took heart from a number of political and ideological transformations that were taking place outside Brazil. First among these transformations was the establishment of the black republic of Haiti, which proved that slaves could overthrow white planters and live independently. In addition, the emancipation of over a half-million slaves in the British Caribbean and many more in the French and Dutch West Indies encouraged abolitionists to push forward with their campaign. Finally, the U.S. Civil War showed that antislavery forces could arouse popular support and destroy the most powerful slave society in the Americas.

British moral suasion in particular helped spread antislavery activities after midcentury. Religious groups and intellectuals in Great Britain obliged political leaders to work toward ending slavery around the world. After the end of the slave trade to Brazil, the British turned their attention to the widespread use of slaves in cities and plantations. Criticism helped ensure the passage of Brazil's Law of Free Birth in September 1871, which provided freedom to all offspring of slaves.

The example of the United States after 1865 also spurred abolitionism in Brazil. Debates in the national Parliament and in provincial assemblies showed that representatives followed events in the United States closely. The political elites hoped that Brazil could avoid a civil war by adopting a program that would not alienate influential slaveholders. For their part, the antislavery minority appealed to their opponents to recognize that slavery went against the forces of progress and modernization. Some discussions centered on the benefits that emancipation gave to both former owners and former slaves in the United States.

The Paraguayan War of 1865–1870 heightened the need for action on the slavery question in Brazil. In this conflict Brazil, Argentina, and Uruguay united against their smaller neighbor, Paraguay, and some two hundred thousand men, women, and children lost their lives. Mounting slave resistance during the depths of the war forced the government to promise tangible antislavery measures afterward. Thus, the Paraguayan War was a decisive juncture in the quest for freedom by Brazil's million and a half slaves.

Government agents worked tirelessly to conscript tens of thousands of men from cities and rural areas into military service in Paraguay. Such impressment sweeps often employed brutal tactics and imprisonment of unmarried men, who ironically were called *voluntários da pátria* (volunteers for the nation). Besides lower class recruits, thousands of slaves were sent to the front. Landowners often sold their slaves to government agents to prove their patriotism, meet troop quotas, and protect their own sons from conscription. In November 1866 Pedro II offered freedom to all slaves who enlisted in the armed forces, after which many more slaves took advantage of enlistment to escape from their masters and gain their freedom.

When it became clear that the war would be protracted, opposition groups increasingly decried the government's stance on the slavery issue. They were joined by a small chorus of British, French, and U.S. abolitionists. To offset criticism, in May 1867 Pedro announced a gradual emancipation of the slaves and other initiatives once the war was over. This announcement did not satisfy his opponents, who issued three manifestos between 1869 and 1870. Besides immediate emancipation of slaves, their demands included greater provincial autonomy, direct elections, and freedom of religion. Shortly before leaving on a trip to Europe, Pedro told his daughter, Princess Isabel, that something had to be done to counteract the growing polarization of political opinion.

Popular opposition to the government climaxed during the war. Low morale dogged the young men, who had been forced to fight in a conflict they did not understand. Moreover, provincial officials did not fulfill promises of free land and financial assistance to veterans and their families. Former slaves who survived the war returned home determined to protect their new liberty. *Libertos* (freedpersons) surely spoke to others about fighting alongside black soldiers from Argentina and Uruguay who had long enjoyed their freedom. Complicating matters was the decision of several planters to go to court to force the return of escaped slaves, despite their service in the war. Not surprisingly, a malaise seemed to settle over the country in the late 1860s.

Military officers also became disenchanted with the government, having returned to civilian life disillusioned with the incompetence of imperial leaders and their policies. Officers who had earned their ranks through hard work and bravery felt closer to the emerging business and professional middle classes in the cities than to the traditional planter families who predominated in imperial circles. Thus, the slave issue became enmeshed in the general disaffection with the government.

Serious economic problems plagued the country in the 1870s. After the war, Brazilian troops were greeted with public festivities but soon found they had little chance of getting jobs since the war industries that had been set up to make uniforms, food, tents, and other gear had now cut back their workforces. The good prices enjoyed by the export sector in the 1870s were not enough to relieve the social inequalities, because slaves and people of African descent did not benefit from plantation profits. Visible signs of development, like railroads and port facilities, merely enriched a small minority of Brazilians and exposed the hardships suffered by the masses.

In the months following the end of the war, slaves, in particular, experienced great difficulties. Newspapers described widespread slave resistance in the provinces of São Paulo, Minas Gerais, and Espírito Santo. Police in Sergipe were unable to disperse recently formed runaway camps—*quilombos*. In the Recôncavo region around Salvador, slaves began attacking their masters in the early 1870s. Even in Pernambuco, whose sugar economy was undergoing modernization and transition to free labor, planters feared slave violence once the war ended.

The Paraguayan War, then, proved a major turning point for the black population. It eroded the authority of the state and encouraged civil disobedience among the enslaved and poor. Although slavery was not a main cause of the war, as it was in the United States, the instability and distress it engendered set in motion new currents of abolitionism.

◆ URBAN ABOLITIONISTS AND THE LAW OF FREE BIRTH

Urban antislavery forces organized many societies in the late 1860s, adding to the government's problems. These societies drew their members from many circles, including intellectuals, businesspeople, professionals, and government officials, and often raised money to purchase freedom for slaves and publish antislavery literature. Many used dramatic tactics, unusual in Brazil, such as holding public meetings to protest slavery. These societies tended to be conservative in that they did not expect to see slavery end immediately. Viewing the emperor as an adept administrator, they thought he would find a solution to the problem.

Most of the men and women who joined these early abolitionist societies had light skin and belonged to the middle or upper classes. Many abandoned the societies after passage of the Law of Free Birth in 1871. They had joined the societies for a variety of reasons. The affluent among them viewed the movement as a counterpoint to more radical elements, who demanded an immediate end to slavery in Brazil. Elites in the cities of Fortaleza, Recife, Salvador, Rio de Janeiro, and São Paulo recognized the dangers of the slave question and sought to bring about reforms without violence. Others saw gradual abolition as a way to promote modernization and the growth of urban professions. Still others were motivated by personal, family, or racial experiences, and many undoubtedly believed in the Enlightenment ideals of the eighteenth century. These societies did not welcome the downtrodden and black masses, who remained at the fringes of politics.

Many rural landowners who had witnessed slave uprisings blamed the abolitionist societies for contributing to the crisis. To prevent wider upheavals, slaveholders, with the support of some merchants and government officials, employed repressive tactics against slaves, including hiring gangs to capture runaways, attack quilombos, torture rebellious slaves, and prevent the dissemination of abolitionist pamphlets to the country-side.

When some early abolitionists chose methods of direct confrontation, such as protest meetings, planters and urban elites alike were further alarmed by these radicals. The Bahian poet Antônio Frederico de Castro Alves, for example, joined two of the original abolitionist societies in Recife and Salvador between 1866 and his death in 1871. He wrote poems that depicted the terrible conditions that black and mulatto slaves faced daily. Often he recited his poetry before outdoor gatherings and in large auditoriums in order to mobilize popular opinion against powerful slaveholders.

Castro Alves's genius and passionate commitment to the antislavery cause is clear from the images evoked by his poetry. In the poem "América" he urged:

Wake up, mother country. Don't bow your head . . .

It won't take much. Shake off the chain
that you call wealth. It mars what could be good.
Don't stain the page of the nation's story
with foul displays of slaves' blood.

If you'll be poor, so what? Be free,
as noble as the condor of high lands.
Remove the weight from Atlas's shoulders.
Lift the cross from God's hands.

In "Salute to Palmares," he paid homage to the thousands of fugitives who joined and defended that famous seventeenth-century quilombo. He suggested that slave resistance was a legitimate way to weaken the slave regime.

Palmares! I salute you . . .

You've unveiled the thunder,
Let loose the blast of wind
And released the furled banner
To the sound of sailors' howls
on the waves of slavery.

During and after the war, Luiz Gama also gained prominence as a radical journalist, poet, lawyer, and advocate of immediate abolition. Having been sold into slavery at the age of ten by his father, Gama ended up as a domestic slave in an affluent home in São Paulo where he learned to read and write and eventually studied law. After obtaining documents proving that he had been illegally enslaved, Gama fled from his master and lived free for the rest of his years. In 1864 he founded a humorous periodical called *Lame Devil*, which ran antislavery pieces and satirical articles about the Paulista elite. He also gained notoriety by defending African and creole slaves in the courts of São Paulo, even without a law degree. His determined efforts enabled hundreds of slaves to gain their freedom.

After the war, Gama and his followers campaigned to end slavery immediately. The Law of Free Birth raised their hopes that full emancipation would soon follow, but this optimism was dashed when the planter class closed ranks to protect slavery. Continued high profits from agriculture, as well as the scarcity of blacks and mulattoes in the abolitionist movement, limited the law's effectiveness. As a result, Gama and others opted for more radical approaches.

Fearing that the abolition campaign might get out of hand, some moderates opted for watered-down changes that would avoid drastic alterations in the monarchy, land tenure patterns, and the preeminence of the white minority. Joaquim Nabuco, the best known moderate, joined the movement to achieve emancipation without deeper changes. Well-meaning members of the elite tried to channel Afro-Brazilian leaders like Luiz Gama into an opposition movement of limited goals.

The emperor and his associates viewed the 1871 Law of Free Birth as a way to protect the property rights of slaveholders while appearing to be responsive to abolitionist criticism. After four months of intense debate in Parliament and in the press, the bill passed. Specifically, it provided that (1) children of slaves be freed upon attaining the age of eight or twenty-one, at the discretion of the owner; (2) an emancipation fund be created to free slaves and compensate owners; (3) slaves be allowed to save money to pay for their emancipation at prices set by courts; and (4) all slaves be recorded on special rolls kept by the provinces. Portrayed as a decisive step toward emancipation, the Law of Free Birth had mixed results. It did little to reduce the number of slaves, for the first newborns were eligible for freedom only after 1879. Masters, whose power was undiminished, became adept at bypassing the law. Moreover, the emancipation funds rarely had enough money to purchase slaves' freedom.

The law did, however, encourage increased resistance in urban areas. Slaves quickly became aware of new rights to manumission under the Law of Free Birth. In one instance, in July 1871 the slave Maria petitioned her master, José Joaquim de Franca, for the right to purchase her freedom. Franca agreed to a price of 1400 milreis (about $700 U.S.), but she was unable to save that amount. Later, after passage of the Law of Free Birth, Maria challenged Franca's price in court and received a favorable judgment that enabled her to purchase her freedom for half the earlier price.

With few exceptions, the impact of the Law of Free Birth was reactionary. It effectively ended the abolitionist threat that had arisen at the end of the war. Fledgling abolitionist societies floundered, radical newspapers disappeared, black leaders lost their audiences, and street demonstrations diminished. Meanwhile, the government deflected international criticism by pointing out that the Law of Free Birth was more favorable to slaves than the Moret Law passed by Spain. By breaking the momentum of the abolitionist movement, then, planters protected their dominion over the slaves and reinforced their political power.

◆ AFRO-BRAZILIAN ABOLITIONISTS IN THE 1880s

After 1880, descendants of slaves played a vital part in reviving abolitionist activities. Afro-Brazilians spread the abolitionist word by founding radical newspapers, writing prolifically against slavery, organizing public meetings, and traveling throughout the nation. Their success in forging an effective movement added to the violence of the struggle. Planters, merchants, and politicians dreaded the thought of educated blacks and mulattoes leading former slaves in a free Brazil. The fierce reactions of most slaveholders against emancipation can be traced directly to the effectiveness of Afro-Brazilian leaders.

A major strategist, organizer, and orator in the struggle to overthrow slavery in Brazil was the mulatto José do Patrocínio. Born in the province of Rio de Janeiro to a slave mother and a Portuguese priest, Patrocínio early gained his freedom, was educated, and worked as a pharmacist and tutor. In the late 1870s he began writing newspaper articles and a few plays. With money he received from an inheritance and from business partners, Patrocínio purchased two small newspapers. In one, the influential *Afternoon Gazette*, he criticized the treatment of slaves and freedmen in Rio de Janeiro. Patrocínio astutely attacked problems that affected the growing middle class—for example, high food prices and urban crime—to which he pitched his antislavery ideas. His depictions of cynical government leaders provoked angry and racist responses that confirmed his assertions.

In 1880 Patrocínio united several provincial groups and urban abolitionists into the Abolitionist Confederation, which, unlike the more elite Brazilian Antislavery Society, appealed to a cross section of the urban middle class, including medical students, printers, journalists, and commercial employees. It soon became the most radical abolitionist group in Brazil, advocating direct political action, more efficient government, an end to the planters' domination of political life, and immediate abolition of slavery. The Abolitionist Confederation forced the abolitionist debate out of government circles and into the streets, and Patrocínio's role in this group greatly enhanced his growing fame as a radical.

In October 1882 Patrocínio traveled to the ports of Salvador, Recife, and Fortaleza, where he encouraged his listeners to organize and take action against slaveholders. Patrocínio's travels had immediate and extensive effects. In João Pessoa an abolitionist society demanded the immediate end of slavery in Paraíba. Its members founded a newspaper, *The Emancipationist*, that continued until the imperial decree of 1888. During his three-month visit in Fortaleza, Patrocínio displayed methods activists could use to disrupt urban slaveholders and merchants. When the capital city of Ceará halted interprovincial slave exports, it became the first city in the nation to end slavery.

Patrocínio, aware that the racist values pervading Brazilian culture influenced even committed abolitionists, encouraged slaves and freedmen to organize themselves and to buy freedom for slaves. He stressed the need to educate freedmen to allow them to compete in a free society. In scores of public lectures, Patrocínio castigated proslavery forces for their manipulation and callousness. In several forums where opponents deplored the number of mulattoes in the movement, Patrocínio extolled the talents of Afro-Brazilians and their contributions to the nation. By the late 1880s, Patrocínio had gained a reputation as an urban leader with a national following.

André Pinto Rebouças, another mulatto intellectual, contributed much to the abolitionist resurgence after 1880. Born free in the province of Bahia, Rebouças studied civil engineering at the Escola Militar in Rio de Janeiro. With his father's support, Rebouças traveled to France and England for further training. Although a brilliant writer and engineer, he often encountered discrimination while in Europe, the United States, and back in Brazil. Nevertheless, through his talents and hard work he attained financial success, personal fame, and acceptance in the highest circles of the imperial government.

In September 1880 Rebouças joined Joaquim Nabuco to found the Brazilian Antislavery Society, an organization that would give Rebouças the opportunity to organize and write against slavery in the newspaper *The Abolitionist*. With Nabuco's departure for London, responsibility for the society fell primarily to Rebouças. To challenge the slavocracy, Rebouças and José do Patrocínio created the Abolitionist Confederation discussed above. This marked an important turning point in Rebouças's career. Now instead of advocating parliamentary debate and legal tactics, he turned to direct action, encouraging slave flight and civil disobedience by confederation members. He wrote at least one hundred and twenty articles about emancipation, addressing such topics as land redistribution, quilombos in Rio de Janeiro, and the importance of abolitionist Luiz Gama. Rebouças, together with Patrocínio, helped to make the Abolitionist Confederation the most important antislavery group in the 1880s.

Rebouças's career exemplifies some personal difficulties and complex questions confronting Brazilians of mixed race. An intellectual trained in fine universities, Rebouças internalized the values of Brazil's upwardly mobile citizens. For example, he viewed abolition as necessary to ensure the modernization of his nation and to improve the black and mulatto underclass. Rebouças had a number of blind spots, however. Foremost among these was his friendship with the emperor, which led him to believe that each individual could successfully overcome obstacles and achieve personal fulfillment. Unfortunately, Rebouças's acceptance of white elite values distanced him from the Afro-Brazilians he sought to defend. He also tended to be short-tempered and prejudiced against them. All in all, Rebouças simply did not possess the leadership qualities necessary to achieve his high goals. When the emperor was overthrown in 1889, Rebouças decided to leave the country rather than attempt to defend the interests of former slaves. Rebouças's travels and writings in Europe and Africa, where he committed suicide in 1898, reveal a man torn by doubts about racial inequality and the meaning of freedom.

The mulatto medical professor Luís Anselmo da Fonseca was yet another well-known figure in the antislavery movement in Brazil. An astute observer of social life in the northeast, Fonseca joined a small group of militant abolitionists who challenged the slaveholders controlling Bahia. He encouraged his students to participate in the struggle, and he traveled to the countryside to meet secretly with slaves. Often in Salvador, he publicly condemned the slavocracy and the slow pace of emancipation. Fonseca used his considerable talents to educate other persons and to organize popular demonstrations in favor of abolition.

During the waning months of slavery, Fonseca, with his own funds, published *Slavery, the Clergy and Abolition*, an analysis of the abolitionist struggle that was among the most influential of his day. His survey of Brazilian history exposed the reactionary character of the Catholic church. While blaming planters and urban masters for the poor treatment of slaves, he criticized religious leaders for not playing greater roles in the abolitionist campaign. By including a wide cross section of the political spectrum, this book departed from other nineteenth-century studies of slavery. For example, Fonseca presented the most conservative proslavery opinions, along with the perspectives of lower class whites who had returned from the Paraguayan War searching for work.

Fonseca's insights are impressive even today. He roundly criticized free Afro-Brazilians who did not take part in the abolitionist crusade, and he pointed out that many libertos and mulattoes purchased slaves themselves or joined the infamous *capitães do mato* (bush captains) to search for fugitives. He also stated that uneducated Afro-Brazilians had been deluded by a manipulative elite into accepting the racist subordination inherent in a slave society. He emphasized that the poor performance of masses of

Francisco do Nascimento organized a boycott of the internal slave trade in the Brazilian state of Ceara during the 1880s.

blacks and mulattoes was due to lack of education and employment opportunities. Still, Fonseca noted many significant contributions made by Afro-Brazilians, not the least of which was a decisive role in the abolitionist movement itself. He continued to work on behalf of former slaves for more than a decade after emancipation.

Afro-Brazilian libertos and free persons joined the abolitionist movement in cities and towns throughout the nation. In Fortaleza, for example, libertos Francisco José do Nascimento and José Napoleão led protests by port workers, which culminated in halting the export of slaves to destinations in the south. In Salvador, the African liberto Emygdio stole slave registration lists from postal sacks so that their masters could not legalize their ownership. The most dynamic members of the Abolitionist Confederation in Rio de Janeiro came from two brotherhoods, the Freedmen's Club and the José do Patrocínio Liberty Fund, composed of libertos and free blacks. These groups raised money to purchase freedom for slaves and gave legal, educational, and financial support to freedpersons. In the province of São Paulo, blacks and mulattoes helped abolitionist Antônio Bento de Souza e Castro transport escaped slaves to safe havens.

After 1880, Afro-Brazilian activists generated abundant protest and propaganda literature, forcing the slavery issue into political debate at all levels. Like their U.S. counterparts, black and mulatto abolitionists developed strategies and tactics distinct from those of white abolitionists. Their initiatives often reinforced growing discontent with the imperial government among military officers, businesspeople, professionals, urban workers, and the poor. Afro-Brazilian leaders hammered at the idea that the time had come to challenge recalcitrant planters and merchants who were motivated solely by profits.

♦ THE POLITICAL ECONOMY AND EMANCIPATION

While the governments of Europe and the United States played less active roles in the late emancipation struggle after 1870, foreign writers and intellectuals conveyed the message that slavery was not acceptable to the civilized world. Although international businesspeople considered free labor more efficient for developing Brazil's resources, Brazil's economy prospered from money earned from plantation commodities like sugar, coffee, cacao, and cotton, all of which relied on African slave labor. Foreign influences canceled one another, condemning slavery on philosophical grounds and yet encouraging it by buying tropical goods.

With such conflicting advice, most slaveholders decided to retain their slaves as long as they could be worked profitably. Therefore, abolitionists decided to force the issue by combining their actions with resistance by slaves. This approach produced violent confrontations that made it impossible for masters to operate with slave labor.

Agricultural expansion in the late nineteenth century strengthened the planters' resolve to hold on to slavery. The sugar industry, for example, modernized production by building *usinas* (large mechanized mills) that could compete with Cuban *centrales* and with beet sugar in international markets. Coffee production spread to new frontier regions in São Paulo, Minas Gerais, Rio de Janeiro, Espírito Santo, and Bahia. Tobacco and cacao output also increased in the 1880s. These crops had a long history of slave-based production in Brazil, and planters did little to find new sources of labor.

Planters, merchants, and landowners who owned slaves defended their profits from the institution until its final days. In Paraíba, for example, cattle ranchers employed hundreds of slaves on their estates and thwarted efforts by abolitionists to end the interprovincial slave trade. In Pernambuco, in spite of sharp decreases in the slave population, the urban and rural elites called abolitionists dangerous subversives. Planters in Bahia, Espírito Santo, Rio de Janeiro, and São Paulo proved just as obstinate. They and urban merchants alike continued to regard capitalism and slavery as fully compatible.

European ideology did not always oppose slavery. For example, the British St. John d'el Rey Mining Company near Belo Horizonte continued to employ slaves in the 1870s, despite an 1845 prohibition against Britons owning slaves. Over 60 percent of the labor force in the largest mine was composed of male and female slaves. Local labor shortages, together with the profitability of their operations, prompted the directors to retain their slaves. When the situation became untenable in the early 1880s, the company converted to free labor to assure a steady supply of workers.

The Sexagenarian Law, passed by Parliament in 1885, revealed growing polarization over the slavery issue. As with the Law of Free Birth, planters hoped that token reforms would deflect the rising tide of abolitionism and slave resistance. The central provision of the law granted freedom to slaves at age sixty, with the stipulation that they remain under the tutelage of their masters for three years or until age sixty-five. The law overestimated the worth of slaves in order to enhance the value of the planters' investments. Planters who freed slaves under the age of sixty retained the right to their labor for five years. The law also established fines for persons who helped slaves to flee or provided shelter to fugitives. Like its 1871 predecessor, the Law of Free Birth, the Sexagenarian Law contained complex wording that made it impossible to carry out the provisions fully. Meanwhile, a temporary lull in abolitionist activities led planters to believe that they had escaped the threat of emancipation.

Radical actions by abolitionists and slaves soon rendered the 1885 law irrelevant. Lawyers and judges challenged the rights of slave owners. Antônio Bento helped hundreds of slaves to escape by train and foot to protected enclaves such as the huge quilombo in the port of Santos. João Clapp and his supporters in Rio harbored fugitives or transported them to safety outside the province. In Bahia, abolitionists Eduardo Carigé and Luís Anselmo da Fonseca visited plantations at night to inform slaves of locations where they could receive help. Such actions led Bahian planters in late 1887 to vilify those "pseudo-abolitionists who only wish to agitate and destroy." The fact that abolitionists could travel in the countryside distinguished the final years of slavery in Brazil from conditions elsewhere in the Americas.

Despite the growing boldness of abolitionists and the support they found in the legal system, slavery remained an integral part of Brazilian society in the 1880s. At the time of the Sexagenarian Law, for example, slaves still accounted for 10 percent of the total population: 1,240,906 out of 12 million. Slavery was still profitable in the plantation sector, particularly in expanding frontiers. Seen in this setting, the imperial emancipation decree of May 1888 was a belated response to social pressure and instability that would not go away. Afro-Brazilian intellectuals and thousands of enslaved blacks and mulattoes stood at the forefront of this movement.

The end of slavery came quickly once the imperial family decided to abolish it. In 1888, when the emperor traveled to Paris to treat his diabetes, the Princess Regent Isabel, convinced that the problem had grown too dangerous to postpone, decreed the end of slavery with a simple statement on 13 May:

Art. 1. From this date slavery is declared extinct in Brazil.

Art. 2. All provisions to the contrary are revoked. She orders, therefore, all the authorities to whom the knowledge and execution of the Law belong to carry it out, and cause it to be fully and exactly executed and observed.

The decree has become known as the *Lei Aurea,* or Golden Law.

Unfortunately, the imperial government failed to establish institutions or policies that might have helped the 1.2 million slaves freed after 1885, and so it was that distribution of land, an idea that André Rebouças had considered so important, never took place. Nor did the imperial or provincial governments fund training programs that might have taught former slaves skills to compete better in urban areas. On all fronts, political, economic, and social, black and mulatto men and women faced tenuous circumstances.

◆ THE AFTERMATH OF SLAVERY

In 1888 freedpersons and abolitionists celebrated emancipation in public plazas, churches, and private ceremonies throughout the land. The Golden Law, the result of over two decades of organized resistance, meant that owners could no longer use government agencies and the courts to control the labor of other human beings. Although the decree did not guarantee political rights and citizenship to freedpersons, similar to those afforded to white Brazilians, it did ensure that Afro-Brazilians had legal rights to defend against infringements of their civil liberties.

As in other postemancipation societies, a tug of war ensued between the white elite and the recently freed in which the new freedpersons fought for independence in all aspects of their lives. Moreover, in the months following abolition former slaveholders made seventy-nine appeals to Parliament seeking indemnification for their slaves. Their failure suggests that abolitionists had succeeded in completely discrediting their position.

In November 1890, after the emperor had been deposed, Minister of the Treasury Ruy Barbosa ordered the destruction of federal documents pertaining to slavery. Exactly three years after emancipation, officials carried out the decree, and two years after that, government officials and former abolitionists in Salvador watched as thousands of documents burned. A police band played in the background. Concerned officials wished not only to avoid payments to former slave owners, but also to erase the very memory of slavery from the national psyche.

Although the planters and merchants lost their struggle to maintain slavery or receive indemnification, their fears of a breakdown of the traditional social order proved unfounded. With the military coup of November 1889, new alliances emerged between regional landed interests and the central government, and most abolitionists disappeared from the scene. José do Patrocínio's hope of restoring the empire by deploying *capoeira* groups—the so-called black guards who practiced an Afro-Brazilian martial art—in the streets failed. In the 1890s, repression of black organizations, marginalization of Afro-Brazilians in the cities and countryside, and grinding poverty turned blacks into an underclass.

Former slaves understood that with abolition they could now negotiate labor contracts with landowners and employers, and they were accordingly determined to defend their personal and family interests to the best of their abilities. In reaction, rural farmers and urban factory owners sought to limit the ability of blacks and mulattoes to organize. In São Paulo, for example, the farmers and owners sponsored the immigration of Europeans. Moreover, when labor conflicts arose in the 1890s, government officials always took the side of the employers. As one scholar wrote, emancipation meant that the great mass of black men and women had made the short transition from slaves to proletarians.

As in the U.S. South, Afro-Brazilians placed a high priority on formal education once they could move about freely. Night schools that often included parents and their children in the same classroom sprang up in the 1890s. The fact that libertos and free blacks could congregate at night to learn to read and write without fear of being attacked clearly distinguished postemancipation social life from earlier times. In addition, brotherhoods provided their members with educational opportunities and cultural events where they could meet and socialize, and in the countryside, black women tried to give their children rules and values by which to live as respectable adults.

The abolitionist Eduardo Carigé, in a letter to the president of the province of Bahia, described the fears and aspirations of two Afro-Brazilian women.

Victória, a Creole, mother of 12-year-old Victorina, 6-year-old Eutrópio, and 10-year-old Porcina, in wishing to give an education to her children, claims that her former master Marcos Leão Velloso, owner of the sugar mill Coité in the region of Inhambupé, refuses to give up these children, preferring to have them work in the sugarcane as if they were slaves and subject to punishments. . . . The African Felicidade of the nation Nagô also requests that her grandchildren be freed from the control of the same owner. . . . Since this fact is an attack upon the natural right of liberty ensured by the act of the 13th of May that ended slavery in the Empire, the supplicants request the help of Your Excellency, certain that he will help, if only because they wish to educate their children to the benefit of the nation.

The decade following emancipation in Brazil witnessed a widespread resurgence of Afro-Brazilian culture. Houses of *candomblé*, a Bahian version of an African religious practice, flourished. Often held at night in remote locations, candomblé sessions afforded poor blacks and mulattoes places to gather, share mutual concerns, and forge communal bonds. The world-famous *Carnaval* festivity became an annual event in the 1890s, when blacks would join the street parades of Salvador and Rio. Observers from the period noted that clubs composed of Africans and their descendants put on lavish displays with costumes and floats to celebrate their heritage.

Most of these expressions of Afro-Brazilian culture met with open or subtle forms of repression by the elite and fledgling middle class. Their responses ranged from police invasions of candomblé meetings to newspaper articles portraying Carnival as an uncivilized practice that refined persons should avoid. It was not until the 1930s that Brazilian officialdom adopted a more permissive attitude toward black people and their culture.

♦ CONCLUSION

Four million Africans literally built Brazil out of the plains, mountains, and jungles. Their very success profited their masters and postponed their liberation until scarcely a century ago. By the time emancipation came in 1888, hundreds of thousands of Brazilians of African descent had already won their freedom and made up a large underclass of persons of mixed race. Because the system of slavery was so entrenched in the economy and society, it took generations to tear it down. Without an elite faction willing to go to war (as in St. Domingue) or to risk separation (as in Great Britain) over the issue, slavery dragged on until the late years of the nineteenth century. Equally tragic was the lack of interest of all Brazilians in the fate of the recently freed people. No program, no law, no appropriation was created to ease the transition to freedom. Instead, the government burned its records trying to forget the terrible legacy of slavery. Ironically, that very act of suppression may have created racial problems that were more difficult to solve than elsewhere in the Americas.

PART IV

Africans in the Americas since Abolition

T he legal prohibition of chattel slavery in the Americas marked the culmination of generations of agitation, producing emancipation according to the principles and rules of law, but not necessarily according to the practical realities that determined everyday life. The prohibitions commonly called abolition were not themselves effective emancipation, nor was emancipation itself equality. The transition from slavery to full citizenship with equal opportunity for self-determination, self-development, and equal protection under the law continued long after Brazil became the last state in the Americas to outlaw slavery and involuntary servitude.

Abolition changed the countenance of the Americas by producing notable population movements, as African Americans, determined to improve their life circumstances and conditions, entered both local and long-distance migrations. The so-called Great Migration of Afro-Americans in the United States from 1910 to 1940 redistributed millions of blacks from the U.S. South to the North. Similarly, in Brazil millions of Afro-Brazilians massed into the cities from the countryside. Throughout the Caribbean, interisland migration and migration to the United States transformed the atmosphere and attitudes. The diaspora continued.

The various migrations reflected the African Americans' efforts to transform the traditional race-dominated regimes of the Americas. For example, they shunned the old plantation order. Refusing the travail of slave ways,

they sought independence on the lands, wanting to work for themselves. But their efforts were variously rewarded and thwarted.

Most African Americans found few openings to acquire their own lands, but where they did they seized the chance. In the West Indies, for example, a black peasantry developed. Haiti perhaps exemplified the pattern of smallholdings. Haitians laid claim to one- or two-acre plots, enough to eke out garden produce for sustenance but too little to carry on commercial farming with any prospects for cash. In Cuba, where most former slaves remained in rural areas, some Afro-Cubans settled newly opened plots in the mountainous areas of the east that would serve as a haven in the 1950s to the insurgent Fidel Castro. In the U.S. South, about one in eight of the Afro-American families in 1910 worked their own land.

Economic restrictions gripped most African Americans. The rural settings in which most remained offered limited opportunity at the hands of the old plantation elites. Yet, moving to the cities did not always offer better answers to old questions. In Brazil, for example, labor market forces used new European immigrants to squeeze Afro-Brazilians into menial, poor-paying jobs in the major urban areas of Rio de Janeiro and São Paulo. In the United States, the move from the rural South to northern cities sharpened segregation in a sense—if not in the de jure means of the South, then in the de facto measures of the North. Until 1945, urban race riots littered the U.S. landscape north and south, from Brownsville, Texas, and Atlanta, to East St. Louis and Chicago, to Detroit and Harlem.

The increased urban residence of African Americans reflected a shift in economic and social organization in the Americas. The basis of the change was the wage relationship and the new industrial order. Both the effects and pace of change accelerated as African Americans joined in building the infrastructure of modern industrial economies throughout the Americas. They built railroads in the U.S. South and throughout Central and South America, with their most massive handiwork being the Panama Canal, which used West Indian laborers.

Throughout the Americas, although industrialization offered African Americans new occupational and entrepreneurial opportunities, the impact was hardly even. Conspicuous divergence continued to separate African Americans from whites. For example, the pace of U.S. industrialization provided Afro-Americans job opportunities that were unmatched elsewhere. Yet suffering, like success, did not spread itself evenly, as the effects of the Great Depression of the 1930s demonstrated. Black unemployment levels soared past whites'.

Uneven progress distanced some African Americans not only from their brothers and sisters throughout the Americas but also within particular nations. Marcus M. Garvey emphasized this point in his United Negro Improvement Association (UNIA), as did other organizations that announced the aim of uplifting the black masses rather than catering to colored elites.

In pressing for broad-based development, labor unions and then labor parties proved significant, as illustrated by A. Philip Randolph's Brotherhood of Sleeping Car Porters and Maids in the United States, by T. B. U. Butler's Oil Field Workers Trade Union in Trinidad, and by the Jamaica Labor party or Guiana's Manpower and Citizens' Association. From the first, African American labor was a determining factor in the Americas, and its muscle in the union movement and in the political process showed its continuing importance.

The U.S. civil rights movement of the 1950s and 1960s represented one powerful version of the African American's continuing effort to achieve economic and social equality. The independence in the British Caribbean illustrated another, and perhaps Fidel Castro's regime in Cuba was yet another version, for he relied on vital support from Afro-Cubans as he denounced their continued oppression. Castro's success in gaining power reflected the demise of one more Latin American elite that had relegated African Americans and Native Americans to the socioeconomic scrap heap.

While Afro-Americans were pressing their claims as U.S. citizens, African Americans from Argentina to Mexico were struggling against perhaps even more invidious currents. "Whitening campaigns" instituted in Central and South America sought to diminish the black presence, if not eliminate it, by favoring white immigration and suppressing black culture. In Argentina, for instance, blacks were all but whited out by waves of European immigrants from 1880 to 1914. The African American presence in politics proved sparse throughout Latin America, but the significant variations have reflected the historical development of African American communities such as the Afro-mestizos of Mexico's coast around Veracruz in the east and the Pacific Costa Chica in the west.

The national and regional variegation among African Americans demonstrates the profound influence of historical developments. Yet it has also formed a connection among African Americans, regardless of where they live, and it has created continuing ties between them and ancestral Africa. Pan-Africanism has sought to build on the connections and ties to reunite the elements of the black diaspora as a forceful voice in the contemporary world. Primarily cultural and political, the influence of Pan-African thinking is in evidence throughout the Americas.

Chapter 12

AFRICAN AMERICANS IN POSTEMANCIPATION ECONOMIES

1886	Slavery ends in Cuba.
1888	Slavery ends in Brazil.
1898	United States acquires Puerto Rico and occupies Cuba until 1901 as a result of the Spanish American War.
1904–1914	Construction of the Panama Canal.
1914–1918	World War I.
1917	British end importation of indentured Indian laborers to the West Indies.
1929	Collapse of the New York Stock Exchange begins Great Depression.
1934–1941	President Franklin D. Roosevelt's New Deal.
1937–1938	Labor riots in the West Indies.
1939–1945	World War II.
1954	U.S. Supreme Court *Brown* v. *Board of Education* decision.
1960s–1970s	Caribbean independence movements.
1964	U.S. Civil Rights Act.
1965	U.S. Voting Rights Act.

Between the 1880s and the 1970s, persons of African descent throughout the Americas moved from agricultural labor into a diverse array of urban-industrial occupations and professions. The transformation did not occur evenly; it resulted in part from larger developments in the world economy, from wars, and from the individual actions of persons ranging from government officials to plantation and factory owners and to black leaders in different countries of the Americas. Most of all, however, it reflected the efforts of black laborers to escape poverty, dependence, and degradation and to gain the benefits made possible by the Industrial Revolution.

At the end of slavery, not all people of African descent in the Americas occupied the same status. In fact, even during the days of slavery certain distinctions among black workers were present, the most significant of these differences being the array of occupational and social privileges held by the free black population. Free blacks often practiced skilled trades or professions and operated businesses, at times under the direct patronage of their European relatives. In the period after slavery, these old-line free persons were often able to advance their professional and entrepreneurial status, even as most emancipated slaves struggled to escape the confines of plantation labor.

Changes in the industrial economies of the United States and western Europe during the twentieth century transformed the employment patterns that had developed under slavery. For example, in the United States, beginning with World War I, when the immigration of European workers slowed to a trickle, industrial employers in the North tapped the reserve labor power on southern plantations. The ensuing Great Migration represented only the first wave of such movements of black workers from the south to the north. After a lull during the Great Depression of the 1930s, a second wave accompanied the start of World War II and persisted through the 1960s.

Migrants to the urban North did not merely broaden their employment prospects, they also gained access to material goods, social amenities, educational opportunities, and political rights that were unavailable to them in the South. Although occupational and other kinds of discrimination persisted in the North, a wide gulf separated the overall circumstances of factory workers from those of plantation workers. On the job, black workers were exposed to (and at times affiliated with) trade unions and other specifically working-class organizations. Off the job, a wide variety of nationalist and internationalist movements and parties, ranging from Garveyism and Pan-Africanism to socialism and communism, supplemented the traditional range of church and benevolent organizations that had been the mainstays of rural southern life. In short, black workers and entrepreneurs in the cities could think and do what would have been inconceivable on the plantations.

A family of Southern blacks arriving in Chicago around World War I as part of the Great Migration. Stock Montage.

The emergence of the United States as an economic powerhouse early in the twentieth century affected black workers elsewhere in the hemisphere. Construction of the Panama Canal, for instance, stimulated labor migration from the Caribbean, and such immigration became an increasingly characteristic feature of twentieth-century life in the region. Indeed, migrants from the British West Indies moved to Cuba, to the United States, to Canada, and to England as economic opportunities presented themselves (and as state-imposed restrictions on such migration permitted). This migration increased dramatically following World War II, as did the movement of Afro-Caribbeans from the Spanish islands to the United States and from the French and Dutch islands to their respective European metropoles. At the same time, the growth of new industries and new plantation products throughout Latin America often profoundly affected employment patterns among those persons of African descent who did not migrate.

Black workers in the Caribbean, Central America, and South America responded to many of the same forces that affected black workers in the United States, though often at different times and with different results. By the mid-1960s, however, it was clear throughout the Americas that the old plantation order had been transformed and that black workers had entered industrial employment on a large scale. Much of this change resulted from the international challenge of industrial capitalism to labor-intensive plantation economies. But even more important was the determination of black workers to benefit from the economic, political, and social amenities that industrial-capitalist societies offered.

◆ THE PRE–WORLD WAR I PERIOD

In the 1890s the plantation regime defined the work experience of most persons of African descent throughout the Americas. In every plantation region, the postemancipation struggle between former masters and former slaves had produced a variety of economic groups, including independent landowners, quasi-independent peasant producers and tenants, and dependent sharecroppers and wage laborers. Nonetheless, the plantation as an institution continued to provide the essential context of life as well as labor.

The rise of imperialism presaged drastic changes in this pattern, as the industrialized nations of Europe along with the United States searched the globe for investment markets and sources of raw materials. These new ventures often required mobilizing laborers in new ways, the effects of which would become increasingly apparent as the twentieth century advanced. At the dawn of the century, however, the new patterns developed alongside the old. Railroad contractors and mining and lumbering concessionaires, for example, often took advantage of slack agricultural seasons to obtain laborers. Over time, workers who strung together successions of nonagricultural employment found it possible to break cleanly from the plantation. Still others managed to escape plantation labor by operating small businesses.

In the southern United States, most of the region's 6 million Afro-Americans worked in commercial agriculture, growing cotton, tobacco, sugar, and grains. Although approximately two hundred and eighteen thousand families (representing perhaps one million persons) worked their own land in 1910, most southern black workers were tenants, sharecroppers, and wage laborers who were frequently debt-ridden and who owned little but their clothing and household effects. Despite the fact that the South did not industrialize as the North did during this period, cities were growing throughout the region and extractive industries outside the plantation belt provided opportunities to earn cash wages. By 1900 certain patterns of local and long-distance migration—not necessarily seasonal—

had emerged over much of the South, which suggested the erosion of the planters' monolithic power over the black labor force.

The Caribbean islands demonstrated several other variants of plantation economies. In Barbados and Antigua, for example, the European planters' control over the limited amount of cultivable land gave persons of African descent little choice except plantation labor. Most resided in plantation quarters (with occupancy conditional on labor), supplementing their meager earnings with produce from garden patches. In Jamaica and the larger islands (and British Guiana, too), emancipation enabled black workers to escape the planters' control. For years the planters attempted to rein in the former slaves through such means as vagrancy laws and taxes or, failing that, to replace them with laborers from India. The former slaves effectively resisted these pressures. Denied wage employment, former slaves and their descendants abandoned the plantations and settled on vacant land, where they raised subsistence goods and some marketable surplus. Accordingly, a black peasantry arose on most West Indian islands. In Haiti, where the former slaves had dismantled the plantation system and subdivided the land into one- and two-acre smallholdings, the peasantry was the most numerous as well as the most isolated from larger economic trends in the Caribbean region.

African Americans in Spanish- and Portuguese-speaking regions fared differently, in part because slavery did not end in Cuba and Brazil until the 1880s. In Cuba, most former slaves remained in rural areas, either as wage laborers on the sugar plantations or as settlers on newly occupied lands in the mountainous eastern end of the island. In Brazil, however, the deterioration of slavery gave rise to patterns that persisted well into the postemancipation period. In the sugar plantation region of the northeast, Afro-Brazilians continued to play their customary role as tenants and wage laborers on plantations. In the newer coffee region of the southeast and the urban centers of Rio de Janeiro and São Paulo, the planters' and industrialists' preference for European immigrants squeezed Afro-Brazilians into the most menial and low-paying levels of rural and urban employment. In areas where the black population was traditionally small (in southern South America, for instance), state-sponsored immigration of Europeans and Asians further marginalized persons of African descent. Indeed, in Argentina they virtually disappeared as a distinct group.

In the United States, black communities diversified in response to these larger developments. Entrepreneurs, both male and female, found markets for their goods and services among neighbors and friends and within larger economic networks. Towns and cities provided a supportive atmosphere for the emergence of small but influential groups of professionals, particularly ministers, physicians, teachers, and at times government functionaries. In southern cities, such as Charleston, this elite may have constituted as much as 15 percent of the black working population by 1890. In contrast, in northern cities, such as Philadelphia, its proportion did not exceed 5 percent. Members of this elite occupied precarious positions in their communities. Although some may have functioned autonomously within the larger society, most suffered discrimination of one kind or another that placed them on a par with the masses of black laborers. Discrimination notwithstanding, the elites held themselves aloof, especially when they were distinguishable by light skin, wealth, and education. They tended to socialize and marry among themselves; they educated their children at Howard or Atlanta University or at elite northern institutions; and they formed such self-help organizations as the National Negro Business League and the National Association for the Advancement of Colored People (NAACP).

At the dawn of the twentieth century, U.S. imperialism profoundly affected persons of African descent throughout the Americas. Unlike Europe, which was scrambling for lands in Africa, Asia, and the Pacific during this period, the United States largely avoided acquiring new territories. To be sure, the United States seized Cuba and Puerto Rico after the Spanish American War, repeatedly occupied sovereign states under Theodore Roosevelt's corollary to the Monroe Doctrine, and effectively asserted that the Caribbean was an American lake. Business followed the flag to Central America and the Spanish-speaking Caribbean, constructing railroads and investing in the traditional plantation economies. European capital flowed unevenly into the region—with the British interested in railroads, lumber, and mining, and the French, the Dutch, and the Germans in sugar mill machinery—with correspondingly uneven effects on the established employment structure.

North American and European capital investment in the sugar industry illustrates these trends. New central factories (*centrales* in Spanish) employed advanced engineering techniques to convert cane juice into sugar, and many planters substituted machines for workers in the fields as well. Sugar-growing regions from Louisiana to Argentina witnessed such changes. Mechanization had two broad effects: seasonal labor and unemployment. In Louisiana and Cuba (and to a lesser extent Puerto Rico and Martinique), it created reliance on seasonal wage workers, giving rise to migrations at harvest time into the sugar regions by men unaccompanied by their families. In most of the British West Indies, however, where such change occurred more slowly, resident plantation workers experienced underemployment and unemployment. Even when planters did not attempt to economize by introducing machines, they reduced costs by consolidating operations and rationalizing production. For example, the number of sugar estates in British Guiana declined from about four hundred in the late 1830s to forty-six in 1904, at which time the four largest plantations controlled 60 percent of the industry. Consolidation meant loss of jobs, and black workers had no other choice but to seek alternative employment.

Both governments and private businesses invested heavily in infrastructure, particularly railroads and shipping facilities. Black workers often found employment on these projects. Throughout the southern United States, for example, railroad contractors employed black laborers to clear land, lay track, build bridges, and mine tunnels. In some instances, the laborers were recruited locally—they included convicts as well as seasonally employed agricultural laborers—but in Arkansas, Louisiana, and Texas, gangs of railroad workers developed migrant-labor patterns that took them from one construction site to another, with periodic stints at logging camps and lumber mills in between. The opening of railroads in Central and South America produced similar results. From the Guianas to Honduras, black workers built the railroads and then extracted the timber, gold, and other resources from the interior.

The most massive of these projects was the Panama Canal. As early as 1904, some forty-four thousand workers from the West Indies (primarily Barbados and Jamaica) were at work on the canal, and by the time the project was completed in 1914 several times that number had migrated to the Isthmus for a tour of work, which usually lasted about a year and a half. Over time, a West Indian community took root in Panama; by 1914 it numbered perhaps fifty thousand persons. Its core consisted of those who set up small businesses to serve the needs of migrant workers in the Canal Zone.

European and American investors also underwrote assorted projects aimed at extracting natural resources in the region. Prior to World War I, the major products were timber and minerals. But the dawn of the age of automobiles and electricity brought U.S. and European oil interests into the Caribbean Basin, especially to Trinidad, Aruba, and Curaçao, and aluminum producers into Jamaica and Guiana. Despite its initially small scale, employment in oil and mining signaled the growth of an industrial wage-labor force that was unattached to plantation agriculture. Miners, oil workers, roustabouts, seafarers, dockworkers, and day laborers, as well as the small-scale entrepreneurs who served them, would in time transform the political landscape of the entire region.

In some places, like the northern United States and southern Brazil, industrial employers favored European immigrant workers over those of African descent, even though most of the Europeans hailed from rural backgrounds and differed culturally from the rest of the population. In the United States, the growth of industries in the cities of the Northeast and Midwest, and the steady increase of North–South rail traffic began to lure Afro-Americans northward. By 1900 large black communities existed in Boston, New York, Philadelphia, Pittsburgh, Buffalo, Cleveland, Detroit,

Chicago, and Milwaukee, not to mention the border state cities of Baltimore, Louisville, and St. Louis. Most black workers in the North were laborers and servants, but small numbers of entrepreneurs and professionals also appeared, representing at most 15 percent of the population. Although real, discrimination in the North took a less blatant form than the Jim Crow practices springing up across the South. Hence, when the outbreak of World War I created job opportunities in northern industries, Afro-Americans had social and political as well as economic reasons to leave the South en masse.

◆ World War I and the Great Depression

Between 1914 and 1939, the various black laboring classes in the Americas continued to diverge, owing largely to the uneven pace of industrialization, the varying effects of World War I and the Great Depression, and the differing responses of the respective nations to the war. In North America, where the industrialization of the black labor force proceeded the farthest, war production increased the need for workers at precisely the time that conscription was thinning their ranks and the war in the North Atlantic was curtailing immigration from Europe. Black workers in the South saw an opportunity to escape the economic ravages of the boll weevil and the social and political disabilities of segregation and disenfranchisement. Black migrants to the northern cities, where southern-style Jim Crow legislation did not apply, entered a new relationship with government structures at the local, state, and federal levels. Following the war, as the United States assumed world economic leadership, black workers continued to benefit from industrial employment. When the depression began late in 1929, black workers, like their counterparts of other colors and nationalities, turned to the state for assistance.

The West Indies witnessed a similar, though less dramatic, process of industrialization and urban migration, especially in and around the port cities. In 1917 British authorities interdicted the importation of contract laborers from India, thereby at least theoretically creating the possibility of more jobs for workers of African ancestry. But the plantation sector, where most of the contract laborers were employed, stagnated after World War I. Displaced rural workers moved to the cities, found what employment they could, and began fashioning a movement that soon spread in a number of directions. In large measure it was a labor movement, but in its struggle to exact concessions from employers and the colonial state, it had political ramifications.

For Brazil, the other region that experienced industrial development between the two world wars, the specific effects of industrialization on black workers cannot be easily assessed. Industrial and agricultural output increased and commerce expanded, largely thanks to coffee exports. As in earlier periods, however, such developments did not necessarily work to the benefit of black laborers, who for the most part remained a marginalized agricultural work force, despite the fact that the black population in the cities was growing. Like their counterparts throughout the Caribbean, black city dwellers in Brazil worked in assorted trades and performed unskilled labor and domestic service. With but few exceptions, factory employment remained the preserve of European immigrants.

Apart from such differences from one region to another, differentiation proceeded within regions as well. In the United States, for instance, several million Afro-Americans migrated to the urban North between 1910 and 1940, and those who remained behind tended to resettle in cities rather than in rural areas. Occupations varied between South and North and between rural and urban areas; so, too, did educational attainments and entrepreneurial opportunities. As persons of African descent moved in new directions, they often came into contact with other ethnic groups with whom they had had little, if any, prior experience. In the Harlem of the 1920s, for example, a former sharecropper from the South might rub shoulders with a West Indian poet. Similar differentiation occurred in Caribbean and Latin American areas, though on a less dramatic scale.

Although in some respects this differentiation signaled strength, in others it represented weakness. In the United States, for example, established black communities did not always welcome the new migrants with open arms. At times, fear of competition for scarce jobs or social services fueled this tension. However, much of it followed cultural lines, with groups that had become acculturated to urban life looking askance at the crude ways of the newcomers. Government officials as well as employers could exploit these tensions. Larger social and cultural differences among different groups of workers enabled employers to play one group against another, as steel manufacturers, for example, did with Anglo-American, northern European, eastern European, and Afro-American workers. Such a strategy of capitalizing on ethnic divisions within the work force closely resembled the preferred strategy among employers in such multiethnic plantation regions as Peru, Cuba, and the British West Indies.

In the United States, World War I dramatically altered the status of black workers. The most significant impact of the war was to close off European immigration that northern industrialists had come to rely on so heavily. To fill the need for laborers, they soon turned to the untapped black labor-power resources of the South. Even before the United States declared war in 1917, recruiters representing such concerns as United States Steel in Gary, Indiana, the Westinghouse Electric Company in Pittsburgh, and the Ford Motor Company in Detroit had begun canvassing the South, offering jobs and often transportation to prospective migrants to the North. After circumventing such barriers as astronomical state and local licensing fees, recruiters tapped into existing networks within black communities, for instance, by making contact with a man who had a network of relatives, friends, or workmates interested in migrating. Typically, recruiters established ties with ministers and owners of small businesses who could place them in contact with large numbers of prospective migrants.

Once set in motion, the migration took on a life of its own, as workers who had already migrated sent money and information home. Workers returned home to assist the move northward of family members, neighbors, or friends. In black communities throughout the South, prospective migrants formed clubs to exchange information and to save money for the trip. In some cases, communities of relatives or neighbors reconstituted themselves hundreds of miles from their original homes. Church congregations re-formed, as did benevolent societies and social organizations of every description. Entrepreneurs often followed their customers north.

Not all migrants were prepared for the challenges that faced them on the job, no matter how carefully they had planned their move. Job experiences such as foundry work for men and domestic service for women were transferable to the North, but agricultural work provided few skills relevant to industrial employment. Work in steel mills and slaughterhouses had little in common with farming. Farm workers followed patterns governed by the sun and the seasons, whereas factory workers had to keep pace with machines and punch a time clock. Moreover, factory work entailed artificial lighting, foul air, and noise. Some workers found the new settings exciting, but most longed for the sights, sounds, and smells of the outdoors, if not necessarily for southern sharecropping.

In some respects, the new circumstances replicated the old, and in most cases, men and women had to find remunerative employment to support their families. Informal patterns of segregation consigned black workers to crowded tenements, many of which lacked proper sanitary facilities. Public services for blacks such as schools, water and sewer facilities, and garbage removal left much to be desired. On the job, similar patterns of discrimination prevailed. The consignment of black workers to the lowest paying, dirtiest, and often the most dangerous jobs seemed to replicate patterns typical of the South. Moreover, the gap between take-home pay and the cost of living necessitated that both parents support their families. But the northern setting also marked a clean break with the South in a number of ways. Workplaces and neighborhoods displayed an ethnic diversity for which there were few counterparts in the South. By the same token, few northern institutions could replicate the aura of the plantation.

If conditions in the factories called for amelioration, the factory setting provided fertile ground for labor organizations. But black workers viewed unions skeptically at best. With only few exceptions, southern unions systematically discriminated against black workers, either excluding them from membership outright or relegating them to separate locals. In the

North, industrial employers had a long history of employing black substitute workers to break strikes conducted by white workers, thus exacerbating racial and ethnic tensions among workers. As a result, black workers in meatpacking plants, steel mills, automobile assembly plants, and the other mass industries often kept their distance from organizing campaigns. To reinforce these misgivings, employers such as Henry Ford deliberately cultivated an image of paternal concern for black workers. Ford went out of his way to establish contacts with black ministers and other community leaders, who in turn recruited potential workers for Ford's plants but also opposed an auto workers' union. Even in the absence of such calculated paternalism, many black workers steered clear of union organizers to protect their jobs. Yet despite all these influences, small numbers of black workers began seeing the unions as a source of collective strength whereby they could improve their working conditions. Hard economic times increased their numbers significantly.

For black workers in the Caribbean, World War I did not bring about such dramatic change. The pattern of uneven development in the sugar economies continued to create labor shortages in some islands and unemployment in others. The war did make seasonal interisland migration difficult. On islands such as Jamaica, where commercial agriculture remained viable and peasant agriculture stagnated even after the war, many peasants became agricultural wage workers, at least seasonally. Moreover, thousands also became laborers on docks or on road crews, petty merchants, and roadside vendors, in rural as well as urban areas. Still others found employment in the new industries (oil in Trinidad and bauxite in Jamaica) that began operations in the post–World War I era. Overall, however, because of the slow rate of industrialization in the Caribbean as a whole, the economies of the region were unable to absorb the expanding number of people who were looking for work off the plantations.

This structural crisis in the plantation economies of the Caribbean did not impede the process of professionalization within black communities. It was not simply that the number of physicians, writers, and civil servants increased, but their influence grew as well. Education assumed new importance, and the war brought into public debate such topics as imperialism and communism. Military service in France, as well as international intellectual movements, including Garveyism, Pan-Africanism, and the Harlem Renaissance, began sprouting seeds throughout the Caribbean. Whether as workers or entrepreneurs, persons of African descent began formulating demands for enhanced government services such as health and education and for fuller participation in political affairs.

During the 1920s, interisland migration advanced the transformation of the Caribbean region even further. Like their counterparts in North America, Caribbean migrants received information about job prospects from networks of families, neighbors, and friends. As the Pullman porters had done in the United States, Caribbean seafarers spread news about available jobs to dockside workers who passed it along. Whereas local authorities in the U.S. South tried to block northward migration, British officials in the Caribbean were only too happy to facilitate migration to relieve unemployment and to gain needed foreign exchange from wage remittances.

Between the two world wars, Cuba replaced Panama as the destination of migrant laborers in the Caribbean. Cuba's large agribusinesses—mainly sugar centrales—desperately needed workers and attracted as many as four hundred thousand Jamaicans and Haitians between 1913 and 1928. The United Fruit Company in the Dominican Republic and Central America and the United States Sugar Company in Florida also recruited migrant laborers from the islands. Thus did the postwar influx of U.S. capital into the Caribbean Basin continue to transform traditional labor patterns in the region.

When they returned with their earnings, these migrants often invested them in repairs to their cottages or in purchases of small lots of land. The movement of workers among the islands and to the shores of the mainland loosened the plantation's hold on their labor and their lives.

Permanent migration from the Caribbean to the United States (especially to New York City) persisted after World War I, although restrictive immigration laws passed during the 1920s slowed the movement. Up to that time, the total number of immigrants to the states was about one hundred and thirty-thousand persons. Though largely from urban areas rather than plantation districts in the Caribbean, these migrants were similar to their counterparts from the American South in their lack of industrial experience. Considerable numbers of West Indians in Harlem and Brooklyn became entrepreneurs, however, and as such they fared somewhat better than migrants from the South. During this period, some black Cubans, Dominicans, and Puerto Ricans also began migrating to Miami and New York City.

More than simply prompting population movements, World War I affected black workers throughout the Americas in other ways. For example, it drew several hundred thousand black men into military service, large numbers of whom saw combat in France. Besides representing a way to escape plantation employment, such service exposed the soldiers to a larger world and the exhilaration of having helped to liberate Europe. With such memories fresh in their minds, returning soldiers did not take kindly to resuming their inferior positions at home. Tensions in the United States reached fever pitch during the infamous "Red Summer" of 1919, when race riots embroiled over a dozen cities. Even in the absence of such violence, it was clear throughout the Americas that the fires of war had created "a New Negro."

The war also advanced the process of internal differentiation within black communities. In the United States, growing urban populations created demands for assorted services that were filled by black entrepreneurs, professionals, and politicians. Businesspeople, physicians, attorneys, and politicians, in turn, exerted pressure on public officials to respond to the needs of their communities. Moreover, they placed a high premium on higher education, which resulted in the flowering of Howard, Fisk, and Atlanta Universities and the matriculation of Afro-American students at leading universities throughout the nation. The Harlem Renaissance represented the flowering of postwar black intellectual life. Like the broader movement of Pan-Africanism, which also flourished after World War I, the renaissance celebrated the African heritage and provided a supportive context wherein black artists could express their creativity. Such cultural expressions as jazz and the blues furnished vehicles that allowed working-class Afro-Americans to participate in the new spirit of the age.

Political-cultural movements such as Marcus Garvey's Universal Negro Improvement Association (UNIA) similarly thrived among black workers in the cities. A complex movement that defies easy generalization, Garveyism promoted pride in the African heritage through a variety of subsidiary organizations, a newspaper (the *Negro World*), and a back-to-Africa movement. Much like his hero, Booker T. Washington, Garvey emphasized entrepreneurism. Shaky business ventures, particularly the Black Star Steamship Line by which he intended to establish commercial connections with Africa, opened Garvey to persecution from the government. U.S. agents convicted him of mail fraud in connection with stock subscriptions, and he was deported upon his release from prison in 1927. Although his movement faltered thereafter, it left a legacy of black pride on which later generations would draw liberally.

The sleeping car porters and maids, the men and women hired by George Pullman to work on the railroad sleeping cars that bore his name, also merit special mention. Their duties were deceptively straightforward, yet complex. Pullman charged them to fulfill every request of railroad passengers quickly and cheerfully, and in the process they had to endure the countless humiliations to which persons in service are generally exposed. Any sign of insubordination resulted in instant dismissal. The Pullman porters were a select group that often included college graduates, for whom the Pullman Company represented steady work and steady income despite its assorted disadvantages.

The Pullman porters distinguished themselves in other ways besides their exceptional backgrounds. Under the inspired leadership of A. Philip Randolph, they organized a union, the Brotherhood of Sleeping Car Porters and Maids, which became an important vehicle not only for their demands regarding wages and working conditions but also for issues affecting their families, their communities, and Afro-Americans generally. Typically, they carried news and information along the routes they

Marcus Garvey organized the United Negro Improvement Association, a successful black business, pressure group, and back-to-Africa movement during the late 1910s and 1920s. Brown Brothers.

traveled, and in this way they were able to disseminate copies of newspapers published by Afro-Americans throughout the nation. They also reported information on living and working conditions in the various locales with which they were familiar.

Other groups of Afro-American workers also took up the concerns of the Pullman porters. Following passage of New Deal labor legislation, large numbers of black workers entered the emerging industrial unions affiliated with the Congress of Industrial Organizations (CIO). Many joined Communist party–affiliated unions in the steel, rubber, tobacco, and electric industries, and some joined the party itself. As a reflection of their strength in the manufacturing sector, black workers played a critical role in pressuring the administration of Franklin D. Roosevelt to enact legislation guaranteeing certain rights to workers, particularly collective bargaining, a minimum wage, unemployment benefits, and governmental compensation during retirement (or social security). In return, most black voters changed their party allegiance from Republican to Democratic during the late 1930s.

Elsewhere in the Americas, the depression affected black workers differently. In Brazil, where continuing coffee exports helped finance internal industrial development, neither coffee growers nor industrialists made a point of hiring black workers. Black workers, however, abandoned declining agricultural areas for the cities and took whatever jobs they could find. Afro-Brazilians in cities such as Rio de Janeiro formed social and cultural organizations, some of which asserted black and mulatto consciousness, at times with clearly African inspiration.

In Latin America and the Spanish Caribbean, the depression had varying effects. Although the prices of plantation products had collapsed, the Cuban sugar centrales continued to provide employment for black as well as mestizo workers. However, urban unemployment increased, with direct repercussions for the black Cubans who had migrated to the cities over the previous two generations. Many workers allied themselves with radical syndicalist, socialist, and communist organizations with links to the Soviet Union or to the working classes of western Europe. This was especially the case in Cuba and the Central and South American regions, some of whose traditions of political radicalism dated from their wars of independence in the nineteenth century. Yet, as of 1939, neither in Brazil, Cuba, nor any other Latin American countries did black workers improve their condition as did those workers associated with the Pullman Company or with the CIO unions in North America.

Throughout the Americas, the depression altered traditional relationships between workers and officials of the state. Nowhere outside the United States did the government take such comprehensive action to ameliorate workers' grievances in the interest of avoiding social unrest. In much of Latin America, including Cuba and Haiti in the Caribbean, dictators manipulated state power to serve their selfish interests, often at the direct expense of their respective working classes. Black workers lost jobs, as a result of political manipulation as well as direct economic dislocation, and black entrepreneurs felt the effects as the purchasing power of their clienteles decreased. The prototypical dictator of this period, Getulio Vargas of Brazil, refused to countenance independent unionism. Neither did he initiate policies to relieve the suffering wrought by the depression. As a result, all Brazilian workers suffered, but, given their previous marginalization, black workers arguably endured more additional hardship than their white counterparts did.

In the English-speaking Caribbean, the depression created the preconditions for mass political mobilizations that increasingly challenged the legitimacy of colonial rule. The first step in this process was the crisis of plantation agriculture, which had prompted large-scale unemployment and migration to the port cities. There, continuing unemployment and low wages offered fertile ground for protest movements.

Colonial officials sought to appease insurgent workers with alternate appeals to platitudes and brute force rather than jobs. The shadow of Marcus Garvey loomed large. While the exiled leader's health deteriorated, his movement took on new strength, serving as a catalyst for black workers throughout the British Caribbean and Central America. The *Negro World* provided propaganda for the growing rebellion. Many of the leaders of the violent outbursts against European businesses in particular and British colonial rule in general were veterans of World War I and organizations associated with the UNIA. Rarely in the history of the postslavery period did solidarity between black workers and black petty entrepreneurs in the region bring about such a high level of governmental concern. States from the Canal Zone to the Windward Islands moved to coordinate action against the movement, banning the *Negro World* and other incendiary publications and suppressing workers' associations.

The depression gave rise to various social and welfare organizations among expatriate West Indians. Whether known as self-help organizations in the West Indies or ethnic organizations in New York City or London or cells of Garvey's UNIA throughout the Atlantic world, these associations built networks among Caribbean workers and entrepreneurs. Most of these groups combined internationalist and nationalist ideology and politics. In New York City, for example, the most radical elements affiliated with socialists and communists, hoping to bring attention to the international plight of West Indian workers. Yet, in the vein of Garvey's own infatuation with ethnic nationalism, these groups also envisioned nationalist solutions to the problem of colonialism, and they affiliated strongly with West Indian organizations in the city. George Padmore and Cyril Briggs, to name only two of the most prominent examples, were expelled from left-wing parties for supporting "Negro petty bourgeois nationalism." Because of their small numbers and their tendency to insulate themselves, West Indian workers and entrepreneurs retained a separate identity within the growing black population of New York City. A shared interest in Garveyism did not overcome the cultural and other differences between West Indians and southern migrants.

Between 1919 and 1929, production of bauxite and petroleum buoyed the regional economy of the Caribbean. This industrial expansion stimulated trade, which redounded to the direct benefit of both workers and entrepreneurs and made possible the development of industrial unions. The depression reversed these trends, creating widespread unemployment among the increasingly urbanized working class. Lacking access to the garden plots that had helped mitigate the effects of unemployment in the past, these workers turned increasingly to British authorities for relief. When officials failed to respond, workers began challenging the legitimacy of colonial rule itself.

The new activism that appeared in the 1930s surfaced first in the extractive industries but spread rapidly through the urban working class and beyond to plantation laborers. The 1937 Butler riots in Trinidad provide a good example of this phenomenon in the British West Indies. The riots took their name from T.B.U. Butler, an expatriate Grenadian who had formed an independent union to rival one sponsored by the managers of the U.S.-owned Leasehold Oil Company and sanctioned by British authorities. The company's failure to restore pay cuts precipitated the outbreaks. Between 1929 and 1936, the company had reduced the pay of workers by 30 percent; by the last year, the oil industry had recovered, but Leasehold's managers refused to return to the 1929 rates on the grounds that they were too high. When the government refused to respond to their demands, the workers took to the streets. Workers in the sugar industry were in an even worse position as wages decreased and unemployment surged. They quickly joined the ranks of the insurgents. The 1938 report of the Moyne Commission, established by the Colonial Office to identify the sources of unrest among West Indian workers, pointedly faulted the government's lack of a policy to combat the effects of the depression. As a result, the British Parliament passed the Welfare Development Act to promote economic recovery and thereby lessen the threat of worker agitation. Yet, popular rebellions of this type continued throughout the islands during the 1930s.

◆ From World War II to Civil Rights

World War II completed the transformation of plantation laborers throughout the Americas into urban industrial workers. In the United States, a threatened march on Washington in 1942 guaranteed black workers access to employment in war industries, which in turn prompted mass migration to the Northeast, Midwest, and Pacific coast. In the two decades following the war, a successful struggle for civil rights overturned the entrenched system of Jim Crow and established political equality among citizens. At the same time, the federal government declared a war on poverty, which to some extent was intended to reverse the damage caused by decades of systematic discrimination against Afro-Americans.

In the Caribbean, the war produced a similar transformation. Economically, the islands experienced the continuation of some older trends and the growth of entirely new ones. As earlier, bauxite extraction and petroleum production accounted for the region's heavy industry. Secondary industries such as local manufacturing alternately flowered and wilted in response to changes in local, regional, and international markets. Under the auspices of metropolitan capital, bananas replaced sugar as the major export of several islands, while most plantations became agribusinesses that increasingly relied on machines and chemicals to perform work previously done by humans. With so many displaced workers, the conditions of structural unemployment and political unrest that had characterized the 1930s were reproduced. Politically, the postwar period witnessed the formal end of colonial domination and the emergence of independent states.

In every instance, workers' organizations played a critical part in the independence process.

As had been the case earlier, black workers in Brazil struggled to adapt to changes over which they had little control in a political and social climate that did not acknowledge their special needs. Under Vargas, Brazilian industry and agriculture diversified, on the whole mitigating the ravages of the depression, though not necessarily the endemic marginalization of black workers in rural and urban areas. After World War II, these trends continued but with the additional phenomenon of new waves of displaced smallholders and agricultural laborers to the cities, where they faced poverty and crowding in *favelas,* or shanty towns.

In the United States, the outbreak of World War II accomplished what the New Deal had proved incapable of doing, namely, ending the depression. Only in late 1939, when England declared war on Germany and the United States became the "arsenal of democracy," did unemployment begin to decline. Spurred by orders for military goods, factories sought additional workers, relying first on their unemployed former employees. Lest employers discriminate against black workers in the rehiring process, A. Philip Randolph began organizing a march on Washington to force President Roosevelt to integrate the armed forces and prohibit discrimination in the defense industry. Although the president stopped short of abolishing Jim Crow in the services, he accommodated the demand for nondiscriminatory practices among defense contractors and established the Fair Employment Practice Committee to monitor compliance.

When the United States entered the war in December 1941, military production skyrocketed and with it the demand for additional defense workers. As manufacturers had discovered during World War I, black migrants from the South were fine workers. The war against Japan also spurred the growth of war industries on the West Coast, an unknown phenomenon in the earlier war, and so black workers migrated in unprecedented numbers to the centers of the shipping and aircraft industries: the metropolitan areas of San Diego–Los Angeles, San Francisco–Oakland, and Seattle and Portland. During the 1940s, an estimated 1.6 million Afro-Americans abandoned the South for other regions of the nation. Even within the South, however, the growth of defense industries along the South Atlantic and Gulf coasts attracted large numbers of black migrants from declining plantation regions.

The new migration both resembled and differed from the earlier one. As in the earlier period, black workers often had to settle for overcrowded and expensive housing and scanty public services. Now, however, employment opportunities tended to cluster in manufacturing and service, and large numbers of women gained access to manufacturing jobs due to the size of the military call-up. The migrants also encountered ethnic groups with whom they had had little previous contact—Chicanos and Asians, as well as Europeans—and at times social tension resulted. The rapidly changing demography and shifting balance of employment opportunity and political power in Detroit led to a riot there in 1942 that was every bit as bloody as the clashes during the Red Summer of 1919.

The war left a mixed legacy. When the hostilities ended, the shipping and aircraft industries entered a period of retrenchment, with other primary industries (such as automobile assembly) and secondary industries not always able to pick up the slack. Although the shipyards never recovered, other industries did, and the manufacturing economy of the northern and western United States remained vigorous through the 1960s. Hence, migration continued. In the 1950s a total of 1.5 million black persons left the South, and during the following decade an additional 1.4 million migrated.

In the Caribbean, different economic patterns emerged in the aftermath of World War II. Plantation agriculture underwent a major transformation, virtually collapsing in some areas, consolidating into highly capitalized agribusinesses in others, and experiencing a combination of collapse and consolidation elsewhere. Throughout the region, the proportion of workers employed on plantations declined, often precipitously. In Trinidad and Barbados, for example, plantation employment shrank from more than half of all workers before the war to 22.8 percent and 16.7 percent, respectively, by the late 1940s. As a result, workers migrated, often in response to governmental policies. During much of the postwar period, Haitian and Dominican officials connived in the seasonal movement of semislave Haitians to the Dominican sugar fields. Although the Walter-McCarran Immigration Act of 1952 restricted the immigration of West Indians to the United States, agricultural interests lobbied successfully for admission of short-term agricultural laborers. These workers, who numbered in the thousands by the early 1960s, cut sugarcane in Florida and (with other migrants from Mexico and the American South) followed the vegetable and fruit harvests from the Gulf states to Canada. Temporary migrants—who in immigration jargon came to be known as H-2s after the provision of the law under which they were admitted—performed some of the most undesirable work possible under the control of exploitative and racist employers. They had virtually no legal rights and could at will be fired and deported for "unsatisfactory" performance of their duties. During the 1950s and early 1960s, several thousand West Indians also entered the United States and Canada as domestic servants.

Throughout the Caribbean, migration of various kinds became the order of the day, including permanent, semipermanent, and seasonal, both within the region and beyond. In the most striking of these patterns, migrants left the islands for metropolitan areas of North America or Europe: Puerto Ricans came to New York City; British West Indians to Toronto, New York City, and London; and French West Indians to Paris.

By the early 1960s, as many as three hundred thousand persons per year migrated from the region, but not all permanently. Many had adopted a strategy of temporary migration as a hedge against economic downturns or as a source of ready cash. The earnings accumulated by migrant workers, like the money sent home by those who had moved permanently to industrial countries, enabled significant numbers to purchase homes and small parcels of land and to help maintain families who remained in the islands.

For workers who remained in the Caribbean, the collapse of the plantation system both made possible and necessitated a diversification of skills, some of which had clear entrepreneurial application. Men became jacks-of-all-trades, moving from one trade to another as need dictated. As petty traders, women fashioned elaborate networks with both suppliers and customers to keep their businesses afloat. Flexibility was the key—being able to respond to changing conditions quickly by moving from island to island and by resorting to a range of skills and contacts.

As the postwar years advanced, black workers developed an ever more sophisticated political consciousness. They challenged the status quo and joined forces with Garveyites and the emerging intellectual elite, best personified by Eric Williams in Trinidad. As working-class leaders increasingly challenged the legitimacy of the colonial state, they engineered the transformation of their unions into political parties. In Jamaica, Bustamante's Industrial Union became the Jamaica Labor party. The Oil Field Workers Trade Union associated with Butler in Trinidad underwent a similar transformation, as did the Manpower and Citizens' Association in Guiana. Moreover, the expanded urban and nonpeasant sector made up the bulk of the membership of the new political parties such as the People's National party in Jamaica, the Progressive League in Barbados, and the West Indian Nationalist party—later the People's National party—in Trinidad. The experience of labor leaders and the support of workers made possible the victories of black-dominated political parties beginning in the early 1960s.

The civil rights movement in the United States paralleled these developments. The Montgomery bus boycott, which launched the career of Martin Luther King, Jr., was triggered by Rosa Parks, a seamstress, and organized by Jo Ann Robinson, a college professor, and E. D. Nixon, a Pullman porter. Black workers bore the brunt of the hardships that the boycott entailed, even as they devised an alternate transportation system to help sustain their protest. As the movement for equal civil and political rights swept across the South, black workers in both rural and urban areas played a similarly critical role. They risked injury and death sheltering organizers, registering to vote, and engaging in nonviolent protests against discrimination. Even after the enactment of the Civil Rights Act of 1964 and the Voting Rights Act of 1965, southern black workers, professionals, and entrepreneurs continued to risk life and limb asserting the freshly guaranteed rights.

From the mid-1960s onward, the mounting frustration of northern black workers pressed the movement beyond civil and political rights toward such economic rights as jobs, housing, and unemployment relief. Urban unrest in Watts, Detroit, Newark, and other manufacturing centers stemmed not so much from interethnic conflicts as earlier, but from resentment against pervasive discrimination even in areas where Jim Crow laws had not applied. Industrial workers faulted their unions as well as employers and elected officials for failing to address systematic inequality. The Dodge Revolutionary Union Movement (DRUM) in Detroit was only one of many such grass-roots movements among black unionists that took inspiration from international struggles for national liberation and sought a radical transformation of the economic and political structure.

Such movements had mixed success in altering traditional patterns both within their respective industries and the broader society. They did provide the foundation for electing black mayors in such industrial cities as Gary, Indiana; Detroit; Newark; Chicago; and Los Angeles. But this political achievement accompanied the economic transformation, wherein corporations closed factories in urban areas, leaving unemployment and its resulting social consequences behind. Black workers only recently removed from the collapse of the southern plantation system now faced the collapse of the factory system.

From the mid-1960s onward, similar developments affected the Caribbean. When they could no longer resist the demand of colonial subjects for national independence, Britain and the other colonial powers reluctantly conceded it. However, political self-determination by itself did not infuse new life into the regional economy. Only in Trinidad among the English-speaking Caribbean islands did the black workers' and intellectuals' control of the state inaugurate a period of economic boom. On that island, prosperity resulted from nationalization of the petroleum industry and exploitation of natural gas reserves. In the islands that lacked such resources, workers and entrepreneurs continued to pursue a variety of employment and business options both in the Caribbean region and on mainland North America and Europe.

In the Spanish Caribbean and Central America, black workers and entrepreneurs experienced similar upheavals after World War II. The United States' foreign policy played as large a part in this process as did its economic policy. Puerto Rico's special status made possible a mass exodus of displaced workers to the mainland, particularly to New York City. In Central America and the Dominican Republic, U.S. armed forces intervened against popular leftist movements whether led by government officials or opposition forces. In many of these countries, dictatorships and military regimes took root with the blessing of the United States. With the investment climate thus stabilized, U.S. capital poured into the region, with a primary objective of producing and transporting plantation products. In South America, where the United States did not intervene militarily, it nonetheless remained a dominant economic force.

For various reasons, these changes produced a heightened awareness of race among persons of African descent throughout Spanish America. At one level, black workers became more outspoken in their resentment against white creole domination of the managerial and technocratic cadres as well as most of the skilled trades. At another level, they increasingly criticized government officials who ignored the significance of race in the formulation of public policy. Moreover, pockets of English-speaking West Indians who had migrated to the Latin countries over the years also contributed to a greater awareness of race, especially in such places as Nicaragua and Costa Rica, where they remained largely apart from the Spanish-speaking population.

This explosion of racial consciousness among workers went farthest in Cuba, in part through the support of Fidel Castro. On the eve of the Cuban Revolution, for example, more than 60 percent of the blacks and mulattoes in Cuba lived and worked in urban areas. Racial discrimination excluded them from certain trades, such as baking and pastry-making, though not from the construction trades. Most Afro-Cubans, however, were unskilled rather than skilled workers, and they experienced high unemployment, with approximately 45 percent of the work force permanently unemployed or at work only intermittently during the late 1950s. Castro's pointed criticism of such discrimination made his movement attractive to black workers. Indeed, blacks and mulattoes became the staunchest supporters of communism in Cuba in hopes that socialism would eliminate racism in the workplace as well as society. A survey in 1962 showed that an estimated 80 percent of the Afro-Cuban population supported Castro, as against 67 percent of the whites.

The economic blockade that the United States imposed on Cuba and the mass exodus of thousands of white Cubans to the mainland in the 1960s and 1970s eventually allowed black workers to benefit under Castro's socialist policies. The Cuban government initiated jobs programs for black workers, and, just as important, it sponsored a host of Afro-Cuban cultural programs, many organized through the workplace. Hence, support for his regime remained strong over time.

Black workers and entrepreneurs in Brazil also struggled against economic marginalization but in a very different setting from that of Cuba. Whereas Castro actively sought the support of black workers and integrated them fully into the armed forces and the manufacturing sector of the economy, Brazilian policymakers largely ignored Afro-Brazilians in their larger aim to achieve world standing as an industrial nation. Black workers thus had no institutional means of gaining industrial skills. To the extent that officials took into account the concerns of workers, they uniformly did so within the traditional structure of political parties and labor unions wherein Afro-Brazilians lacked a distinct voice. As a result, the postwar industrial boom largely bypassed black workers, and the development of agribusiness in the countryside continued to displace tenants and small farmers. As of 1952, Afro-Brazilians made up a significant part of the 42 percent of the agricultural labor force that was unemployed, and in the 1960s the percentage was still growing. But Brazilian industrialists—in marked contrast to their North American counterparts—did not take advantage of this windfall of potential laborers from the rural areas. As a result, Afro-Brazilians working in nonagricultural occupations remained overwhelmingly concentrated in low-paying manual labor, often working intermittently at best. Not surprisingly, the rate of employment among Afro-Brazilians in the major urban centers such as São Paulo made up a tiny portion of the total labor force in many of the leading businesses. In the better paying skilled occupations, Afro-Brazilians were underrepresented or even totally absent.

Unlike other areas of the Americas, in Brazil urbanization did not foster political mobilization. Rather, it produced large-scale poverty as displaced rural folk crowded into favelas in the major metropolitan areas. To the extent that Afro-Brazilians had formed racial-political organizations in São Paulo and elsewhere, these remained largely underground until the 1970s. Only in the cultural realms of music and dance did Brazilian society at large recognize a distinct African contribution.

In short, Afro-Brazilians never gained access to jobs or exercised the democratic rights on a scale comparable to that of black workers elsewhere in the Americas. Economically, politically, and socially marginalized, Afro-Brazilians did not benefit from the nation's industrial expansion following World War II. Thus, by the 1960s the achievements of Brazil's black workers fell far short of those beginning to be made by their counterparts in the United States, the Caribbean, and even Cuba.

◆ CONCLUSION

Between the 1880s and the 1970s, black workers in the Americas underwent a profound transformation from plantation laborers to a diverse group of industrial and service workers, professionals, and entrepreneurs. Many descendants of slaves struggled against low pay and other kinds of exploitation, which in some respects rendered their position structurally similar to what it had been under slavery. In the United States and Brazil in particular, racial discrimination exacerbated this situation. Yet overall, the years brought unthought-of improvement in the status of black persons throughout the Americas. In the United States, federal civil rights legislation gave black workers the tools to fight discrimination in unions, on shopfloors, and in neighborhoods, and to take part in the political life of the nation. In the independent Caribbean islands, black workers constituted a majority of the citizens; in Cuba, their support for the Castro regime brought them victory against restrictive employment patterns in law and custom. All over the Americas, mobility within and between areas made black workers a significant factor in the economic and political life of postindustrial societies. Although not immune to reversal, these achievements represented the outcome of struggle, originating in emancipation and persisting through the imperialist environment that followed.

Chapter 13

RACE AND POLITICS IN THE UNITED STATES

1830s	Beginnings of Negro Convention Movement.
1864	Blacks begin to vote Republican in presidential elections.
1872–1901	First blacks serve in Congress and southern state legislatures.
1909	National Association for the Advancement of Colored People founded.
1932	Blacks shift toward Democratic party in presidential elections.
1941	National Negro Congress founded.
1954	U.S. Supreme Court decision known as *Brown* v. *Board of Education* overturns separate but equal doctrine.
1955–57	Montgomery bus boycott; emergence of Dr. Martin Luther King, Jr., as civil rights leader.
1958–1960	Student sit-in movement begins.
1961	Congress of Racial Equality reinvigorates Freedom Rides, ignites larger youth involvement.
1964	Mississippi Democratic Freedom party challenges the Democratic party convention.
1964	Congress passes Civil Rights Act.
1964	Birmingham movement of Southern Christian Leadership Conference.
1966	Black Power movement emerges from Student Nonviolent Coordinating Committee.
1971	Congressional Black Caucus founded.

1972	Black Political Convention held in Gary, Indiana.
1984, 1988	Jesse Jackson makes first credible campaigns by an Afro-American for presidency.

I n the United States Afro-Americans have had to struggle against the oppression of the overarching political culture ever since their ancestors were forcibly introduced into the Americas. The oppression expanded during their enslavement, and it continued after emancipation. At each historical juncture blacks had to adjust their strategies for survival, considering the discrete aspects of oppression and emerging opportunities to establish themselves as a viable community.

The dominant elements of black politics have emerged in the interaction with the larger and alien political culture. One aspect has been the manifestation of strong race pride which has led to a politics of self-determination within the United States and has also forged linkages to Africa. A second element has been the development of pressure tactics using massive protest demonstrations. A third has been the effort to participate in the formal political system. Using the vote and membership in the major political parties, blacks have sought both elected and appointed office. By exploring these three thematic elements—self-determination, mass protest, and electoral participation—during the civil rights struggle, we will see how black politics have developed historically in the United States.

◆ EARLY MOVEMENTS

The Negro Convention Movement lasted from 1830 to 1854 and initiated a primary stage in black politics and the movement for civil rights in the United States. The series of meetings began in Philadelphia. Black delegates, predominantly from Delaware, Maryland, New York, Pennsylvania, and Virginia, convened in the City of Brotherly Love "to devise ways and means for bettering our Condition." They declared their fidelity to the United States and their intention to work out their destiny within its borders, and they also declared their grievances, of which slavery was foremost, followed closely by lack of access to education and the vote. The participants' expression of black attitudes and intentions became a platform for black political action.

The Thirteenth Amendment to the U.S. Constitution in 1865 announced the achievement of the Negro Convention Movement's number one priority. Suffrage became the next priority, which the black abolitionist and political leader Frederick Douglass promoted by founding the early civil rights organization known as the Equal Rights League. Blacks entered electoral politics in the post–Civil War South by supporting Reconstruction Era projects and the politics of the Republican party. With the vote in hand, they won elective and appointed office. Their postwar electoral participation proved short-lived; by 1900 both the Democratic and Republican parties had turned against blacks.

To defend themselves against renewed subjugation, especially in the South, blacks created new organizations at the turn of the century, the most important of which were the Afro-American Council (1895), the Niagara Movement (1905), the National Association for the Advancement of Colored People or NAACP (1909), the National Urban League (1911), and the National Liberty party (1904). Most of these organizations fought threats to bodily survival, for this was the era of lynching. They also pressed against segregation and discrimination in every phase of life.

To fight racial discrimination in labor relations, in both the North and South, A. Philip Randolph helped to found the National Negro Congress in 1941. He later headed this civil rights organization, pushing to achieve its broad objectives. Among the most dynamic of Randolph's projects was a march on Washington for civil rights, which was designed primarily to protest the exclusion of blacks from jobs in World War II industries. The march was never held inasmuch as the threat of a massive demonstration sufficed to desegregate some war industries. The goals and tactics of this protest foreshadowed the 1963 March on Washington.

The Congress of Racial Equality (CORE), founded in 1942, thrust a cadre of nonviolent leaders like James Foreman and Bayard Rustin into the forefront of the civil rights movement. CORE was an outgrowth of the Fellowship of Reconciliation, a Christian pacifist group that followed the ideas of the South African and Indian nationalist protest leader Mahatma Gandhi. CORE became one of the first organizations to use direct, nonviolent action against restaurants and recreational facilities that discriminated against blacks. Its chapter in Chicago fought against segregation at the University of Chicago Hospital housing and at the University Barbershop. In 1947 its members engaged in a national protest called the Journey of Reconciliation to test compliance with a 1946 U.S. Supreme Court decision outlawing segregation in interstate travel.

CORE's protest methods produced the most intensive and sustained action in the civil rights movement in the 1950s and 1960s, the culmination of decades of litigation in the courts and of direct action against segregation. The 1946 methods served as a model for the first so-called Freedom Rides that CORE initiated in 1961.

Perhaps the most important organization of the pre-1960s period was the NAACP. Within a short period, it scored a series of important legal victories that set the stage for the 1960s. NAACP suits particularly set precedents in voting rights and education. For example, it won invalidation of both the Grandfather Clause as a requirement for voting (1915), and the all-white primary in *Smith* v. *Allwright* (1944). It also won victories against segregated school systems in *Missouri ex rel. Gaines* v. *Canada* (1938) and in *Sweatt* v. *Painter* (1950). The NAACP's most important victory came in the 1954 U.S. Supreme Court decision known as *Brown* v. *Board of Education* in which the Court outlawed the so-called separate but equal doctrine enshrined in *Plessy* v. *Ferguson* (1896), the bedrock of southern law and life in segregation.

Thus, as the civil rights movement entered the 1960s, it stood on decades of solid and hard-won groundwork as well as on the NAACP's successes in court. The direct action strategies of the 1943 march on Washington movement and the 1946 Journey of Reconciliation served as models for the first Freedom Rides. Thus, historical experience and preparation had supplied the civil rights movement's strategies and tactics.

◆ THE MODERN CIVIL RIGHTS MOVEMENT

The modern stage of the civil rights movement is commonly said to extend from the 1955 bus boycott in Montgomery, Alabama, to the assassination of the Rev. Dr. Martin Luther King, Jr., in 1968. This period was marked by strong black national organizations and leaders, as well as a national political mood conducive to black protest. In the 1960s the United States was especially receptive to black protest, which took on a special legitimacy in those years. The movement thus unfolded in a context of long-term historical developments and short-term opportunities.

Seizing the opportunity, the civil rights movement advanced its goal of attaining for black Americans the rights guaranteed to all U.S. citizens under the Constitution. Inherent in this goal was the notion that the Afro-American cause was a decisive test for democracy. The full political participation of blacks was crucial to the very survival of democracy in the United States. To obtain and guarantee equal access to the benefits and rewards of all U.S. institutions, black leaders adopted racial integration as their central objective, for it would guarantee blacks the prosperity of the American dream of which they were equally deserving.

For a long time, the modern civil rights movement was seen mainly in terms of national organizations, and the local activities that provided the base and resources for the national effort were dismissed. It was assumed that national leaders almost entirely coordinated and directed the black insurgencies of the 1955–1968 period. A more accurate assessment reveals a larger role for local organizations. In thousands of black communities, grass-roots leaders were at the forefront of building support for change.

Local movement centers provided the internal organization that enabled the campaign to gather momentum and withstand repression. Specifically, the local centers furnished money, leaders, and communications networks, and acted as social organizations within communities, targeting their activities at defined goals.

The black churches were the most important grass-roots institutions in sustaining the momentum of the modern civil rights movement. They became the movement's institutional backbone because of several key characteristics, namely, their autonomy from the white power structure, their organized mass base, their leadership cadres in their clergy, their available finances, their psychological support and commitment from the community, their communications network, and their ability to supply meeting places. The local and national black church structure thus became crucial to the movement.

While the Montgomery bus boycott is generally credited for triggering the national modern civil rights movement, the Baton Rouge bus boycott of 1953 marked the real beginning. It set the model for Montgomery. The protest in Louisiana's capital occurred when bus drivers went on strike rather than abide by a municipal ordinance for first-come-first-served seating. Louisiana's attorney general sided with the drivers and ruled the ordinance illegal because it conflicted with the state's segregation laws. The satisfied drivers returned to work, but blacks refused to ride. Led by the Rev. T. J. Jemison, pastor of Mount Zion Baptist Church, blacks mobilized through the local black churches and established a mass boycott of the buses. After six days in June 1953, the boycott forced a compromise first-come-first-served seating on buses.

The famous Montgomery bus boycott began on 5 December 1955 after Rosa Parks, a seamstress and an active member of the NAACP, was arrested for refusing to give up her seat to a white man on a Montgomery bus. Urged on by the Women's Political Caucus, the black community mobilized and drew near-total unified support.

In Montgomery, as in Baton Rouge, the network of black churches and civic organizations created a unified structure to lead the action. In Baton Rouge the United Defense League provided leadership, whereas in Alabama direction came from the Montgomery Improvement Association (MIA), whose chairman was the twenty-six-year-old pastor of the Dexter Avenue Baptist Church, Martin Luther King, Jr. King coordinated local efforts and national assistance. His church organized car pools to transport blacks who had depended on the buses, maintained an information network to keep residents informed, and held fund-raising events to finance these efforts.

The NAACP handled the legal aspects of the boycott. It defended Rosa Parks against a suit by the city of Montgomery, and it attacked Montgomery's segregated bus service. Representing the MIA, the NAACP filed for

By refusing to give her bus seat to a white, Rosa Parks sparked the 1955 Montgomery bus boycott, which lasted several months and was a major success of the early Civil Rights Movement. This photograph was taken in December, 1956. UPI/Bettman.

an injunction against segregated bus service, which violated the Fourteenth Amendment. The federal courts agreed with the NAACP's argument. Finding for them on 4 June 1956, the U.S. District Court declared the municipal bus segregation laws in Alabama unconstitutional. Montgomery appealed, but three months later the Supreme Court affirmed the district court's decision.

The Montgomery boycott victory proved to be more powerful than that in Baton Rouge, because it was not a compromise. Legal segregation on buses was over in Montgomery.

The successful 382-day bus boycott gave King and his associates the confidence to confront segregation throughout the South. For that broader effort they founded a larger organization—the Southern Christian Leadership Conference (SCLC). Led by Martin Luther King, Jr., the SCLC set as a goal the racial integration of the entire South. Its founding signaled the

Martin Luther King is pictured leading the march from Selma to Montgomery in 1965 to protest violent opposition to their voter registration campaign. UPI/Bettman.

adoption of direct action tactics to complement legal efforts to end racial segregation.

In ruling for the MIA, the Supreme Court reaffirmed its stance against segregation. The highest level of the federal judiciary had backed the boycott's principles and had also hinted at passing laws to underwrite new aspects of the antisegregation drive. Then, in April 1957, Congress passed the first civil rights act since 1875. The executive branch showed little sign of enforcing the act, however. Then president Dwight D. Eisenhower even called for local and state action to oppose federal court antisegregation efforts.

The president initially offered no protection for civil rights protestors facing white hate groups such as the Ku Klux Klan and the White Citizens Councils, which had mobilized to oppose the *Brown* v. *Board of Education* decision of 1954. The successful mobilizations of the bus boycotts further fueled antagonism. Segregationist forces launched an all-out attack on the NAACP, prompting many southern states to outlaw the organization. In addition, violence flared against blacks in the South. Yet President Eisenhower merely appealed to those who were initiating violence to exercise common sense. His administration remained neutral and declined to enforce the Court's decisions until violence erupted at Central High School in Little Rock, Arkansas, in September 1957.

The federal government's failure to protect civil rights protestors in the South fostered new protests. Black youth, many of whom attended segregated colleges in the South or were members of NAACP groups, began to play more active parts in this new phase. Their special innovation was the sit-in movement to force establishments to comply with the 1957 Civil Rights Act.

Lunch counter sit-in demonstrations began in Wichita, Kansas, in 1958, then moved to Oklahoma City in 1959, and from there spread to North Carolina. The February 1960 sit-in in Greensboro, in particular, captured national attention. There students from North Carolina A & T College challenged lunch counter segregation at the Woolworth store, and shortly afterward they were joined by the NAACP, CORE, and SCLC. The sit-in tactic had proven its value.

Experience with sit-ins encouraged protesting college students to form their own organization, the Student Nonviolent Coordinating Committee (SNCC), whose first mission was to spawn more protests throughout the South. Working together, the SCLC and SNCC targeted communities for desegregation demonstrations, one of which was in Albany, Georgia, about 150 miles southwest of Atlanta. In the fall and winter of 1961, they attempted to break segregation in the Albany bus terminal, which was out of compliance with a recent ruling by the federal Interstate Commerce Commission. Local authorities unleashed violence on the protestors and arrested two thousand people without any interference from federal officials.

The Albany campaign was a turning point, for it hardened the SCLC and SNCC ranks and tested their tactics for a broad offensive against segregation. The next battleground was Birmingham, Alabama. Located in the heart of the old Confederacy, the so-called Pittsburgh of the South took pride in its reputation as the most segregated city in the United States.

SNCC and the SCLC came to town early in 1963 determined to desegregate Birmingham. They held sit-ins at segregated lunch counters; they held mass marches to demand the right to vote; they conducted voter registration campaigns; and they confronted Bull Connor, the city's commissioner of public safety, who on 4 May 1963 unleashed dogs on the protestors. In a display of naked brutality, Connor's minions battered protestors with torrents from fire hoses and clubbed and beat them. These scenes, carried into livingrooms on millions of television sets, riveted national attention. Birmingham became a national center and symbol of the civil rights movement.

The high point of 1963 came in the nation's capital on 28 August 1963 as the March on Washington drew two hundred and fifty thousand Americans of all colors to the Lincoln Memorial. The massive demonstration displayed nationwide popular support for the civil rights movement and forced a reluctant President John F. Kennedy publicly to align himself with civil rights goals. The presidential alliance with civil rights extended to Kennedy's successor, Lyndon B. Johnson.

The sit-in campaigns and the events from Albany to Birmingham to Washington, D.C., laid the basis for the omnibus Civil Rights Act of 1964 and the Voting Rights Act of 1965. They also elevated civil rights leaders such as Rev. Martin Luther King, Jr., to national and international prominence and put the civil rights movement on a new stage.

◆ PARTY POLITICS AND LEGISLATION

Securing the right to vote in practice stood as a traditional goal of the civil rights movement. The Kennedy administration supported the goal, emphasizing citizenship preparation as the focus of the southern movement. With its eyes on a key voting constituency of white southern Democrats, the administration hoped such an approach would deemphasize direct challenges to segregationist social practices. Citizenship preparation meant confrontation, however, as events in Mississippi showed.

Having operated Freedom Schools (where prospective black voters could learn to pass qualifying tests) and other campaigns in Mississippi since 1961 convinced SNCC of the need to confront that state's Democratic party. Therefore, it initiated an effort that resulted in the Mississippi Freedom Democratic party (MFDP). The MFDP held a convention in 1964 and established itself as a statewide organization. In challenging the state Democratic party, the MFDP targeted the seating of an all-white delegation from Mississippi at the National Democratic Party Convention. Concerned about his reelection fortunes, President Johnson engineered a compromise with the help of national civil rights leaders to avoid the credentials challenge that the MFDP had planned. The deal was to give the MFDP two seats in the Mississippi delegation and to claim victory for the principle of desegregating Mississippi's Democratic party. The MFDP rejected the sham. Embittered at being sold out for convenience, MFDP workers rededicated themselves to contesting the power of the state's regular Democratic party.

The SCLC also pressed for electoral reform, targeting central Alabama's Dallas County, where blacks formed the majority but made up only 3 percent of the registered voters. So stark a contrast dramatized the need for national voting rights legislation, the SCLC argued. SNCC had worked the area since 1962. In January 1965 the SCLC campaign made Selma, fifty miles west of Montgomery, the scene of the most significant challenge to barriers against black voting in the South.

Violence immediately met the SCLC efforts. In March 1965 Alabama state troopers set upon civil rights activists attempting to march from

Selma to Montgomery. The onslaught attracted national sympathy for voting rights. Within days the Johnson administration proposed a bill before Congress to protect the right of blacks to register and vote. The bill authorized the U.S. attorney general to challenge in federal court any state or local voting practices specified as racially discriminatory. It also provided for federal registrars to assure the blacks' opportunity to enroll as voters and for federal marshals to guarantee that blacks could cast their ballots. On 4 August the president signed the bill into law as the Voting Rights Act of 1965.

Another stage of the movement had thus begun. The next major legislative achievement of the civil rights movement would be the Fair Housing Act of 1968, the year Martin Luther King, Jr., was assassinated.

◆ THE BLACK POWER AND BLACK NATIONALISM MOVEMENTS

Four days after President Johnson signed the Voting Rights Act, blacks in the Watts section of Los Angeles moved civil rights violently into the streets for the first time outside the South. Their action signaled the need for new strategies and tactics.

Racial barriers outside the South were much harder to confront with protest demonstrations, because they were based on customs, not laws. In areas outside the South, discrimination was more subtle and required more comprehensive approaches. In the North, for example, inequality arose from the exclusion of blacks from white power centers, which had to be confronted with black power. The Black Power concept popularized in 1966 was the response to black needs outside the South, and it generated such momentum that it temporarily displaced the civil rights movement, at least in the media.

The Black Power movement emerged from SNCC, the early 1960s civil rights organization in the South, and its most prominent spokesman was one-time SNCC chairman Stokely Carmichael. Its program called for more militant action than the civil rights movement had provided. Black Power aimed to establish an independent community in which blacks could shape their own political and economic destinies.

Black Power reverberated with the centuries-old, if sometimes muted, message of black self-determination. Its self-help theme superseded the call for integration as the priority for some blacks. For others it completely replaced what they viewed as the futile hope of becoming integral players in America's essential institutions. It encouraged a desire among some blacks to restore the integrity of their own civilization and to project their role within it as their only true salvation. Such a projection was no mere back-to-Africa fantasy. Afro-Americans had long understood that a return to their ancestral continent was impractical for the masses. Instead, black nationalism sought to define black Americans as Africans who formed a "nation within a nation."

The black nationalism that became a central theme of Black Power carried traditional African American core values and was a product of the historical attempt to survive slavery and other oppression. It sought some autonomy and independence outside the sociocultural and political institutions fashioned by white power. In the ebb and flow of black ideological expression, the black nationalist tradition maintained general acceptance within Afro-American communities.

Although most Afro-Americans never joined the ranks of any black nationalist organization, many tended to associate their political aspirations and their critique of American democracy with that offered by black nationalists. Most blacks embraced the central elements of black nationalist thought, believed in a common cultural heritage, and espoused racial solidarity. In addition, most felt ambivalent or hostile toward outside groups. While some supported efforts to create an autonomous territory for blacks, a greater number believed in the need to become an independent political force. No blacks have ever rejected economic self-sufficiency. Thus, if few blacks espoused every tenet, most held firmly to one or more.

The various emphases produced variants of black nationalism that were usually labeled as cultural, religious, revolutionary, and economic. Cultural nationalism insisted on the presence of a distinctive African or African American aesthetic and asserted that effective political and economic change necessarily depended on a renaissance of traditional values. Religious nationalism sought to resurrect sacred African imagery and doctrine, rescuing it from condemnation by white supremacist religious dogma. Revolutionary nationalism combined class and race analyses to reject the pursuit of black liberation within the existing American political economy. Finally, economic nationalism held that the material salvation of blacks required black solidarity to achieve economic development and individual self-reliance.

♦ MARCUS GARVEY

Henry Highland Garnet, Edward Wilmot Blyden, Martin Delany, Bishop Henry McNeil Turner, and other black stalwarts of the 1800s all forcefully articulated black nationalism, but it was Marcus Garvey who captured the popular imagination and developed the largest black nationalist organization and movement in history.

Garvey immigrated to the United States from the Caribbean island of Jamaica in 1916. Arriving in New York City, he perceived that post–Reconstruction pogroms against them had left blacks feeling powerless and demoralized. Seizing on the hopelessness and despair, particularly among blacks fleeing to the urban North from an inhospitable South, within a few years Garvey emerged as a legitimate leader of working-class blacks.

Garvey propagated a powerful new perspective on Africa and Africans dispersed in the black diaspora. He offered a commanding vision of redemption, and he articulated it through his audacious Universal Negro Improvement Association (UNIA). The power of his vision was displayed fully at UNIA's first International Convention of the Negro Peoples of the World in August 1920, which drew twenty-five thousand delegates from twenty-five countries to New York City. In addressing the conditions of blacks, the convention adopted Garvey's global outlook and issued a Declaration of Rights that sought to improve the conditions of all black people.

Garvey popularized the idea that through their solidarity blacks could amass power; politics followed power, he insisted. To get the kinds of public policy they needed blacks had to exercise power, for people who had power got what they wanted and those who had no power were left wanting. That was Garvey's message, and it rang with great clarity among oppressed blacks everywhere.

Garvey spoke to the various nationalist constituencies, and through his UNIA, which included the African Orthodox Church, the Black Cross Nurses, the Black Star Steamship Line, and the *Negro World* newspaper, he offered something for everyone. The UNIA, something of a microcosm of a black nation-state, had cooperatives and mutual aid societies and promoted small businesses. Its structure inculcated the assumptions and philosophy of continental black nationalism and of Pan-African nationalism.

UNIA's structure, principles, and objectives reflected Garvey's view of redemption. Simply put, it offered Africa as the locus of a black empire and made Africa not only the future of the black man and woman, but also their past and present. Contrary to the popular belief, it was no mere back-to-Africa venture. For Garvey, Africa was "the Black Star," standing for direction and not necessarily as a destination. Garvey did not prescribe a mass black removal to Africa, and suggestions that he did so were usually aimed to dismiss him.

Garvey's activities had an overwhelming impact on the self-esteem of African Americans. He influenced blacks' political behavior, and he created a legacy for black leadership. When the establishment became aware of Garvey's dynamic appeal, he came to be seen as extremely dangerous. So it was that the federal government prosecuted him for mail fraud connected with his failed Black Star Steamship Line and upon conviction sent him to prison in 1924. By the time President Calvin Coolidge pardoned him in 1927, Garvey's movement was broken, and so the prosecu-

After joining the Nation of Islam, Malcolm X became a fiery and effective spokesperson for aggressive action on behalf of oppressed blacks. UPI/Bettman.

tion and prison had clearly served their purpose. Although the UNIA's memory long remained a force, its power soon waned. Deported from the United States in 1927, Garvey died in London in 1940.

◆ MALCOLM X

The son of a former UNIA organizer, the man born Malcolm Little in 1925 became the most articulate disciple of black nationalism after Marcus Garvey. Malcolm X developed a fierce racial pride while serving as a leading minister in Elijah Muhammad's Nation of Islam, a black nationalist Muslim organization structured much like the UNIA.

In the context of the growing urgency of the early 1960s, Malcolm X captured the imagination of black youth both in the streets and in the universities. Especially in the urban North his message rang true against a racism that differed in form, if not in outcomes, from that in the South. He offered a lucid view of the blacks' predicament, and he articulated that view with a compelling sincerity. He did not shy away from issues, and he was particularly adept at exposing the ideological contradictions of black leaders in traditional groups like the NAACP and CORE.

Malcolm X developed a mass appeal among blacks because, like Garvey, Malcolm internationalized the black liberation struggle, at once linking Soweto, South Africa, and Selma, Alabama. The oppression was the same, he said, and he insisted that blacks in Soweto and Selma alike needed self-determination. The black community everywhere needed to become independent—politically, socially, and economically. Only then could it effectively address its problems.

The dynamic Malcolm X outgrew his role as minister under Elijah Muhammad and broke with the Nation of Islam in 1963 after his comment on the 1963 Kennedy assassination, that "The chickens have come home to roost." Malcolm X commenced his independent mission by forming the Organization of Afro-American Unity (OAAU) in March 1964. He opened the first chapter in the African republic of Ghana during his *hajj*—the pilgrimage to Mecca that Islam requires of every devout Muslim at least once in a lifetime. While on his trip, Malcolm visited various African countries and became the first African American invited to address the Organization of African Unity (OAU). He championed Pan-African solidarity and the international struggle against racism.

Like Garvey, Malcolm was misunderstood and criticized by public opinion makers who cast him as a fierce firebrand and extremist. Fearing his impact on the Afro-American masses, they urged whites to negotiate with moderate black leaders. Better the nonviolent tone of Christian love espoused by Martin Luther King, Jr., they suggested, than the aggressive and seemingly un-American Muslim brotherhood of Malcolm X. Not since Garvey had an individual so decisively altered the political direction of the black freedom movement. Like Garvey, Malcolm discouraged assimilation, and in doing so he helped change the political consciousness of Afro-Americans. College campuses and northern ghettos in particular reverberated with Malcolm's demanding self-reliant tone in the mid-1960s. Even his assassination in New York City in 1965 failed to quiet his voice, and today it continues to echo.

Malcolm X's message and tone infused both old and new organizations and personalities. Former SNCC leaders Stokely Carmichael and James Foreman openly acknowledged Malcolm's influence on their thinking and behavior. Through the remainder of the 1960s, other notable nationalist organizations were created or formed from existing ones. Roy Innis, for example, acknowledged Malcolm's influence in transfusing black nationalism into CORE, a generation-old civil rights organization. Malcolm X also inspired the creation of a series of new nationalist organizations. Among the most radical of these were the Republic of New Africa (RNA), the Revolutionary Action Movement (RAM), and the Dodge Revolutionary Movement (DRM), all of which proclaimed the self-determination theme and advocated that blacks be given a political state of their own within the United States. They also promoted the idea of armed defense to secure black liberation. Such bold initiatives for Afro-American independence made Malcolm an icon.

Malcolm X and Marcus Garvey gave black nationalism a cast and character for the twentieth century, translating an ideology of racial solidarity, self-help, and self-determination from mere beliefs into behavior for millions of African American peoples. They moved not only blacks in the United States but also African peoples elsewhere in the Americas and in Africa. They insisted that, whether decolonizing or desegregating, autonomy was the solution to the problems of African peoples everywhere.

Garvey and Malcolm also illustrated the historical function of black nationalism as a barometer in the United States. Both figures had remarkable charisma and captivated the popular imagination, able to inspire allegiance through their special qualities of personality. Neither, however, stood for a personality cult. The key to their ability to inspire lay in their insightful deduction of historical reality from the facts of black experience. Their followers multiplied because their message affirmed daily truths, and their ideology embraced the substance of racial subordination as the masses felt it. They accepted no compromise. They showed that black nationalism has flourished when blacks have felt the most marginalized.

◆ BLACKS IN NATIONAL POLITICS

The appeal of nationalist autonomy has competed with, but never overshadowed, that of inclusion. Afro-Americans have persisted in their struggle to become part of the legislative and administrative processes of the United States. In their efforts to win elected and appointed public office, they have succeeded in part and have accordingly gained access to the negotiation of political interests and a role in establishing national policy. This inclusion has been a necessary goal of black political strategies.

Their road to suffrage and full political participation has been a long and difficult one. From their earliest beginnings in America until the Civil War, only a few free blacks were allowed to vote. Even in the North, where by the 1820s slavery no longer existed above the Mason-Dixon line, free blacks suffered political restrictions that prevented them from voting and exercising other rights and privileges. The Civil War finally introduced some changes in their status that affected their political participation. The Thirteenth Amendment, ratified in 1865, abolished the slave status. The Civil Rights Act of 1866 declared blacks "born in the United States and not subject to any foreign power . . . to be citizens of the United States," and it entitled them as citizens "to full and equal benefit of all laws and proceedings for the security of person and property, as is enjoyed by white citizens." The Fourteenth Amendment in 1868 confirmed blacks' citizenship status and equal protection under the law. That reinforced the mandates of the Congressional Reconstruction Acts of 1867 that blacks in the ex-Confederate states be granted the vote on the same bases as whites. The provisions affected only blacks in the South, however; those outside the South received no federal mandate until the Fifteenth Amendment in 1870.

Southern blacks plunged into politics in 1867. Overwhelmingly, they supported the Republican party, which reputedly had caused the war and emancipation. Black votes contributed handsomely to Republican presidential victories in 1868, 1872, and 1876. They also elected their own to local and state offices; between 1868 and 1901 they sent twenty blacks to the U.S. House of Representatives and two blacks—Hiram R. Revels and Blanch K. Bruce—to the U.S. Senate, both representing Mississippi.

Political participation also boosted blacks to appointed office. Frederick Douglass and other blacks served in diplomatic and administrative posts from the 1860s to the 1890s. Their presence was initially felt most in the South, where in 1860, 95 percent of all blacks in the United States lived; about 80 percent still lived there in 1900. Even before the so-called Great Migration that began in 1910 shifted blacks from the rural South to the urban North, blacks outside the South established political bases. In Indiana, Kansas, Michigan, and Ohio, blacks made inroads, particularly in the Republican party, serving as committee members, national convention delegates, ward constables, and other state party officers.

The 1890s initiated a long period of increased black exclusion. Wholesale disenfranchisement swept the South, and blacks not explicitly barred from voting were threatened with lynching if they tried to exercise their rights. Although both parties turned their backs on black people, they refused to give up. They formed so-called black and tan factions to defend their interests, and they kept their hands in local organizing. Such work won Oscar DePriest election to Chicago's city council in 1915, making him the first black in the new century elected to the House of Representatives. In 1934 Arthur W. Mitchell became the first black Democrat in the House when he unseated the Republican DePriest in Illinois' First Congressional District. Mitchell's victory signaled not only the reemergence of black political participation but also a shift in party allegiance.

Franklin D. Roosevelt wooed black voters in 1932, building on a coalition his Democratic forebear Al Smith had begun forging in 1928. Blacks remained loyal to Roosevelt during his unprecedented four election victories. With considerable urging from his wife, Eleanor, Roosevelt included blacks in his programs to pull the nation out of the Great Depression.

Roosevelt put blacks in charge of so-called Negro affairs departments in most major federal agencies, through which members pooled information and offered proposals to the president. Black appointees and others organized what they called a federal council, and some called the black cabinet. Mary McCleod Bethune, director of Negro affairs for the National Youth Administration, headed the council, and Robert Weaver, director of Negro affairs for the Federal Housing Authority, served as vice-chair. The council developed a five-part program that tested Roosevelt's commitment to blacks' rights: (1) integration of the armed services; (2) abolition of the poll tax that barred so many blacks from voting by pricing it beyond their means; (3) "100 percent elimination" of anti-Negro job discrimination by the federal government and by unions; (4) through the Fair Employment Practice Committee (FEPC), punishment of employers who discriminated; and (5) appointment of more blacks to policymaking boards and advisory committees.

A. Philip Randolph's planned march on Washington in 1943 added pressure for the council's program and pushed Roosevelt to take them more seriously. In all the years between 1929 and 1945, however, there was never more than a single black representative in Congress, and so no legislative pressure emerged for the black cabinet's agenda.

Executive goodwill turned on calculations of how great an impact blacks would have on presidential elections. In 1948 they showed that strength by contributing to Harry Truman's upset victory over Thomas E. Dewey. And it was Truman who issued the executive order to desegregate the armed forces. Republican Dwight D. Eisenhower owed blacks little and gave them less during his two terms. Then in 1960, when black voters gave John F. Kennedy a seven-to-three margin over Richard M. Nixon, their support proved decisive in a close election. Kennedy won the presidency by a bare 112,827 votes out of 68.8 million cast. The narrow victory left Kennedy receptive but hesitant to act on blacks' civil rights demands until 1963, which proved to be his last year as president. The following year blacks strongly backed President Lyndon Johnson, who sponsored the 1964 Civil Rights Act and addressed many racial problems with his Great Society initiative.

Black voters were not decisive in the presidential contest of 1968, when Richard Nixon defeated Hubert H. Humphrey by less than 0.1 percent. Race was an issue that year, however, for nearly ten million persons voted for Alabama's segregationist governor and third-party candidate George C. Wallace. Nor were blacks an electoral factor in Nixon's 1972 landslide victory over George S. McGovern, a U.S. senator from South Dakota. But blacks proved crucial in Jimmy Carter's narrow victory over incumbent Gerald R. Ford in 1976.

Carter rewarded his supporters by appointing more blacks to his administration than any president since Franklin D. Roosevelt. Carter appointed nearly half the 141 blacks who served in high-level executive branch positions between 1960 and 1980. (Presidents Kennedy and Johnson had made 29 percent of the black appointments, and Nixon and Ford 32 percent.)

The black contribution to President Carter's election in 1976 manifested the growing black presence in politics and particularly in the Democratic party. By 1976 blacks formed one-fourth of all Democratic voters and had become a force in the national party organization and in several state parties. They were also an increasing presence in federal courts, where the NAACP had fought to gain equal protection of the law.

The growing black presence was especially evident in elected offices. In Congress, whereas only three blacks had sat in the federal legislature at the end of the 1950s, six at the end of the 1960s, and fourteen by the 1970s, in 1990 twenty-six blacks were elected.

In 1971 black representatives formed the Congressional Black Caucus (CBC), which over the years has grown in both size and clout, reflecting its members' rising seniority. By 1990 CBC members chaired five major standing committees and thirteen subcommittees. The CBC has also sponsored important legislation for blacks, including the Full Employment and Balanced Growth Act of 1976 and the Martin Luther King, Jr., Holiday Act of 1981. The CBC also insisted on provisions to strengthen the Voting Rights Act of 1982; secured an amendment to the Public Works Act of 1985, setting aside portions of projects to assure minority participation in government-contract jobs; and sponsored the Anti-Apartheid Act of 1986. Along with its legislative initiatives, the CBC presented annual budget proposals as alternatives to the federal budgets submitted by presidents Ronald Reagan and George Bush.

The CBC symbolizes the distance blacks have traveled in U.S. politics. Over the last twenty years, it has provided direction and support for national black priorities and several of its members have emerged as national, and not merely black, leaders. One of its most shining members, Shirley Chisholm, a Democrat from Brooklyn, in 1968 became the first black woman to serve in the House of Representatives. In 1972 she also became the first black candidate for the presidential nomination of a major party in the United States, campaigning for public policies that addressed the nation's social needs. Her bold crusade marched beyond race, color, or previous condition of servitude.

◆ THE JESSE JACKSON PHENOMENON

Chisholm's challenge tested strategies and tactics that the Rev. Jesse Jackson summoned in his 1984 campaign for the Democratic party's presidential nomination. A former aide to Martin Luther King, Jr., Jackson has established himself as a leader in his own right. He first gained national attention directing Operation PUSH (People United to Save Humanity), a self-help group based in Chicago, and after some initial struggles finally disproved the proposition that whites would not vote for a black candidate for president.

Jackson's campaign in 1984 far exceeded expectations. He won nearly 3.3 million votes in the Democratic primaries, which gave him 384 delegate votes in the convention, but placed him a distant third, behind former senator Gary Hart of Colorado and former vice president Walter F. Mondale, who won the nomination. Jackson had nonetheless offered a vision of the future.

In 1988 Jackson won impressive victories in the southern regional primary called Super Tuesday, and he also garnered some delegates in the Alaska, Michigan, and Vermont primaries. His showing surprised pundits who had said he would draw significant support only in states with large black populations. His remarkable showing put him in a league with other candidates.

Although Jackson placed second to Massachusetts governor Michael Dukakis, his campaign had a major influence on the issues and national agenda. After the election, for example, his strong presence compelled the new Reagan administration to address the topic of South Africa at least weakly. Similarly, Jackson agitated to move U.S. policy on the Middle East away from its traditional, almost automatic, pro-Israeli stance, and he gave new impetus to a national urban policy to deal with rapidly deteriorating cities and the fight against drugs.

Jackson's 1988 presidential campaign made a lasting impact in its success in registering millions to vote and crossing old lines to form new coalitions. Most importantly, it disproved the notion that white voters would never vote black candidates into high offices. Douglas Wilder's election as governor of Virginia in 1989 and David Dinkins' election as mayor of New York City in 1989 further discredited such theories. Jackson's success showed that, as both voters and candidates, Afro-Americans are forces to be reckoned with in contemporary U.S. politics.

◆ CONCLUSION

Blacks have made substantial progress through politics. In 1992 nearly eight thousand of all elected officials in the United States were blacks. The Congress of 1993 had thirty-nine Afro-American members, and the first cabinet of the Clinton administration contained four blacks. In addition, thousands of Afro-Americans have sat on city and county councils and in state legislatures. Many blacks have also served as mayors of the nation's largest cities. The Congressional Black Caucus has made the Afro-American presence felt on the national scene. Blacks have gained seats in state courts, including several state supreme courts, and have increasingly served in the federal judiciary. Remarkably, two blacks have filled seats on the U.S. Supreme Court. They have sat at the highest levels in the federal executive departments.

Yet their struggle has not ended, for the national political culture has remained largely unresponsive. As impressive as the rise in the number of black elected officials has been, Afro-Americans still make up only a little more than 2 percent of elected officials, and their share in appointed office has never risen even to that level. Moreover, even in office blacks have often been unable to push through measures essential to their constituents.

Participation in politics has not been an end in itself; rather, it has served as a means to relieve racial oppression. The strategies of black politics have sought to move public policy to give Afro-Americans the same rights, privileges, and opportunities available to any Americans. The goals of equality and social justice remain distant. In the 1980s and early 1990s, the national political culture increasingly cast blacks' interests as antagonistic and became less receptive. For most Americans, solving national social concerns appeared to give way to solving their personal socioeconomic concerns. Again, the struggle against the overarching political culture has shaped the blacks' present and future.

Chapter 14

RACE AND POLITICS IN LATIN AMERICA

1791–1825	Independence movements.
1853–1854	Final emancipation in mainland Spanish America.
1886–1888	Emancipation in Cuba and Brazil.
1910	Mexican Revolution begins.
1890–1930	Positivism dominates elite philosophy.
1930s	Gilberto Freyre's writings become popular.
1940s–1960s	Populist politicians govern most of Latin America.
1950s	São Paulo school of race studies challenges Freyre.
1959	Fidel Castro's revolution triumphs in Cuba.
1980–1993	Black movements appear in Brazil and other countries.

At the turn of the twentieth century, elites in all Latin American nations fell under the influence of racist doctrines that emanated from Europe and the United States. One of the most pervasive of these doctrines was the theory known as positivism. On the issue of race, most of the positivist theorists—especially Herbert Spencer, Arthur de Gobineau, Gabriel Tarde, Walter Bagehot, and Gustave Le Bon—suggested that nonwhites were inferior to whites. Based on such thinking, Latin American elites assigned African Americans and Native Americans to the bottom of the social scale. They attributed negative characteristics to blacks, which they ascribed to the effects of genetic inheritance.

During the first third of the twentieth century, blacks were victims of such thinking. From Mexico to Argentina, elites convinced themselves that they had to whiten their populations if they wanted to achieve their nations' highest destinies. In the process, they relegated African Americans to the scrap heap of history, and for that reason, they encouraged massive immigration from Europe. They sincerely believed that increased miscegenation combined with waves of white immigration would lead to the eventual disappearance of blacks and Amerindians as separate groups.

Economic factors also exacerbated the problems faced by black and mulatto Latinos. For the most part poor, they lacked the education and skills needed in the developing industrial sectors of Latin America. During most of the first half of the century, their poverty condemned them to low-paying agricultural work. Even there they did not enjoy steady employment or stable conditions. Illiterate, malnourished, and propertyless, they had little job mobility.

In the cities, blacks faced equally difficult times. Official government policies favored European immigrants and light-skinned nationals over blacks, a prejudice that became increasingly strong as blacks moved up the occupational ladder. Whereas many managed to find industrial jobs, they met with almost no success when they competed for white-collar positions in government and the private sector.

Just as blacks in Latin America have suffered economic and social discrimination, they have failed to gain political power commensurate with their numbers, either as individuals or as ethno-racial groups. While a few have gained important positions as ministers, ambassadors, and even presidents, the bulk of the black population between Mexico and Argentina has been systematically excluded from the political arena, especially at the upper levels of national affairs.

Because of widely varying demographic differences between nations, no generalizations about African American political participation hold for the entire region. Black experiences vary from country to country. For instance, an avalanche of European immigration between 1880 and 1914 buried Argentina's black population and virtually led to their disappearance as an influential group in the capital city of Buenos Aires.

In sharp contrast, Brazil's black and mixed population is the second largest African population in the world. Afro-Brazilians make up approximately one-third of the nation's population and racially mixed people another third. But despite their numbers, Brazilian blacks have not made their political mark as a group during the twentieth century.

The Andean nations of Ecuador, Colombia, and Venezuela have had different racial histories, especially compared with those of Brazil and Argentina. In those nations, as in the Central American republics, black enclaves dotted the coastal areas, but no African American movements occurred, nor did individual blacks play significant roles during recent history.

Even the Caribbean experiences varied. These African Americans constitute the majority, but in the Dominican Republic, where as much as 90 percent of the inhabitants have some African ancestry, whites and light-skinned mulattoes monopolized national politics and excluded blacks in the process. In Cuba, an abortive effort to organize an Afro-Cuban political party failed in 1912. Until 1959, blacks endured repressive white administrations. The Cuban Revolution slowly brought the nation's black population into the political mainstream and offered some hope that Afro-Cubans will hold high offices in the post-Castro era.

Haiti, in desperate poverty throughout the century, is a black republic. Struggles between blacks and mulattoes have characterized the nation's politics and thus hardly represent a quest for black power.

There is one generalization, however, that may be made for all of Latin America; namely, throughout the twentieth century, only a few individual blacks achieved prominence as political leaders. The vast majority failed altogether to escape the chains of poverty and prejudice. The few exceptions prove the point. Between 1899 and 1908, blacks such as Manuel Corao, Antonio Fernández, and Benjamín Ruíz served as cabinet members and generals under Venezuelan dictator Cipriano Castro. In Peru, during the early 1930s, Luis Sánchez Cerro briefly held the presidency before his assassination in 1933. Cuban intellectual Juan Gualberto Gómez and labor leader Jesus Menéndez Larrondo were also significant national figures. But few other African Americans ever accomplished what these individuals did.

Any understanding of race as a political factor depends on recognizing that race has defined only one dimension of individual or group identity in Latin America. Class, education, gender, and occupation have played equally important roles in assigning social status, and so, too, has geographic location. Although they were excluded from national politics for reasons of race, blacks held positions of power at local levels.

This was especially true in the small black enclaves that lie scattered throughout South and Central America. Many date from the slave era, when runaways founded isolated havens. These enclaves, variously known as *cumbes, palenques, quilombos,* and maroon communities, survive to the present day and are especially common in the former plantation regions of coastal South America, coastal Central America and Mexico, and the Caribbean islands. In some cases, such as in the Esmeraldas district in Ecuador, the Chocó and northern coastal parts of Colombia, and the Barlovento region of Venezuela, blacks make up most of the population in entire states, provinces, or districts. In other cases, such as maroon communities in Mexico and the Black Carib or Garífuna sections of Honduras and Guatemala, they live in small towns or communities next to Amerindian and mestizo settlements.

African Americans in most parts of the Caribbean coast of South and Central America became *ladinos,* or hispanicized blacks, although some preserved their African heritage and daily rituals. Examples are the descendants of slaves who live in southern Suriname and French Guiana. In these situations, African Americans controlled their local affairs. Despite government interference on issues of national importance, blacks served as mayors, chiefs, and administrators on local councils and organizations. Although some analysts have criticized these enclaves as "racial cysts," these areas provided safety and comfort for African Americans who merely wished to live as farmers, traders, fishermen, hunters, and gatherers. During the last decades of the twentieth century, some have even turned their quaint villages into tourist attractions. Recently, however, young African Americans have left these enclaves in increasing numbers to seek employment and modern life elsewhere.

◆ MESO-AMERICA

Mexicans view themselves racially as mestizos. Especially since the 1910 revolution, the official rhetoric has held that European and Amerindian mixtures formed the bedrock of the Mexican citizenry. In propagating this myth, Mexicans have suppressed the fact that some Africans and their descendants made their homes in the nation. Approximately 3 percent of the population has African origins. Today, several Afro-Mexican communities exist, the remnants of maroon settlements. The people who live in these maroon communities, who have maintained cultures with distinctly African characteristics or at least traditions, are called Afro-mestizos. (Elsewhere in Latin America they are called *zambos,* signifying a mixture of African and Amerindian.)

Many Afro-mestizo communities dot the Gulf coast region of Veracruz and the Pacific Costa Chica, between the states of Guerrero and Oaxaca. On the Gulf side, the pueblos of Mata Clara and Coyolillo continue to preserve Afro-mestizo traditions. On the Costa Chica, at least sixteen independent towns are descended from maroon camps.

In colonial times these communities managed to obtain guarantees of autonomy from local authorities, but such arrangements had a price. For instance, in return for freedom they had to agree not to take in other runaways. They also helped to quell Amerindian uprisings against Spanish rule. Because most of the original maroons were men, they mated with local Amerindian women and created racially and culturally mixed offspring.

Until recently, Mexican authorities chose to ignore this small Afro-mestizo presence. Today, however, local officials have begun to organize carnivals to celebrate the foundations of such towns, playing up African vestiges in attempts to attract tourists from Africa. Afro-mestizo artisans, musicians, dancers, and storytellers have gained deserved recognition, for both their talents and the history they have preserved. One contingent even participated in the Smithsonian Institution's Quincentenary Folklife Program in 1992, joining other maroon groups from the Americas in celebrating the lives of Africans and their descendants in the hemisphere.

For the most part, Mexicans of Afro-Amerindian descent have chosen to emphasize their native origins. Afro-Mexicans have become assimilated into the prevailing mestizo culture. This curious behavior in a nation where whites denigrate natives even more than blacks remains a puzzle of race relations in Latin America. The idea seems to be, better mestizo than Amerindian, zambo, or black; better black than Amerindian, despite strong antiblack sentiments. The answer lies partly in the fact that over the centuries Afro-Mexicans—and Afro-Latinos in general—have absorbed the cultures of the elites more thoroughly and completely than have Amerindians and therefore tend to eschew links with Africa.

Blacks make up less than 1 percent of the population in Central America. Most are descendants of West Indian laborers who were recruited to build railroads and ports and to work in the banana plantations along the Caribbean coast. The first major group came in the 1880s to work with Minor C. Keith on the Limón–San José Railroad. Faced with construction delays, the workers began planting bananas for export. Gradually the market grew, and bananas became as important as the railroad for the coastal economy. In 1899 Keith incorporated several smaller operations into the United Fruit Company, which became the de facto government along the entire coast. Refrigerated company ships serviced company towns where black workers prepared the fruit for embarkation.

The United Fruit Company continued to recruit new workers for the banana business, drawing in other West Indians, Amerindians, Spanish Americans, and occasional Asians. Other firms, as well as logging companies, located in the region. In general, the longer the immigrant group had been there, the higher its members moved up on the occupational scale. By the 1950s the original West Indians and their descendants had become a labor elite, while many others had become farmers and petty merchants in the port towns along the coast. Not all the settlements prospered, however, because disease and the vicissitudes of the market closed down some plantations. There black residents adopted subsistence strategies or moved elsewhere in search of work. Large numbers resettled in the United States, forming a diaspora within the diaspora.

West Indian blacks in Central America have played little part in national politics during the twentieth century, for their activities have been limited to the Caribbean towns. Their political affiliations, if any, have been with national parties, none of which has recognized the needs of blacks as a distinct group.

◆ THE HISPANIC CARIBBEAN

Three-tiered racial structures exist on these islands. As elsewhere in Latin America, whites and blacks sit at opposite poles of a racial spectrum, with a rich variety of racially mixed groups arrayed between them. Both class and race determine an individual's status. Rich blacks become mulattoes, and rich mulattoes become whites.

As much as 60 to 70 percent of the Dominican population has some African heritage; another 12 to 13 percent are black; and whites make up around 15 to 20 percent. The class structure clearly follows racial stratification. Upper- and middle-class Dominicans classify themselves as white, although they may be dark-skinned. Mulattoes and blacks belong to the lower class. Money connotes whiteness, poverty blackness. Success implies white European features, real or assumed.

Such differentiation takes on larger significance given the Dominicans' proximity to Haiti, which occupies the western half of the island. Relations between the two republics have historically been strained. Dominicans do not like to think of themselves as in any way similar to their neighbors. For that reason, they have always emphasized their origins as Spanish to distinguish themselves from black Haitians.

As a rule, Dominicans have sought to erase their black characteristics and emphasize whitening. Since social prestige depends in large part on whiteness, even poor blacks try to whiten their progeny whenever possible. Given the preponderance of mulattoes, Dominicans should be able to avoid racial conflict and embrace the concept of racial democracy. But mulattoes still covet whiteness and despise blackness, making it impossible to reach a completely harmonious racial situation. Given the prevailing poverty and the unequal distribution of wealth in the hands of a white elite, it is difficult to imagine improvement of class or race relations soon.

Despite their racist views, the vast majority of Dominicans believe that individuals belong to a national community, not to racial groups. They argue that their identities depend on Dominican characteristics, not those of specific ethnic, class, or racial factions.

Politically, until the late 1960s nonwhite Dominicans remained outsiders. Ruled by a series of brutal dictators until 1961, when Rafael Trujillo was assassinated, the Afro-Dominican population lived in poverty and fear. Trujillo did allow a few dark-skinned army officers into his coterie of close associates. Otherwise he appealed for support from the white elite, courted their attention, and served the interests of foreign powers, especially the United States and its corporate investors.

Since Trujillo's death, little has changed in the Dominican Republic. The nation's two leading political rivals, both anti-Trujillo figures, vie with each other for power and largely ignore the impoverished masses. Between 1961 and the present, Joaquín Balaguer and Juan Bosch have battled for control of the government. Both are racially mixed, as is common in the Dominican Republic, but neither has aligned with a black power group or sought votes with racial appeals. Nor have Afro-Dominicans held top positions under either leader. As elsewhere, Afro-Dominicans are politically active at lower levels, such as city and district offices, and occasionally as governors. Some black officers hold high ranks in the military, and a few belong to organizations such as the Rotary and the YMCA. But as a group and as individuals, blacks remain conspicuous for their absence in high places. One exception is José Francisco Peña Gómez, former mayor of Santo Domingo, who in 1993 was a leading candidate in the 1994 presidential elections. He has been the target of racist barbs because his parents were Haitian. Another exception, Heredia Boneti, the nation's leading international lawyer, serves as director of the American Chamber of Commerce, an otherwise mostly white organization.

Racial antagonism permeates a book written by Joaquín Balaguer, entitled *La isla al revés* [The topsy-turvy island], in which he not only attacks the Haitian national character but also echoes the disdain of Dominican whites for their black compatriots, whom he describes in derogatory terms.

◆ CUBA

The black struggle for recognition and political influence in Cuba began in 1907, when Evaristo Estenoz and Pedro Ivonet founded the Cuban Independent Party of Color. These veterans of the war for independence (1892–1898) joined other disgruntled Afro-Cubans who felt that the new government under the tutelage of the United States excluded them from holding influential positions. Moreover, the founders of the party wanted other benefits for all Afro-Cubans, including land, jobs, and access to higher education. Between 1907 and 1912, the party agitated for basic social reforms that would give former slaves and their descendants opportunities to improve their living standards.

Ironically, opposition to the Party of Color came not only from whites but also from many influential Afro-Cubans and mulattoes. Two of these, Juan Gualberto Gómez and Martín Morúa Delgado, argued in favor of national rather than racial identity. Gómez, a leading black Cuban intellectual and politician, wrote: "We are all Cubans, nothing more." By that he meant that Afro-Cubans should not form a separate political movement around race.

Morúa Delgado, who feared that whites would create an all-white party and ultimately resort to racial warfare, went even further in his opposition to the colored party movement. Elected president of the Cuban Senate in 1909, he introduced a bill (passed in 1910) that banned the establishment of parties based on race.

Ignoring this law, Estenoz and Ivonet continued their efforts to organize an Afro-Cuban party. Frustrated by the arrest of these two leaders in 1912, party members, led by agricultural and urban workers, began an abortive revolt demanding better wages, working conditions, and social mobility. President José Miguel Gómez, with the support of U.S. officials, used the revolt to crush the outlawed party. He massacred thousands of party loyalists, including women and children. Both Ivonet and Estenoz died in the bloody conflict. With their deaths, Afro-Cubans ceased being a political faction. A few lighter-skinned Cubans held minor positions, but the bulk of the Afro-Cuban population remained chained by poverty. Illiterate, uneducated, underfed, underemployed, and generally disaffected, Cuba's blacks remained outside political circles.

During the 1920s and 1930s, many Afro-Cuban intellectuals and labor leaders joined the Cuban Communist party. Some, such as the renowned poet Nicolás Guillén, have remained party loyalists to this day. The party drew into its ranks such well-known blacks as the writer and teacher Salvador García Aguero and labor organizers Lázaro Peña (Confederation of Cuban Workers), Arascelio Iglesias Díaz (chief of the Havana dock workers), and Jesús Menéndez Larrondo (of the sugar workers' federation). Menéndez, who led the one-third of the sugar workers who were unionized, gained many benefits for the sugar workers, including honest representation, wage increases that exceeded inflation, equal pay for all seasons, compensated rest periods, a social security program, retirement pensions, and profit-sharing from the sale of sugar byproducts.

Afro-Cubans also organized several small groups that fought against racial prejudice. For example, the Committee for the Rights of Blacks and the National Federation of Black Societies in Cuba used legal and social activities to promote racial awareness. But these efforts fell short of the mark. None attracted significant membership, and they engaged only a small minority of urban blacks to carry on their efforts. The nation's uneducated and alienated rural blacks remained largely untouched by such movements.

In 1933 Fulgencio Batista came to power. Of mixed racial origins himself, Batista claimed to be a friend of Afro-Cubans. His friendship extended to his belief in Santería, an Afro-Cuban religion, and to his support of individual blacks who benefited from the island's prosperity under his rule. In 1940 he supported a constitution that included provisions prohibiting racial, gender, and class discrimination. However, he never enforced such provisions, and he did little to improve the lives of blacks. Exclusive clubs kept their doors closed to dark-skinned Cubans.

A handful of black professionals lived in Havana and Santiago. A few served in congress, whereas others held minor positions in the governmental bureaucracy. The military also promoted some Afro-Cuban officers, including General Gregory Querejata. Yet neither Batista nor the governments he supported went out of their way to alter the situation of blacks.

In 1959 Fidel Castro came to power as the leader of a leftist revolution vowing that the Cuban Revolution would at once eliminate racial discrimination, among other objectives. Without doubt, the revolution did reverse centuries of injustice by incorporating poor blacks into one of the best educational systems in the Americas. Improvements in public sanitation, living standards, health care, and school facilities have contributed to the betterment of Afro-Cubans. In addition, over a million white middle- and upper-class professionals left after the 1959 revolution. Cuba immediately became more mulatto and black than before, and available public services and aid were shared more equally among the remaining population.

The revolution made tremendous strides in eliminating racism and sexism, which proved especially helpful to Afro-Cuban women. Socialism replaced capitalism and reduced the economic gap between whites and

Fidel Castro, leader of the 1959 Cuban Revolution, attempted to eliminate racial discrimination and later sent troops to several countries in Africa. Brown Brothers.

blacks. Moreover, Castro eventually gave blacks access to political power, at least at the local level. Most important, educational and other social reforms produced a generation of healthy and literate young Afro-Cubans with the energy and will to enter the mainstream. Thus, the revolution created a more equal playing field for Afro-Cubans. Although racism persists, especially among older Cubans, it no longer circumscribes the fate of Afro-Cubans. Many Afro-Cubans have moved into high-ranking military positions and formed a bulwark of the Cuban Communist party.

Some observers, however, cast doubt on Cuba's antidiscrimination campaign. Both Elizabeth Sutherland of the United States and Barry Reckford of the British West Indies contended that the revolution had eliminated the worst manifestations of racism but had not erased some whites' perceptions that blacks were inferior. Black Power exiles like Robert Williams, John Clytus, and Eldridge Cleaver were more outspoken. They expressed outrage at the lack of progress made by Afro-Cubans under the Castro regime. Their ideas of Black Power and Pan-Africanism obviously affected their views of the less confrontational approach in Hispanic societies.

A number of Afro-Cuban observers of race relations have reached opposite conclusions. Nicolás Guillén, for instance, remained in Cuba and believes the revolution has eliminated racism. But he represents intellectuals who played no active political roles and therefore are not frustrated by the fact that the entire upper echelon of the government remains white. For their part, Afro-Cuban exiles like Carlos Moore and Juan René Bettancourt concluded that the Cuban government had conspired to keep blacks out of high positions. Moore continues to charge the Cuban authorities with falsifying data to make Cuba appear whiter than it is. Bettancourt, former director of the Federation of Black Societies in Cuba, even accused Fidel Castro of having killed off the black movement in Cuba.

Without doubt, the 1959 revolution radically altered the political rights and power of Afro-Cubans. As anticipated, in each generation blacks have displayed more active and visible participation in the political process. Still not seen in top governmental positions, Afro-Cubans do hold posts within the Communist party and the Soviet. Afro-Cubans have served as ambassadors and commanders in Africa and as high officials in the Ministry of Foreign Affairs. In fields such as education and agriculture, they increasingly make their presence felt as policymakers.

◆ VENEZUELA

Today's Afro-Venezuelans are descended from several distinct immigrant groups, one of which goes back to the slaves imported during the colonial era and a second to the Caribbean islands, where poverty in the late nineteenth century drove many to migrate to the mainland in search of jobs. Within several generations, these West Indian blacks became thoroughly hispanicized. A third group arose from the steady arrival of Guyanese blacks, who have not assimilated and hence have suffered from ethnic and cultural discrimination. Natives criticize the Guyanese for speaking a different language, worshiping in different churches, and following foreign customs.

As elsewhere in the hemisphere, Venezuelan blacks had historically been prevented from rising socially or politically, a situation worsened by their disparate origins and cultures. Still, individual blacks exercised some power in the past. For example, at the beginning of this century several skilled Afro-Venezuelans served as generals in the army. However, when dictator Juan Vicente Gómez began to professionalize the officer corps in 1908, black generals began to disappear. New educational requirements in the military academies tended to favor cadets from white or mestizo families.

Gómez followed whitening policies that reduced the presence and influence of Venezuela's blacks. To accomplish this objective, the government continued the ban on nonwhite immigration begun in 1892. Furthermore, it mounted a campaign to discourage black West Indian laborers from staying, although they were the backbone of the agricultural, mining, and petroleum work forces. With assistance from the U.S. and British governments, Gómez also prevented the agents of Marcus Garvey's UNIA and Samuel Gompers's American Federation of Labor from entering Venezuela.

The systematic exclusion of blacks from politics abated after Gómez's death in 1935. Opposition parties sprang up in the more moderate atmosphere. One of these, the Acción Democrática (AD), adopted a strategy of including all classes and races in its ranks. The AD was led by individuals of mixed race, such as Rómulo Betancourt, Andrés Eloy Blanco, and others. Its leaders were partly inspired by the Alianza Popular Revolucionaria Americana (APRA), organized in the 1920s by Peruvian Víctor Raúl Haya de la Torre. AD set out to create an alliance of middle- and working-class followers, including many of the nation's *pardo* (racially mixed) and black masses. It launched a new era in Venezuelan politics.

From the beginning, the AD was dedicated to improving workers' rights and to supporting political and racial democracy. To accomplish this goal, AD leaders campaigned to change the immigration codes. Rómulo Betancourt outlined his party's position:

> Our immigration policy followed a definite sociological concept. We wanted the immigrant to increase our production and to fill the country. We did not consider the white man as such or the European as superior to the Venezuelan of mixed blood. We were not interested in the transfer of civilization as one might bring some Swiss pine saplings to give style to a tropical garden, filled with our mango and tamarind trees.

The AD deserves much credit for translating an intellectual doctrine of racial tolerance into a platform to improve the lives of millions of nonwhite Venezuelans.

Betancourt and the AD built their multiracial platform on a body of social thought developed during the previous half-century. The positivist intellectual and politician José Gil Fortoul first introduced the notion of social race, or race as a cultural rather than a purely physical phenomenon, in the 1890s. Since then, Venezuelans have considered themselves a *café con leche*, or brown-skinned, people. Gil Fortoul recognized the mixed racial origin of Venezuela's majority but argued that the bulk of Venezuelans belonged to a mestizo rather than a mulatto or Negroid racial group.

Venezuelan positivists brought a new dimension to discussions of race in Venezuela by introducing European and North American theories. Although they rejected blatant racial determinism, they embraced the mechanistic premise of social progress. They agreed that race, along with hygiene and technology, were important factors in the evolution of modern societies. They also associated dark skin with backwardness and underdevelopment.

Ultimately, the postivists' study of race and its influence on national development led them to advocate a policy of whitening the population. While they did not deny their Amerindian and African heritage, they judged the mixed racial majority—made up of pardos, blacks, and Amerindians—to be incapable of governing itself under a democratic order. Like their contemporaries in Mexico and Peru, who reached similar conclusions about Amerindians, the Venezuelan elites believed that the bulk of their population belonged to an inferior racial group. To correct this condition, they advocated whitening the population through massive immigration of Europeans. Like Gil Fortoul, they also held that most of the miscegenation in Venezuela was between Europeans and Amerindians, which they considered a less degraded mixture than the others.

Despite his historically inaccurate explanation of Venezuela's society, Gil Fortoul deserves recognition as the first major Latin American intellectual to describe racial mixing in positive terms. His idea that racial mixing could produce robust racial types contrasts with the writings of Justo Sierra of Mexico, Alejandro O. Deustua of Peru, José Ingenieros of Argentina, and Sílvio Romero and Raimundo Nina Rodrigues of Brazil—all of whom regarded miscegenation as an obstacle to national progress. For Gil Fortoul, more mixing with stronger, white Europeans would further improve the Venezuelan mestizo stock.

Although he held strong antiblack sentiments, Gil Fortoul believed that the crossing of races could lead to offspring that were better suited than their parents to the environment of Venezuela. His idea of "social race" embodied the belief that cultural factors played a larger part than genetic factors in determining the evolution of a society. For him, the term *race* described only the degree to which an individual had become incorporated into the prevailing culture. In Venezuela, this meant the hispanicized segment of the population. Thus, the process of evolution was driven by the emergence of a new and stronger race owing to mestizos mixing with European immigrants.

Gil Fortoul's basic theories prevailed throughout most of the twentieth century and helped promote the myth that a racial democracy exists in Venezuela. Subsequently, the few scholars who have written about race, or about Afro-Venezuelans, have accepted his view that during the colonial era Afro-Venezuelans lost their African heritage and became hispanicized. According to the myth, blacks gained parity with other Venezuelans, so that race alone no longer played a major role in deciding social status.

When the AD leaders came on the scene in the 1930s, however, Venezuela's blacks remained alienated by their poverty. In rural areas, their physical isolation exacerbated their social exclusion. Without education, and living in a society where elites preferred whiteness, the black population found itself victimized by silent racism, with its subliminal prejudices and covert forms of discrimination. White Venezuelans described blacks as inherently lazy, inclined to criminality, and stupid, people who caused problems wherever they lived in large numbers. Whites treated predominantly black regions of the nation, such as the Barlovento district east of Caracas, as pieces of Africa.

Race relations began to change noticeably after Rómulo Betancourt and the AD party came to power in 1945 and became effective advocates for the nation's tricolored masses. They immediately passed an antidiscrimination law and began liberalizing the nation's immigration laws to allow the entry of nonwhites into Venezuela. They frequently referred to their fellow Venezuelans as the café con leche people. AD rhetoric voiced opposition to a predominantly white oligarchy linked to foreign imperialists who tried to dominate the Venezuelan economy. In these and other ways, the AD provided blacks access to political influence and put some in high offices, without necessarily breaking down all racial barriers.

Since 1958, Venezuela has lived under a two-party democracy. To their credit, Venezuelans have removed many racial barriers that existed before that time. Blacks now make up significant percentages of the students at previously white high schools and universities; they hold more jobs in national and state government; and they have served as state governors and have held high positions within the political parties. Individuals of mixed blood, or café con leche complexions, as the Venezuelans describe it, have run for the presidency and even served as president. And while they have not breached all social barriers, they have made progress within a nonrevolutionary framework.

Although the military officer corps continues to be an all-white bastion, blacks in cities such as Caracas and Maracaibo make up the bulk of the police and their officer ranks. Blacks serve as deputies in the national congress and hold positions as mayors and city council members. Race alone no longer proscribes the blacks' political opportunities in Venezuela. Perhaps that is the closest approximation to racial democracy that the hemisphere is likely to see.

◆ THE ANDEAN COUNTRIES

During the era of slavery, the countries along the spine of the Andes, from Colombia down to Bolivia, received far fewer Africans than did Venezuela or the Hispanic Caribbean. Moreover, African Americans in the Andes have always been heavily outnumbered by Amerindians, which tended to ally whites and blacks against the native masses. This peculiar situation in the Andes diminished the African influence seen elsewhere in modern times, yet it also reduced hostility and discrimination against blacks found in those same places.

In Colombia and Ecuador, blacks remain concentrated along the coasts and in a few highland pockets, geographically separated from the main seats of power and wealth. Intellectuals have taken little pride in their nations' black heritage, and their history texts overlook the roles of African slaves and their descendants in nation-building.

Colombia's black enclaves along its Pacific and Caribbean coasts are located in old plantation and mining regions. From Buenaventura on the Pacific coast, through the Chocó district south of Panama, to the northern coast of Colombia, remnant maroon communities still exist. Other villages lie along the lower reaches of the Magdalena River, once a major transportation artery. Blacks also make up a significant portion of the populations of port cities such as Buenaventura, Cartagena, and Barranquilla. Cali, the hub of a major agro-export region in southwestern Colombia, also has many blacks, although they are a minority of the total population.

During the twentieth century, blacks have not risen very high in Colombian politics. Few have served in cabinets, as agency directors, or as military commanders. The two national parties, the Liberals and the Conservatives, have not made any concerted effort to incorporate blacks into their ranks at the national level. They do coerce blacks into taking sides in local politics, however, but this has not led to recruitment into national positions. The same is true of the Catholic church, which has named few blacks to high office.

Nevertheless, African Americans have dominated the municipal politics of cities like Buenaventura and Cartagena, even if white elites there have excluded them from social clubs. In remote pueblos, such as the former palenque of San Bonifacio along the Caribbean coast, descendants of slaves live as fishermen, farmers, traders, and artisans. Blacks run local affairs entirely and have little interaction with the larger national scene.

Political exclusion is partly to blame for inducing the mulatto and mestizo drug lords to bypass the existing structures. The cartels established control over extensive areas of the country and resisted efforts by the national government to break them up. The Cali drug cartel, a segment of Colombia's disaffected African American population, has converted illicit drug profits into legitimate investments. They own chains of pharmacies, department stores, and supermarkets, which guarantees their children the wealth needed for social acceptance and prominence on the political stage.

Black Colombians have also played important roles in organizing rebel forces, such as the M-19. Just as drug lords have recruited blacks into paramilitary forces, so have the Colombian *guerrilleros* recruited blacks into their ranks. As a result, many aspiring blacks have turned to subversive activity to gain some semblance of political power. Though unsuccessful to date, these rebel movements have offered an alternative channel to African Americans who found no opportunity for political advancement through the existing structures.

Panama belongs to northern South America because of its large black population. It has a more complex black population than Colombia, from which it declared independence in 1903. Some Afro-Panamanians call themselves colonial blacks and trace their ancestry back to the era of slavery. Most have assimilated to hispanicized customs over several generations and find little evidence of discrimination.

Most Afro-Panamanians are descended from black immigrants from the West Indies who arrived during the nineteenth and twentieth centuries. Most of them live in the Canal region and have descended from Antilleans who helped build the Panama Railroad and Canal. The Antilleans and their descendants experienced ostracism by the colonial blacks and whites, owing in part to their English-speaking and Protestant heritage. The fact that many lived in the old Canal Zone further removed them from contact with Panama's colonial blacks.

Politically, neither the colonial blacks nor the West Indians made much headway as a group during the twentieth century, partly because of the dominant position of the United States in Panama. Upwardly mobile colonial blacks identified with the white elites, and as they rose up the social ladder they tended to whiten their lineage through association with well-to-do Panamanians. Mulattoes have held prominent positions, both in national administrations and in the nation's military.

In contrast, West Indian blacks had little opportunity to join in the political activities of the Hispanic Panamanians. Earlier in the century, many turned to Marcus Garvey's UNIA movement that swept through the Caribbean. Others maintained close relations with black politicians in the

United States, especially those active in the Harlem Renaissance movement. During the dictatorship of Omar Torrijos (1968–1981), some prominent West Indian descendants joined colonial blacks in supporting the regime. They believed that Torrijos's pluralist nationalism might lead to their integration into the political and social mainstream. That has not occurred, and blacks are a visible but powerless segment of Panama's population today.

In Ecuador, modest remnants of maroon societies remain north of Quito. Also, in the Esmeraldas district along the northwestern coast, blacks make up most of the working poor. These Afro-Ecuadorians are vestiges of the slave economies that existed until the midnineteenth century. Most still live in poverty, victims of racial and economic discrimination. They have not achieved prominence at the national level, nor have the black citizens of Esmeraldas attempted to migrate in large numbers to Quito or other predominantly mestizo and Amerindian cities.

In Colombia, Panama, and Ecuador, race relations ultimately boil down to the acceptance of white phenotypes as natural for elites. Blackness corresponds to poverty and implies negative characteristics. Like most Latin Americans, Andean whites perceive of race as being arrayed on a scale; colored people fall somewhere between the white and black extremes of the scale. As individuals move upward in socioeconomic status, they become increasingly white in the eyes of others. In sharp contrast to the United States, miscegenation is viewed as a way to promote whitening rather than as mongrelization or blackening. Finally, a person's appearance (clothing, grooming, posture, diction, residence) is as important as actual genetic characteristics in deciding race, although phenotype is never ignored.

Several observations apply equally to Colombia, Panama, and Ecuador. Whites predominate among the social, economic, and political elites in these countries, and both whites and mestizos consider coastal African Americans to be biologically and intellectually inferior. To date, the apparatus of the state has favored whites over blacks, especially in legal disputes. Black and mulatto men and women accept the social advantages of whitening and whenever possible try to marry whiter spouses. Blacks have adopted white cultural values, not only in language and social behavior, but also to the extent of referring to Negroid features, like kinky hair, as undesirable.

Although Peru and Bolivia had substantial slave populations during the colonial era, blacks failed to expand numerically during the national period. Bolivia's black population remains virtually invisible, located in the Amazonian foothills and lowland jungle areas of northern Bolivia. In Peru, blacks made up a significant portion of the artisan class during the Spanish colonial administration, but during the last half of the nineteenth century their numbers diminished. Blacks often married into whiter families to escape the prejudices directed against them. By the twentieth century, few blacks participated in public affairs. One, Luis Sánchez Cerro, of mixed racial origins, won the presidency and served for a year in the early 1930s. However, he remains an anomaly in Peruvian politics.

◆ THE SOUTHERN CONE

The largest number of African Americans in the Southern Cone nations (Argentina, Chile, Uruguay, and Paraguay) lives in Buenos Aires. By 1900, some fifty thousand descendants of Argentina's slave population still resided in the nation's capital. Overwhelmed by several million recently arrived European immigrants, they made up a shrinking portion of the city's residents. Throughout the twentieth century, however, Buenos Aires blacks have maintained a separate identity. Their organizations staged carnival parades, and they have continued to publish an African American newspaper.

Yet Argentines prided themselves on being a white people. Indeed, they claimed that blacks had disappeared from their population, because, as they explained, during the nineteenth century warfare, miscegenation, and diseases had eliminated the nation's black population. The remnant black population seemed to disappear, submerged by generations of new Argentines of foreign origin. The myth, as popularized by the positivist intellectual José Ingenieros, held that Argentina had become a Euro-American nation by World War I. In his estimate, this placed Argentina well ahead of other Latin American nations on the evolutionary scale. Unlike Brazil, with its population of "monkeys," Argentina would become a world leader because of its temperate climate, rich resources, and white population.

Uruguayan blacks, who number no more than three thousand, have fared no better than their Argentine counterparts. During the past one hundred years, they have encountered racial and class discrimination that has reduced them to peripheral roles. Deeply embedded racism has kept blacks from rising above menial tasks in Uruguay. Few have escaped the manual agricultural or industrial jobs that their slave ancestors held, and fewer still have graduated from the national university or become professionals.

Afro-Uruguayan intellectuals have tried to address racial discrimination, but their one serious attempt, in 1937, ended in failure. In that year, blacks founded the Indigenous People's party in Montevideo but did not manage to elect any of its candidates to the national legislature. Many cultural and social associations have thrived in the party's wake and have kept alive the racial consciousness of Uruguay's small black populace. Despite their efforts, Afro-Uruguayans have not succeeded in getting Uruguay's white population to admit that racial prejudice and discrimination exist.

In political terms, blacks in the Southern Cone simply do not count and have not held important political positions. In the eyes of their white compatriots, blacks do not even exist. Thus, they have made no impact, either as a group or as individuals, on the political destinies of their respective nations. They simply exist in isolation, either as a few individuals in the cities or as small groups living in remote regions of the interior.

◆ BRAZIL

During the twentieth century, race relations in Brazil have gone through a series of convolutions. From the beginning, elites wished to avoid creating a segmented society, such as existed in the U.S. South, and so they evaded discussions of race relations and even stopped tabulating race in the census from 1900 to 1980. Yet they also worried about the large black and brown population, which made up the majority, and so, in the end, they moved toward a compromise on race. On the one hand, they accepted the mixed origins of their people and rejected most of the deterministic theories about race. On the other, they steadfastly maintained that whitening had to occur for Brazil to become a great nation. Ambivalence on the race question did not eliminate racial prejudice and discrimination; paradoxically, it led to disguising inequality as racial democracy.

Following abolition in 1888, Brazil's former slaves did not experience much improvement in their living standards. The nation's elites, who controlled both agricultural and industrial capital, enacted policies aimed at keeping blacks in menial, low-wage positions. One researcher concluded that blacks had gone no farther than from slave to proletarian. Employers' wage policies were complemented by subsidized immigration from Europe that expanded the work force and helped to whiten the nation's gene pool.

An extensive oligarchy of landowners, military officers, and business-people dominated regional and national politics in the early decades of this century. Leaders from the states of São Paulo, Rio de Janeiro, Minas Gerais, and Rio Grande do Sul controlled the national government, dismissing the democratic intent of the constitution. Local planters, called *fazendeiros*, ran their districts as feudal lords, virtually beyond the jurisdiction of any government. Thus, blacks moved from slavery to freedom in an environment that excluded over 90 percent of the population from political participation.

During these years, the efforts of a few black and brown intellectuals to generate movements like those in Cuba met with defeat. As early as 1925, São Paulo blacks had called for the creation of a racial pressure group. In 1927 they founded the Palmares Civic Center, which sponsored meetings and lectures and soon began a campaign to change legislation that prohibited blacks from enlisting in the state militia. Unfortunately, the un-settled politics of the late 1920s and their own internecine squabbling frustrated their attempts to exert political force. Other efforts to improve conditions for Afro-Brazilians, such as labor unionization and other forms of social and political dissent, also met with failure. The elites simply relied on force to keep workers—black and white—in their places at the bottom of the economic system. As one president said, "The social question is a matter for the police."

The political situation improved for most Brazilians when Getúlio Vargas came to power as the result of a brief civil war that he termed the 1930 revolution. Vargas, who hoped that cultural nationalism would forge a nation out of Brazil's disparate parts, later accepted the ideas of Gilberto Freyre and others who held that Brazilians had formed a new race in the tropics, a people of mixed origins. The idea of racial democracy eventually became the official doctrine of the Vargas regime and its successors.

In the early 1930s, sociologist Gilberto Freyre had supplied an agreeable racial theory for Brazilian elites. Brazil's strength, he wrote, resulted from the mixed racial origins of its population; indeed, he implied, Brazil was a racial democracy. Although it is not entirely clear what he meant by this term, he suggested that race did not decide an individual's status. By inference, after the abolition of slavery, blacks could operate in Brazilian society on equal terms with whites.

According to Freyre, the lack of racial prejudice and discrimination flowed from the less harsh nature of Brazilian slavery. The fact that Portu-guese masters felt no shame in cohabiting with African slave women also reduced awareness of race. Over the centuries of slavery, extensive mis-cegenation eroded race prejudices and created a mixed racial majority. Freyre believed that racial commingling had made a positive contribution to the formation of Brazilian society and its culture. His so-called Bahian school, which served as the orthodox view of race relations in Brazil, held that Brazilians, a tricolored race in the tropics, did not have prejudices or discriminate by race.

In common usage, however, racial democracy really meant that people could whiten themselves. Race embodied a social and cultural meaning as well as physical connotations, such as Gil Fortoul's social race in Vene-zuela. Thus, blacks who progressed economically and socially could whiten themselves culturally, a process called *branqueamento*. In this fash-ion, their progeny would become equals with the whites. Brazilians also say, "money whitens."

Vargas, himself a product of the landowning class in Rio Grande do Sul, had little feeling for the race question and no desire to stir up trouble. He did, however, make a bid for labor support, which meant winning over urban voters, many of whom were black. Because of the instability of the country in the 1930s, he also wished to avoid divisiveness at all costs.

Therefore, he appealed to urban workers and offered to improve their conditions regardless of race or national origins. He opened new opportunities for education, and he also reduced immigration quotas, which alleviated some problems stemming from the importation of cheap foreign workers. Most Afro-Brazilian activists chose to work with the Vargas administration.

Given the signs of greater receptiveness to improving the racial climate after 1930, Afro-Brazilian leaders decided to press for reforms by organizing a black political movement. In late 1931 Arlindo Veiga dos Santos convened a series of meetings in São Paulo to found a black political organization. Previously, dos Santos had worked with the Congress of Black Youth and the Palmares Civic Center. The upshot was his launching of the Brazilian Black Front, which was devoted to fighting the injustices experienced by persons of African descent.

The Brazilian Black Front won widespread support throughout São Paulo, southern Minas Gerais, and Espírito Santo. In Bahia and Rio Grande do Sul, Afro-Brazilians founded independent black fronts. In 1933 dos Santos ran for the city council of São Paulo but was not elected. The Front also sponsored literacy and vocational courses for adults, set up educational facilities for children, built clinics to provide inexpensive medical treatment, and offered legal counseling to blacks who had disputes with landlords and employers.

Despite its success at these endeavors, the Front failed to gain any political power. In part, the gap between its upwardly mobile leaders and its working-class followers weakened its appeal. For various reasons, between 1931 and 1937 the Front did not register enough voters to elect any candidates to office. It succeeded only as a lobbying group by addressing matters of secondary concern, such as admission into the state militia. Otherwise, it failed to take a clear political path, and it stirred up trouble by allying itself with highly nationalistic and xenophobic political movements, similar to European fascism. The end came in late 1937, when Vargas banned all parties, including the Front, and ended electoral politics. Race ceased to be a topic of public discussion until after the war.

By midcentury it was clear to some observers that racial inequality existed in Brazil, although it was neither institutionalized nor segregationist. The absence of state-sanctioned race discrimination allowed a more insidious racism to arise. Unlike the overt kinds found in the United States, Brazilian racism appeared in unpredictable and capricious ways. For that reason, it has taken Brazilian scholars decades to discover what Afro-Brazilians have known all along, that prejudice and discrimination do exist.

As in the United States, race relations in Brazil differed from region to region and between rural and urban settings. In the agricultural northeast and central coastal areas, through the plantations and ranches of Rio de Janeiro, Minas Gerais, São Paulo, and Espírito Santo, a more paternalistic racial pattern has existed. After the abolition of slavery in 1888, former slaves and free blacks experienced discrimination aimed at keeping them in their places as low-paid rural workers. Blacks who moved to cities, especially the industrial cities of the southeast, experienced more competitive conditions. But industrialists, like planters, wanted to coerce workers into accepting their terms of employment. Both groups found that racial competition served their purposes by maintaining Afro-Brazilians in subordinate positions.

Beginning in the 1950s, sociologist Florestán Fernandes and his colleagues at the University of São Paulo disputed Freyre's notion of racial democracy, although they also traced Brazil's racial dilemma back to the slave experience. Having grown up in São Paulo, with its modern industrial and agro-commercial economy, Fernandes and his collaborators observed obvious racial inequality around them. This so-called Paulista school of researchers exposed discrimination, which they attributed to the destructive nature of the slave experience. In their eyes, slavery turned white masters into authoritarians who asserted their racial and cultural superiority over their slaves. This treatment turned the slaves into illiterate, unskilled workers who abhorred disciplined labor. The legacy of the slave experience meant that succeeding generations of Afro-Brazilians became marginalized. The descendants of slaves were incapable of fitting into a modern society and economy, while the white master class harbored deep-seated prejudices against blacks.

Fernandes was optimistic, however. He predicted that blacks who worked in industrial settings would overcome their aversion to disciplined work and that modern urban life would outgrow the prejudices and inefficient behavior of the past. Advanced societies simply had no place for racial discrimination, and Brazil would soon shrug it off along with other forms of traditionalism.

Today few students of race relations deny the existence of a permanent racial hierarchy in Brazil. Census and survey data, again tabulated by race, prove the existence of patterns of discrimination in schools, jobs, and government services. Recent studies show that whites, mulattoes, and blacks of equal age, education, and class do not receive equal pay or promotions in the workplace. Blacks predominate at the bottom of the socioeconomic pyramid, while the elites are virtually pure white. Freyre's racial democracy simply does not exist in either the public or private job market, and Fernandes's modernization has failed to eliminate racial inequality. Brazilian whites maintain a standard stereotype of blacks as lazy, pernicious, stupid, vain, untrustworthy individuals. They expect blacks to excel only as athletes—like the renowned soccer player Pelé—or as entertainers. Such attitudes pose a covert barrier to the blacks' efforts to improve their status and to achieve racial equality.

Since the end of World War II, Brazilian blacks have not organized themselves effectively into national political groups. In 1956 congress passed the Alfonso Arinos Law prohibiting racial discrimination, but it was virtually never invoked because of the covert ways prejudice works. Several black movements have appeared in recent decades, and some six hundred existed as of the 1990s. Yet none mounted effective political campaigns, and few sent leaders to congress or executive office. Class differences, as well as geographic isolation, have hampered the efforts of Afro-Brazilians to establish anything like the Black Power movement of the United States. In the absence of an overt segregationist system, they have been unable to unify their followers.

In 1964 the Brazilian army installed an autocratic regime that lasted until 1985. During those years, conservative elites proved unreceptive to social advancement for blacks or any other disadvantaged group. During the 1980s, as the military retreated from rule, blacks became political activists again. Many joined the Christian-based communities organized by liberal Catholic priests and laypeople throughout Brazil. This liberation theology movement did not serve as a black movement per se, but it attracted predominantly nonwhite members. The liberation theology leaders addressed several issues concerning Afro-Brazilians, including racial discrimination and the need to eliminate racial injustice in Brazil.

Other black activists joined mainstream movements, such as the Party of the Brazilian Democratic Movement. They struggled to raise the awareness of fellow party members about the plight of Afro-Brazilians and often won the support of party leaders. As a result, in 1982 the governor of São Paulo created a state agency known as the Council for the Participation and Development of the Black Community. Individual blacks have also achieved some national prominence. In 1933 one served as governor of Espírito Santo, and Benedita da Silva, an Afro-Brazilian member of congress, ran for mayor of Rio de Janeiro. In these and other cases, it should be noted, the individuals belonged to mainstream political parties, not black movements.

Brazilians who hoped to eliminate injustice and racism in their country had believed that they did not need the measures adopted in the United States, like civil rights legislation, affirmative action, and regional and community development programs. The Freyre and Fernandes theses suggested that if difficulties existed, they would take care of themselves. Recent analyses, however, suggest that social problems laden with racial implications—sharp income gaps, blocked mobility, unfavorable media images, rising criminality, and urban deterioration—are getting worse. The prospects for laissez-faire solutions, or for a general reorientation of Brazilian thinking about race, appear faint.

◆ CONCLUSION

Few countries in Latin America have experienced the racial divisiveness and violence that have assailed the United States for over a century. Latin American race confrontations were mitigated by many factors, including lower ratios of blacks to whites in most places, sustained genetic mixing over centuries, flexible social categories, agile elite accommodation, and nation-building rationales that repudiated racism. Prejudice and discrimination still exist, but they are so subtle and veiled that they rarely come into the open. In several countries, writers have invented myths of racial democracy to explain away racial inequities. In others, they have devised myths of disappearance about once numerous African descendants. Latin America simply does not have the overt, public, confrontational race problems that exist in the United States.

Afro-Latinos have a difficult time pinpointing discriminatory behavior, and they often choose to defend their cultural and diasporic traditions instead of fighting an elusive racism. Afro-Panamanians, for example, struggled to preserve their West Indian origins amid Hispanic ostracism; Brazil's blacks asserted their right to worship African deities without harassment; and Jamaican followers of Marcus Garvey created a socio-religious movement oriented toward Ethiopian beginnings. In many parts of Latin America, preservation of the black identity in the face of assimilationist pressures looms larger than combating discrimination.

Because the European colonies in the Americas fragmented into dozens of nations, some no more than tiny islands like Grenada, the possibilities of a united black movement have been nil. As time passed, geographical and social differences among the new countries enlarged the ethnic variety already existing among ancestors of African slaves. Those African descendants who care about questions of ethnic identity are more likely to look to Africa or even to the United States than to other Latin American countries. But the truth is that the vast majority of Afro-Latinos no longer see themselves in relation to the outside world; their daily struggles are set in towns, regions, and cities, and involve Hispanics, mestizos, and Amerindians.

Whether the Latin style of racial accommodation will prove to be more successful or satisfying than the U.S. approach cannot yet be determined. Latin America, however, has witnessed very distinctive ways for people of different races to come together and eventually form multicultural societies.

Chapter 15

THE AMERICAS' CONTINUING TIES WITH AFRICA

1890s	John B. Small's mission work in West Africa leads to founding of AME Zion Church.
1890s	Tuskegee Institute development mission to Togo.
1919	First Pan-African Congress.
1921	Second Pan-African Congress.
1923	Third Pan-African Congress.
1927	Fourth Pan-African Congress.
1920s	Height of Marcus Garvey's UNIA movement.
1930	Emperor Haile Selassie crowned in Ethiopia.
1930s	First black cultural conferences in Brazil.
1935	Kwame Nkrumah enrolls in Lincoln University, Pennsylvania.
1950s	Independence movements begin to succeed in Africa.
1960s	Cuba's revolutionary government engages in African liberation struggles.
1962	U.S. Peace Corps begins sending volunteers to Africa.
1960s	Black Power movements on U.S. college campuses begin.
1975	Cuba sends troops to Angola and other parts of Africa.
1978–1990s	New black cultural awareness movements in Brazil.
1991	New Pan-African movement.

T he history of the Americas' ties with Africa falls into several major periods. During the nineteenth century, Pan-African sentiment infused the antislavery crusade. The next phase embraced the Pan-African conferences held outside Africa between 1919 and 1950. Black cultural awareness movements in Brazil in the 1930s and 1940s added a new dimension, as did *negritude* currents in the Caribbean. Pan-African conferences held in Africa after the onset of independence in the 1950s began a new phase. This was followed by the powerful civil rights movement in the United States and the Cold War intervention by U.S., Soviet, and Cuban agencies in the 1960s. Finally, international aid efforts to promote stability, democracy, and economic development in the continent mark the most recent period.

◆ PAN-AFRICAN MOVEMENTS

Only a month after the abolition of slavery in Brazil, deposed West African King JaJa of Opobo arrived in St. Vincent in the Windward Islands. The year was 1888. Born a slave but able to win his freedom and build a lucrative export business, JaJa had become too successful in the eyes of the British Colonial Office, and so was removed to this remote southeast corner of the Antilles to allow uncontested British control over what was becoming their colony in Nigeria.

Word of JaJa's coming had spread throughout the island and caused great expectation. The former king represented an African past most Vincentians had been cut off from by slavery. Moreover, people on the islands lived in isolation and tended to inflate the riches and opportunities available abroad, even in Africa at the onset of the colonial conquests. So King JaJa symbolized ancestral connections with Africa and possibly access to great wealth—he had been the richest palm oil trader in West Africa.

Huge crowds thronged the docks to greet JaJa, in hopes of speaking with or touching him. For weeks afterward, visitors called on him to learn of his past and find out what he could do to help them. The British officials in St. Vincent discouraged this contact but were unable to isolate him. In time, however, the Vincentians' fascination with their African celebrity diminished, and JaJa was eventually moved to Barbados for medical care. He died en route back to Africa and was buried in Nigeria.

Episodes like these, in which persons of African descent thirsted for knowledge and contact with their ancestral homeland, were repeated thousands of times throughout the Americas. In the course of the twentieth century, many African Americans forged links with Africa, which were emotional, religious, economic, political, and personal.

Pan-Africanism grew out of the nineteenth-century campaigns to end the slave trade and slavery itself. Former slaves who served in the British West Indies regiments resettled in Sierra Leone, as did captives liberated from the slave trade. Freedpersons from the United States established the nation of Liberia in the 1820s and received U.S. protection throughout the oppressive days of colonialism. Abraham Lincoln and others imagined repatriating former slaves to tropical lands during the U.S. Civil War. These and other initiatives recognized an African legacy among American blacks, as well as a need to change the negative perceptions, stereotypes, and attitudes toward them.

In this century, Pan-Africanism became anti-imperialist, supporting efforts to liberate Africa from the devastating effects of European colonialism. It also created and disseminated an appreciation of the rich African contributions to world cultures. Finally, it promoted solidarity among the peoples of Africa and the diaspora.

Contacts and linkages between Africans and African Americans were carried out by universities (especially historically black ones), government-sponsored travel, international congresses of all sorts, individual studies and research, business dealings, and personal connections. Pan-Africanism, then, ranges from organized and focused to informal and scattered.

* * *

Organized Pan-Africanism was born in the West Indies and raised in the United States. W.E.B. Du Bois, the originator of the movement, was of Haitian parentage, and leaders like Marcus Garvey, George Padmore, Sylvester Williams, and Claude McKay sprang up in the British West Indies. The movement seemed to flourish where colonialism appeared unjust and yet where British political rights permitted dissent.

People of African descent in the French islands were less confrontational and sought political and social justice within the French colonial system. They considered themselves black Frenchmen and valued cultural ties with France more than with Africa. As a result, African solidarity in the French West Indies took the form of the negritude movement, which was more literary and cultural than political. Writers in the negritude genre, popular after World War I, included Aime Lesaire, Leopold Senghor, Frantz Fanon, Reme Maran, Gaston Monnerville, and Jean Price-Mars. Only later did the movement become political and it engaged in the independence struggles of Guinea and Mali in the late 1950s.

During World War I, W.E.B. Du Bois (1868–1963), journalist, author, and educator, emerged as the most articulate spokesperson of the Pan-African movement. Reports of inhumane treatment of black soldiers by American military officers in France prompted the NAACP to send Du Bois to France to investigate. He did so partly to participate in the Paris Peace Conference scheduled to begin shortly. He wanted to draw attention to the injustice of European colonialism in Africa, treatment of the black soldiers, and the need for representation of people of African descent at the peace conference.

W. E. B. DuBois, a leading black intellectual in the United States, helped found the NAACP (1909) and the post-World War I Pan-African Conferences. The Bettman Archive.

With the support of the Senegalese high commissioner to France, Du Bois gained the permission of the French government to organize the first Pan-African Congress, held in Paris in February 1919. Sixteen black Americans attended, despite official opposition to the congress by the governments of the United States and Great Britain. The Caribbean nations sent twenty-seven official delegates, while Africa was represented by twenty (from Senegal, Nigeria, and Ghana). France, Belgium, and Portugal officially recognized the event and also sent delegates.

Encouraged by the enthusiasm displayed at the 1919 congress, Du Bois and other Pan-Africanists continued to develop political and cultural ties with Africa. Their efforts led to the second Pan-African Congress, held in London, Brussels, and Paris between 29 August and 6 September 1921. They now concentrated on the problems of European colonialism and hence achieved a higher degree of unanimity than at the first congress. Their recommendations on colonialism were later presented to the League of Nations and the International Labor Office. The third Pan-African Congress was held in London, Lisbon, and Paris in 1923, and the fourth in New York City in 1927.

Virtually simultaneously with Du Bois's work promoting Pan-Africanism, Marcus Garvey mobilized his UNIA and conducted its black pride and back-to-Africa campaigns, sketched in Chapter 13. The two movements appealed to different audiences: Du Bois's to middle-class intellectuals and Garvey's to the working masses.

Garvey's activism had an unexpected offshoot in the Americas: the Rastafarian movement. Garvey stated that the ascension of Prince Ras Tafari Makonnen to the Ethiopian throne in 1930, as Emperor Haile Selassie, fulfilled his prophecy that a black Christ would appear who would redeem the children of the diaspora. Selassie's followers, especially those in Jamaica, worshiped him as a messiah and named their faith Rastafarianism. Widely known for the reggae music and dreadlocks popularized by its Jamaican followers, the faith continues to grow in the Caribbean and some East Coast U.S. cities. As a serious African American religion and philosophy of life, however, Rastafarianism deserves a place beside other mass movements in the Americas, like Cuba's Santería, Brazil's Umbanda, and Haiti's voodoo.

Pan-Africanism, overshadowed by the independence struggles of the midtwentieth century, languished for many years. African Americans were caught up in the civil rights campaigns, while Africans themselves faced the formidable challenges of rebuilding their societies and economies. Most restored African countries fell under the rule of dictators who discouraged foreign contacts. As a result, little solidarity existed before the closing decades of the twentieth century.

In general, middle-class blacks in the United States have tended to view Africa as instrumental in terms of raising issues of foreign policy, self-determination, and economic development. Few have conceived of Africa as a homeland in a personal sense. Many blacks throughout the hemisphere, on the other hand, have felt emotional attachment to the idea of Africa as a place of origin and of spiritual inspiration. Yet they have tended to have very little information with which to favor policy choices.

Flows of poor and biased information between Africa and the Americas have been constant through history. In general, however, the U.S. population has access to more information than any other hemispheric society. The Latin American media depend heavily on Eurocentric news agencies. Oddly, Africans know more about African Americans—especially those in the United States—than vice versa.

Recently, widespread economic distress in Africa has engendered a new Pan-African movement. The economic crisis has occurred because commodities that enjoyed high prices in the 1970s—cocoa, copper, coffee, and palm oil—are now a glut on the market. Loans undertaken ten to fifteen years ago have pyramided into oppressive debts. Most of the debt is held by governments in the developed countries and by multilateral agencies, making collection unlikely, but because of the indebtedness little new money is available for development projects. Meanwhile, foreign investment has declined over the last twenty years because today's businesspeople are pessimistic about long-term profits in Africa. Tragically, much of the continent is worse off today than in the 1960s, owing to myriad factors.

In view of this situation, Africans began taking on more responsibility for solving their social and economic development problems and formed the New Pan-African Movement (PANAF) in the 1990s. PANAF consists of periodic high-level meetings by heads of state and development officials who are attempting to confront African problems head on. PANAF's first African and African American summit was held in Abidjan, Ivory Coast, in April 1991. PANAF met again in Gabon in mid-1993. The organization consists of several thousand members from various countries and institutions. The coordinating committee, headed by the Rev. Leon H. Sullivan, is a loosely defined group of professionals from throughout Africa and the West.

PANAF's two summits analyzed and discussed ways to promote African unity, this time including participation by and aid from the people of the diaspora. In the context of the 1990s, these efforts embrace democratization, freer trade, international solution of political problems, and privatization of government enterprises.

◆ GEOPOLITICS

Since gaining their independence in the late 1950s and 1960s, most African nations have experienced grave political turmoil, often at the hands of military dictators commanding one-party regimes. Many analysts trace this authoritarianism to the oppressive and exploitative colonial rule of the preceding century. Others blame it on Cold War politics that supported dictators like Mobutu Sésé Sekó of Zaire, Idi Amin of Uganda, Mohammed Siad Barre of Somalia, Hasting Kamuzu Bandu of Malawi, Samuel Doe of Liberia, and Mengister Haile Mariam of Ethiopia. These men chose sides by declaring their loyalty to either the Soviet Union or the United States, in exchange for money, military assistance, and diplomatic support. As a result of superpower rivalry, countless billions of dollars and rubles poured into Africa after 1960.

Twenty wars have been fought on African soil since 1960, resulting in some seven million fatalities and five million refugees. Many more millions have been the victims of poverty, drought, overpopulation, corruption, vanishing natural resources, and overcrowded living quarters. African leaders today are confronted with economic chaos and political instability. Foreigners often express pessimism about the Africans' ability to organize themselves, yet most educated Africans are capable managers and able businesspeople. The problem appears to be bad government left over from colonialism and the Cold War.

Cuban intervention in civil wars throughout Africa has been an important theme in the Cold War struggle there, but with Pan-African overtones. From 1960 on, Cuban premier Fidel Castro aided independence fighters against the colonial powers, as well as leftist regimes against pro-Western ones, and he justified Cuban involvement on both ideological and ethnic grounds. Castro supported pro-Soviet, and later pro-Chinese, movements; Cuban officials professed a special sympathy for African liberation forces because of the large proportion of Cubans of African descent. Cuba's activities included guerrilla training, foreign aid, diplomatic leadership, trade, and eventually military intervention.

In November 1975 Fidel Castro dispatched twenty-eight hundred combat troops to Angola to train and assist the Soviet-backed Popular Movement for the Liberation of Angola (MPLA). This force would eventually total forty thousand men. Meanwhile, the United States supported the Front for the National Liberation of Angola (FNLA), which allied with the South Africa–backed National Union for the Total Independence of Angola (UNITA). The foreign sponsorship of civil war contenders raised the level of bloodshed and international confrontation.

Cuban intervention in Angola had a number of outcomes. First, it aided rebel leaders in Namibia, who fought for and eventually achieved total independence from South Africa. Second, South Africa suffered several major defeats in Angola and ultimately withdrew, leading to a negotiated settlement formally ending the war. That settlement also included the departure of all Cuban troops from the continent.

Brazil's government became involved at about the same time Castro's did, though in a different way. In 1961 President Jânio Quadros initiated a policy of strengthening ties with the newly liberated countries of Africa in the hopes of enhancing Brazil's international standing. His policy involved brokering African votes in international bodies and tapping the rich natural resources of that continent. The next several presidents of Brazil, including military generals, followed this geopolitical strategy, regardless of ideology.

Surprisingly, Brazil recognized the leftist government of Angola in 1975, before any of the major powers did. In this way, the military hoped to gain preferential access to Angolan oil, at a time when the Organization of Petroleum Exporting Countries (OPEC) had dramatically forced up the world price. Brazil also cooperated with oil-producing nations in northeastern Africa for the same reason. Counter to these contacts, however, Brazil also cooperated with South Africa in a quasi-military defense alliance during the late 1970s.

A final episode of outside intervention in Africa had a more positive outcome. After decades of publicizing the cruelty and injustice of South Africa's system of apartheid, African leaders succeeded in enlisting the support of influential European and U.S. figures in pressuring the Johannesburg government to change. Economic boycotts involving trade and investments during the 1980s caused significant hardships in South Africa and rallied African Americans to the cause. The end of the Cold War also contributed to phasing out apartheid. Once the specter of communism in the region evaporated, the Western powers no longer needed South Africa as a military ally. Great Britain and the United States, in particular, stepped up their insistence, and the government of South Africa finally agreed. By mid-1993 apartheid was rapidly being dismantled.

Few other countries in the Americas have reached across to Africa the way the United States, Cuba, and Brazil did, for most do not claim strong ties of social and cultural identity.

◆ MULTILATERAL PROGRAMS

Educators and reformers throughout Africa have worked for decades to overcome illiteracy and to adapt their schools' curriculums to the realities of Africa, a process called *Africanization*. External aid agencies, such as U.S. Agency for International Development (USAID), the Ford Foundation, the Rockefeller Foundation, UNESCO, UNICEF, and the Fulbright-Hays Program, have assisted the ministries of education and culture in many nations. In most cases, educational reformers must dismantle colonial systems and mentalities before they can construct new ones appropriate for their countries. This effort has often required a revolutionary commitment and zeal.

In the late 1970s, African educators and ministry officials met in Dakar, Senegal, for a series of seminars on educational goals and theories in Africa under the auspices of UNESCO. One purpose of the seminars and workshops was to study traditional systems of education that might prove serviceable in the new nations. A second goal was to amalgamate traditional learning systems with modern curriculum organization and teaching methods.

Donor organizations in the United States have provided opportunities for African students and educators to study in U.S. universities. For example, the U.S. Academy for Educational Development, an independent, nonprofit organization, focuses on designing, implementing, and evaluating educational programs in emerging nations. Its projects during the 1980s included the Radio Language Arts Project in Kenya; the Primary Education Project in Liberia; the Basic and Nonformal Education Systems Projects in Lesotho; the Human Resources and Institutional Development Project in Malawi; the Gender Resource Awareness in National Development Project in Senegal; the Management and Development Project in Somalia; and the Basic Education and Skills Training Project in Zimbabwe.

The Peace Corps is another technical assistance organization that has fostered productive relationships between African nations and the United

States. Tens of thousands of volunteers have served since the program began in 1961. By the early 1990s, over two thousand young professionals were working in such areas as basic and special education, teacher training, public administration, energy conservation, engineering, industrial arts, family nutrition, maternal and child care, agriculture extension, natural resources development, and small business management.

◆ INTELLECTUAL AND CULTURAL CONNECTIONS

For over seventy-five years, historically black U.S. colleges and universities (HBCUs) have been training African students in fields deemed important for the progress of their respective homelands. Meanwhile, contractual agreements between these institutions and several African nations have enhanced educational and cultural linkages through study-abroad exchanges. At first HBCUs that were also land-grant institutions predominated, so that agricultural and home economics studies proved the most popular among African students. Today Africans take the entire gamut of academic offerings.

Since the turn of the century, HBCUs have carried out research and extension work in Africa as well. In the 1890s, for example, the renowned scientist-educator George W. Carver of Tuskegee Institute undertook cotton and peanut research programs in Togo. Since that time, innumerable institution-to-institution programs and educational projects have been carried out between historically black universities and African universities. Examples include:

University of Maryland, Eastern Shore, with Zambia University

Virginia State University with Egerton College in Kenya

Alabama A & M, Florida A & M University, and the University of Maryland, Eastern Shore, in collaboration with the International Institute of Tropical Agriculture working in Cameroon

Every year dozens of persons from Africa and the Caribbean convene at Clark Atlanta University for conferences on a wide variety of topics, including women and development management; health service programs; rural development; environmental and natural resources management; entrepreneurship; and democratization. The seminars are conducted in both English and French. Similarly, special management training courses have been offered in the Ivory Coast, Burundi, Zaire, and the Central African Republic. Conferences conducted under the auspices of U.S. HBCUs often receive financial support from the participants' governments or multilateral agencies.

In addition to professional training programs, a number of HBCUs and other universities have enriched our knowledge about and involvement in

Africa. Temple University, for example, has pioneered an Afrocentric approach in the humanities and social sciences. Some of the Ivy League schools have developed strong graduate programs in African literature and liberal arts. Michigan State's African Diaspora Research Project has promoted a hemispheric approach to understanding and uplifting blacks in many ways. The universities of Maryland and Minnesota link black studies programs with community development efforts. Finally, a number of traditional African studies programs in such universities as Emory, Clark, UCLA, Michigan, Florida, and Boston maintain strong connections with African counterpart schools.

The impetus for African-related university programs often came from the bottom up. When student movements were at their peak in the late 1960s and early 1970s, African American students pressured college administrators to create black studies programs that would tailor educational experiences to their needs. Black students wished to explore the sociocultural, political, and economic realities of black people in the United States, the Caribbean, and Africa. The first phase involved establishing academic concentrations in black studies, but after 1968 attention shifted to new courses, programs, and even departments.

African American studies programs sought to raise students' consciousness by introducing them to values and curriculums that would foster solidarity among people of African descent. Amiri Baraka (formerly Leroi Jones) and student leader Ron Karenga recommended seven principles for organizing black studies, keyed to Swahili terms:

KUJICHA-GULIA (Self-determination)

NIA (Purpose)

IMANI (Faith)

UJAMAA (Cooperative economics)

UMOJA (Unity)

KUUMBA (Creativity)

UJIMA (Collective work and responsibility)

These authors emphasized the need to impart skills that would be useful in African development programs and to imbue students with positive images of Africa and of people of African descent.

By late 1970 approximately eighty colleges across the United States had instituted black studies curricular offerings. A decade later, more than two hundred and fifty schools had black studies degree programs, usually listed as black studies, Afro-American studies, Pan-African studies, African studies, and African American studies. These programs were sometimes housed in existing departments, but increasingly they became separate units. Black studies programs faced continuous scrutiny as new and interdisciplinary creations, yet those at major schools have attained considerable legitimacy.

* * *

In 1986, inspired by the success of Alex Haley's *Roots*, the National Council of Negro Women initiated annual meetings called the National Reunion of African American Families. This program of African revivalism fostered appreciation of African cultural legacies among descendants of the diaspora. Headquartered in Washington, D.C., the council provided its membership with growth experiences through participation in national socioeconomic and political institutions. The council's International Division, led by Dorothy Heights, helped to provide African women access to educational and counseling resources. It worked through corresponding councils of women in Kenya, Lesotho, Swaziland, Mozambique, and Senegal.

Another effort to reconnect with roots began in the 1960s, when African American activists created an ethnic celebration called *Kwanzaa*. This Swahili word, meaning first fruit, evokes certain East African harvest festivities. In U.S. usage, Kwanzaa spreads the principles enunciated by Baraka and Karenga, mentioned above. Kwanzaa, observed during the seven days following December 25, consists of family gatherings that feature cultural heritages. It has become an African American occasion for giving gifts, clothing, and food to the needy and homeless.

Other important linkages between Africa and the Americas were forged by missionary activities in Africa and by Islamic movements in America. The African Methodist Episcopal Zion (AME Zion) and the Christian Methodist (CME) churches have worked to strengthen ties with Africa's people through mission work. John B. Small, a pioneer in the Methodist program in West Africa, was representative of efforts by men like Alexander Crummell and Bishop Turner to introduce Christianity and development to Africa.

Small, a West Indian who traveled to the Gold Coast as a clerk around 1863, became devoted to mission work in Africa. In 1875 he returned to the West Indies to prepare himself. He eventually traveled to the United States and joined the AME Zion church. In 1896 he was promoted to bishop, a position that enabled him to expand his programs in Africa.

Through Small's work, the AME Zion church in West Africa was well established by 1900. At Livingstone College, its divinity college at Salisbury, North Carolina, it operated a student-exchange program under which African students came to the United States to study theology. One of those invited was James E. K. Aggrey, considered one of Ghana's foremost educators.

Aggrey returned to Ghana in the early 1930s and continued his work as a missionary and educator. His most famous student and protégé was Kwame Nkrumah. In 1935 Aggrey convinced Nkrumah to enroll at the predominantly black Lincoln University in Philadelphia. After graduating, Nkrumah stayed on as a faculty member and in 1945 was voted "outstanding professor of the year" by students and faculty. That year he returned to Ghana to carry on the long fight for his country's independence.

Although the Christian missions sometimes competed excessively for converts, they made many positive contributions: conducting literacy programs; recording and writing many of the approximately eight hundred separate African languages; publishing and distributing textbooks in African languages; and building and maintaining quality primary and secondary schools.

The U.S.-based Nation of Islam was another religious group that supported linkages with Africa. Founded as the Black Muslim Organization by Elijah Muhammad and later joined by Malcolm X, the movement became influential in the black community during the civil rights movement. The Black Muslims stressed traditional Islamic philosophy and disciplined religious observance. Controversy and racism plagued the organization, however, and the assassination of Malcolm X by church members led to the demise of the Nation of Islam. Elijah Muhammad's son, Wallace Muhammad, later revived the organization as the American Muslim Mission, devoted to educational programs based on the principles of Islam.

◆ BRAZIL AND THE BLACK CONSCIOUSNESS MOVEMENT

As was seen in Part II, Africa left a significant cultural imprint on Latin America. Brazil, in particular, was said to have the body of America and the soul of Africa. This remained true despite vigorous campaigns since the nineteenth century to "de-Africanize" the country. For example, early-twentieth-century Brazilian intellectuals spoke of whitening, which still meant reducing African influence. Nevertheless, Africa remains powerful in Brazil's contemporary music, customs, traditions, cuisine, and religious practices.

A wealth of research now shows that blacks in Brazil do suffer the effects of subtle racial discrimination. The peculiar juxtaposition of a popular African heritage and official desires to suppress it meant that few spoke up for recognizing that legacy. These features were highlighted in 1988 during the centennial commemoration of the abolition of slavery. For example, a 1988 survey on the situation of Afro-Brazilians by the Brazilian Institute for Geography and Statistics showed a depressing portrait of socioeconomic discrimination against blacks in the Brazilian society.

The plight of Afro-Brazilians has given rise to three major black movements:

Brazilian Negro Front (FNB) in São Paulo during the 1930s

Negro Experimental Theatre (TEN; Teatro Experimental do Negro) founded by Abdias do Nascimento in the 1940s

United Black Movement (MNU), which has been active since 1978

The current movement seeks to promote the awareness, appreciation, recognition, and preservation of the Afro-Brazilian cultural heritage, customs, and traditions. It also fosters solidarity among Brazilians of African descent for the purpose of improving their socioeconomic situation and life chances.

Brazil's black awareness movements have been spurred by Pan-African activities, U.S. civil rights campaigns, and back-to-Africa sentiments throughout the hemisphere. Intellectually, they drew on Afrocentric theories popularized by Molefi Asante, a professor of African history at Temple University. Culturally, they built on the pioneer work of Abdias do Nascimento, who called his doctrine *Quilombismo*, after the maroon camps of colonial times. Black thinkers in Brazil naturally stressed solidarity with others of African descent, but they went further to suggest that they must avoid wholesale adoption of European culture, which is antithetical to African traditions. Afrocentric modernization should seek harmony with nature, humanness, and rhythm. Finally, African-American society ought to adopt a form of communalism or socialism in the way wealth is produced, owned, and distributed.

◆ CONCLUSION

Continuing ties between Africa and the Americas in the twentieth century have been primarily political and cultural. The most impressive of these ties have been the Pan-African congresses and Garveyism, the civil rights movement and its discovery of Islam, and African revivalism in the United States and its cultural analogue in Brazil.

Although sometimes dismissed as escapism, the back-to-Africa sentiments of African Americans really constitute black nationalism. Widespread oppression, segregation, and discrimination even after the centuries of emancipation struggles led black people throughout the hemisphere to identify with one another. Racial pride and the courage that came from solidarity naturally fostered identification with Africa. Outward signs of re-Africanization were black-is-beautiful styles like Afro hairdos, African and Muslim names, and African clothing. The desires of African Americans to reestablish links with Africa were not trendy gestures but rather drew on the frustrations of many generations of black Americans.

AFTERWORD

N orth Africans, living near the Mediterranean Sea, have always played important roles in history. African societies developed advanced civilizations, which exchanged culture, material goods, and people with Middle Eastern and southern European societies. Africans even pioneered sea exploration. For example, some evidence suggests that Africans reached meso-America thousands of years ago. About twenty-six hundred years ago, a Phoenician fleet reportedly circumnavigated the continent. And in the century before the Portuguese explorations, the emperor of Mali was said to have sent fleets of war canoes west, eventually making contact with America. Even when the political and economic importance of these societies declined, North Africans continued to trade and interact with other regions, and they left recorded histories.

Africans who lived to the south of the Sahara Desert, however, were isolated from other civilizations and kept fewer written records of their activities. Only after the development of long-distance travel in modern times did most sub-Saharan Africans come into sustained contact with outsiders. Regular commerce developed between sub-Saharan Africa and the outside world, first with the camel and later with sailing ships, especially the lateen-rigged dhow and the European nao. In this way, Africa became interconnected with Asia, the Middle East, Europe, and the Americas. The growing interaction between the outside world and the peoples of sub-Saharan Africa, while sometimes detrimental to the latter, also led to new and powerful states that traded in slaves and export commodities and exchanged technology with other societies.

Africans in regions distant from the Mediterranean became more engaged in world history after the fifteenth century. West-central Africa became a battleground on which the religious and cultural soldiers of Christianity and Islam fought for converts and conquest. European and Islamic states competed to appropriate the valuable resources of the continent, including its human beings. Slave-trading Euro-Americans joined in this process by taking slaves across the Atlantic. Without African slaves, many European colonies in the Americas would have atrophied or remained insignificant. Meanwhile, Africa supplied a substantial portion of the world's gold and ivory in the sixteenth and seventeenth centuries.

The Middle Passage, the portion of the slave trade from Africa to the Americas, moved more than ten million Africans to the Americas. It was the largest migration in history before the European exodus of the nineteenth century. The continuous arrival of so many Africans over several centuries left an indelible imprint on the history of the Americas, probably more than their departure affected Africa. Furthermore, the movement of Africans helped to make possible the massive transfer of plants, technology, microorganisms, and animals that became known as the Columbian exchange.

Later, in the second half of the nineteenth century, Europeans employed the newly invented military weapons of the industrial age to commandeer African lands and resources. This development marked a sharp break with the past, for Africans had previously dealt with Europeans on an equal footing. Imperialism destroyed that relationship. Hundreds of thousands of Africans died trying to prevent the imposition of European rule. The slave trade era must have seemed civilized in comparison. Ironically, the descendants of those victimized by the trade to America often went on to achieve freedom and comfortable livings by the late nineteenth century, thereby escaping the horrors of the imperialist wars across the Atlantic in Africa.

Only in recent times have Africans begun to recapture control of their political and economic destinies. The plight of Africa today is more the result of the disastrous policies of imperialism than of the slave trade.

We have framed this book as a confirmation of Africa's enduring and vital contribution to the Americas. Traveling from Detroit to Rio de Janeiro, from New Orleans to Cartagena, from Luanda to Veracruz, we find evidence of an African-inspired ethos, a way of life that reflects the multicultural origins of the Americas. To be sure, strong regional variations exist, which we term African American cultures. Taken as a whole, however, they truly constitute an African American civilization.

* * *

A major organizing concept in the study of African American history is the diaspora, or dispersion, of African peoples around the world in the slave trade. Large numbers of Africans were taken to the Middle East and Asia during the medieval era. At that time they were simply another agrarian people captured and forced to farm, herd, or soldier by Muslims and Christians. The trans-Saharan trade to the Middle East and the stream to Asia may have equaled in size the total sent later to the Americas.

The huge dispersion of Africans to the Americas began soon after Columbus's voyages of the 1490s. Columbus began the process of spreading knowledge about the Americas to the European public and thus helped launch that hemisphere on its fateful incorporation into global contacts. The diaspora was a byproduct of the encounter of two worlds and was a major current in the Columbian exchange.

The Portuguese, who had pioneered the use of African slaves in sugar production in their Atlantic islands, soon took Africans to Brazil. There they developed sugar plantations that became models for other New World colonies. Later, the Dutch pushed into the Caribbean and South Atlantic and joined the slave business, also introducing slavery into some of their American colonies. In the second half of the seventeenth century, the English and French colonies in subtropical and tropical regions also used African slaves to produce goods for export to Europe. At first merely an alternative to other labor systems (Amerindian, tenant, and indentured, for example), chattel slavery eventually became the main labor system of the tropics. European descendants shaped their societies around its requirements, but slaves also played a major role in the making of the Americas.

The diaspora continues. The uprooting, transplanting, and exploitation of African peoples for hundreds of years were built on profound injustices and new forces that determine American peoples' behavior down to modern times. The northward migration of blacks from the U.S. South during and after World War I was a subcurrent of the diaspora. So too are the recent arrivals of Afro-Cuban and Haitian refugees in the United States.

The great sweep of world history that we call the African diaspora contains many important components. Foremost are the African contributions to art and technology, religion and literature, music, science, and material civilization in the Western world. In addition, Africans' roles in the settlement and development of the Americas affected the course of history in the hemisphere and in other world areas. For example, the gold, sugar, cotton, and tobacco that African slaves produced in Brazil helped drive the commercial and financial expansion of northern Europe in modern times. In addition, the Haitian Revolution of the 1790s inspired antislavery movements throughout the hemisphere. Indeed, through a complex chain of causality, Haiti influenced the civil rights movement, a major episode in twentieth-century U.S. history. Antillean laborers, descended from slaves, worked on the Panama Canal that helped establish the United States as a great power in the early twentieth century. Black artists and intellectuals in the Americas have also produced a distinguished body of creative work that commands universal recognition.

These examples are not meant to exaggerate the historical importance of African Americans. The fact that for long periods of time the majority were slaves prevented greater "historic" accomplishments. After all, slaves did not own the mines, the weapons, the machinery, or the capital that helped drive political economy. Only in Haiti did African Americans make leadership decisions. Overall, the African American experience shows how people who are politically and economically disadvantaged may still play key parts in historical events. This book attempts to portray objectively the experiences of all those who shared the common legacy of forced removal from Africa to labor and settle in the Americas.

The history of Africans and their descendants in the New World—what we call African American history—challenges our ability to restore and interpret the past. The slaves brought to the New World usually did not read and write (nor did most of the world's population). Even when they did, they were discouraged from inscribing their thoughts and knowledge. Their descendants became acclimated to their new homelands, and many attained the status of free persons. Yet their societies restricted them from taking roles that might have been recorded in history books. African Americans who excelled had to wage a constant struggle against such limitations; it was a struggle for survival.

Even after the African slave trade ended in the nineteenth century and the remaining slaves won their freedom, barriers of all sorts made it difficult to achieve results that attracted the interest of historians of those eras. African Americans' lives, then, were inherently significant, yet the biased historical record does not reveal this importance. From today's perspective, African American history should be seen as a main current of world history.

Finally, the social, economic, cultural, and philosophical processes of African American history were enduring. They changed more slowly than political or military events in traditional narratives and could not be altered simply by decree. For example, slavery existed in many societies, including those of Africa and the Middle East, long before the advent of the Middle Passage. It persisted afterward for generations, despite existing legislation. The exploitation of one people by another did not begin or end in discrete moments. Religious practices and beliefs from Africa endured in the Americas despite attempts to suppress them. Prejudices harbored by one people about another lasted centuries, resisting scientific and humanistic evidence to the contrary.

◆ AFRICA AND EUROPE SINCE THE FIFTEENTH CENTURY

Most Africans, and especially those swept up in the diaspora, had undergone nation-building processes distinct from those of Europeans during their early modern times. The African empires that arose between five hundred and a thousand years ago were religious and familial in leadership and increasingly used Islamic methods of statecraft. Rulers were merchants who supported and furthered the commercial activities of their kin. Gold, salt, ivory, and slave shipments enriched kings and protected their realms. Territorial expansion took place by conquest, largely to gain control over more trade routes and goods. Alliances were fashioned from religious affinities, yet wars still broke out among the states. Legal systems were often segmented, with laws for Muslims (a privileged elite), foreigners, and non-Muslims. The West African empires with which Europeans came into sustained contact were loosely united territories governed by elites more interested in distant trade than in conquest. The principal nationalism in Africa (in the European sense) was Islam, and it was restricted to the ruling classes. Today, elites are often Christian and the masses Islamic.

In Europe, Portugal and Spain became nation-states in the fifteenth century, France and England in the sixteenth, and the Netherlands in the seventeenth. There, nation-states enforced common laws on most persons residing within a jealously guarded territory and required absolute loyalty from their subjects. State revenues came increasingly from taxes, not trade, and the governments organized overseas conquests in order to enrich their tax base. Religion helped to justify conquest for the Catholic kings, just as it did for Muslims, although the British, French, and Dutch colonies often served as outlets for dissidents. In time, the Europeans' allegiances became focused on the state, whereas in Africa they continued to align according to family, religion, and ancestral homeland. Thus, European nationalism had an aggressive outward thrust and exerted more loyalty demands on citizens than did African empires.

The international economies forged by European expansion since the sixteenth century may eventually doom human survival on the planet, owing to their voracious consumption of resources and people. But in the late nineteenth century, European powers, flush with industrial advancement, found African states institutionally and psychologically vulnerable to European conquest. Imperialism in Africa, though beyond the scope of this book, is one of the most tragic episodes in modern world history.

Most African Americans did develop a sense of nation, to which Europeans and American creoles referred in their own terms: nation, nação (Portuguese), nación (Spanish), and so on. The term referred to ethnic and cultural identity as much as geographical territory. These bonds were forged in Africa and tempered by the common experiences of the Middle Passage and slavery. The sense of belonging to a particular "nation" equipped slaves with a priceless defense against spiritual death. Slaveholders disliked and mistrusted such attachments with good cause: Most forms of resistance drew on this national identity.

In modern times peoples of African descent continue to share a kind of nation-spirit. Weak allegiance to place (say, to Colombia or Jamaica) is replaced by a broader identification with others of African ancestry. This link to Africa has been manifested in many movements—for example, Pan-Africanism, the Black Panthers, the NAACP, Muslim revivalism, and negritude. Rather than nostalgic attachments, these identities have empowered black people to organize and achieve momentous change. Still, African American nationalism remains fragmented, with African Americans divided in their loyalties, means, and goals.

Africans possessed many other attributes that affected their adaptation to a new continent. For example, many were herders and farmers, and they had resistance to many viral and bacterial diseases common in the Old World. Such characteristics made Africans suitable substitutes for Native Americans, who nearly died out from exposure to European diseases and work regimes. So although the mortality in the slave trade was high, it became the largest wholesale human replacement in history.

Africans survived in American rain forest and savanna environments at a time when Europeans regarded the tropics as virtually uninhabitable. Many prized goods in world commerce—sugar, spices, cacao, tobacco, rice, and later bananas—could only be grown in such climates, and therefore by African laborers.

Throughout these chapters we have emphasized the contribution Africa made to the settlement and development of the New World. Its people, plants, animals, and resources helped build the Americas of today. We have also stressed the extent to which uprooted peoples took spiritual solace in African cultures that they brought, looking back and sometimes returning to remembered homelands. Yet with the end of the slave trade, the linkages grew weaker. Subsequent generations lost touch with their past and felt pressures to assimilate to the dominant, usually Euro-American, culture.

Yet because social and cultural traditions change slowly, Africa was never fully lost to them. A few attempts were made to renew the ties. Some former U.S. slaves founded the Republic of Liberia in the 1820s, and in Sierra Leone the British resettled former soldiers and Africans they freed from the slave trade. Substantial numbers of Afro-Brazilians returned to West Africa and became merchants in the South Atlantic trade. Christians and Umbanda worshipers traveled to Africa to seek their roots. Such sporadic links were enough to keep alive an image or ideal of an African homeland despite the terrible ordeal of colonialism.

◆ AFRICAN AMERICAN SLAVERY AND RACE RELATIONS

Discussing the slave trade and forced labor regimes requires certain suppositions about the use of coercion. Since long before Columbus, slaves were imprisoned and sold by African traders, generals, and rulers, mostly for profit but occasionally to get rid of criminals and war prisoners and to settle debts. Traders from Europe and the Americas did what they could to encourage tribal raiding, warfare, and capture of people, so that the supply would be abundant and less expensive.

Once African slaves arrived in the Americas, they were subjected to different kinds of coercion to make them work and obey their owners' rules of conduct. Coercion was now applied mostly by non-Africans. As slaveholders, Europeans and their descendants created the work and living regimes and decided on the measures that would be used to enforce

them. Even here, however, African Americans (often of mixed race) usually served as overseers and meted out sanctions. Like most complex organizations, American mines, plantations, workshops, and other businesses
had established lines of authority, with those at the top white and those at
the bottom black. Coercion, as rewards and punishments, flowed from
white to mulatto to black. Racism, in the form of anti-African ideology,
infused entire slave societies.

All social institutions, including the slave regimes of the past, relied on
the recognition and enforcement of rules to function. Labor systems, as
forms of social organizaton, employed coercion to achieve their goals.
Modern societies, however, usually discourage inhumane means to oblige
people to work, for example, physical punishment, imprisonment, or
denial of food and shelter. Before the nineteenth century, all these means
were regularly applied to workers, and not just to slaves. It is important to
remember, then, that coerced labor has existed ever since ancient states
arose.

Labor was necessarily a major part of the African American experience,
since the slave trade arose to supply workers for New World enterprises.
African American slaves between the sixteenth and nineteenth centuries
underwent a variety of experiences, both positive and negative, designed
to encourage or enforce labor and to suppress resistance. Contemporary
critics and historians have rightly focused on the brutal, and sometimes
murderous, methods used by slave owners. They do so because the extremes of an institution conveyed the latent possibilities its victims had to
live with. Yet, many slaves also could regularly expect positive rewards
and hope for a better life. This was especially true when they did not
perform heavy labor. This minority held in its minds and hearts the future
of Africans in the New World.

The endurance of African American traditions depended on the fortunate few whose duties and life chances allowed them to create culture,
raise children, exercise leadership, and define the future of their communities in the New World. Conditions under which African slaves and
their descendants suffered were more oppressive than those of most contemporary workers, but the means for their survival and liberation were
similar. While the African experience in the Americas included great
hardships, cruelty, and suffering, it did not extinguish this people's will to
live. Their pride, their desire to procreate and multiply, their hunger to
express themselves, their urge to control their own destiny, and their
power to organize endured. At times they could seize decisive forces in
their history.

The slave trade originally brought more males than females to the
Americas, since the males were favored for their physical strength. Yet
during most of the trade period, the male/female ratio remained fairly low
and became inverted in the nineteenth century. In addition, from a quarter

to over a third of the Africans brought were children, especially in the last decades of the trade. Women played extremely important roles in the diaspora by trying to establish stable homes for a new life, preserving traditions, and building an African American culture. Women also worked in fields and factories, mediated between owners and slaves, and raised crops on the side. They achieved manumission more frequently than men and joined the ranks of free blacks, forming the mainstays of their communities.

In addition, the vitality of the African cultures transplanted to the New World modified European and Native American cultures, creating hybrids and new strains that are very influential today. Such blending processes took place slowly, sometimes secretly, and they included complex exchanges among the American peoples. None of the parent cultures remained unaffected; each was enriched by borrowing from the others.

Interracial blending occurred in the Americas on a scale perhaps unprecedented in human history, synthesizing new cultures and socially defined races. The ultimate effects of these interactions will perhaps not be known for centuries. In some places, however, they appear to have promoted racial tolerance and acceptance, in comparison with European and Asian societies. The more widespread the mixing, the more complex the mechanisms developed to accommodate it and the less divisive relations among the races.

Societies dealt with racial mixing in distinct ways. Some accepted it as natural, others banned it, and still others discouraged it. Persons of mixed background faced different treatment, depending on the prevailing ideas of race. More or less racial mixing produced two main patterns of race relations in the Americas, which may be labeled as Latin and North American. These were, in turn, based on cultures from southern and northern Europe.

Where the Spanish and Portuguese settled, race became identified with culture, religion, and behavior. Persons were defined as white, for example, not only by their phenotype but also by their European language, Christianity, class, formal learning, and style of life. Europeans occupied the highest social positions, followed by persons of mixed race, and then by either blacks or Indians, depending on local circumstances. Acquiring European ways whitened the individuals and enhanced their status; losing such attributes lowered their standing. These societies offered powerful incentives to shun non-European behavior and yet also diluted the importance of race in assigning status. Racial characteristics weighed less heavily in the calculation of rank. This conception is sometimes called social race.

This Latin pattern of race relations encouraged the development of middle classes of persons of mixed ancestry and culture, persons who were mulattoes and mestizos by birth as well as by training. Because of higher status and better life chances, their population grew more rapidly, and they often came to outnumber persons clearly of a single race. By the twentieth century, some emerging national ideologies even approved of racial mixing as a way to create homogeneous, hybrid citizenries. Some examples are Vasconcelos's Cosmic Race in Mexico, Freyre's racial democracy in Brazil, and Gil Fortoul's tricolor population in Venezuela. Race as a determinant of socioeconomic status in these societies never disappeared, however.

Racism in Latin societies, then, promoted whitening and European behavior and rewarded them with better (though not fully equal) social status. This pattern may be called multiracial. In this configuration, some white blood denoted a process of racial redemption and was seen as good. Rigid race lines were avoided, as was open discussion of racial preferences.

In contrast, in most areas settled by the English, French, and Dutch, African ancestry continued to be a major criterion in social relations. People of mixed race were not considered capable of Europeanizing completely (and therefore whitening). Interracial marriage was discouraged and sometimes outlawed, and persons of mixed race were regarded as retrograde. African physical features marked persons as inferior, whatever their social learning. Even the slightest African heritage classified a person as a lesser human being and subject to laws and rules of separation.

Since no ethic or ideology arose to favor interracial unions or racially mixed persons, a legitimate intermediate class could not develop. Racial barriers arose, rules codified segregation and inequality, and interracial contact was discouraged. These societies experienced the greatest racial divisiveness and conflict, and miscegenation did not improve the situation. This pattern may be termed biracial, or simply racist. Perhaps because of the racial inflexibility of these societies, civil rights movements attracted huge followings to battle for the interests of African Americans and others seeking justice and equality.

These two variations of race relations, multiracial and biracial, here greatly simplified, had endless subtypes throughout the Americas, as was seen in the separate chapters of this book. They are an important component of the African legacy in the New World.

Throughout the Americas, even at the height of the slave economies, many persons of African descent were free, not slaves, and much of the story of Africa in the Americas was theirs. So this book is not about slavery but about the African Americans, only some of whom were slaves. Free blacks made significant contributions to American development, as soldiers, craftspeople, inventors, artists, scientists, and entrepreneurs. They led their communities through the difficulties faced by any transplanted people. And, when necessary, they gave up their lives to end oppression and exploitation.

♦ THE AGE OF EMANCIPATION

The clearest sign of the African Americans' will to control their lives, despite racism and the continued enslavement of many, was the high level of resistance they displayed throughout the hemisphere. Year after year Africans and their descendants individually and collectively fought against abusive labor and social systems. This behavior took many forms, ranging from feigned sickness and work slowdowns to mass escape and even political rebellion. Resistance was also an attitude toward endurance and preservation of African traditions.

At its peak, African American resistance was diverted into the armed struggles for liberation from European colonialism and oppression. Black battalions fought in the U.S. War of Independence, the Haitian Revolution, the War of 1812, the Latin American independence wars, and the U.S. Civil War. In this way, African Americans exercised great control over their destinies.

Emancipation broadly defined means the growing autonomy and self-determination of African Americans during the past three centuries. In fact, five interconnected and hemispheric emancipations have occurred. The first consisted of continuous struggles and rebellions to secure freedom and well-being. The second banned the slave trade coming from Africa. The third ended slavery in the New World. The fourth brought political freedom to African Americans in former European colonies. The fifth and still ongoing, the struggle for civil rights, seeks to eliminate prejudice and discrimination against people of African descent. To the extent that the five struggles overlapped in time, motivation, and leadership, they formed a continuous process of gaining freedom.

This is not to say that African Americans won every struggle and took control over their destinies, or that they acted in isolation. Only a few rebellions led to complete freedom (Haiti is the best example), and the institutions and forces of exploitation proved powerful and resourceful. Episodes of limited rebellion, group flight, and uncooperative behavior did not usually succeed. Yet they did put pressure on elites and won sympathy from nonslave allies. Arising as they did during an overall rejection of European colonialism and slavery in the Americas, the African American struggles were most forceful there.

What is more, many non-Africans joined in at critical moments to lend support and even leadership to emancipation campaigns. At such times, a more general quest for human dignity and equality seemed to overcome divisiveness based on color, origins, and status.

Finally, the African American emancipation movements inspired and were stimulated by similar crusades elsewhere: for example, abolitionist campaigns in the United States, the West Indies, and Brazil reinforced antislavery themes in the Cuban independence struggle of the 1870s and sparked anti-imperialist movements in Africa. Such broad liberation movements have stood near the mainstream of New World history for the last two centuries.

We need to understand these several emancipations comparatively and to note instances when they interacted. For example, the drive to end the slave trade was led and executed largely by Europeans for ideological, religious, and economic motives, whereas the abolition movements were directed by African Americans and their white allies. Latin American emancipation proved peaceful in comparison with that in the United States. The various civil rights movements in this century, though less insurrectionist than the previous ones, borrowed from them a spirit of resistance and defiance. Such differences were variations on a main theme.

◆ TWENTIETH-CENTURY PERSPECTIVES

The African American experience in the twentieth century, especially in the realms of politics, race relations, the arts, labor, and business, carried forward the central story of this book. These last chapters did not seek to celebrate recent African American achievements: many persons covered here have already attained worldwide attention and have been the subjects of books, films, and plays. They need no acclamation here. Instead, their lives and accomplishments deserve to be put into the larger perspective of African American history. To the extent that an African American civilization has resulted from the diaspora, these people and subjects stand as testimony to its existence.

In the twentieth century, African Americans in the countries most deeply influenced by the diaspora—Brazil, Haiti, Cuba, and the United States—established new contacts with Africa that were discussed in Part IV. The connections were no longer simple, for Africa had been colonized and oppressed, while African Americans had achieved a middling socioeconomic status in international comparisons. With time, African Americans lost immediate knowledge of the homeland and had to create mythic versions to muster support for struggles of national liberation. Islam made renewed efforts to penetrate Central Africa, and communism spread as a rival doctrine. Asians resettled by the colonial powers exacerbated African social problems. For most African Americans today, Africa is an ideal, a memory, an ancestral allegiance, but not a place to which they might return. African American civilization owes much to Africa and yet has become a self-sustaining presence in the modern world.

* * *

World history must recognize Africa's many roles in the development of the Americas. Some modern nations—for instance, Cuba, Brazil, and most

Caribbean islands—correctly trace part of their origins, people, and culture to African roots. Others, like the United States, coastal portions of South America, and Central America, were profoundly influenced by Africans. Historians and intellectuals have not always acknowledged these legacies, because of a desire to emphasize European heritage. This book adds to the multicultural perspective and gives a focus to the African American contribution to world history. The Americas would have been far poorer—materially and culturally—without Africa's children.

GLOSSARY

Afro-mestizo   Mexican descendants of African and indigenous parents, known as *zambos* elsewhere.

Alcaçovas, Treaty of (1479)   Spanish permit Portuguese to supply slaves.

Alforria   manumission of a slave. Some slaves were able to save money after years of work and purchase their freedom.

Allada   a people located in modern Benin who speak Ewe-Fon languages.

Angola   Portuguese colony in west-central Africa, founded in 1575; also general name in seventeenth and eighteenth century for coast from Gabon to Angola. Independent since 1975.

Antillean   resident of the Greater and Lesser Antilles.

Australopithecines   the earliest form of humanity known, remains of which were found only in South and East Africa. Considered origin of our species. Also known as *homo Africanus.*

Bantu   literally, the people; cultural and linguistic term referring to the largest single language group in Africa, ranging from central to the southernmost regions.

Black and tans   Black Republicans in the United States who organized on their own in opposition to their exclusion from the party by the so-called "lily white" Republicans at the turn of the century.

Black cabinet   group of high black government officials appointed by President Franklin D. Roosevelt from 1934 to 1944.

Black Power/Black Nationalism   strong belief in pride of race, cultural autonomy, community, and self-development, and militant defense of blacks from racism.

Blanquear (Sp.), branqueamento (Port.)   literally, whitening, but often used to describe cultural as well as racial characteristics.

Bozales (boçaís, bossales)   newly arrived, unacculturated slaves.

BSCP   Brotherhood of Sleeping Car Porters, a trade union of railway porters, founded by A. Philip Randolph.

Caboclo   a term that connotes a person from the interior of Brazil with Indian blood. It often implies that a person is of mixed Indian and African descent.

Candomblé   popular Afro-Brazilian religion based on practices from West Africa. Maintained African culture in Brazil and embodied resistance to white domination.

Capitães do mato   men often employed by plantation owners to hunt down fugitive slaves in Brazil.

Capoeira   a style of fighting with hands and feet, developed by Brazilian slaves and now preserved as a ritualized martial art.

Casta   persons thought to be of any type of racial mixture on the basis of their physical appearance.

Ceddo   Senegambian slaves holding military and administrative positions.

Centrales, usines, usinas, central factories   large manufacturing plants for converting sugarcane juice into sugar crystals.

Cimarrón   a runaway slave.

CIO   Congress of Industrial Organizations, an umbrella federation of unions established along industrial lines.

Civil rights movement   mass movement by U.S. blacks in the 1960s to attain legal and political rights to citizenship.

Code Noir   1685 laws promulgated in France to regulate slavery in its Caribbean colonies.

Compromise of 1850   set of agreements, including a stringent new Fugitive Slave Act, that postponed collapse of negotiations over admission of new slave territories to statehood.

CORE (1942)   Congress of Racial Equality.

Courts of Mixed Commission   international courts set up by Britain and other countries to adjudicate cases of illegal slave ships.

Creole   an ethnic designation denoting American origin and attachment to American regional culture; it was applied to both European- and African-descended peoples.

Crioulo   a slave born in Brazil of either African or Brazilian-born parents.

Cumbe, palenque, quilombo   runaway slave communities, also known in English as maroon communities.

Dahomey   West African state active in the slave trade.

Dred Scott Decision   1857 proslavery ruling by the Supreme Court that undermined the Compromise of 1850 and helped precipitate the Civil War.

Emancipation Act (1833)   began manumission in British colonies.

Emancipation Proclamation (1863)   U.S. decree that freed slaves in secessionist states and encouraged black enlistment in Union armies.

Engenho   a sugar mill, which in Brazil implied a sugar plantation (*ingenio* [Sp.]).

Ethnicity   throughout colonial mainland Spanish America was primarily defined on the basis of acquired characteristics related to culture such as language, religion, norms, and values.

Factory (feitoria)   European trading establishment on the African coast.

Fazendeiro   owner of a medium-sized or large estate who produced food and commodities for consumption within Brazil or for export.

Feijoada   one of the most popular meals in Brazil today, based on Afro-Brazilian cuisine.

Free Birth, Law of   1871 Brazilian law liberating children born to slave mothers.

Freedom Schools   1960s workshops sponsored by civil rights groups to teach the meaning of voting and other citizenship rights.

Fugitive Slave Act   originally passed in 1793 to allow runaway slaves to be returned to their owners; another version passed as part of the Compromise of 1850.

Gabriel's Rebellion   1800 slave uprising in Virginia.

Gabu   initially, a secondary or tributary state of Mali made up of Mandingo-speaking people as early as the fourteenth century.

Gang system   method of organizing production where slaves spent all their time in production of cash crops, lived in barracks, and had little free time.

Gold Coast region of modern Ghana, center of trading for many European nations.

Great Awakening eighteenth-century Christian movement that converted many North American slaves.

Great Depression economic depression that gripped the world during the 1930s.

Great Migration mass movement of Afro-Americans from U.S. South to the urban-industrial North during and after World War I.

Great Negro Plot 1741 slave conspiracy in New York.

Haitian Revolution 1791 slave revolt that culminated in independence in 1804.

Harlem Renaissance Afro-American cultural movement centered in Harlem between World War I and World War II.

Hispaniola Caribbean island where the Spanish first settled; today shared by the Dominican Republic and Haiti.

Islam a world religion, based on the teachings of Mohammed, that spread throughout North Africa and Asia; its followers are called Muslims.

Juula (Wangara) African commercial group.

Kongo important Central African kingdom, converted to Christianity in the late fifteenth century.

Kush the ancient state found in Nubia, which at its height ruled all of Egypt and the northern Sudan.

Ladino hispanicized blacks on the Caribbean coast of South and Central America.

Liberto or liberta a former male or female slave who attained freedom.

Lower Guinea coast west coast of Africa from Liberia to Cameroons.

Lynching murder of blacks in the United States, by hanging without judicial process, as a form of oppression and intimidation.

Mali the great West African savanna kingdom that reigned from about 1235 to about 1468.

Manumission societies associations to promote freedom for slaves, founded in most U.S. states during the 1770s to 1790s.

Maroon runaway slave.

Mason-Dixon line 1760s survey that separated slave and free U.S. states.

Mestizaje a Spanish term referring to racial and cultural mixture.

Mestizo person of European and Amerindian ancestry.

Middle Passage the sea voyage from Africa to the Americas on slave ships.

Missouri Compromise (1820) pairing slave and free states for admission to the union.

Morbidity incidence of disease.

Moret Law (1870) began emancipation of newborns in Cuba.

Mulatto mixture of African and European; a person thought to be of black-white racial mixture on the basis of his or her physical appearance.

NAACP National Association for the Advancement of Colored People, founded in 1909 to promote the interests and improve the image of black people in the United States.

Nation social grouping of slaves from the same language group in Africa for mutual aid and selection of leaders.

Ndongo important Central African kingdom that fought long series of wars against the Portuguese in Angola.

Negro Convention Movement national meetings of black male leaders that took place annually from 1830 to 1854 to establish the national agenda for the black community.

Negro World the official newspaper of the Universal Negro Improvement Association.

Neolithic period starting with the rise of domesticated animals and plants, in Africa after about 7000 B.C.

New Deal the package of legislation sponsored by U.S. President Franklin D. Roosevelt in the 1930s to rejuvenate the economy and to dampen political and social unrest.

Nubian ethnic group descended from the people of Kerma and Kush, quite distinct from Egyptians, residing in the upper Nile Valley.

Palenque runaway slave settlement.

Paleolithic Old Stone Age; from the period when *Australopithecines* used stone tools to that when *Homo sapiens* employed finely chipped flint blade tools.

Paraguayan War 1865–1870, Brazil, Argentina, and Uruguay versus Paraguay; also the War of the Triple Alliance.

Pardo term for a mulatto in Brazil.

Paulista resident of the state of São Paulo, Brazil.

Peasant system method of organizing production on estates in which slaves are given tasks to perform plus time to raise their own food.

Pharaohs the kings, or rarely queens, of ancient Egypt, spanning the period from 5100 to 2300 years ago.

Phoenicians ancient Lebanese traders who navigated the Mediterranean Sea and the Atlantic. Established a powerful base at Carthage. Some scholars claim they circumnavigated the African continent and reached the New World.

Quakers members of an English Protestant sect who settled in Pennsylvania in the seventeenth century; began abolitionist campaign.

Queiroz Law (1850) Brazil effectively ended slave trade.

Quilombos escaped-slave communities in Brazil. The most famous, Palmares, flourished in the interior backlands of Pernambuco from the 1590s until 1694.

Race throughout colonial Spanish America was primarily defined on the basis of physical appearance, most notably skin color.

Rights of search power of one country to board and search the vessels of other nations. Belligerents assumed this power in wartime, but in time of peace it had to be negotiated.

Sahel the long strip of savanna grasslands between the Sahara Desert and the forest areas of West Africa, home to the great kingdoms of Ghana, Mali, Songhai, Bornu, Darfur, and the Funj. Means edge or border lands in Arabic.

Samba a famous dance in Brazil whose African origins led officials to ban it for centuries. Now central to carnival celebrations.

Sexagenarian Law (1885) Brazilian legislation that freed persons over sixty-five years of age.

Shipmates slaves who bonded while crossing the Atlantic on the same ship, often becoming lifelong friends and an important social group.

Stono Rebellion 1739 slave uprising in South Carolina.

Ten Years' War 1868–1878 insurrection in Cuba that raised the issue of emancipation.

Tight-packing   the practice of forcing African slaves into the holds of slave ships of inadequate size.

Tordesillas, Treaty of (1494)   made Africa a Portuguese sphere and the Americas a Spanish sphere; thereafter the Portuguese dominated slave trade.

UNIA   the Universal Negro Improvement Association, the nationalist organization founded by Marcus Garvey in 1914.

Upper Guinea coast   west coast of Africa from Senegal to Liberia.

Zambo   person of African and Amerindian ancestry.

BIBLIOGRAPHIC ESSAY

PART I AFRICA, EUROPE, AND THE AMERICAS

The most authoritative introduction to African history is the eight-volume collection organized by Unesco, entitled *General History of Africa*, and published jointly by Heinemann and the University of California Press (1981–). Volumes 2 to 4 cover from the ancient civilizations of Africa to the end of the sixteenth century. The earlier eight-volume collection, *Cambridge History of Africa* (Cambridge, Eng.: Cambridge University Press, 1975–1986), is still extremely useful.

A thoughtful work on Africa's place in world evolution is Cheikh Anta Diop, *The African Origin of Civilization: Myth and Reality* (New York: L. Hill, 1974). On cultural and intellectual development in Africa, consult the ten-volume series edited by Joseph Ohiomogben Okpaku, Alfred Esimatemi Opubor, and Benjamin Olatunji Oloruntimehin, entitled *The Arts and Civilization of Black and African Peoples* (Lagos, Nigeria, and New York: Third Press International, 1986). The volumes correspond to these topics: arts, philosophy, literature, African languages, history, pedagogy, religion, science and technology, African government, and the mass media.

Shorter general surveys that cover the pre-1500 period include Basil Davidson, *Africa in History*, rev. ed. (New York: Macmillan, 1991); J. Ajayi and M. Crowder, eds., *History of West Africa*, vol. 1 (London: Longman, 1972); R. Oliver and B. Fagan, *Africa in the Iron Age, c. 500 BC to 1400 AD* (Cambridge, Eng.: Cambridge University Press, 1975); R. Oliver and A. Atmore, *The African Middle Ages, 1400–1800* (Cambridge, Eng.: Cambridge University Press, 1981); and vol. 1 of Harry A. Gailey, Jr., *History of Africa*, 3 vols. (Melbourne, Fla.: Krieger, 1970–1989).

A useful survey-anthology is Robert O. Collins, *African History*, 3 vols. (Princeton, NJ: Markus Wiener, 1990). The respective volumes cover West Africa, East Africa, and Central and South Africa. See also the materials gathered in Graham W. Irwin, ed., *Africans Abroad: A Documentary History of the Black Diaspora in Asia, Latin America, and the Caribbean During the Age of Slavery* (New York: Columbia University Press, 1977). A detailed account of the spread of Islam in the Mediterranean is Abdulwahid Dhanun Taha's *Muslim Conquest and Settlement of North Africa and Spain* (New York: Routledge, 1988).

West Africa sustained the closest contact with the Americas, and its societies became more engaged with the Atlantic world than other regions.

See the fine study by John Thornton, *Africa and Africans in the Formation of the Atlantic World, 1450–1680* (Cambridge, Eng.: Cambridge University Press, 1992). The interconnected character of the domestic and international economies is covered in Philip Curtin, *Cross Cultural Trade in Comparative Perspective* (Cambridge, Eng.: Cambridge University Press, 1984). The survey by John Blake, *West Africa: The Quest for God and Gold, 1454–1578* (London: Curzon Press, 1971) is more descriptive. Specific regions are analyzed in Philip Curtin, *Economic Change in Pre-Colonial Africa: Senegambia in the Era of the Slave Trade*, 2 vols. (Madison: University of Wisconsin Press, 1975); John Vogt, *Portuguese Rule on the Gold Coast, 1469–1682* (Athens: University of Georgia Press, 1979); and David Birmingham, *Trade and Conquest in Angola* (Oxford, Eng.: Oxford University Press, 1966). See also the studies in Claude Meillassoux, ed., *Trade and Markets in West Africa* (London: Oxford University Press, 1972); Richard Gray and David Birmingham, eds., *Pre-Colonial African Trade: Essays on Trade in Central and Eastern Africa before 1900* (Oxford, Eng.: Oxford University Press, 1970); Robert Harms, *River of Wealth, River of Sorrow: The Central Zaire Basin in the Era of the Slave and Ivory Trade, 1500–1891* (New Haven, Conn.: Yale University Press, 1981); and Ray Kea, *Settlements, Trade and Policies on the Seventeenth Century Gold Coast* (Baltimore: Johns Hopkins University Press, 1982).

On the development of Mozambique, see M.D.D. Newitt, *Portuguese Settlements on the Zambezi: Exploration, Land Tenures, and Colonial Life in East Africa* (London: Africana, 1972), and David Elkiss, *An African Eldorado* (Waltham, Mass.: Crossroads Press, 1981).

An excellent guide to the physical and spacial evolution of Africa is G.S.P. Freeman-Grenville, *The New Atlas of African History* (New York: Simon & Schuster, 1991). See also C. Fluehr-Lobban, Richard Lobban, and J. Voll, *Historical Dictionary of the Sudan* (Metuchen, N.J.: Scarecrow Press, 1992).

On gender issues in this period, see Martin Klein and Claire Robertson, eds., *Women and Slavery in Africa* (Madison: University of Wisconsin Press, 1984).

Slavery, central to the history of persons transported to the Americas, is covered in Paul Lovejoy, *Transformations in Slavery in Africa* (Cambridge, Eng.: Cambridge University Press, 1982); Leonie Archer, ed., *Slavery and Other Forms of Unfree Labour* (New York: Routledge, 1988); and William D. Phillips, Jr., *Slavery from Roman Times to the Early Transatlantic Trade* (Minneapolis: University of Minnesota Press, 1985).

Early navigation around Africa is the subject of two recent books, Lionel Casson, *The Ancient Mariners* (Princeton, N.J.: Princeton University Press, 1991), and Felipe Fernandez-Armesto, *Before Columbus: Exploration and Colonization from the Mediterranean to the Atlantic* (London: Macmillan, 1987).

A vast literature covers the Atlantic slave trade itself. Among the best places to start are Philip D. Curtin, *The Atlantic Slave Trade: A Census* (Madison: University of Wisconsin Press, 1969), a classic in the field, and the narrative survey by James A. Rawley, *The Transatlantic Slave Trade: A History* (New York: W. W. Norton, 1981).

The long-term impact of the slave trade on Africa is hotly debated. Among the best works in this vein are Patrick Manning, *Slavery and African Life: Occidental, Oriental, and the African Slave Trade* (Cambridge, Eng.: Cambridge University Press, 1990), which argues that it had negative results in Africa; and the essays in J. E. Inikori, ed., *Forced Migration: The Impact of the Export Slave Trade on African Societies* (New York: Africana, 1982). See also Walter Rodney, *How Europe Underdeveloped Africa* (Washington, D.C.: Howard University Press, 1974).

Some scholars explain the trade as a global phenomenon arising from the spread of international trade. The essays in Barbara L. Solow, ed., *Slavery and the Rise of the Atlantic System* (New York: Cambridge University Press, 1991), stress such economic forces.

Sugar was central to the rise of the slave trade in the sixteenth century. Philip D. Curtin's *The Rise and Fall of the Plantation Complex: Essays in Atlantic History* (Cambridge, Eng.: Cambridge University Press, 1990) provides a sweeping interpretation of the means of production and its effect on Africa and the Americas. Two fine general histories of sugar itself are J. H. Galloway, *The Sugar Cane Industry: An Historical Geography from Its Origins to 1914* (New York: Cambridge University Press, 1989) and Sidney Mintz, *Sweetness and Power: The Place of Sugar in Modern History* (New York: Viking, 1985).

Several books look more closely at the trade to the Americas and Africans' adaptation there. See, for example, Vincent Bakpetu Thompson, *The Making of the African Diaspora in the Americas, 1441–1900* (London: Longman, 1987); Herbert S. Klein, *African Slavery in Latin America and the Caribbean* (New York: Oxford University Press, 1986), and *The Middle Passage: Comparative Studies in the Atlantic Slave Trade* (Princeton, N.J.: Princeton University Press, 1978); and Mario Azevedo, ed., *Africana Studies: A Survey of Africa and the African Diaspora* (Durham, N.C.: Carolina Academic Press, 1993).

PART II THE SLAVE TRADE AND SLAVERY IN THE AMERICAS

The excellent overviews of the Atlantic world by Curtin, Thornton, and Solow, cited in the bibliographic essay for Part I, should be supplemented by Franklin Knight and Peggy Liss, eds., *Atlantic Port Cities: Economy, Culture, and Society in the Atlantic World, 1650–1850* (Knoxville: University of Tennessee Press, 1991).

The best broad treatment of slavery in Latin America is Herbert Klein's *African Slavery in Latin America and the Caribbean* (New York: Oxford University Press, 1986). For a good general discussion of runaways and rebels, see Eugene Genovese, ed., *From Rebellion to Revolution: Afro-American Slave Revolts in the Making of the Modern World* (Baton Rouge, Louisiana University Press, 1979). On runaway communities, the best introduction is Richard Price, ed., *Maroon Societies: Rebel Slave Communities in the Americas*, 2nd ed. (Baltimore: Johns Hopkins University Press, 1979). A useful reference work is Benjamin Nuñez, *Dictionary of Afro-Latin American Civilization* (Westport, Conn.: Greenwood Press, 1980).

Literature on Caribbean slavery abounds. Excellent places to start are Bonham C. Richardson, *The Caribbean in the Wider World, 1492–1992* (Cambridge, Eng.: Cambridge University Press, 1992), Margaret E. Crahan and Franklin W. Knight, eds., *Africa and the Caribbean: The Legacies of a Link* (Baltimore: Johns Hopkins University Press, 1979), and Hilary Beckles and Verene Sheperd, eds., *Caribbean Slave Society and Economy* (Kingston: Ian Randle, 1991).

The many studies of slavery in the British Caribbean reveal a great diversity of African experiences. For much of the period Barbados was the model plantation system in the region; see: Hilary Beckles, *White Servitude and Black Slavery in Barbados, 1627–1715* (Knoxville: University of Tennessee Press, 1989) and *Black Rebellion in Barbados* (Bridgetown: Antilles Publications, 1984). Slavery in other islands is covered by vol. 1 of Michael Craton and Gail Saunders's recent *Islanders in the Stream: A History of the Bahamian People* (Athens: University of Georgia Press, 1992), and by David Barry Gaspar, *Bondmen and Rebels: A Study of Master-Slave Relations in Antigua* (Baltimore: Johns Hopkins University Press, 1985). B. W. Higman provides an exhaustive demographic portrait of the region in *Slave Populations of the British Caribbean, 1807–1834* (Baltimore: Johns Hopkins University Press, 1984).

From early on, the growing numbers of free blacks and mulattoes, who formed a middle socioracial group in the islands, have attracted the attention of historians. See the articles in David W. Cohen and Jack P. Greene, eds., *Neither Slave nor Free: The Freedmen of African Descent in the Slave Societies of the New World* (Baltimore: Johns Hopkins University Press, 1972), and the more detailed work by Jerome S. Handler, *The Unappropriated People: Freedmen in the Slave Society of Barbados* (Baltimore: Johns Hopkins University Press, 1974).

Three recent studies focus on slave women in the Caribbean: Barbara Bush, *Slave Women in Caribbean Society, 1650–1832* (Bloomington: Indiana University Press, 1990); Marietta Morrissey, *Slave Women in the New World: Gender Stratification in the Caribbean* (Lawrence: University of Kansas Press, 1989); and Hilary Beckles, *National Rebels: A Social History of Enslaved Black Women in Barbados, 1627–1838* (New Brunswick, N.J.: Rutgers University Press, 1989).

The best general treatment of slave resistance is Michael Craton, *Testing the Chains: Resistance to Slavery in the British West Indies* (Ithaca, N.Y.: Cornell

University Press, 1982). See also Mavis C. Campbell, *The Maroons of Jamaica, 1655–1796* (South Hadley, Mass.: Bergin & Garvey, 1988).

Richard Price has provided intimate and moving studies of slavery and colonialism in Dutch Guiana, modern Suriname. See especially his *Alabi's World* (Baltimore: Johns Hopkins University Press, 1990) and *First Time: The Historical Vision of an Afro-American People* (Baltimore: Johns Hopkins University Press, 1983).

Brazil has long been a favorite subject for comparative slavery perspectives. Good introductions are José Honório Rodrigues, *Brazil and Africa*, trans. Richard A. Mazzara and Sam Hileman (Berkeley and Los Angeles: University of California Press, 1965); Stuart B. Schwartz, *Sugar Plantations in the Formation of Brazilian Society: Bahia, 1550–1835* (Cambridge, Eng.: Cambridge University Press, 1985) and *Slaves, Peasants, and Rebels: Reconsidering Brazilian Slavery* (Urbana: University of Illinois Press, 1992). See also the dated but still useful overview by Charles R. Boxer, *Race Relations in the Portuguese Colonial Empire, 1415–1825* (Oxford, Eng.: Clarendon Press, 1963).

Superb accounts from the African perspective are Katia M. de Queirós Mattoso, *To Be a Slave in Brazil*, trans. Arthur Goldhammer (New Brunswick, N.J.: Rutgers University Press, 1986), and Phyllis Galembo, *Divine Inspiration: From Benin to Bahia* (Albuquerque: University of New Mexico Press, 1993). The flavor of the times comes through nicely in Robert Edgar Conrad, ed., *Children of God's Fire: A Documentary History of Black Slavery in Brazil* (Princeton, N.J.: Princeton University Press, 1983).

On the slave trade, see Joseph C. Miller, *Way of Death: Merchant Capitalism and the Angolan Slave Trade, 1730–1830* (Madison: University of Wisconsin Press, 1988), and Robert Edgar Conrad, *World of Sorrow: The African Slave Trade to Brazil* (Baton Rouge: Louisiana State University Press, 1986).

Mary C. Karasch, *Slave Life in Rio de Janeiro, 1808–1850* (Princeton, N.J.: Princeton University Press, 1987), depicts the intense experience of Afro-Brazilians in the largest city in the South Atlantic and the largest importer of slaves. A.J.R. Russell-Wood examines free blacks as well as slaves in *The Black Man in Slavery and Freedom in Colonial Brazil* (New York: St. Martin's Press, 1982).

For general overviews, besides Klein (cited above), see Magnus Morner, *Race Mixture in the History of Latin America* (Boston: Little, Brown, 1967); Leslie B. Rout, Jr., *The African Experience in Spanish America* (London: Cambridge University Press, 1976); Rolando Mellafe, *Negro Slavery in Latin America*, trans. J.W.S. Judge (Berkeley and Los Angeles: University of California Press, 1975); Marvin Harris, *Patterns of Race in the Americas* (New York: Walker, 1964); and Robert Brent Toplin, ed., *Slavery and Race Relations in Latin America* (Westport, Conn.: Greenwood Press, 1974).

For the African experiences in several Spanish colonies, see Patrick Carroll, *Blacks, Race, and Regional Development in Colonial Veracruz, 1570–*

1830 (Austin: University of Texas Press, 1991); Frederick Bowser, *The African Slave in Colonial Peru, 1524–1650* (Palo Alto, Calif.: Stanford University Press, 1974); Colin Palmer, *Slaves of the White God: Blacks in Mexico, 1570–1650* (Cambridge, Mass.: Harvard University Press, 1976); and William F. Sharp, *Slavery on the Spanish Frontier: The Colombian Chocó, 1680–1810* (Norman: University of Oklahoma Press, 1976).

Donald R. Wright's *African Americans in the Colonial Era: From African Origins Through the American Revolution* (Arlington Heights, Ill.: Harland Davidson, 1990) provides a succinct overview of the black experience in colonial British North America. On the background of cultural developments, Melville J. Herskovits's *The Myth of the Negro Past* (New York: Harper, 1941) remains the best introduction to the elements that Africans retained and contributed to American cultures. Leland Ferguson, *Uncommon Ground: Archaeology and Colonial African America* (Washington, D.C.: Smithsonian Institution Press, 1992) describes the evidence and impact of black retentions and contributions to material culture. Mechal Sobel, *The World They Made Together: Black and White Values in Eighteenth-Century Virginia* (Princeton, N.J.: Princeton University Press, 1987), illustrates the experience of attitudinal interactions, as does John B. Boles, ed., *Masters and Slaves in the House of the Lord: Race and Religion in the American South, 1740–1870* (Lexington: University Press of Kentucky, 1988).

Winthrop D. Jordan's *White Over Black: American Attitudes Toward the Negro, 1550–1812* (Chapel Hill: University of North Carolina Press, 1966) remains the benchmark for understanding the attitudinal framework in which African Americans existed in British America. Gary B. Nash, *Red, White, and Black: The Peoples of Early America*, 3d ed. (Englewood Cliffs, N.J.: Prentice Hall, 1992) offers a synthesis of the interaction among Africans, Native Americans, and Europeans. Nash continues the time of interaction in his *Race, Class, and Politics: Essays on American Colonial and Revolutionary Society* (Urbana: University of Illinois Press, 1986).

Each colony has its own history. Among the best are Edmund S. Morgan's now near-classic *American Slavery, American Freedom: The Ordeal of Colonial Virginia* (New York: Norton, 1975); Gwendolyn Midlo Hall, *Africans in Colonial Louisiana: The Development of Afro-Creole Culture in the Eighteenth Century* (Baton Rouge: Louisiana State University Press, 1992); Charles Joyner, *Remember Me: Slave Life in Coastal Georgia* (Athens: University of Georgia Press, 1989); Daniel C. Littlefield, *Rice and Slaves: Ethnicity and the Slave Trade in Colonial South Carolina* (Urbana: University of Illinois Press, 1981); Julia Floyd Smith, *Slavery and Rice Culture in Low Country Georgia, 1750–1860* (Knoxville: University of Tennessee Press, 1985); Betty Wood, *Slavery in Colonial Georgia, 1730–1775* (Athens: University of Georgia Press, 1984); and Peter H. Wood, *Black Majority: Negroes in Colonial South Carolina from 1670 Through the Stono Rebellion* (New York: Knopf, 1974). For an example of some fluidity in early race relations, see Timothy H. Breen and Stephen Innes, *"Myne Owne Ground": Race and Freedom on Virginia's Eastern Shore, 1640–1676* (New York: Oxford University Press, 1980).

Regional studies complement the studies of individual colonies and the overviews of development. Allan Kulikoff's *Tobacco and Slaves: The Development of Southern Culture in the Chesapeake, 1680–1800* (Chapel Hill: University of North Carolina Press, 1986) describes the relationship among place, product, and population, as does Ronald L. Lewis, *Coal, Iron, and Slaves: Industrial Slavery in Maryland and Virginia, 1715–1865* (Westport, Conn.: Greenwood Press, 1979), for example. Lorenzo J. Greene's still reliable classic, *The Negro in Colonial New England* (New York: Columbia University Press, 1942), William D. Piersen's *Black Yankees: The Development of an Afro-American Sub-culture in Eighteenth Century New England* (Amherst: University of Massachusetts Press, 1988), and Edgar J. McManus's *Black Bondage in the North* (Syracuse, N.Y.: Syracuse University Press, 1973) describe slavery and Afro-American life from Pennsylvania northward. Gary B. Nash, *Forging Freedom: The Formation of Philadelphia's Black Community, 1720–1840* (Cambridge, Mass.: Harvard University Press, 1988), provides a view of black life in a northern city, as does Thomas J. Davis, *A Rumor of Revolt: The "Great Negro Plot" in Colonial New York* (New York: Free Press/ Macmillan, 1985), which also treats the theme of slave resistance.

More broadly on resistance, Herbert Aptheker's classic, *American Negro Slave Revolts*, 5th ed. (New York: International Publishers, 1987), continues to serve as an introduction. Sylvia R. Frey, *Water from the Rock: Black Resistance in a Revolutionary Age* (Princeton, NJ: Princeton University Press, 1991), explores the centrality of African American defiance in defining the emerging U.S. culture, particularly in the South and during the era of the U.S. War of Independence, for which the essays in Ira Berlin and Ronald Hoffman, eds., *Slavery and Freedom in the Age of the American Revolution* (Charlottesville: University of Virginia Press, 1983) are also helpful.

Fugitives proved the most massive overt form of black insurgency as illustrated in the materials in Paul Finkelman, ed., *Rebellions, Resistance, and Runaways within the Slave South* (New York: Garland, 1989), and in Gerald W. Mullin, *Flight and Rebellion: Slave Resistance in Eighteenth-Century Virginia* (New York: Oxford University Press, 1972). A composite of the fugitives emerges in Lathan A. Windley, comp., *Runaway Slave Advertisements: A Documentary History from the 1730's to 1790* (Westport, Conn.: Greenwood Press, 1983), and Billy G. Smith and Richard Wojtowicz, comp., *Blacks Who Stole Themselves: Advertisements for Runaways in the Pennsylvania Gazette, 1728–1790* (Philadelphia: University of Pennsylvania Press, 1989).

African American resistance to slavery deeply implicated the legal system, as U.S. Court of Appeals Judge A. Leon Higginbotham, Jr., *In the Matter of Color: Race and the American Legal Process* (New York: Oxford University Press, 1978), demonstrates in detail. Philip J. Schwarz, *Twice Condemned: Slaves and the Criminal Laws of Virginia, 1705–1865* (Baton Rouge:

Louisiana State University Press, 1988), illustrates local dimensions. Paul Finkelman, ed., *Fugitive Slaves and American Courts: The Pamphlet Literature* (New York: Garland, 1988), provides ample documentary examples. The chief source of documentary case material remains the five volumes of Helen T. Catterall, ed., *Judicial Cases Concerning American Slavery and the Negro* (Washington, D.C.: Carnegie Institution, 1926–37).

The African American position during the colonial period continues to stand in the shadow of antebellum development. Robert William Fogel, *Without Consent or Contract: The Rise and Fall of American Slavery* (New York: Norton, 1989), offers an overview of the U.S. institution and its colonial forebears. It does not, however, supplant his and Stanley L. Engerman's *Time on the Cross* (Boston: Little, Brown, 1974) in presenting the considerations and controversies in dealing with African American experience with the so-called Peculiar Institution. For an alternative view to Fogel and Engerman's, see Herbert Gutman, *Slavery and the Numbers Game: A Critique of Time on the Cross* (Urbana: University of Illinois Press, 1975) and Paul David et al., *Reckoning with Slavery: A Critical Study in the Quantitative History of American Negro Slavery* (New York: Oxford University Press, 1976). To appreciate the historiography on the institution demands attention to at least four works: U. B. Phillips's apologetic but no less influential *American Negro Slavery* (New York: D. Appleton, 1918), Kenneth Stampp's *The Peculiar Institution* (New York: Knopf, 1956), Stanley Elkins's *Slavery: A Problem in American Institutional and Intellectual Life*, 3d ed. (Chicago: University of Chicago Press, 1956), and John W. Blassingame's *The Slave Community: Plantation Life in the Antebellum South* (New York: Oxford University Press, 1972).

PART III ENDING THE SLAVE TRADE AND SLAVERY

A number of fine general works deal with the various emancipations, among them David Brion Davis, *The Problem of Slavery in the Age of Revolution, 1770–1823* (Ithaca, N.Y.: Cornell University Press, 1975); Jane H. Pease and William H. Pease, *They Who Would Be Free: Blacks' Search for Freedom, 1830–1861* (Urbana: University of Illinois Press, 1990); Howard Temperley, *British Antislavery, 1833–1870* (Columbia: University of South Carolina Press, 1972); Seymour Drescher, *Capitalism and Antislavery: British Mobilization in Comparative Perspective* (New York: Oxford University Press, 1986); J. R. Ward, *British West Indian Slavery, 1750–1834: The Process of Amelioration* (New York: Oxford University Press, 1988); William A. Green, *British Slave Emancipation: The Sugar Colonies and the Great Experiment, 1830–1865* (Oxford, Eng.: Oxford University Press, 1976); Ronald K. Richardson, *Moral Imperium: Afro-Caribbeans and the Transformation of British Rule, 1776–1838* (Westport, Conn.: Greenwood Press, 1987); Robin Blackburn, *The Overthrow of Colonial Slavery, 1776–1848* (London: Verso, 1988); Barbara Solow and Stanley Engerman, eds., *British Capitalism and Caribbean Slavery* (Cambridge, Eng.: Cambridge University Press, 1987); Robert Brent Toplin, ed., *Slavery and Race Relations in Latin America* (Westport, Conn.: Greenwood Press, 1974); Gordon K. Lewis, *Main Currents in Caribbean Thought: The Historical Evolution of Caribbean Society in Its Ideological Aspects, 1492–1900* (Baltimore: Johns Hopkins University Press, 1987); and Paul E. Lovejoy, *Slow Death for Slavery* (New York: Cambridge University Press, 1993).

On the campaign to end the trade, see David Eltis, *Economic Growth and the Ending of the Transatlantic Slave Trade* (New York: Oxford University Press, 1987); David Murray, *Odious Commerce: Britain, Spain, and the Abolition of the Cuban Slave Trade* (Cambridge, Eng.: Cambridge University Press, 1980); and E. Philip LeVeen, *British Slave Trade Suppression Policies, 1807–1865* (New York: Arno Press, 1977).

The struggle to end slavery in a disputed borderland is dealt with in Randolph B. Campbell, *An Empire for Slavery: The Peculiar Institution in Texas, 1821–1865* (Baton Rouge: Louisiana State University Press, 1989).

Many blacks in the Americas had gained their freedom before the nineteenth century. Their experience in Jamaica is recounted in Gad J. Heuman, *Between Black and White: Race, Politics, and the Free Coloreds in Jamaica, 1792–1865* (Westport, Conn.: Greenwood Press, 1981). See also Stanley L. Engerman, Manuel Moreno Fraginals, and Frank Moya Pons, eds., *Between Slavery and Free Labor: The Spanish-Speaking Caribbean in the Nineteenth Century* (Baltimore: Johns Hopkins University Press, 1985). For the United States, consult Ira Berlin, *Slaves Without Masters: The Free Negro in the Antebellum South* (New York: Pantheon, 1974), and Herman Belz, *A New Birth of Freedom: The Republican Party and Freedmen's Rights* (Westport, Conn.: Greenwood Press, 1976).

Slave resistance in the campaigns for emancipation is treated in Gary Y. Okihiro, ed., *In Resistance: Studies in African, Caribbean, and Afro-American History* (Amherst: University of Massachusetts Press, 1986). Their general participation in military life is the subject of Gary A. Donaldson, *The History of African-Americans in the Military* (Melbourne, Fla.: Krieger, 1991). The special case of armed African slaves is covered in Roger Norman Buckley, *Slaves in Red Coats: The British West Indian Regiments, 1795–1815* (New Haven, Conn.: Yale University Press, 1979).

The story of emancipation in specific islands is covered in Claude Levy, *Emancipation, Sugar, and Federalism: Barbados and the West Indies, 1833–1876* (Gainesville: University Presses of Florida, 1980); Franklin W. Knight, *Slave Society in Cuba during the Nineteenth Century* (Madison: University of Wisconsin Press, 1970); Rebecca J. Scott, *Slave Emancipation in Cuba: The Transition to Free Labor, 1860–1899* (Princeton, N.J.: Princeton University Press, 1985); Mary Turner, *Slaves and Missionaries: The Disintegration of Jamaican Slave Society, 1787–1834* (Urbana: University of Illinois Press, 1982); Thomas C. Holt, *The Problem of Freedom: Race, Labor, and Politics in Jamaica and Britain,*

1823–1938 (Baltimore: Johns Hopkins University Press, 1991); Kenneth F. Kiple, *Blacks in Colonial Cuba, 1774–1899* (Gainesville: University Presses of Florida, 1976); Robert L. Paquette, *Sugar Is Made with Blood: The Conspiracy of La Escalera and the Conflict Between Empires over Slavery in Cuba* (Middletown, Conn.: Wesleyan University Press, 1988).

Abolition movements on the mainland have attracted some attention. See John V. Lombardi, *The Decline and Abolition of Negro Slavery in Venezuela, 1820–1854* (Westport, Conn.: Greenwood Press, 1971); Peter Blanchard, *Slavery and Abolition in Early Republican Peru* (Wilmington, DE.: Scholarly Resources, 1992).

The greatest slave rebellion of all is covered in Thomas Ott, *The Haitian Revolution, 1789–1804* (Knoxville: University of Tennessee Press, 1973), and Carolyn E. Fick, *The Making of Haiti: The Saint Domingue Revolution from Below* (Knoxville: University of Tennessee Press, 1990). Compare also David Geggus, *Slavery, War, and Revolution: The British Occupation of Saint Domingue, 1793–1798* (New York: Oxford University Press, 1982).

A large literature deals with emancipation in Brazil. On the end of the trade, see Leslie Bethell, *The Abolition of the Brazilian Slave Trade: Britain, Brazil and the Slave Trade Question, 1807–1869* (Cambridge, Eng.: Cambridge University Press, 1970). João José Reis narrates a fascinating episode in *Slave Rebellion in Brazil: The Muslim Uprising of 1835 in Bahia* (Baltimore: Johns Hopkins University Press, 1993). On the abolition movement, see Robert Conrad, *The Destruction of Brazilian Slavery, 1850–1888* (Berkeley and Los Angeles: University of California Press, 1972); Robert Brent Toplin, *The Abolition of Slavery in Brazil* (New York: Atheneum, 1972); and Rebecca J. Scott et al., *The Abolition of Slavery and the Aftermath of Emancipation in Brazil* (Durham, N.C.: Duke University Press, 1988).

Literature has often been used as a lens for viewing racial conceptions. Three excellent examples are David T. Haberly, *Three Sad Races: Racial Identity and National Consciousness in Brazilian Literature* (Cambridge, Eng.: Cambridge University Press, 1983); David Brookshaw, *Race and Color in Brazilian Literature* (Metuchen, N.J.: Scarecrow Press, 1986); and William Luis, *Literary Bondage: Slavery in Cuban Narrative* (Austin: University of Texas Press, 1990).

Mary Elizabeth Thomas, *Jamaica and Voluntary Laborers from Africa, 1840–1865* (Tallahassee: Florida State University, 1974), deals with the peculiar case of postemancipation immigration from Africa to the Caribbean.

Good general studies on the emancipation movement in the United States include Derrick A. Bell, Jr., *Race, Racism and America*, 2d ed. (Boston: Little, Brown, 1980); Sylvia R. Frey, *Water from the Rock: Black Resistance in a Revolutionary Age* (Princeton, N.J.: Princeton University Press, 1991); Herman Belz, *Emancipation and Equal Rights: Politics and Constitutionalism in the Civil War Era* (New York: Norton, 1978); Robert W. Johannsen, *Lincoln, the South, and Slavery: The Political Dimension* (Baton Rouge: Louisiana State

University Press, 1991); Don E. Fehrenbacher, *The Dred Scott Case: Its Significance in American Law and Politics* (New York: Oxford University Press, 1978); Eric Foner, *Nothing but Freedom: Emancipation and Its Legacy* (Baton Rouge: Louisiana State University Press, 1983); Vincent Harding, *There Is a River: The Black Freedom Struggle in America* (New York: Harcourt Brace Jovanovich, 1981); Donald G. Nieman, *Promises to Keep: African Americans and the Constitutional Order, 1776 to the Present* (New York: Oxford University Press, 1975); James Brewer Stewart, *Holy Warriors: The Abolitionists and American Slavery* (New York: Hill and Wang, 1976); Thomas P. Slaughter, *Bloody Dawn: The Christian Riot and Racial Violence in the Antebellum North* (New York: Oxford University Press, 1991).

Abolition in a specific region is dealt with in Lynda J. Morgan, *Emancipation in Virginia's Tobacco Belt, 1850–1870* (Athens: University of Georgia Press, 1992).

Biographies of exceptional people appear in R.J.M. Blackett, *Beating Against the Barriers: The Lives of Six Nineteenth-Century Afro-Americans* (Ithaca, N.Y.: Cornell University Press, 1986), and Leon Litwak and August Meier, eds., *Black Leaders of the Nineteenth Century* (Urbana: University of Illinois Press, 1988). Wilson Jeremiah Moses, in *The Golden Age of Black Nationalism, 1850–1925* (New York: Oxford University Press, 1978), traces the writings of black activists into the early twentieth century. Compare also Willard B. Gatewood, *Aristocrats of Color: The Black Elite, 1880–1920* (Bloomington: Indiana University Press, 1990).

The period following the Civil War is covered by Eric Foner, *Reconstruction: America's Unfinished Business, 1863–1877* (New York: Harper and Row, 1988); C. Vann Woodward, *The Strange Career of Jim Crow*, 3d ed. (New York: Oxford University Press, 1974); Jay R. Mandle, *Not Slave, Not Free: The African American Economic Experience Since the Civil War* (Durham, N.C.: Duke University Press, 1992); Frank McGlynn and Seymour Drescher, eds., *The Meaning of Freedom: Economics, Politics, and Culture After Slavery* (Pittsburgh: University of Pittsburgh Press, 1992); and Roger L. Ransom and Richard Sutch, *One Kind of Freedom: The Economic Consequences of Emancipation* (Cambridge, Eng.: Cambridge University Press, 1977).

David R. Roediger, *The Wages of Whiteness: Race and the Making of the American Working Class* (London: Verso, 1991), looks at the effects of racism on the behavior and outlook of laborers since the last century.

Studies of the blacks and race relations in specific settings include Eric Arnesen, *Waterfront Workers of New Orleans: Race, Class, and Politics, 1863–1923* (New York: Oxford University Press, 1991); Edmund L. Drago, *Black Politicians and Reconstruction in Georgia: A Splendid Failure* (Athens: University of Georgia Press, 1992); Kenneth L. Kusmer, *A Ghetto Takes Shape: Black Cleveland, 1870–1930* (Urbana: University of Illinois Press, 1976); Howard N. Rabinowitz, *Race Relations in the Urban South, 1865–1890* (New York: Oxford University Press, 1978); Leonard P. Curry, *The Free Black in Urban*

America, 1800–1850: The Shadow of the Dream (Chicago: University of Chicago Press, 1981); William Cohen, *At Freedom's Edge: Black Mobility and the Southern White Quest for Racial Control, 1861–1915* (Baton Rouge: Louisiana State University Press, 1991); and Joel Williamson, *The Crucible of Race: Black-White Relations in the American South Since Emancipation* (New York: Oxford University Press, 1984).

Women's experiences are the focus of Melton A. McLaurin, *Celia a Slave* (Athens: University of Georgia Press, 1991); Sally McMillen, *Southern Women White and Black in the Old South* (Arlington Heights, Ill.: Harlan Davidson, 1991); Cynthia Neverdon-Morton, *Afro-American Women of the South and the Advancement of the Race, 1895–1925* (Knoxville: University of Tennessee Press, 1989); Susie King Taylor, *A Black Woman's Civil War Memoirs: Reminiscences of My Life in Camp*, 2d ed. (Princeton, N.J.: Markus Weiner, 1985).

Michael Newton and Judy Ann Newton provide a useful outline in *Racial and Religious Violence in America: A Chronology* (Hamden, Conn.: Garland, 1991).

PART IV AFRICANS IN THE AMERICAS SINCE ABOLITION

Comparative studies are particularly rich sources for understanding the African diaspora. The following are recommended: Leo Spitzer, *Lives in Between: Assimilation and Marginality in Austria, Brazil, West Africa, 1780–1945* (Cambridge, Eng.: Cambridge University Press, 1989); Carl N. Degler, *Neither Black nor White: Slavery and Race Relations in Brazil and the United States* (New York: Macmillan, 1971); Robert Brent Toplin, ed., *Freedom and Prejudice: The Legacy of Slavery in the United States and Brazil* (Westport, Conn.: Greenwood Press, 1981); Sidney W. Mintz and Richard Price, *The Birth of African-American Culture* (Boston: Beacon, 1992); and Pierre L. Van den Berghe, *Race and Racism: A Comparative Perspective*, 2d ed. (New York: Wiley, 1978).

On Pan-African movements, see David Rooney, *Kwame Nkrumah* (New York: St. Martin's Press, 1989); Robert G. Weisbord, *Ebony Kinship: Africa, Africans, and the Afro-American* (Westport, Conn.: Greenwood Press, 1973); and Judith Stein, *The World of Marcus Garvey: Race and Class in Modern Society* (Baton Rouge: Louisiana State University Press, 1986).

General works on people of African descent in the United States abound. Among the best are Joseph E. Holloway, ed., *Africanisms in American Culture* (Bloomington: Indiana University Press, 1990); F. James Davis, *Who Is Black? One Nation's Definition* (University Park: Pennsylvania State University Press, 1991); Molefi Asante and Mark T. Mattson, *Historical and Cultural Atlas of African Americans* (New York: Macmillan, 1991); and Charles Johnson, *Being and Race: Black Writing since 1970* (Bloomington: Indiana University Press, 1988).

Studies of race relations in general include Bruce M. Tyler, *From Harlem to Hollywood: The Struggle for Racial and Cultural Democracy, 1920–1943* (Hamden, Conn.: Garland, 1992); and Ralph E. Luker, *The Social Gospel in Black and White: American Racial Reform, 1885–1912* (Chapel Hill: University of North Carolina Press, 1991); Willard Gatewood, *Aristocrats of Color: The Black Elite, 1880–1920* (Bloomington: Indiana University Press, 1990).

The U.S. South has always been the focus of much research on African Americans. See, for example, Hans A. Baer and Yvonne Jones, *African Americans in the South: Issues of Race, Class, and Gender* (Athens: University of Georgia Press, 1991); David R. Goldfield, *Black, White, and Southern: Race Relations and Southern Culture, 1940 to the Present* (Baton Rouge: Louisiana State University Press, 1990); Joel Williamson, *The Crucible of Race: Black-White Relations in the American South Since Emancipation* (New York: Oxford University Press, 1984); William Cohen, *At Freedom's Edge: Black Mobility and the Southern White Quest for Racial Control, 1861–1915* (Baton Rouge: Louisiana State University Press, 1991); and Richard A. Couto, *Ain't Gonna Let Nobody Turn Me Round: The Pursuit of Racial Justice in the Rural South* (Philadelphia: Temple University Press, 1991).

Religion played an important part in the African experience in the United States. See C. Eric Lincoln, *Race, Religion and the Continuing Dilemma* (New York: Hill and Wang, 1984); and Michael Newton and Judy Ann Newton, *Racial and Religious Violence in America: A Chronology* (Hamden, Conn.: Garland, 1991).

Politics and civil rights marched hand in hand for most of this century. See Merl E. Reed, *Seedtime for the Modern Civil Rights Movement: The President's Committee on Fair Employment Practice, 1941–1946* (Baton Rouge: Louisiana State University Press, 1991); Steven F. Lawson, *Running for Freedom: Civil Rights and Black Politics in America Since 1941* (New York: McGraw Hill, 1991); Charles P. Henry, *Culture and African American Politics* (Bloomington: Indiana University Press, 1992); and Steven F. Lawson, *Black Ballots: Voting Rights in the South, 1944–1969* (New York: Columbia University Press, 1976). Henry Hampton, producer of the award-winning documentary *Eyes on the Prize*, offers a fascinating collection of reminiscences in *Voices of Freedom: An Oral History of the Civil Rights Movement from the 1950s Through the 1980s* (New York: Bantam, 1990).

Many studies have examined black workers in order to understand the economic dimension of the diaspora experience. Especially recommended are Eric Arnesen, *Waterfront Workers of New Orleans: Race, Class, and Politics, 1863–1923* (New York: Oxford University Press, 1991); Jay R. Mandle, *Not Slave, Not Free: The African American Economic Experience Since the Civil War* (Durham, N.C.: Duke University Press, 1992); Robin Kelley, *Hammer and Hoe: Alabama Communists During the Great Depression* (Chapel Hill: University of North Carolina Press, 1990); August Meier and Elliot Rudwick, *Black Detroit and the Rise of the UAW* (New York: Oxford University Press, 1979);

Joe William Trotter, Jr., *Black Milwaukee: The Making of an Industrial Proletariat, 1915–1945* (Urbana: University of Illinois Press, 1984).

A subset of U.S. labor studies concerns the Great Migration that lasted from World War I until the Great Depression. Some fine works in this vein are Peter Gottlieb, *Making Their Own Way: Southern Blacks' Migration to Pittsburgh, 1916–1930* (Urbana: University of Illinois Press, 1987); James Grossman, *Land of Hope: Chicago, Black Southerners, and the Great Migration* (Chicago: University of Chicago Press, 1989); Carole Marks, *Farewell— We're Good and Gone: The Great Black Migration* (Bloomington: Indiana University Press, 1989); Joe William Trotter, Jr., *The Great Migration in Historical Perspective* (Bloomington: Indiana University Press, 1991); and Earl Lewis, *In Their Own Interests: Race, Class, and Power in Twentieth Century Norfolk* (Berkeley and Los Angeles: University of California Press, 1991).

Labor studies in the Caribbean Basin increasingly treat race as a major factor in wages, benefits, and industrial organization. See Walter Rodney, *History of the Guyanese Working People* (Baltimore: Johns Hopkins University Press, 1981); Clive Thomas, *The Poor and the Powerless: Economic Policy and Change in the Caribbean* (London: Latin America Bureau, 1988); Alec Wilkinson, *Big Sugar: Seasons in the Cane Fields of Florida* (New York: Knopf, 1989); Thomas C. Holt, *The Problem of Freedom: Race, Labor, and Politics in Jamaica, 1832–1938* (Baltimore: Johns Hopkins University Press, 1992).

Some good works on the period prior to 1930 include August Meier and Elliot Rudwick, *From Plantation to Ghetto* (New York: Hill and Wang, 1970); and Leonard J. Moore, *Citizen Klansmen: The Ku Klux Klan in Indiana, 1921–1928* (Chapel Hill: University of North Carolina Press, 1991).

The 1930s proved pivotal in U.S. black history. Compare John B. Kirby, *Black Americans in the Roosevelt Era* (Knoxville: University of Tennessee Press, 1980).

An especially rich literature covers the period after World War II. Consult Taylor Branch, *Parting the Waters: America in the King Years, 1954–1963* (New York: Simon and Schuster, 1988); Robert F. Burk, *The Eisenhower Administration and Black Civil Rights* (Knoxville: University of Tennessee Press, 1984); Clayborne Carson et al., *The Eyes on the Prize Civil Rights Reader*, rev. ed. (New York: Penguin, 1991); Adam Fairclough, *To Redeem the Soul of America: The Southern Christian Leadership Conference and Martin Luther King, Jr.* (Athens: University of Georgia Press, 1987); Alan B. Anderson and George W. Pickering, *Confronting the Color Line: The Broken Promise of the Civil Rights Movement in Chicago* (Athens: University of Georgia Press, 1986); Ronald P. Formisano, *Boston Against Busing: Race, Class, and Ethnicity in the 1960s and 1970s* (Chapel Hill: University of North Carolina Press, 1991); August Meier, Elliot Rudwick, and John Bracey, Jr., eds., *Black Protest in the Sixties* (Princeton, N.J.: Markus Weiner, 1991); Keith D. Miller, *Voice of Deliverance: The Language of Martin Luther King, Jr., and Its Sources* (New York: Free Press, 1991); Kenneth O'Reilly, *"Racial Matters"*:

The FBI's Secret File on Black America, 1960–1972 (New York: Free Press, 1991); Albert E. Stone, *The Return of Nat Turner: History, Literature, and Cultural Politics in Sixties America* (Athens: University of Georgia Press, 1992); Bruce Perry, *Malcolm, The Life of a Man Who Changed Black America* (Barrytown, N.Y.: Station Hill Press, 1991); Fred Prowledge, *Free at Last?: The Civil Rights Movement and the People Who Made It* (New York: HarperCollins, 1992); Linda Reed, *Simple Decency and Common Sense: The Southern Conference Movement, 1938–1963* (Bloomington: Indiana University Press, 1991); and John Hope Franklin, *The Color Line: Legacy for the Twenty-First Century* (Columbia: University of Missouri Press, 1993).

A growing number of studies examine women's perspectives in the diaspora, among them Nancie Caraway, *Segregated Sisterhood: Racism and the Politics of American Feminism* (Knoxville: University of Tennessee Press, 1991); Cynthia Neverdon-Morton, *Afro-American Women of the South and the Advancement of the Race, 1895–1925* (Knoxville: University of Tennessee Press, 1989); Kesho Yvonne Scott, *The Habit of Surviving* (New York: Ballantine, 1991); and Olive Senior, *Working Miracles: Women of the English-Speaking Caribbean* (Bloomington: Indiana University Press, 1992).

State and community-level studies help to illuminate the daily experiences and challenges of black Americans. The classic by St. Clair Drake and Horace R. Cayton, *Black Metropolis: A Study of Negro Life in a Northern City* (New York: Harper, 1962), can be complemented with Richard W. Thomas, *Life for Us Is What We Make It: Building Black Community in Detroit, 1915–1945* (Bloomington: Indiana University Press, 1992); David R. Colburn, *Racial Change and Community Crisis: St. Augustine, Florida, 1877–1980* (Gainesville: University Presses of Florida, 1985); Douglas Henry Daniels, *Pioneer Urbanites: A Social and Cultural History of Black San Francisco* (Berkeley and Los Angeles: University of California Press, 1980); Chandler Davidson, *Race and Class in Texas Politics* (Princeton, N.J.: Princeton University Press, 1992); James W. Button, *Blacks and Social Change: Impact of the Civil Rights Movement in Southern Communities* (Princeton, N.J.: Princeton University Press, 1992).

Biographies penetrate the black experience from the vantage of individual leaders. Especially useful among the many fine studies are Wayne J. Urban, *Black Scholar: Horace Mann Bond, 1904–1972* (Athens: University of Georgia Press, 1992); W. Burghardt Turner and Joyce Moore Turner, eds., *Richard B. Moore, Caribbean Militant in Harlem, Collected Writings, 1920–1972* (Bloomington: Indiana University Press, 1988); Walter L. Hawkins, *African American Biographies: Profiles of 558 Current Men and Women* (Jefferson, N.C.: McFarland, 1992); Roger Goldman and David Gallen, *Thurgood Marshall: Justice for All* (New York: Carroll and Graf, 1992); and Thomas T. Lyons, *Black Leadership in American History* (Menlo Park, Calif.: Addison-Wesley, 1971).

Latin American race relations and black history have attracted a wide range of scholars. Useful introductions are available in Frank Tannenbaum, *Slave and Citizen*, 2d ed. (Boston: Beacon, 1991); Harry Hoetink, *Slavery and Race Relations in the Americas: An Inquiry into Their Nature and Nexus* (New York: Harper and Row, 1973), and *Caribbean Race Relations: A Study of Two Variants* (Oxford, Eng.: Oxford University Press, 1971); Franklin Knight, *The African Dimension in Latin American Societies* (New York: Macmillan, 1974); Roger Bastide, *African Civilization in the New World* (New York: Harper and Row, 1971); Ann M. Pescatello, ed., *Old Roots in New Lands: Historical and Anthropological Perspectives on Black Experience in the Americas* (Westport, Conn.: Greenwood Press, 1977); Richard Graham, ed., *The Idea of Race in Latin America, 1870–1940* (Austin: University of Texas Press, 1990); and Leslie B. Rout, Jr., *The African Experience in Spanish America* (Cambridge, Eng.: Cambridge University Press, 1976); Sidney Kronus and Mauricio Solaun, *Discrimination Without Violence: Miscegenation and Racial Conflict in Latin America* (New York: John Wiley, 1973); Richard L. Jackson, *Black Writers in Latin America* (Albuquerque: University of New Mexico Press, 1979); and Thomas M. Stephens, *Dictionary of Latin American Racial and Ethnic Terminology* (Gainesville: University Presses of Florida, 1989).

A smaller number of books treat individual countries or regions of Latin America. The most important are Winthrop R. Wright, *Café con Leche: Race, Class, and Natural Image in Venezuela* (Austin: University of Texas Press, 1990); George Reid Andrews, *The Afro-Argentines of Buenos Aires* (Madison: University of Wisconsin Press, 1980); Norman Whitten, Jr., *Black Frontiersmen* (New York: John Wiley, 1974); Nancie L. Solien Gonzalez, *Sojourners of the Caribbean: Ethnogenesis and Ethnohistory of the Garifuna* (Urbana: University of Illinois Press, 1988); Peter Wade, *Blackness and Race Mixture: The Dynamics of Racial Identity in Colombia* (Baltimore: Johns Hopkins University Press, 1993).

Because of its similarities to the United States, Brazil has been studied by a larger number of researchers. Among the excellent books available are Roger Bastide, *The African Religions of Brazil: Toward a Sociology of the Interpenetration of Civilizations* (Baltimore: Johns Hopkins University Press, 1978); George Reid Andrews, *Black and White in São Paulo, 1888–1988* (Pittsburgh: University of Pittsburgh Press, 1991); Florestan Fernandes, *The Negro in Brazilian Society* (New York: Columbia University Press, 1969); Martha K. Huggins, *From Slavery to Vagrancy in Brazil: Crime and Social Control in the Third World* (New Brunswick, N.J.: Rutgers University Press, 1985); Rowan Ireland, *Kingdoms Come: Religion and Politics in Brazil* (Pittsburgh: University of Pittsburgh Press, 1992); Thomas E. Skidmore, *Black into White: Race and Nationality in Brazilian Thought* (Durham, N.C.: Duke University Press, 1993); and Pierre-Michel Fontain, ed., *Race, Class, and Power in Brazil* (Los Angeles: UCLA Center for Afro-American Studies, 1985).

Labor studies about Afro–Latin Americans are more rare. See Philippe I. Bourgois, *Ethnicity at Work: Divided Labor on a Central American Banana*

Plantation (Baltimore: Johns Hopkins University Press, 1989); Michael L. Conniff, *Black Labor on a White Canal: Panama, 1904–1981* (Pittsburgh: University of Pittsburgh Press, 1985); and Ken Post, *Arise Ye Starvelings: The Jamaican Labour Rebellion of 1938 and Its Aftermath* (The Hague: Institute of Social Studies, 1978).

On continuing linkages between Africa and the Americas, see Imanuel Geiss, *The Pan-African Movement: A History of Pan Africanism in America, Europe, and Africa* (New York: African Publishing, 1974); Jahneinz Jahn, *Muntu, African Culture, and the Western World* (New York: Grove Press, 1961); José Honório Rodrigues, *Brazil and Africa* (Berkeley: University of California Press, 1965); John N. Paden and Edward W. Soja, *The African Experiences* (Evanston, Ill.: Northwestern University Press, 1970); Manuel Moreno Fraginals, ed., *Africa in Latin America: Essays in History, Culture, and Socialization* (Paris: Unesco, 1977); and Margaret E. Crahan and Franklin W. Knight, eds., *Africa and the Caribbean: Legacies of a Link* (Baltimore: Johns Hopkins University Press, 1979).

INDEX

Italicized page numbers identify maps, line drawings, or photographs.

ABOUT THE AUTHORS

Patrick Carroll is a history professor at Corpus Christi State University. He has authored a book, *Blacks, Race, and Regional Development in Colonial Veracruz, 1570–1830* (1991), and numerous articles, essays, and professional papers on the Afro-Mexican experience.

Michael Conniff teaches history at Auburn University, where he also directs the Institute for Latin American Studies. His books include *Black Labor on a White Canal, Panama 1904–1981* (1985), *Urban Politics in Brazil* (1981), *Modern Brazil* (1989), and *Panama and the United States* (1992).

Thomas J. Davis teaches history and African American Studies at the State University of New York at Buffalo. His books include *The New York Conspiracy* (1971) and *A Rumor of Revolt: The "Great Negro Plot" in Colonial New York* (1985).

David Eltis received his Ph.D. from the University of Rochester in 1979. He is the author of *Economic Growth and the Ending of the Transatlantic Slave Trade* (1987) and other important works on economic history. He is a professor of history at Queen's University, Kingston, Ontario.

Patience Essah teaches African American and African history at Auburn University. She holds degrees from the University of Ghana and UCLA. Her book *Slavery and Freedom in Delaware* will be published in 1994.

Alfred D. Frederick is a professor of education at the State University of New York at Oswego. After receiving his B.A. from Northern Illinois University, he earned an M.A. from Columbia University and a doctorate from the University of Brussels. He has researched and taught in West Africa and Brazil. He is author of *Curriculum and the Socio-Cultural Context* (1988).

Dale T. Graden teaches Latin American history at the University of Idaho. He received his Ph.D. from the University of Connecticut in Storrs, where he studied with Dr. Hugh M. Hamill and Dr. Francisco Scarano. He is presently completing a manuscript on the abolition of slavery and its aftermath in the northeastern state of Bahia, Brazil.

Linda M. Heywood is associate professor of history at Howard University. She received her Ph.D. degree in history from Columbia University. Professor Heywood is the author of several important articles on the history of Angola and editor of *The African Diaspora* (1989–1990). She is currently completing a manuscript on the state in Angola, 1850–1940.

Richard Lobban is professor of anthropology and the director of the Program of African and Afro-American Studies at Rhode Island College. He has done extensive research and writing on the Nile Valley nations, and on West Africa. He is especially interested in ancient Egypt and Kush and comparative systems of slavery. Among his many works are historical dictionaries on the Sudan, Cape Verde, and Guinea-Bissau.

Colin A. Palmer is William Rand Kenan Jr. professor of history at the University of North Carolina at Chapel Hill. He is author of *Slaves of the White God: Blacks in Mexico, 1570–1650* (1976) and *Human Cargoes: The British Slave Trade to Spanish America, 1700–1739* (1981), and co-editor of *The Modern Caribbean* (1989), among other works. His book *Passageways: An Interpretive History of Black America* is forthcoming from Harcourt Brace Jovanovich.

Joseph P. Reidy is associate professor of history at Howard University. He received his Ph.D. degree in history from Northern Illinois University. Professor Reidy is co-editor of *Freedom: A Documentary History of Emancipation, 1861–1867* (4 vols., 1982–1993). He is also the author of *From Slavery to Agrarian Capitalism in the Cotton Plantation South: Central Georgia, 1800–1880* (1992).

John Thornton was educated at the University of Michigan and UCLA, receiving his Ph.D. in 1979. He has taught at the University of Zambia, Allegheny College, and the University of Virginia, and is associate professor of history at the University of Pennsylvania in Millersville. A specialist in African and Atlantic history, he is the author of *The Kingdom of Kongo: Civil War and Transition* (1983) and *Africa and Africans in the Making of the Atlantic World* (1992).

Ronald Walters is professor and chairman of the political science department at Howard University. He is the author of many scholarly articles and four books, one of which, *Black Presidential Politics in America* (1988), won the Ralph Bunche Prize. His co-authors were Karin Stanford, a postdoctoral fellow at the University of North Carolina, and Daryl Harris, a doctoral candidate at Howard University.

Ashton Welch is associate professor and chairman of the department of history at Creighton University, where he also coordinates the program in black studies. He received his Ph.D. in African history from the University of Birmingham, England. His research focus is social and political change in the African diaspora, as well as religion and social change in Africa.

Winthrop R. Wright is professor of Latin American history at the University of Maryland. He has written two books, *British-Owned Railways in Argentina* (1974) and *Café con Leche: Race, Class, and National Image in Venezuela* (1990), in addition to numerous articles.